White Power

George Lincoln Rockwell

White Power

George Lincoln Rockwell

sspress

— 2024 —

SSPress, LLC

Special Services Press, LLC, is a non-profit educational publisher.

Library of Congress Cataloging-in-Publication Data

Rockwell, George Lincoln
White Power
Reprint of original 1967 edition, with corrections and minor edits

p. cm.
Includes bibliographical references

ISBN 978-1963-1431-02
(pbk.: alk. paper)

1.   White studies, 20th century

2.   Jewish Question

Printing number: 9 8 7 6 5 4 3 2 1

Printed in the United States of America on acid-free paper.

CONTENTS

EDITOR'S PREFACE

White Power was completed yet unfinished at the time of Rockwell's death on 25 August 1967. The full text was written but the final edits and final 'polish' had not yet been done. As a result, the book was published posthumously in a rather rough form; all existing editions have numerous typos, grammatical errors, and textual flaws that would have been caught by a good editor. The present edition seeks to provide a polish to the text and to issue it as a fully professional production, all without deviating in the slightest from the spirit of the original. With very minor exceptions, the following contains the entirety of Rockwell's first-edition text.

In order to improve the flow of the book, one change in chapter sequence was made: the original Chapter 14—"White Revolution"—was moved to the front, and here constitutes Chapter 1. The reason is clear: this chapter provides an excellent overview and introduction to the chapters to follow (it was originally intended as a kind of recap). This eliminates the need for an invited Introduction by an outside party; and in any case, the best introduction to a book is often that of the author himself.

A few other improvements have been made to the text. Numerous footnotes have been added, all by the editor, except for a few original notes (marked as "GLR"). Many section breaks have been inserted at appropriate points ("卐 卐 卐") in the text, in order to improve readability. In the original, when Rockwell wanted emphasis, he put the text in all capital letters, but these have been changed to italics, which is more in line with modern professional standards. Much of the original text was evidently composed in short, choppy "paragraphs" of just one or two sentences, and these have been frequently merged into single larger paragraphs—again, to give it a more polished style. And as noted, spelling errors, typos, and other flaws have been largely remedied. Though not perfect, we think this edition is the best yet of Rockwell's magnum opus.

Finally, five substantial and important appendices have been added; these are not mere after-thoughts but rather provide essential insight into Rockwell's life and work. Appendix A provides a detailed biography, written by a man who knew Rockwell personally: William L. Pierce, a significant figure in his own right. Appendix B is one of Rockwell's most famous essays, originally titled (in Latin) *In Hoc Signo Vinces*—which means "By this sign, we will conquer." (The 'sign' in question is the swastika.)

Appendix C is the full, and infamous, 1966 *Playboy* interview—surely one of the most amazing interviews ever printed in a major American magazine. Appendix D offers a few select pages from Rockwell's self-published periodical, *The Rockwell Report*. And Appendix E is a relatively recent (2017) *Washington Post* article discussing Rockwell in some detail; though horribly slanted, it shows something of the on-going influence of the man, now some 60 years after his untimely death.

White Power stands as an utterly unique and unmatched accomplishment: a brutally honest assessment of the situation of the White race in America (and globally), and a roadmap to restore greatness to this beleaguered global minority. In many ways, the situation has grown significantly worse for Whites in the intervening decades; Rockwell's words are needed now more than ever.

CHAPTER 1

WHITE REVOLUTION

Before starting out, let's briefly review the plan of the present book. In the following chapters, I will show that:

- Western society is sick, rotten, and dying but most of its citizens don't seem to care. (Chapter 2 - "Death Rattle")

- Our people, especially our youth, are spiritually lost—empty. (Chapter 3 - "Spiritual Syphilis")

- This sick, rotten, spiritually-empty state of our people is not natural degeneration but the result of the efforts of a gang of "liberal" liars—the "chart forgers." The purpose of these lying chart forgers is to pile up Western Civilization on the rocks, so that, like the old-time ship wreckers, they can loot and enslave our people. (Chapter 4 - "Chart Forgers")

- To hurry our "ship of state" onto the rocks, the ship wreckers have installed as our "captains" nothing but crooks and traitors working with the ship wreckers. (Chapter 5 - "Crooked Captains")

- The chart forgers and ship wreckers are led by a breed of people called "Jews." (Chapter 6 - "The Ship Wreckers")

- The Jewish breed is leading the ship wreckers, crooked captains, and chart forgers in a conspiracy to smash Western Civilization and the White Race because they are mentally ill; they suffer from mass paranoia; they believe they are "God's Chosen People" and always innocent "scapegoats"—the classic symptoms of paranoia. They have developed these crazy ideas into a "religion" because they are basically parasites that will not work and must get a living off other people, like tapeworms. Healthy societies always purge these human tapeworms. Jews can live only in an unhealthy society, just as tapeworms can live only in an unhealthy and unclean body. Jews, therefore, foster every kind of degeneracy and chaos so that they can suck the blood of an unhealthy people. (Chapter 7 - "A Close Look at the Crooks")

- There are two segments of this world Jewish conspiracy, both aiming at world conquest and both using the strategy "divide and conquer." One segment, the "friends of the *captain*," is Zionist and capitalist. They promote the world Jewish conspiracy by gathering up gold by fake speculation and unfair merchandising, then using the gold to buy up newspapers and other media with which to brainwash the people. They also exaggerate upper-class arrogance and wealth, thus promoting class war. (Chapter 8 - "Friends of the Captain")

- The other segment of world Jewry operates as "friends of the *crew*." They preach violent class war from below: communism = mutiny. The communist/Marxist Jews believe they can thus fulfill the ancient Jewish prophecies of world domination by the bloody violence of world revolution. They need endless masses of easily-manipulated humanity. So the Jews promote, first, the breeding of the huge colored swarms, and then their incitement to a Marxist mutiny against the elite White minority. (Chapter 9 - "Friends of the Crew")

- To destroy the hated Whites and thus advance their violent world revolution, the Jews promote the endless breeding, arming, and organizing of the colored world. They move hordes of Blacks into urban areas, forcing them into competition with Whites; and then, when the Blacks fail, the Jews convince them that they are being "oppressed." This produces riots and finally armed rebellion, both in America and elsewhere. As a result of this Jewish promotion of colored breeding, the colored birthrate is skyrocketing while the best of the Whites are killing each other off in fratricidal wars and by birth control. The end will be world racial warfare, in which the swarming colored races will be pitted against the minority of Whites for survival. Either the colored swarms, led and inflamed by the Jews, will overwhelm the White minority and inherit a ruined world, or we will smash them. It's "them or us." (Chapter 10 - "Black Plague")

- The Negro masses are biologically inferior and easily manipulated. But the Jews can't as easily manipulate White men, so they are doing everything possible to destroy the idea that there is any such thing as "race," with the intention of breeding the White man—and especially the Nordic—out of existence. (Chapter 11 - "The Facts of Race")

- Ahead lies all-out world race-war, with Blacks mutinying in the armed forces, with the Whites paralyzed by "love" and integration propaganda, and with the fearful weapons of modern White technology falling into the hands of Black terrorists and being used against their White creators to create a Marxist-mongrel-Jewish U.N.-dominated America. (Chapter 12 - "Nightmare")

- In the face of this hideous threat, the only White response has been 50 years of failure, because our side has insisted on "fighting" only within the Jewish-built conservative "playpen," never mentioning the Jewish enemy, and never fighting on the only grounds which can unite our squabbling side: *race*. Conservatives have been suckered into 50 years of fighting on the Jews' favorite grounds: economic manipulations. "Conservatives" drive our own masses away from us by preaching economic "royalism," just as the Jews want. In spite of this conservative stupidity, the healthy racial instincts of our working people have been leading them steadily to the right, until a substantial portion are now following George Wallace.[1] But even Wallace accommodates the Jews by denying race, and by cooperating with the devilish Jewish enemy. No leader, even Wallace, who stays in the Jewish playpen, can hope to win. Only a leader who tells the revolutionary truth—all of it—can win. And that includes the facts that Adolf Hitler fought the Alamo of our White Race and that the enemy is *Jewish* and *Negro*. (Chapter 13 - "Fifty Years of Failure")

Instead of such honesty, however, the conservative movement is used and manipulated by Jews who pose as our "leaders."

Those who have followed these facts and arguments must now be asking themselves (as I once did) "What does it all mean? What are we to

---

[1] Wallace (1919-1998) was a three-time governor of Alabama who ran for president several times on a conservative, segregationist platform.

do? Can we win? And, if so, how?" The purpose of this chapter is to show the reader that there is a historically-proven method of smashing these arrogant Red Jews and their colored troops. Hitler did it—which is precisely why they hate him and revile his name and anything connected with him so bitterly.

Germany found itself in exactly the same revolutionary mess we now face. We have been forced into a crazy Vietnam War that we aren't allowed to win.[2] Mobs here at home are sabotaging the kids out there fighting. They even attack troop trains and ammunition ships and get away with it.

German troops, fighting at the front in World War I, found themselves sabotaged from the rear by a Jewish-Marxist revolution, just as we have here now. Jews caused a vast ammunition strike, so the troops had nothing to shoot, and stirred up a mutiny in the German Navy at Kiel.

Here in America, Jews and their allies promote draft-dodging, give aid and comfort to the enemy, and promote outright rebellion among Negroes, who shout "Hell no, we won't go!" We find Jewish scum hanging up the Viet Cong (communist) flag in our streets and burning our American flag.

In the states of Bavaria, Hesse, and Saxony, in Germany, the Reds seized governments. They hung up their hammer-and-sickle rags and dragged the German flag in the mud. In Germany, the Jews had used the methods of capitalism to gather up almost all the wealth, to become almost all the professors, almost all the lawyers, almost all the doctors, and to push Germans out of the professions. Jews dominated Germany through the press, the professions, and the power of money.

Here in America, we have the same thing happening, with the percentage of Jews in high positions going up, and, Jews quietly dominating America through control of the press, professions, and money.

While rich German Jews were seizing all the top professional jobs, the Marxist-Jew labor agitators were turning millions of German working men into enemies of their own people—into rabid, violent communists, just as Jews are doing to many US laboring men, through rotten, Red unions.

The Jews in Germany, like typical parasites, devoured the wealth of the nation so greedily they wrecked the economy and ruined the currency, bringing on catastrophic inflation.[3] We have precisely the same thing going on here, with only the degree of crisis not yet the same as it was in

---

[2] The Vietnam War ran in earnest from about 1963 through 1974.

[3] German hyperinflation raged in 1923 and 1924, destroying families' savings.

Germany. But all-out inflation is just ahead. The Jews in Germany had almost total control of the press and all other media for reaching the minds and hearts of the people and were using this power to sow degeneracy, chaos, and mindless hedonism among the Germany people.

Is it any different here in America, today?

The Jews in Germany, with their Marxist lies and propaganda, had incited and inflamed millions of Germans to hatred of their fellow Germans. Without understanding what was causing their poverty and misery, they filled the German streets with violent, rioting mobs.

Is it any different here in America, today?

The Jews in Germany, before World War II, were pushing homosexuality, loose morals, filthy "literature," crazy "dances" fresh from the African jungles, insane "art," Marxist "music," and self-indulgence for youth.

Is it any different here in America, today? *No!*

The Jews wrecked Germany. They have almost wrecked America.

In Germany, at the last minute, from out of the soul of the German people, came forth a man with the spiritual power and leadership to reassert the supremacy of the German majority, restore German honor, and build a healthy, wholesome society.

A simple German corporal arose and gathered about him brave comrades who would rather die than watch their people smashed and enslaved by Jews. Adolf Hitler launched a gigantic renaissance of the people that astonished the whole world! Hitler used the eternal laws of revolution and counter-revolution to smash illegal Jewish power and reassert the legitimate power of the majority of the German people.

The reason our side in America has done nothing but retreat in such a disgusting and cowardly manner for 50 years is that, so far, no one on our side has ever applied these eternal laws of *revolution, power,* and *mass politics* to our problem. Our side has been too powerful and wealthy for too long to be able to feel any real possibility of defeat and death. Our side has been playing kid games of economic conservatism, while the enemy— professional revolutionaries almost to a man—has been systematically destroying our power, our wealth, and our ability to resist. Every day, every year, we get weaker and they get stronger.

The continued existence of Western Civilization and the White Race depends on whether enough Americans are sufficiently concerned about imminent catastrophe to do something professional and revolutionary about it—rather than continue to play the easy, kosher-conservative, playpen games of the last 50 years.

We are facing a *revolution,* and a bloody one at that.

"States' rights," "conservatism," "Wallace-ism," and even the Klan are only crumbling Maginot lines, walls which may delay the brutal advance of the enemy a bit, but which will never stop him. *Only an attack can do these things*—and no half-hearted, Vietnam-style "attack," either, but the old-fashioned kind in which our purpose is simple and direct: to *annihilate* the enemy: to smash him, beat him down, and exterminate him, until he is no longer a threat.

The reason our people are unable to see the urgent, desperate need for a revolution, instead of the silly, conservative shilly-shallying in the Jewish playpen, is that almost all of our people, on both sides, left and right, have fallen victims to Jewish propaganda against "extremism" and radicalism.

The attack upon us is called, even by the enemy, a "Black Revolution." It is communist and Marxist. It is lawless. *It is radical, violent, and bloody!* The only defense that even has a prayer of succeeding must be equally radical. When someone is shooting at you, only counter fire can succeed.

Anyone might be pardoned for believing for a few minutes, or even an hour or so, that he might be able to talk his way out of a gun fight. But when the shooting goes on and on, gets more and more bloody, and the enemy openly proclaims his intention of wiping you out, as the Blacks are doing, it is madness and suicide to keep depending on the easy, "nice," "moderate," conservative" methods of survival. The way you "shoot back" in a revolution is with a revolution of your own. *They have started a Black revolution. Only a White revolution can stop it!*

And that's what this book is all about.

卐 卐 卐

Over the past 20 years, I have run the course from "Republican," to "hard-shell Republican" to "anti-communist" to "McCarthyite" to "Birch-type Conservative" to sneaky Nazi!—and finally to all-out National Socialist Hitlerite! I have become a revolutionary as dedicated to professional, hard-boiled, White Man's anti-communist revolution as any Marxist is dedicated to his bloody revolution. And to succeed, a White Man's anti-communist revolution must be something more than just against the other side. It must be a revolution for something so grand and noble that a man can give his life heroically fighting for it.

Men will talk about almost anything. Men will fight for very few things. And men will fight to the death for only the most basic of motives. They will fight heroically (that is, with supreme self-sacrifice—which is what "heroism" means) only for idealistic aims they hold greater and more holy than their own personal survival. Only when you can make a man feel, deep in his heart, that survival of his loved ones, his honor, or his whole people are in deadly danger, will he risk his life to do battle against overwhelming odds, where his own personal survival is unlikely.

The Jews are filled to overflowing with this "family" feeling, so that they not only stick together, as is well known, but they sacrifice and give for each other too, as the records of any Jewish fund appeal will show, and the rush of Jews even to fight for their precious Israel shows this even more. Pointedly, it is this fanatic "family feeling" which makes the Jews such a power in this world.

The Blacks, today, have also been filled by Jewish agitation with this same feeling of fighting for their family, for "their own," to the point where they go out by the thousands and face beatings, fire hoses, jails, and even death to advance the revolution of their "soul brothers."

But America's anti-communist leadership, so far, is so hung up on money, security, comfort, luxury, and Sunday evening, tea-sipping anti-communism that nobody will sacrifice much for such disgusting material-ism, let alone give his life heroically for such cowardly "leaders." The masses of working people, especially, are not only not won over to fight for their own side by the "Bloomers" Buckley, "Rabbit" Welch, "Fatty" Hargis, and "Dry Goods" Goldwater economic approaches, but the masses are positively repelled and disgusted by this selfish money-madness of the would-be, anti-communist "leadership."

To fire up our people to fight the flaming counter-revolution, we must launch at the Jewish and Negro enemy, we must give our people an over-whelming sense of *family*—an urgent, self-sacrificing, idealistic drive to draw together and fight for "our own." "Wallace-ism" is the next-to-last step toward that goal. But Wallace-ism must fail, as have all the other half measures, because it lacks the guts and honesty to give the masses that powerful, *open* feeling of "family," without which it is just one more (even if temporarily more successful) effort to sneak up on the Jewish enemies without naming them, and even by cooperating with them.

The fuel that feeds the fires behind Wallace-ism is *racism*, the very feeling of family of which I have written. But Wallace endlessly repeats, "I am not a racist; racism is evil!"

The people don't believe him of course. The enthusiasm he generates is racial family feeling, not political. Wallace is the best racial symbol of our White Family that has been allowed by the Jews (through compromise) to rise as a national and somewhat respectable figure. But that very com-

promise by which Wallace has achieved some "respectability" will eventually give the Jews the power to destroy Wallace (and destroy him they
will)—just as they have crushed all the other compromisers for 50 years.[4]

It is not the compromisers and respectable "nice guys" who have the
power to inflame and lead the masses of people in times of bloody revolution, but the wild, rabid, flaming extremists—the Patrick Henrys, the
Lenins, the Garibaldis, the Kenyattas, and the Hitlers—the men most hated
and cursed by whatever power they are fighting.[5] Lenin the Bolshevik won
in Russia, over the more moderate Mensheviks, precisely because he was
exiled and jailed as the most violent and extreme among all the competing
leaders. Jomo Kenyatta, the Mau-Mau leader, won power in Kenya precisely because he was tossed in jail as the most violent, radical, and bloody
cannibal leader.

Here in America, Stokely Carmichael and H. Rap Brown are inevitably winning the hearts of the Black masses precisely because they are the
most violent, radical, and extreme Black leaders and will probably go to
jail, which will help make them all the more the leaders of the Blacks.

On an absolutely different plane, Adolf Hitler won the hearts of the
German people, and won power precisely because he, too, was thrown in
jail as the most extreme, most radical, and uncompromising of all the competing "nationalist" leaders.

These ultimate leaders of revolution are always hated and cursed by
the compromisers and cowards on their own side because the cowards and
compromisers are desperately eager to avoid the bloody terrorism of the
enemy. So the compromisers try to win the enemy's temporary favor by
blasting away at the genuine revolutionaries, who alone can win what these
parlor revolutionaries pretend to fight for.

Thus, we find almost every anti-Marxist leader in America, from
Buckley to Welch, slyly spreading the lie that I am working for the Jews
and communists by "provoking" the enemy. Sure, I provoke the enemy,
just as a soldier provokes the enemy—by shooting at him! The compromisers and kosher conservatives hope that by blasting me viciously
enough, they will win the trust and love of their Jewish pals (although every major Jewish organization and leader in America is viciously blasting

---

[4] Wallace was shot by a would-be assassin, Arthur Bremer, in 1972. Wallace
survived but was paralyzed for the rest of his life.
[5] GLR: Let me make it clear that I am not implying that these men are anything alike. My point is that each of them succeeded against a starting lineup of
dozens of other would-be leaders only because they were the most *extreme*.

away at Welch, Buckley, Hargis and the rest of the "my-best-friends-are-Jews" bunch). How can you fight—and win—without provoking the enemy?

卐 卐 卐

Deep in their hearts, the masses of people—and many of the leaders—already feel that the Jewish, Negro, and Marxist problem has gone far, far past the point where we can talk the enemy out of power. The ordinary workingman knows the enemy has forced us into a *fight* to survive and keep what we have built, when he sees what the Blacks are doing in America. If our people are to have any hope of eventual victory, we must have a hard-core revolutionary cadre organized and ready to assume leadership when Wallace-ism, the last hope of the compromisers, folds up.

To organize and train that hard-core cadre of revolutionary White leaders is, and has been, my naked purpose in building the American Nazi Party.

When the Marxists had had enough of Kerensky's hanky-panky, Lenin was able to grab power, even though he had to come from far behind in the leadership race, because he stuck resolutely to the hard, tough, no-compromise line, and was ready when the time was ripe, in spite of all jails and persecutions.

When the Germans had had enough hanky-panky with Von Papen, Bruning, et al., Hitler was able to win power, even though he had to come from far behind in the leadership race, because he stuck resolutely to the hard, tough, no-compromise line and was ready when the time was ripe, in spite of jails and persecutions.

When the wild Blacks in Kenya had had enough of the hanky-panky of the "moderate," pro-British Black leaders, Jomo Kenyatta was able to come from behind in the leadership race, because he stuck resolutely to the hard, tough no-compromise line and was ready when the time was ripe in spite of the fact that he was then doing a long jail sentence.

No matter how we suffer and go to jail, starve, and are cursed by our own side today, I know with historical certainty that the Nazi party will have the strength to come from far behind when the time is ripe and our people are finally disgusted with the endless compromisers.

When they want to fight, when they are ready to sacrifice anything rather than bow to Negroes and Jews one more day, *nothing can stop us*. For we shall have behind us the mightiest force on this planet: millions and millions of fighting-mad White men, filled with that holy and revolutionary sense of family which has proven unconquerable down through the ages.

The situation, with the revolutionary, bloody Blacks forcing the calling out of the army in Detroit even as I write these words, has now gone past the point where a Wallace can deal with it on a "states' rights" basis. Already, it is clear that it will take a massive and unified federal effort to restore order and sanity.

When our people have had enough Black Revolution and conservative cowardice, then we will be ready to smash the enemy with *White revolution*.

Chapter 2

DEATH RATTLE

Consider several examples of cultural degeneracy:

Sitting in the darkened theatre, you are at first conscious of the audience coughing, and whispering. Then there is the rustling noise of the curtain going up—a very quiet noise, but you can hear it. The stage is pitch black. A powerful spotlight stabs into the darkness. It reveals a live chicken crucified on a miniature cross. You hear the audience gasp almost in unison.

Then a young girl in leotards comes out, slashes the throat of the chicken, unties its wings and legs from the cross, and lets it run around the stage with its blood spurting until it falls dead. The stage lights up. The girl takes off her leotards, and picks up a large doll. Howling and giggling, she twists the arms and legs off the doll. Then she lies down, naked, and a huge Black male comes out with a razor and shaves the White girl's private parts. They get into a burlap bag and, standing up, engage in sexual intercourse. Finally, the girl emerges from the bag and her naked flesh is rubbed all over with wet spaghetti.

You have just been to a performance of the "New Theatre," a "happening"—a classic example of the way Shakespeare has been "improved" by Jean-Jacques Lebel, the producer of the above nightmare.

Not to be outdone by "Whites," the Negro race is doing its share to create the same sort of "New Theatre." *Time* magazine reports that Le Roi Jones, the Negro "playwright," puts on a play appropriately called "The Toilet." As the curtain goes up, we see a White boy being held with his head in a urinal by a Negro, while other Negroes actually urinate on the White boy on stage. According to Le Roi's play, the White boy has been trying to get the Negroes to engage in homosexual acts with him, and the Negroes are chastising him by beating him up, stuffing his head in the urinal and actually urinating on his face. Not only was this play actually staged, without public protest, but US tax payers subsidized this degeneracy with $40,000 in federal funds.[1]

---

[1] *US News and World Report*, December 13, 1965.

In Berkeley, California, the newspaper at the University of California advertises naked sex orgies of the Sexual Freedom League. There are advertisements such as "Slave wants Master," in which masochists want sadists to chain and beat them. These degenerates now brazenly push for naked sex and homosexuality—*in public*. Their program states, "We would rather see a sex organ in the hands of a child than a war toy." They do not specify *whose* sex organ. This is distributed freely to innocent young girls on the campus.

Time magazine, 11 Mar 1966, p. 66

In San Francisco, under the auspices of a rabbi, the homosexuals hold a formal "ball." In Washington, DC, in the Sheraton-Park Hotel, the homosexuals, both "male" arid "female," hold an official convention, and lobby against any restrictions on their spreading filth. They picket the White House for freedom to "marry" each other. Queers *do* get "married" and live together in public. And nobody really protests!

Women have been wearing pants for such a long time that it is no longer noticed. But now the *American Observer* newspaper reports that "men" are taking to long hair, cosmetics, perfume, lipstick, and feminine clothes as "high fashion," until it's hard to tell males from females anymore among so-called young "mods." Finally, the first skirts are appearing on men!

The Associated Press tells us, on May 22, 1966, that there is a huge, million-dollar business in making *false eyelashes* for US businessmen!— not just for queers, but ordinary businessmen!

Time magazine for December 9, 1966, describes a Boston opera production including a wild and completely nude *sex orgy* on stage. Herds of animals are slaughtered and naked men and women run riot! This is taken seriously as "art." The police do nothing.

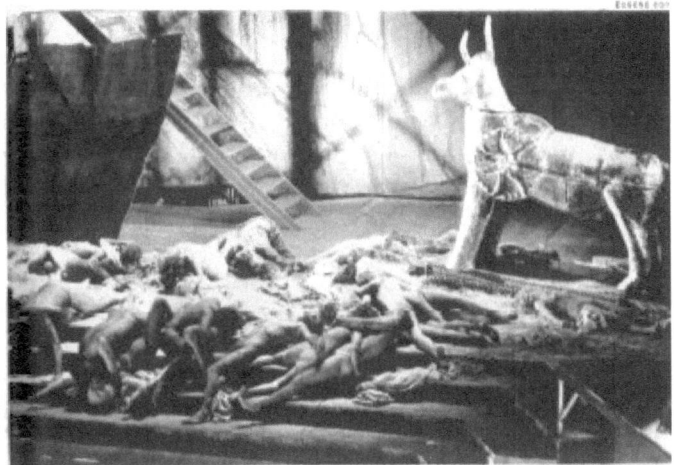

After the orgy – *Time*, 9 Dec 1966, p. 95

UPI reports that Richmond Professional Institute, with lovely White girls in attendance, has chosen a negress, Beatrice Wynn, as "Beauty Queen" in once-proud Richmond, Virginia. Again, no protest!

In Middlesex, England—a White nation even further along on the road to degeneracy than the USA—the *District Post* for March 25, 1965, presents a photograph of a college play about Christ and the Disciples. Christ is portrayed by a Jamaican Negro, while all the White Disciples are shown on their knees before this arrogant black buck, posing as Jesus Christ.

A Negro preacher halts traffic in Boston, dares the police to arrest him, and tells the black mob that if he *is* arrested, they will "rock Boston." This "gentleman" is not arrested. (*Boston Record*, June 18, 1966)

In Dos Palos, California, UPI reports that Jack E. Mulkey, Superintendent of the Poverty War in that area, was "fighting poverty" by buying tuxedoes for Negroes so they can go to dances in style!

Associated Press and Reuters report that a chimpanzee named Cindy-Lou in the Worcestershire Zoo, near London, has "astonished the art world with a series of dazzling abstract paintings." A descendant of master painter Sir Joshua Reynolds reports that these "wonderful" ape-paintings are worth hundreds of dollars each!

In Cleveland, Philadelphia and many other cities, police officers are forbidden to interfere with Negroes openly looting stores. For centuries, looting has been dealt with by shooting all looters, out of hand. Our "leaders" do nothing.[2]

All over Washington, our top diplomats and dignitaries engage in drunken orgies of dancing the "frug" and the "Watusi." Photos are made of our leaders appearing in sexual poses exactly like those of naked cannibals in Africa.

In San Francisco, a Negro named Harry Dedrick runs a shoeshine parlor. He has hired topless, White girls to shine Negroes' shoes!

---

[2] This obviously recalls the infamous "Black Lives Matter" riots of 2020.

Feeling the Truth

CANNIBALS AND CHRISTIANS by Norman Mailer. 400 pages. Dial. $5.95.

Norman Mailer writes so obsessively, and says so many silly things, that the crowds he draws have learned to come with their pockets full of ripe eggs. He makes an irresistible target, like a Hyde Park orator who seems to ask for, if

HENRY GROSSMAN

NORMAN MAILER
Bloodhound of the men's room.

not necessarily to deserve, just what he gets. It is worth noting, however, that he always gets a crowd.

The literary firing line will probably pepper his latest book, which presents targets in gratifying profusion. *Cannibals and Christians* is mostly warmed-over Mailer: a scatter of pseudo poems (he calls them "short hairs"), essays, dialectic, sermonizing, book reviews, literary criticism and political reportage. The principal new material is some italicized mortar troweled in to support the notion that this pile of used bricks rose and took form from a blueprint, which of course it did not.

His short hairs are best ignored. His excursions into philosophy, all taken in Jean-Paul Sartre's second-class compartment, begin at the level of the college bull session and follow a descending route. "*Coitus interruptus* is evil," announces Mailer in the course of a *Playboy* magazine panel discussion on sex. Food has a soul, he writes; fresh food has more soul than canned food. Terminal cancer cases can be arrested by reading William Burroughs: "Bet money on that." The now-notorious Mailer sense of smell, which got such a bloodhound workout in his last novel, *An*

Time magazine reports on September 2, 1966, that one of America's top writers, Norman Mailer ("The Naked and the Dead"), now concentrates on the bowel. "Man's nature," says this Jewish playwright, "can be divined by the color, the shape, the size of the movement of his bowel contents!" This "artist" regularly appears on national TV and has his books published. No outraged protest.

In Berkeley, California, students kidnap a female dean and hold her hostage overnight, while the police and administration do nothing. When the police finally arrest one student, mobs surround the car. They imprison the officers for more than a day and most of a night, using the top of the police car as a platform for speeches blasting the university and the police. The prisoner is released! Nobody is disciplined in any way for all this hell. Then the same students parade around the university with signs reading "F-ck!" and other "freedom" words. Still no discipline or resistance!

In the middle of the United States, we have set up the world's biggest spy and subversion center, the "United Nations." The first General Secretary of this infamous "Trojan horse" in our midst, was none other than Alger Hiss, since convicted of perjury and exposed officially as a Soviet spy, working to destroy the United States of America, while he was a top officer of "our" state Department and the Secretary General of the United Nations in San Francisco. Not only does nobody protest, but last year, when this convicted traitor spoke at Princeton University, he was *cheered* by Americans!

Richard Wagner's great opera, *Tannhauser*, is performed in Bayreuth, Germany, with "Venus" played by a Negress, Leontyne Price.

Walter Jenkins is arrested for soliciting homosexual degeneracy in the men's room of the Washington, DC YMCA. It turns out that Mr. Jenkins is the closest personal aide to President Johnson, who does everything possible to cover up the arrest.

Meanwhile, Jenkins and the President are famous for conducting nude swimming parties in the White House pool, and almost forcing other top US administrators to strip and swim naked with them. After the hullabaloo dies down, Jenkins moves from Washington to a few miles from LBJ's ranch in Texas. No mention in the press.

The Santa Barbara High School puts on the play "King Arthur's Round Table." Sir Lancelot, the lover of Queen Guinevere, is played by a six-foot Negro football player.

In literally tens of thousands of jobs, White men are fired or passed over for promotion, especially in the federal government, to make jobs available to admittedly incompetent Negroes! Harry Golden recommends $100 billion be given outright to Negroes by White taxpayers! Negro labor leader

A. Philip Randolph goes before Congress and demands a $185 billion "Freedom Budget" gift to Negroes! Americans accept this arrogance meekly.

> As these and other programs swell the number of productive workers, cut down unemployment and increase consumption, the private sector of our national economy will inevitably grow also.
>
> The Freedom Budget recognizes that full employment by itself is not enough to eradicate poverty. Therefore, it also proposes — and budgets for — a $2-an-hour Federal minimum wage covering everyone within Federal jurisdiction; a new farm program to provide adequate income to the 43 per cent of farm families who now live in poverty; and immediate improvements in Social Security, welfare, unemployment compensation, workmen's compensation and other programs designed to support those who cannot or should not work.
>
> Where will the money come from?
>
> The Freedom Budget recognizes that we cannot spend what we do not produce. It also recognizes that we must spend wisely what we do produce.
>
> It proposes that a portion of our future growth—one thirteenth of what can reasonably be expected to be available —be earmarked for the eradication of poverty. The Freedom Budget proposed outlay of $185 billion in 10 years sounds like a great deal of money, and it is a great deal of money.
>
> But it will come from the expansion of our economy that will in part be the result of wise use of that very $185 billion. It will build homes and schools, provide recreation areas and hospitals. It will train teachers and nurses.
>
> It will provide adequate incomes to millions who now do not have them. And those millions will in turn buy goods they cannot now buy.
>
> So the wage earner of today will benefit as well. His earnings will go up and his enjoyment of life will be increased. The opportunities for private enterprise will increase.
>
> The breeding grounds of crime and discontent will be diminished in the same way that draining a swamp cuts down

Sammy Davis, Jr., the Negro-Jew entertainer, plays "the fastest gun in the West" in *The Rifleman* TV show. When this one-eyed Jewish Negro appears in the western town, we are shown all the White men running and hiding. Americans swallow this without protest.

In Washington, D.C., police corner a Negro rapist in an elevator, stuck between floors, with his White female victim still terrified in there with the Black rapist. Before police break in to rescue the White girl and capture the Negro, they have to read the criminal a speech about his "rights," his privilege of remaining silent and his right to have a lawyer, for fear he might shout something "incriminating!" Madness!—and nobody cares enough to stop it!

All over the country, although it is not being reported except in isolated incidents, Negroes are using a new robbery technique: 15 or 20 tough Negro males walk into a small store and, at a given signal, run out with armfuls of goods. Nothing much can be done about it, since they are *Black*.[3]

In San Francisco, firemen going into the tinderbox Hunter's Point Negro section are regularly beaten, stoned, and shot at. The firemen can get no protection from cowardly politicians and picket San Francisco City Hall demanding protection. They get none!

---

[3] This was an early precursor to the current fad of Black "flash mobs."

In Boston, Negro schools are so dangerous the Board of Education can't get any teachers to go in among these vicious Blacks. So they offer a thousand dollar bonus for teachers to face the razors, knives, rape and filth—"Combat Pay" it is called in the press. But it is not enough. Teachers still balk at braving the black hell.

$1000 'Combat Pay' Offer Fails To Win Over Boston Teachers

By Bertram G. Waters
Special to The Washington Post

BOSTON, Jan. 12—School teachers here have rejected an offer of up to $1000 extra pay per year to teach in three predominantly Negro schools with a history of violence.

The teachers, polled by the Boston Teachers Union, an AFL-CIO affiliate which represents their interests voted 591 to 494 not to accept the inducement, often called "combat pay." Superintendent William H. Ohrenberger had proposed the pay raise to attract experienced teachers to the city's most difficult classrooms.

The two junior high schools and one elementary school, all located in the Negro core of the city, have been marked by pupil assaults on teachers, high teacher turnover, truancy and rebellion. Nearly half of their faculties are recent college graduates.

The Union vote, representing less than half of the 2400 members polled, was considered a victory for the single salary schedule in effect here since 1958 after a long battle by the teachers. No extra teaching time would have been required to earn the bonus, which would be paid only to teachers with at least four years' experience.

Following two assaults on teachers at the Campbell Junior High School in early December, Superintendent Ohrenberger recommended bonus pay as one step in a 9-point program adopted by the school committee to prevent the spread of violence.

Other measures already under way include recruiting of experienced teachers at regular salaries, the hiring of a full-time child psychologist, and a search for neighborhood parents willing to work as teacher aides.

Union leaders, who vie with two rival groups for teacher memberships, did not challenge Ohrenberger's other measures but called them "long overdue." Ohrenberger predicted that violence would spread through many of the city's 50 Negro schools unless the crash program was adopted.

But the teachers, whose salaries range from $5500 to $10,300 annually, overruled the "combat pay" against the wishes of colleagues at the Campbell school. Many teachers said they would not volunteer to go there even for the added compensation.

Rejection of the incentive measure has caused the Union, which remained officially neutral, to ask the School Committee to seek Federal funds for hand-picked teachers who chose to return to the troubled Campbell.

Special saturation programs for disadvantaged children already are in effect in two other schools under Title 1 of the U.S. Elementary and Secondary Education Act.

Teachers chosen, for these schools work 75 minutes extra each day for $36 additional pay per week. Addition of the Campbell School to the program was proposed by a School Committee member.

Washington Post, 13 Jan 1967

Washington, DC once had the best schools in the nation. Then it desegregated. Now the schools are overwhelmingly Black, after almost all the Whites moved to suburbs. So the DC schools have become among the worst in the country—so bad that the race-mixers who ruined them now claim that children attending them are "deprived." Police officers have to be stationed in the halls of these Negro schools, the rooms and halls smell of urine, windows are all smashed out every year, and it is almost impossible to get good teachers to put up with the attacks and abuse heaped on them by Black pupils.

The government builds tremendous, multi-million dollar "slum clearance" modern apartment buildings, and turns them over to Negroes almost free. The fine new buildings promptly become vile slums, with elevators unsafe and often inoperative from all the Negro urine which literally shorts out the wires and rots the cables and flooring.

Washington, DC papers run advertisements for the new "Watergate Apartments," which boast that these new apartments have closed-circuit TV to guard all passageways, electrified fences, armed guards at all entrances and the rest of the things common to a *prison*. Negro crime is so rampant in the capital of the United States that a congressman is stabbed in his offices by a Black savage.

A Congressman's secretary is stabbed as she kneels in prayer in a church. Women in DC office buildings must use the ladies' rooms only in pairs, because the Blacks lie in wait in rest rooms for unwary, helpless women alone! The Supreme Court of the US provides its secretaries with armed escorts to the women *inside* its building!

High school girls coming to visit their nation's capital in the spring are regularly ravished by sex-crazy Black bucks, and even the White school boys are now victims of gangs of Black teenagers who "shake them down" for money, watches, and other valuables. Nobody dares point out that this is *Negro* crime. Everybody deplores the "crime wave," but it's "hate" to identify the Black criminals, who commit 85% of serious crime (FBI reports).

Tens of thousands of these Blacks, most of them living on "welfare" provided by hard-working White people, have openly organized what they openly call a "Black Revolution," in which they violently attack our cities, policemen, firemen, and anybody who is White. They scream, "Burn, baby, burn!," and loot millions of dollars of goods from stores, right under the noses of our policemen (who are usually ordered by politicians to do nothing). And they boast that, if we don't give them what they want, they will "tear down everything Western Civilization stands for," as the Black Stokely Carmichael puts it. There is no real resistance. In fact, at colleges, Carmichael gets standing ovations from White students for his "Get Whitey" speeches.

On almost any magazine stand these days, you can buy dozens of paperback books and magazines devoted to the most disgusting pornography, depravity, and homosexuality—emphasizing enlarged male genitals and showing nude men caressing each other!

A Negro from the Watts section of Los Angeles wins an art prize with a sculpture consisting of the broken window of an automobile, an old generator, a busted oil can, and some odd, dirty junk, all welded together. Another "great" "sculptor"—Lipshitz—wins another "art" prize and has his work exhibited in the White House.

On October 26, 1965, two Chicago police officers are attacked by two Puerto Ricans. To quote the UPI dispatch of March 8, 1966, "The officers encountered Suarez and Rodriguez in an alley, where they said Suarez was waving a broken beer bottle. They pulled their service revolvers, identified themselves as policemen, and ordered Suarez to drop the bottle. Instead Suarez slashed Officer Desutter in the face. He was scarred for life."

When the case went to trial before Negro Judge Leighton, the judge freed the two colored citizens and cussed out the cops. "The police officer has no business to pull a gun and attack a citizen," said the judge. "What is a citizen supposed to do when he is approached by two officers with a gun? It is not a crime to walk down a street with a broken beer bottle." Nothing is done.

In Leb's restaurant in Atlanta, Negroes invaded the restaurant, urinated on the tables, and defecated on the floors and chairs! None of these people were arrested.

On March 11, 1965, the UPI covered the Negro march on Montgomery, Alabama, reported that "about 200 boys and girls…stood at a given signal and relieved themselves in the street!"

An exhibition of "modern art" features a gigantic statue of a female called "She: A Cathedral." The statue lies on its back, with the breasts touching the ceiling of the exhibition hail, and its legs spread wide. Visitors enter and leave through a tremendous aperture between the legs!

卐 卐 卐

Crucified chickens, naked sex-orgies on stage, bowel-movement prophets, businessmen wearing lipstick and false eyelashes...! As painful as it has been for me, I have steeled myself to set down these almost unbelievable samples of rot and insanity infecting our civilization.

But the real depth of the problem cannot be gauged by these mere symptoms of degeneracy. To plumb the depth of our plunge toward hell, one must examine the less sensational course of our every-day affairs, and the astounding way we tolerate growing horror in our daily lives. Take a look at what *you* put up with every day of the year—what millions and millions of us meekly tolerate!

Just a few generations ago, our forefathers fought a desperate war against the mightiest power on earth—the British army and navy—over relatively minor taxes on tea and some stamps required on legal documents. They fought a bloody war for the right to help set those small taxes.

Today, not only do we have literally thousands of different taxes on stamps, tea, and everything else, but they have *stolen our money too!* Literally! They've done it so gradually that we have actually allowed ourselves to be robbed, just as surely as if it were done by bandits with pistols.

Our grandfathers could guard against future insecurity by saving up actual gold coins. Many young people today have never *seen* a gold coin. They don't miss what they have never experienced. And too few of the rest of us stop to think about it all, so we never remind them. Franklin D. Roosevelt started the robbery by decreeing that *you can't have any gold. Foreigners can get all the us gold they want—but not you!* In the hysteria of a depression, people let Roosevelt and his gang take away every last gold coin we had. It's illegal for you to own them.[4]

People tolerated this outrage because, we were told, the gold was held in safekeeping for us at Fort Knox. It said, right on our paper money, that it was backed by that gold (at Fort Knox). My older readers may remember the "Gold Certificates," which were orange-colored instead of green, and redeemable in solid gold.

Then, after the people had become accustomed to the idea of not being allowed to have their gold, but only the certificates standing for that gold, they went a step further. They withdrew the gold certificates. They took away the gold backing for our paper money, and replaced it with "Silver Certificates." People went along with this, too, since they felt they could always fall back on the solid silver behind the paper.

Then, in 1964, the thieves moved ahead to step three: they changed the paper money again, and took away even the promise to pay for the paper in silver. Take a look at the paper money in your pocket. Unless it is a rarity, it no longer says "Silver Certificate," as it did only a few years ago. Now it just says "Federal Reserve Note." And what does *that* mean? Literally *nothing!* You can get neither gold nor silver coin for the paper.

But still there was actual *silver* in the pockets of Americans; dimes, quarters, half-dollars, and silver "cartwheels." We still had something of real value. Finally, in 1965, they took the last step and *removed the silver from the coinage.* Now the coins in your pocket are as worthless as the paper—just slugs.

And all this time, *foreigners* can and do drain *your* gold—the gold our ancestors sweat and died to win for America. Foreigners take *billions* of dollars' worth of gold in periods of weeks. As I dictate these words,

---

[4] FDR issued Executive Order 6102 in 1933 banning the "hoarding of gold." It was not repealed until 1974 by President Ford.

foreigners have the right to "call" more of our remaining gold at Fort Knox than is available, leaving you—and your country—penniless.

Our great-great-granddaddies fought and won a bloody war over *pennies* and taxes on tea and stamps. Yet the present generation doesn't make any effective protest even when it is *robbed* by its government and given worthless paper and slugs for its gold, while the gold is being hauled out of the country by arrogant foreigners who are getting it *free*—as "foreign aid!"

Meanwhile, even the paper money and credit we still have left is taxed at a higher rate (an average of more than 25% total of all taxes) than anything ever known in history under a supposedly free government. Most Americans meekly work about two days out of every week, not to take care of themselves and their dear ones, or even to help *our* nation—but to send wheat, food, machinery, and our services to Marxists, cannibals, and criminal gangsters posing as "statesmen" in Africa, Haiti, Asia, India, etc., and loafing Negroes in America. Much of what we send to India for instance is devoured by millions of sacred *cows* and rats—while there are hungry Americas right here at home!

Never in history has a great people so meekly submitted to outrageous robbery and payment of tribute to its *enemies!*

Millions of fine American young people who would like to get married, and should be able to, can't—because they can't afford it! So while they work to save enough money to have good American kids, their money is taken in taxes and in gold to enable foreigners and Blacks in Africa and here to have swarms of Black kids on *our* money—on "foreign aid" and "welfare!"

Instead of having a sweet little White American baby, American couples must work hard to produce African kids, Asian kids, and kids of nations which openly hate us, and millions of illegitimate Black babies living on welfare here in America!

Meanwhile, take a ride out on a main road near any big city in what are called the "rush hours." You can't move. You sit, bumper to bumper, jammed in by the enormous crush of *people*. We are almost swamped with people, polluting the air with the cars and manufacturing for too many people, polluting the water with the flood of sewage from too many people, jamming every road, every public and private facility with too many people.[5] And there are such a hellish number *more* people on the way that

---

[5] At the time of this writing, the US population was 195 million; today it is 335 million.

even the liberals and the United Nations experts cringe. They babble about birth control.

But while we already suffer from such a log-jam of population, and limit our own numbers by birth control, our "leaders" are regularly letting down the bars for more and more immigration! We have recently gone all the way in this insanity and opened up the country to the endless millions and millions and millions from teeming Asia and Africa.

If you live in or near a big city, is it necessary for me to inform you of what has been done to our beautiful parks? New York's Central Park is perhaps the most horrifying example in America. This refreshing patch of green in the dingy stone canyons of Manhattan was once a haven for nature-starved humanity toiling and living in the depressing artificiality of a great city. But then came the "love-mongers" with their "equality" propaganda and the resulting flood of savage Africans from Harlem. Today, no amount of policing can make Central Park safe for honest citizens, especially women. The Park has been almost formally given up to the Black Terror—to African savagery!

It is the same in all the big cities. In Chicago, they have had to rip up the shrubbery in the many small parks scattered throughout the city, because the bushes were used by lurking Blacks to attack White passers-by, especially women. Nor is it only the city parks which have been abandoned to the spawn of the jungle by those who created them.

The streets of America, even in small towns, have become the hunting grounds for growing swarms of criminals, almost all of them *black*. In the face of this danger, the obvious, tried and true methods by which police once kept the streets safe have been abandoned, and the police handcuffed with a crazy pattern of restrictions, so that *you* are no longer able to depend on police to protect you. Many policemen, understandably, would rather look the other way than take the chance of jail or losing their job for stopping a Black criminal and then being accused of "police brutality," or starting a riot.

卐 卐 卐

Such examples of depravity and insanity could be multiplied indefinitely. My files bulge with thousands more documented items such as the foregoing. But it should not be necessary. The pattern should be clear to all those who are not determined to be stubbornly blind.

It is not these crazy facts themselves which are horrifying. There have always been nuts and criminals and wickedness, treason and depravity. The difference between all previous times and our times is that the sort of

monstrous insanity I have reported causes no particular outrage or indigna-
tion! These mad and vile things are accepted by most Americans, and the
rest of the world. In fact, many of them are points of pride!

No one has a fit when a Negro gathers our young girls up for a "Sexual Freedom League" and holds naked, interracial sex orgies in Berkeley,
California. No. That is a sign of "freedom" and "progress" today!

No one demands impeachment when the President's top personal aide
of many years turns out to be a filthy degenerate and the President sends
the Jew Abe Fortas around to hush up the story, even when it is discovered
this is not the first time. Instead, the degenerate moves near the President's
home in Austin, Texas (which isn't even reported), and the President wins
a national election by a landslide!

The paintings of apes and the sculptures of madmen and criminals are
pushed at us as "art," and those who deny that such depravity *is* art are
cursed and banished from "decent" society as bigots, "squares," and "phil-
istines."

Other civilizations before us have gone down to collapse and death.
But always before they fell, they have died of senility, of age, weariness,
and centuries of decline. White, Western civilization is not old in terms of
the millions of years of human existence. It is young, especially in America, and should be vigorous, healthy, and aggressive. Instead, it is mortally
sick, weak, feeble, mad, and depraved—dying.

Even Rome, during its decline, never reached the depths to which
America has already sunk. If that sounds hard to believe, just try to imagine the following:

Picture the pomp and splendor of a Roman "Triumph" for a returning
general at the head of his legions; the blaring trumpets, the horses and
chariot wheels clattering on the cobblestones, the roar of the Roman
crowd, the senators in white togas waiting in their dignity on the steps of
the Imperial palace, the marching, armored legions, helmets and swords
flashing in the sun, scarlet banners flying from their eagle, standards.

Now, into the midst of this scene, picture a mob of Black Ethiopian
slaves swarming from the gutter over the palace steps shouting "*F--- Caesar!*,"
carrying signs "Smash Roman Power," and singing "We Shall Overcome!"

Can you *imagine* Rome, at its worst, ever tolerating this outrage? But
wait! . . . There is more!

The trumpets blare and the vast crowd waits for Caesar himself to appear on the balcony high up in the magnificent palace. The great man appears. He raises his hand to still the roars of the crowd. The crowd falls

silent, and mighty Caesar speaks. Caesar shouts the battle-cry of the Ethiopians: "*We shall overcome!*"

The Ethiopian Blacks are still mobbing the steps below the balcony, shouting "*F--- Caesar!*" Suddenly some members of the Roman crowd leap forward and bash the Ethiopians. Caesar immediately orders the Roman citizens seized and executed, *and invites the Black Ethiopians up to the palace so he can apologize over tea and cakes.*

While Caesar is serving tea and cakes to the Ethiopians, they stage a sit-in in the palace, refusing to leave all night, finally urinating on the marble stairs. Is it necessary to draw the picture to the last line?

Can any American forget the scene in the joint session of our Congress in 1965 when our President shouted the slogan of the Black terrorists and revolutionists, "*We shall overcome!*" and our robed Supreme Court rose and applauded? Or when the Negroes held a mass urination in the streets of Montgomery, Alabama?

Did any nation ever sink so low? Where, in the history of all peoples for all time, will you find an equal for the situation in America where our "leaders" openly ally themselves with our enemies and persecute patriots? Where our Attorney General gets down on his knees, begging these Black revolutionists to leave his office? How come? Why? What's happened to our people?

卐 卐 卐

It is not surprising that there are evil forces at work. That has been the case since history began. But in our time, the very victims of the evil are the chief promoters of the evil itself. Our leaders are for the "barbarians" and against us!

Somehow, our people have been brought to the point where the arrogant Soviet, Khrushchev, could boast, rightly, that Americans would soon fall because we have become "too liberal to fight."

It is not the evil itself which is horrifying about our times—it is the way we not only tolerate evil, *but have made a cult of positively worshipping weakness, depravity, rottenness, and evil itself.* It is not the death rattle in the throat of Western civilization which is surprising; it is the fact that millions of Americans believe that the death rattle is a beautiful song!

Too many Americans are doing everything possible to hasten the death of our civilization, to welcome inferior barbarians who openly organize to murder and destroy our kind forever, all in the name of "Brotherhood" and "Freedom." Why? And what can we do about it? I have written this book to seek the answer.

CHAPTER 3
SPIRITUAL SYPHILIS

The guy at the door of Nazi Headquarters was the living embodiment of the national suicide I have set forth in the previous chapter. He seemed young. But you couldn't be sure, because he was wearing a matted red beard. He wasn't wearing clothes, just a raggedy blanket and sandals. "Shades" (sunglasses) covered his eyes. Unkempt hair covered much of the rest of his face.

Our duty officer, sharply uniformed in well-pressed khakis, jump boots and side arm just stood there looking, bug-eyed in amazement. The apparition, his head sort of bobbing and rolling to some rhythm while he snapped his fingers, looked the Duty Officer up and down.

"What's with you Nazi cats?" he said. The Duty Officer stared.

"Say, man, will that thing shoot?" the man-in-the-blanket tried again, pointing a finger with inch-long dirty nails at the Duty Officer's .45.

"Certainly" replied the Duty Officer, finally getting over his first shock. "What can we do for you?"

"I want to join, man. Like I wanna be a Nazi! Wanna gas me a Jew! I wanna sign up! Where's this Rockwell cat?"

I was in a back room, printing. (I had to do much of it myself back then.) I heard all this going on. Although I didn't like to let visitors see me covered with printers' ink, I couldn't resist coming out to see what was at the door. "He wants to join, sir!" the Duty Officer said to me, still flabbergasted. I couldn't resist talking to this thing from outer space.

卐 卐 卐

I have often found that I learn most, not from books and literature, but from people and events themselves. And this guy looked like a whole encyclopedia of everything degenerate.

I invited him in. We talked. He couldn't stay still, but kept moving around the room, seeming to float a few inches above the floor. (I later learned that he was on pills and narcotics.)

After an hour or so of talking, he began to change a bit. He appeared unsure of himself in the presence of something he'd never experienced before—men who were sure of themselves and had a purpose.

A look of unbelieving wonder came over his blue eyes, even through the "shades," as I talked to him of what we really were and why we had given up everything of fun in life to fight for our nation and White Race. Little by little, I began to get the story out of him.

He was only seventeen years old, and had lived an entire lifetime. He'd done everything, tried all kicks, and was already bored to death with an empty life. He'd made a mistress out of his art teacher, he'd run a den of degeneracy and debauchery called "Mule's Pad" where the local beats and wild crowds did anything, including enjoy dope. He'd shot a man, gotten off, and lived as fast and hard as he could until finally, he contemplated suicide in utter despair of finding *anything* worth doing any more all this at seventeen!

Before he committed suicide, he told me, he decided to come to see the Nazi "cats," figuring it might be one last kick. What he found, unexpectedly, was what every human being needs to survive this life a *purpose*—something which gives life more meaning than a constant search for more pleasure and kicks.

He actually convinced me he wanted to try to be a Storm trooper! As a matter of policy, whenever I hear that (as I do every day), I do all I can to discourage the applicant. We want no dabblers, but dedicated, fanatical fighters who will stick through hell itself. With this crazy character, I went even further. I made fun of him. I told him he'd never make it, that we'd run him off the first day. He rose to the challenge.

"You name it, and I'll make it!" he said. Strangely, I could sense a fiercely burning *will* behind the words. I told him he couldn't come up to try life as a Nazi Stormtrooper until he was eighteen. He left, vowing to return in a few months.

He did return—without the beatnik get-up. He turned out to be a blonde, young Viking, built for combat. We poured it to him.

There was no place left inside for him to sleep, so he was assigned to a wrecked car out back. It was still winter and cold. But the kid moved into the wrecked car with a couple of blankets. We put him to work cleaning the toilets, and yard. He worked.

Spring came, and then a broiling summer. He was still in the wrecked car, eaten alive by mosquitoes. I tried him on the printing press, and never saw such a bear for work. He was all dried out of booze, off the pills and dope, exercising plenty, and showing every sign of "making it." He accomplished dozens of dangerous missions against the SNCC, NAACP, communists, and peace creeps. He accompanied me to many a fight—and many a jail.

Within eleven months, faster than almost anybody before or since, this kid became an officer in the Stormtroop section, and led more successful operations against the enemy than any single Party Officer, with one possible exception.

An example of the work of this kid was the time the Black agitators were trying to unseat the White Mississippi delegation, and our own blackface "delegation" sent the Black agitators packing back to Mississippi as laughingstocks. My ex-beatnik managed to race onto the floor of Congress on opening day in blackface, with top hat, loin cloth and cigar, shouting. "I'ze de Mississippi delegation, and ah demands mah seat!"

The young man escaped the vicious circle of despair, boredom and degeneracy of millions of "modern youth" *only* because he happened upon the spiritual life-preserver of Nazi love of Race and Nation before he sank forever into the putrid slime of modern spiritual syphilis.

卐 卐 卐

There will be many who will say that he could have been saved, perhaps even more effectively by religion. Fifty years ago, yes. But I have had five years of experience seeing these lost kids on college campuses all over America. And I can assure the reader that most of these young people are far too cynical and hardened to be able to open their ears and heart even for a moment to *accept* a religious approach. Start talking about religion to such hard-case cynics and you drive them further and further away, no matter how hard you try.

It takes a new and *shocking* approach, a dramatic and powerful approach, to have any hope of making an impression on such lost, bitter kids. We have it, and it works.

Millions and millions of the youth of all Western nations are sinking into various degrees of the misery and degradation of the young "beat" who came to our door in beard, blanket, and sandals. Other millions of good people who don't look like beatniks are lost, without purpose, without confidence, without ambition, without beliefs or religion, without respect for home, flag, country, parents or anything else, without self-control or discipline, without morals or standards of any kind, with neither love for their own people nor hatred for their mortal enemies, without hope and without any real desire to live in any real sense. "Beat" is an apt description.

They have, indeed, had almost everything beaten out of them. They have gotten disgusted with the hypocrisy, disorder, and corruption of our times and quit. In their own words, they have "dropped out."

In *Battle for the Mind* (1957), William Sargant, a top British psychologist, shows how the communists use the principles of Soviet psychologist Pavlov to "brainwash" victims. And the first thing they do is "empty" the minds and souls of the subject. They spiritually "beat" him until he quits. Once he is "empty," it is a relatively easy job for the communist masters to pour back into his head whatever lies they want. That's how the Soviets can produce victims after a year or so in jail, who get up in court and shout that they are guilty, and beg to be punished, as did the victims of Stalin's first great purge.

Our youth, in various stages of "beatnik-ism," are precisely like the victims of Soviet brainwashing—they are empty, or nearly empty, of anything positive. They are sick and disgusted with just about everything. Although they don't realize it, they are desperate to believe in *something*, to become a part of something bigger than they are, to be *worthwhile*, to have a purpose, to have somebody care about them enough to discipline them and to show them something worthwhile to do in this world.

But nobody does show these lost kids anything they can believe deeply. They have been made to feel they are living in a ruined, dirty, hypocritical world about to blow itself to pieces with "the bomb." Many of them have been spoiled rotten. Many know nothing of constructive efforts to earn a living, they are told they are the same as black Negroes (and they try desperately to believe that, but it destroys them inside because instincts are stronger than words).

Worst of all, they have been taught that mature love of *anything*, (except themselves and pleasure) is "corny" and "square." Their family, flag, country, national heroes, race, and even God have been dragged down and ridiculed until there are no fixed stars in their heavens, nothing to aim at, nothing but an aimless wandering for more and more selfish pleasure and "kicks."

Unthinking animals can live from moment to moment on purely animal pleasures and satisfactions. But man has been blessed—or cursed—with consciousness and the ability to imagine the future. Man forms an opinion of himself. This has given him an even greater need than the mere satisfaction of his animal needs. "Man cannot live by bread alone," says the Bible,[1] and no truer words have ever been recorded. Men long for the admiration of other men, and a clear conscience.

Every great religion in the world sets its precepts for human behavior not on mere satisfaction of animal pleasures and "kicks," but on the more

---

[1] Matthew 4:4, copying from Deuteronomy 8:3.

lasting and deeply satisfying joys of outgoing activity, activity to be good and helpful to other people. When men concentrate only on themselves and their own animal lusts, they begin to despise themselves, they become despicable and hated by other men, and they become unhappy and hateful, in turn.

And each generation in Western civilization is being brought up to be more spoiled and selfish than the last. Predictably, each generation is becoming more and more unhappy, until today we have many young people from supposedly "the best" homes going forth into the streets to beat old men to death just for "kicks," while others abandon themselves as "hippies" to drugs, filth, and sloth.

卐 卐 卐

During the Korean War, not *one* American prisoner of war escaped! Many Americans (almost half of them) *cooperated* with the enemy when captured! No matter how vicious the enemy in all previous wars, Americans have never failed to escape in large numbers, and have always resisted every effort by the enemy to make turncoats out of prisoners. But now, the fighting American spirit is dying.

Americans have more cars, more telephones, more televisions, more household appliances and luxuries—more of almost everything than any human beings who have ever lived, or who live now. Yet never have so many had so little inside. Never have there been so many suffering intolerable boredom. Never have people been packed so close as in our giant cities. Yet never have people been so alone, so cut off from one another.

There is a vast ocean of spiritual misery drowning great numbers of our people. Many of them have lost their religion, and there is nothing to fill the black numbing void which freezes the soul of modern, "emancipated" men. They desperately seek escape from this cold hopelessness in alcohol, LSD, dope, or wild, crazy living. It is not physical lacks or hardship which bears down or our people and drives them unconsciously toward national and racial suicide. It is a *spiritual failing*, a disease of the spirit, which has our people down and beaten.

Our people are rotting from the inside, no matter how the outside gives the appearance of prosperity and happiness. Like a man with a diseased heart, the first time America is subjected to a real crisis, unless something changes mighty quickly, America—and all of Western civilization with us—will fold up with a whimper and die. No spiritually healthy people would ever tolerate the sort of horrors catalogued in the last chapter.

Western civilization, as Spengler predicted long ago, and America in particular, are far gone down the road toward decay and death. Nor is there any real resistance. On the contrary, millions have made a "love" cult and a "religion" out of worshipping their own destroyers, and work tirelessly to hasten our national and racial death.

Is this a natural development? Are we, as a civilization and as a nation, dying of old age, senility, and natural decay? Or is there something unnatural about the situation? And if there is something unnatural, if there is something sinister, what is it and who is doing it? And why? Where is all this spiritual syphilis coming from?

CHAPTER 4
THE CHART FORGERS

The affairs of a great nation are often described as the "Ship of State." It is an apt analogy. A nation has a "captain," officers, crew and navigator, who must sail it through endless storms, rocks, shoals and dangers to stay afloat.

In a so-called "free" country, the people are the "navigators." You, the citizen, are supposed to steer the American ship of state. You are supposed to elect a captain who does what you want done. Above all, you are supposed to set the policies of the state by majority rule.

And to do the steering of the American "ship of state," you need *charts*. No matter how wise he may be, the navigator of a great ship cannot steer the vessel safely through rocks and dangers without accurate charts. And you cannot make wise decisions on the policies for the American ship of state, without accurate facts and information—the "charts" of dangers surrounding America.

Can there be any doubt about what would happen if somebody managed to give the navigator of a ship *phony charts*—charts showing rocks, for example, where the channel really was, and showing a clear channel where the jagged rocks lurked to rip out the ship's bottom? And whose fault would it be if a ship piled up on the rocks because the navigator had been given falsified charts? The navigator's? Of course not! The fault would be entirely that of whomever forged the charts and sneaked them over on the honest navigator.

The navigator would think, however, that he must have done something terribly wrong, because who would imagine anyone would be low and vile enough to substitute forged charts? The thought would never occur to most honest navigators.

But that's just what's happening to America. That's why we keep piling up on the rocks of Marxism, crime, corruption and degeneracy. The good people of this great nation have been supplied with nothing but false charts, charts which show a "safe channel" precisely where lie the deadliest rocks, and which pretend that the only possible safe channel is the path to destruction. Trusting and believing in these forged "charts"—the phony "facts" and rigged "news" they are given—our people have innocently driven the once great American ship of state onto just about every shoal and rock there is, producing wreckage and despair.

Our people have been taught that their real heroes and leaders are "haters," "bigots" and "fascists," while the real haters and bigots are exalted by our phony charts—*our press*—as "statesmen" and "world leaders." We have been *forced* onto the rocks of Marxism and degeneracy by the press, TV, books, etc., which have praised every kind of rottenness and filth as "love," "brotherhood," etc., thus ensuring that our people will sail unsuspectingly down the channel onto the rocks. And even when they keep piling up on the rocks, the people still do not suspect that anybody has palmed off forged charts on them. Rather, they naively believe that they simply didn't try hard enough, so that next time, they smash up even harder.

When integration, for instance, produces some of the horrors shown in Chapter 2, our poor, swindled people are taught to believe it is because we need *more* integration. While the liars and forgers are driving our unwitting people up the rock-studded fake "channels," they are also removing all the light houses and buoys which once guided mankind into safe and quiet harbors in the storms. They have ripped up the light houses of religion, family, old-fashioned disciplined education, moral standards, authoritarian fathers and teachers, loving and motherly women, and that precious love of home and country, without which a people lose its bearings.

The chart forgers have been so successful in driving our people onto the rocks time after time, over a period of 40 years, that millions have given up, thrown away all charts, abandoned any effort to steer at all, and are just drifting. Others, more aggressive but equally frustrated, grow beards, wear filthy clothes, mount motorcycles, and race around attacking almost anything in sight.

Still others, the "liberals," have made a cult of shipwreck. They have seen their own lives ruined under the impossible spiritual and intellectual frustrations of the "liberal" lies of the chart-forgers. They haven't got the guts to face the facts of their own mistakes and so they have convinced themselves that no matter how many rocks they hit sailing by the false charts, their charts and lies are right and true, and the fault lies in "extremists," "haters," and "fascists" who are secretly putting rocks in the channel.

Confirmed and rotten old whores and drunkards get a certain relief from their conscience pangs by seducing young innocents into their own rotten ways of life. And in the same way, the liberal victims of the chart forgers, who have had their own lives spoiled and "shipwrecked" by the lies of the chart-forgers, get a depraved satisfaction out of seducing other young innocents, by spreading the same lies and fake charts which wrecked their own miserable lives and are wrecking the life of our young people.

The chart-forgers and their "liberal" army of victims begin their attack on the minds of our people when the child is still in kindergarten. Subtly, the tots are infused with unconscious doubts about the wisdom and methods of their own fathers and mothers. The tiny minds are led to believe that any discipline and order imposed at home is old-fashioned and "tyranny"—although the kids never hear such words.

On through the grades, the process of misleading our new citizens proceeds. American heroes, Washington, Patrick Henry, etc., were not real heroes at all, but greedy little men out for gain or glory. The Constitution is "outdated." Religion is an "opium." Morals are "square."

卐 卐 卐

I didn't notice this subtle forging and distortion of our national heritage and degrading of our heroes and traditions imposed on me at first. It was not until I was a young undergraduate of Brown University in 1938 that I finally made direct contact with these chart forgers, whose identification and overthrow would later become my life work. But I didn't know or even suspect them then. I don't remember even thinking about such a thing, any more than I did Thugee-ism in India. I was still blissfully and totally ignorant of communism, Jews, Negroes, and the assault of the colored masses of the world against the White Race and its elite.

In a way, I am glad of this long-maintained ignorance, because today, when I meet young college men and women who are full of conceit because of their "liberalism" and "understanding" of our social problems, I can be patient with them. I can imagine my own reaction if I had been told as a college-boy, that there was a Jewish or any other kind of world conspiracy. I was sure, at that time, that my "deep" studies into the profundities of knowledge would have long ago revealed any such monstrous conspiracy—and even if not, that my professors and men of learning would surely have known it. I would have been angry at such effrontery, just as most young college kids I meet today are, at first, angry because they've heard only one side.

In 1939, I sat in "Sociology I" class at Brown University and tried my best to make some sense out of it all. I had been happy at the chance to study sociology, as it appeared to me logical that there must be some fundamental principles of the development of the social relationships of life as I had discovered simple basic principles of other affairs I had looked into. I was most eager to learn these basic principles of the operation of human society so that I could understand the events around me, and perhaps even predict sociological occurrences in accordance with the principles I would be taught. I have since learned that there *are* such principles, as will be shown later.

But it would be many, many years before I would fight my way to the simple, fundamental, and logical facts of social life. In Prof. Bucklin's classroom on society at Brown University, all was the most depressing darkness and confusion. It all sounded most enlightening, of course. There were lots of brave new words, "ethnic groups," etc., but try as I might, I could not get to the bottom of it all to find any idea, nor could I get hold of any principle.

Muddiness of mind was not deplored, but glorified. I buried myself in my sociology books, absolutely determined to find why I was missing the kernel of the thing. The best I could come up with in sociology was that human beings are all helpless tools of environment; that we are all born as rigidly equal lumps, and the disparity of our achievements and stations was entirely and 100% the result of the forces of environment; that everybody, therefore, could theoretically be master-geniuses and kings if only we could sufficiently improve everybody's environment.

I was bold enough to ask Prof. Bucklin if this were the idea. He turned red with anger. I was told it was "impossible" to make any generalizations, although all I was asking was for the fundamental idea, if any, of Sociology.

I began to see that Sociology was different from any other course I had ever taken. Certain ideas produced apoplexy in the teacher, particularly the suggestion that perhaps some people were no-good, biological slobs from the day they were born. Certain other ideas, although they were never, never formulated and stated frankly, were fostered and encouraged—and these were always ideas revolving around the total power of environment.

Slowly, I got the idea. At first, I just used it to get better grades. When I wrote my essay answers in examinations, I poured it on heavily that all hands in the civilization in question were potential Leonardo da Vinci's, no matter how black they were or how they ate their best friends for thousands of years—and that with a quick change in environment, these cannibals, too, would be writing arias, building Parthenons, and painting masterpieces.

But then I began to wonder "how come"? Certainly environment was important. Anybody could see that. But it was obviously *negative*. You can make a helpless boob out of a born genius by raising him locked in a dark closet. But you can't make a genius out of a drooling idiot, even by sending him to Brown. Was it just old man Bucklin who was insane with environment? Or was it the whole subject?

I went to the library and read more sociology books. They were universally pushing the same idea. I began to make fun of Sociology in the college paper in my column, and got into more trouble. Some of the columns were "killed" before seeing the light. I was still too ignorant to know that I was fighting Lysenko and Marx and the whole Soviet theory of environmentalism, which has captured and hypnotized or terrorized all our intellectuals. I imagined I was battling just one foolish college course.

During my second year at Brown, my picture of the world darkened, as I discovered more and more the intellectual dishonesty in this university which had at first seemed almost heaven itself to me. I still knew little or nothing about communism, or Marxism, or its pimping little sister, "liberalism." But I could not avoid the steady pressure, everywhere in the university, to accept the idea of *massive human equality*, and *the supremacy of environment*. In every course, I was repulsed by the intellectual cowardice of the faculty in standing up for any doctrine whatsoever.

卐 卐 卐

I majored in philosophy, and, while I admired the intellectual brilliance of my professors, particularly Professor Ducasse, I was hugely disappointed in the headlong retreat of all the faculty whenever they were asked their own opinion as to the objective truth in any matter. I was told that "eternal seeking" is the way to knowledge. (And there is no denying that.) But lively discussion is also vital to any advance, and you cannot have any lively discussion where the opposition either doesn't exist or melts away like a wraith when you seek to take hold of it.

I was running into the social disease of our modern life—cowardice and pathological fear of a strong personality or strong ideas. Dale Carnegie has codified and commercialized this creeping disease as "how to win friends and influence people," which boils down, in essence, to the principle of having no personality or strong feelings or ideas and becoming passive and empty so that the "other fellow" can display *his* ideas and personality. But he, too, is trying to get "popular" by being passive and dispassionate, so that the result is like two dead batteries—no current. Such human robots are suited to enslavement by a *1984*-type society, but not to a bold, free society of men.

I found the same wishy-washy approach in every subject except in the sciences, and for these last, I was very grateful. Here, in geology and psychology, I could find a few principles and laws, which stayed there when I reached out to grasp them. And so I reveled in these subjects, and rebelled to the limit of my capacity in the others.

In sociology, I went so far as to write an insolent examination paper, which almost got me thrown out of Brown. We were asked to write an essay on the factors leading to criminality and delinquency. I wrote a fable about a crew of scientific geniuses who set out for Africa to see what made ants act like ants, searched around until they found a lot of ant-hills, observed them for many years, and finally came up with the discovery that when eggs were hatched in tunnels in a certain kind of hill in Africa, and grew up among six-legged creatures called "ants," they themselves were so affected by this strong environment that they became, themselves, ants, and waved their antennae like ants, scurried around like ants, looked like ants, and *were* ants.

I was hauled up before the administration for this impudence, and almost thrown out. Instead, I was given another opportunity to write the exam. And for the sake of my dear good Grandmother and my patient, loving Aunt Margie, I sat down and wrote what I knew they wanted—a piece showing how unfortunate and most-excellent Negro babies were invariably driven to stealing from their parents, relatives, and friends, robbing strangers at the point of a gun, looting, and finally axing somebody in sheer desperation at their nasty environment.

Meanwhile, I was learning mightily from my endless "bull-sessions" with Vic Hillery and Bob Grabb, my constant companions. Both of them were soused to the ears with the prevailing "liberalism," although I still did not know what it was. I simply discovered that almost all my ideas clashed violently with theirs. My ideas that socially-significant novels were dangerous (because they allowed ideas to sneak into the mind while it was hypnotized by an illusion of "reality") was especially aggravating to them both, as we all aspired to creative careers, they as novelists and writers. My attack on the very social novels they were aiming to write was painful. And their reactions, particularly Hillery's, were most passionate. Far into the night we would battle over this matter, with the usual results—no progress. But in the process, I learned the art of controversy.

At first, I was too sincere and naïve to do anything but try to make my opponent see the truth of my position with the utmost force and honesty. But then I found that I would fall victim of the dirtiest kind of sly tricks. My position would be enormously and ridiculously exaggerated, and then it would be flung in my face in triumph, to the great laughter of the audience of listeners or participants. I could not understand when even my beloved and revered friends did this to me. I was more than once too hurt by such 'liberal' tactics to defend myself.

But, as with everything else in my life, when I discovered the inevitability of such illogical skullduggery. I schooled myself in it and one day turned the tables on my 'liberal' friends.

More and more, at Brown, I came into basic conflict with the prevailing super-liberalism—still without ever realizing what it was all about. My companions, my courses, my professors, and the latest erudite books—everything seemed to me to be touched with madness. I fought it fiercely and, for my ignorance, powerfully, but mostly by instinct. I simply had never heard of communism as anything but a doctrine held by a few fanatics someplace overseas. That the campus, dorms, fraternity houses, and classrooms of Brown University were crawling with the filthy thing, I would never have believed. I would have laughed to scorn anybody who had tried to tell me such a "fantastic" thing—then!

Since this environmental "equality" idea of liberals is literally insane (a delusion, substituted for reality); since men are also creatures who differ by breed just as much as dogs, horses, birds or any other living creatures; since some breeds of men are brighter than others (and some are infinitely stupider than others), it is inevitable that the attempt to organize any useful body of organized facts about human behavior, starting from the insane premise that they are all hereditarily equal, must wind up full of obvious contradictions and insanities. And this is exactly what happens!

If you try to argue with the guy in the nut-house who thinks he is Napoleon, he will not only prove it to you, but he will hate you for doubting his "sacred, holy truth," and believe you are out to "get" him. But if he tries to write his "proofs" that he is Napoleon into a learned "scientific" paper, if he is a "lucid" type nut, he will see that his "proofs" don't look too well in writing. And so he will resort to 'gobbledygook' writing of profound phrases and fancy words to becloud what would be obviously insane if it were clear.

That's precisely what I found going on in "Sociology," only I didn't know it then. I didn't know what was wrong. I only knew that there was no way to get my feet on the ground in "Sociology," no way to come to grips with one, single, sure fact. Everything was, "by and large," "on the one hand...but then on the other hand," "Blatner and Fink say so-and-so, but then Fiddler and Fud say it's the other way around," etc., etc., *ad nauseum*.

I had stumbled head-on into one of the fundamental symptoms of our times, a very literal insanity—a desperate, frantic, pitiful effort by men who pretend to be the most enlightened of all humanity, to cling to the delusion that the only difference between Shakespeare and a savage is environment; that if we only manage to improve the environment enough, every cannibal can be a Chopin, every pygmy a Lord Nelson, every Bantu a Beethoven, and every East Indian ragamuffin a Voltaire. History, biology, political science, economics—every organized body of knowledge must be twisted and wrenched to any extreme to maintain this insane and obvious delusion.

The way those afflicted with this modern insanity cover up their madness from others—and mostly from themselves—is this process of pious scientific muddying of everything about the "sacred" doctrine. It is for this reason we are forever told things are always "grey" in this world, that there are "no simple solutions," that there are "no black and whites."

The fact that many things do exist as "shades of grey" rather than black and white does not mean that there is no such thing as black and white. Yet that is what the modern mad-men of "equality" keep trying to put out, precisely because they don't want any ordinary guy with common horse-sense pointing out that they are full of beans.

Put simply, the "equality" theories of these witch-doctors of "modern science" would be laughed out of countenance by any school boy if they were in plain black and white, simple language. They are idiotic and dishonest, on their face! But in pages of witch-doctor "gobbledygook" they intimidate and impress many of our supposedly highly-trained minds, and produce "liberal" fanatics.

卐 卐 卐

Sociology was an endless sea of grey mud. The only thing I could get clearly was that environment was everything, while heredity was a myth concocted by Southern brutes trying to re-enslave the Negroes.

By nature, I am a rebel. So I rebelled at this insanity. I wasn't sure what it was, or why they were doing it, but I did know for sure that it was crazy. While at Brown, I never did learn why the obviously intelligent and learned men all around me at the college were so all-fired "hung-up" on what seemed to me to be such obvious madness.

Now, more than 20 years and three wars later, I know what was going on, and why. I was surrounded by the most basic of all the lies of the chart-forgers: the lie denying *race*, denying that there is any such thing as breed among men, as there is breed among all other species.

In order for the chart-forgers' scheme to work, (as will be shown later) they must first pull down and destroy the resistance of the captain of civilization, the elite White Race. They must destroy its spirit and its ability to fight. They must fill it full of guilt feelings and degeneracy. Then, and then only, can chart-forgers and their army of mongrels overwhelm the White champion of civilization by sheer numbers.

So the chart-forgers have brilliantly exploited one of mankind's most ancient and deadly failings to produce a mass intoxication with what is actually mankind's last and most dangerous superstition—"humanitarianism." The White Race has been disarmed and poisoned with this clever lie. To get at the truth of the swindle, we have to "unthink" a lot that we have carelessly or, more often wishfully, assumed.

My own youthful experience with a drinking glass in the dish water is a perfect example of the frequent need to "un-think" a misconception. As a boy, I was assigned "chores" around the home. One of them was the dishes. But I don't think I did the dishes like other kids. I experimented and wondered and tried to figure out the "why" of everything. I puzzled for hours why water stayed in a tumbler when you lifted it, upside down, almost out of the dish water. I got in endless trouble over experiments with soap suds. What made them? What were they? Would they be bigger if you added various items? I tried talcum powder, mustard, everything I could get my hands on. The usual result was that somebody got their hands on me for my trouble. I got a licking.

But the investigative turn of mind, which often fetched me out to the woodshed for "experimenting" with the dish water, has stayed with me. One of the dominant passions of my life is and always has been, the effort to discover the natural laws behind what appear, at first, to be a thousand disconnected "wonders"—like the water in the tumbler and the soap suds. I began to discover that there were truly beautiful laws behind these things —that things in this universe are magnificently organized if only we are bright, unprejudiced, and persistent enough to find the laws and the organization. I fell in "love" with the business of discovering and using the laws of the Universe.

I soon discovered, of course, that I was not the original discoverer of this organization of the universe or the methods of learning its laws and system. In high school, I learned that the whole delightful business was called "science," and that a lot of very wonderful men, hundreds of years before me, had been looking into the dish water too and the heavens, and the seas, and into everything else in the universe. I fell upon such knowledge like a starving man and devoured it. Every new morsel was a delight. Even hard-to-digest items were delicacies, once I could intellectually "swallow" them.

That air pressure held the water in the tumbler in the dish water by pressing on all the water outside the tumbler, and thus *pushing it up* inside the glass, instead of the vacuum inside "sucking" it in was a big and tough lump for me to digest. But I got it down, and it was great! This taught me not to be prejudiced, not to be a 'bigot,' not to jump at easy conclusions.

What seemed to be was often simply not true, even though the truth seemed less likely at first. The whole history of man's scientific progress, I learned, has been his struggle to get rid of ideas which, at first, seemed right and were therefore pre-judged to *be* right. In primitive societies, any suggestion that the gods did not exist when everybody *knew* they made the earth, the heavens, the sea, and people, etc. got one promptly burned or sacrificed. Everybody knew for thousands of years that the Earth was flat; you could see it for yourself. And the first few half-wits who suggested it was round were not only laughed out of countenance, but some of them were burned at the stake for such "insanity."

The whole history of humanity is tragically soiled with a million repetitions of the burning of people who dared to suggest the wrongness of a precious prejudice of the times. Each generation in the last few centuries has looked with horror on this history of stupidity and insanity, and then gone about the ruthless business of exterminating the men of its *own* times who dared to question the popular superstitions of the day. The bigots of each era have dutifully shaken their heads in disbelief and horror at the witch-doctors of other eras, and then hunted down and destroyed anybody who dared to question the witch-doctors of their *own* era.

Why do I write this sort of stuff? Is this not the very essence of the arguments of the other side? Is this not "liberalism" at its worst? And the very words 'prejudice,' 'bigotry,' etc., not the chief weapons in the arsenal of the communists and the rest of the enemy apparatus?

Yes, of course. The enemy does inveigh endlessly against the "bigotry" of "racists" and "anti-communists," etc. I am supposed to be the biggest bigot of them all. I "hate" nice Negroes and Jews, "just because of the color of their skins" or because of their "religion." This is the propaganda spread by the enemy. Somehow, goes the superstition of our times, I have developed an unreasoning hate of innocent and equal people who have dark skins or who go to a synagogue instead of a church.

Well, let's examine this idea, as I once examined the soapsuds and the dish water inside the tumbler. It would be a mark of the utmost stupidity to hate something or a person because you didn't like the color of his skin or hair, if there were no other differences. This would be as silly and stupid as hating chocolate ice-cream because it is dark.

I would shrivel up and die of shame before I would participate in any such stupidity and madness. Then why do I head a Nazi Party, and cuss out Negroes and talk about gassing Marxist-Jew traitors? Is this not the worst sort of "bigotry," "hate" and "prejudice?" No!

To repeat: For thousands of years, people suffered from the delusion that the Earth was flat. Those who dared to question the idea got burned or crucified. And for more thousands of years, even now, people are getting burned and crucified for questioning the idea that 'man' is somehow the "center of the universe" and therefore above natural law. That is the whole source of our ideological trouble today, the "liberal" idea that men can disobey natural law.

Copernicus and Galileo fought and suffered for preaching that the Earth was not the center of the universe. Had not God Himself said the Earth was the center of the universe, and Man its crowning glory, the Master of Creation? Of course! Therefore, Copernicus and Galileo were a couple of evil "haters" for suggesting otherwise. Had the word existed, they would doubtless have been called 'fascists."

Since these two gentlemen got "crucified" for their insistence on Natural Law instead of conceited man-made law, facts have piled up to prove they were right. Only nuts, today, dare question that the Earth is round or that it is only a small planet circling a very small sun in a minor galaxy in a very big universe. The battle against that prejudice is all over. We are too "enlightened" today to fall victim to any such stupid prejudice. *Like hell!*

Every time I speak to a university group, there are super-"intellectual" professors there, and the university students are super-enlightened, as is usual at such institutions. No witchcraft or superstition for them. No, sir! They wear beards and beatnik hair-dos to show their contempt for ordinary, stupid, unenlightened, prejudiced, and bigoted dolts like me and other racists.

Their attitudes are precisely those of the ecclesiastical courts which condemned Messrs. Copernicus and Galileo; i.e., they are all conforming slavishly to the prejudice of our times (that every two-legged creature somehow has "dignity" and "rights," and has some mystical "value" just because he can squirm under the wire as "man").

I am portrayed as a wild, raving lunatic, a "nut" and a heretic! Not one of the "enlightened" is able to see that what they are doing to "racists" today is just what the bigots who condemned Copernicus did. Like all bigots, they are right—and tell me so.

One professor at the University of New Hampshire went so far as to admit he *was* a "bigot," when it came to the possibility that he could ever see things my way. "Never!" he gasped, for all the world like the gentle-men of the cloth examining Copernicus and his heretical ideas. I pointed out that anybody could be wrong, and might change—even I. He stuck by his guns. He hated racism, always would, and was proud of it! And there is the point.

Today's liberal intellectuals, who pride themselves on scientific method and being "broadminded," are the most narrow-minded, self-righteous and hate-filled bigots in the history of humanity. No primitive tribe worshiping with its witch-doctor was ever more vicious in its hatred and suppression of heretics than today's Marxist intellectuals, anti-racists and liberals. Their intellectual position is pure, unadulterated superstition and prejudice, and they burn us heretics in the hottest fires of their hate and lies! That, of course, they will deny, puffing and blowing and gasping with utter outrage.

卐 卐 卐

But let's examine it. Let's do as science does with the tumbler full of dish water and see what their position *is*.

Let's start out by exempting from combat the devoutly religious Christians. If you say to me, "God made all humanity in His own image, including savage black cannibals," then I cannot argue with you, because there is no way of proving you are wrong. (However, to me, it is hard to imagine a good God purposely and knowingly dumping into the world, in all innocence, such of his own "Images" as the Australian aborigines and animal-like Congo cannibals. If all "humans" are indeed the "children" of a good God, and were all "created in His image"—then I do not really see how to escape the conclusion that we are all equal and "brothers." Because I can see no fair or honest reason why God would have given the White Man all the brains, good looks, and energy which he has exhibited in histo-ry, while He gave seven times as many Blacks all the stupidity, laziness, ugliness, etc., which they have exhibited for thousands of years.)

Nevertheless, if you postulate God as the "Father of Humanity," then you can go from there to argue that God wants all His "children" to be "equal" and that we racists are mean, "un-Christian" and "prejudiced" if we "discriminate" against some of His children and claim we are superior. (I am not saying, of course, that Christians have to argue that all men are equal. Many of them claim that God designed some to be inferior from birth as part of His plan. I personally cannot believe that a good God would do this to more than 6/7th of humanity. It is impossible for me to believe that God wanted to create a half-animal Congo cannibal when He could have made an intelligent, energetic, and fine-looking White Man, instead —especially when He made at least seven times as many of these colored "Images" of Himself as White Men.)

But it is possible to argue such a position logically from the postulate of a Special Creation of Man as the Image of God just as it is also logically possible to argue the absolute "equality" and "brotherhood" of all men as "Children of God," from the same postulate. Those who postulate a personal God reserve the right to make their own rules, and I cannot argue with them.

But the liberals I have met do not postulate "God." Most of them are arrogant, sneering atheists. And the open Marxists and communists, as everybody knows, are all militant atheists![1] Thus, their belief in equality among men, when it exists nowhere else in nature, is pure superstition.

When we examine the common nature of all superstitions and error from which men have suffered down through the ages, it will be found in every case that the supernatural beliefs of every group of men, from the gloom of the tropical rain-forests of the Congo up to and including some modern religions, contain one constant, permanent factor: *egocentrism.*

---

[1] GLR: Just for the record, I am *not* an atheist. I think atheism is just as much superstition as some religion. The religionist says, "I have examined the universe, and discovered 'God,' and 'God' is such-and-such and all who disagree are heretics and wicked. I alone have the 'truth' in the matter." The atheist says, "I have examined the universe and there is nothing I cannot eventually know and there is no 'super-human-power' who could qualify as a 'God'." To me, the latter statement is just as conceited as the statement of the religious fanatic, maybe worse, because it tries to prove a negative proposition. I don't think either one of them knows a thing. Both are guessing from insufficient data.

What I have been able to observe indicates to me that there are many things that happen which could be (and probably are) the work of a super-human agency, which could be called God. In fact, I believe the preponderance of evidence indicates there *is* some Unknowable Agency at work, and I "believe in" this agency, which I call "Destiny" or "Providence." In this sense, I believe in a God. But I am no bigot on the subject, and seek all scientific data one way or the other.

Technically, I am thus a pro-Christian "agnostic." My answer to the riddle of the universe, which I think is answered with unwarranted certainty by both the religious person and the atheist, is simply "I do not know." My job is not to be a preacher, but soldier in the service of my people. Since most of my people an overwhelmingly Christian, I will fight for their right to keep this White, Christian country, as long as that is the majority will.

They all start from the presumption that the believers are something special, and there are supernatural beings who has a special interest in them, and that if they perform the proper rites and avoid the proper taboos, they will gain special ascendancy in this world, and total ascendancy in the next.

The road-block to progress in science has always been human conceit —the belief that humans are something special. The Earth was the center of the universe, and for anybody to question that was to hurt men's ego, so such heretics had to die. Man had to be a special creation of a special god. And he who questioned that must also die, because if that is not true, then Man was just *Homo sapiens*, an intelligent and communicating form of higher animal who was part of animal nature, and must obey Nature's laws.

It is natural for men to love and admire themselves, and their false beliefs and superstitions have always partaken of this enormous self-love. And this infinite capacity for self-love has always blinded man to scientific truth. For scientific truth reveals that man is mighty near to nothing in the scales of this universe.

The struggle for science has been a constant battle within man himself to see himself *as he is*, not as he likes to imagine himself to be. And that battle is still going on. The last battle in the long struggle is taking place now.

At New Hampshire University, I faced the high priests and cultists of the liberal (and ancient) "Man-is-something-sacred" superstition, and suffered their hatred and scorn for making them look at themselves. But I also found the "Achilles' Heel" of these Marxists and liberals!

Marxists and most liberals are thoroughly *un*-religious. They boastfully and arrogantly deny God. They are their own gods. "Humanity" (themselves) has become their "god." They deny any supernatural agency. So they cannot claim, as humanity has for eons, that God made "Man" as something special. No! The Marxists and liberals are, by and large, materialists—and cannot claim any such thing. This puts them in an absolutely impossible situation, if we will only take advantage of it and press it without mercy.

If man is merely an intelligent animal and thus part of all the rest of nature, which the Marxists and liberals assert, then man is also subject to all the laws of biology and evolution, the same as all other animals. The religious man can and does draw a line between man and the rest of living creation. "God created Man as something special," he says. "And everything above that line can be called 'Man,' and is holy, sacred, and special. *The Marxist and liberal can do no such thing. he can draw no line whatsoever.* He preaches, as the very essence of his doctrine, that everything exists in "shades of greys," not black and white: that there are no arbitrary lines of demarcation between things.

So if we ask the atheist Marxist or liberal about "Man's Natural Rights," or the "Human Dignity" which is so fondly preached by Martin Luther King, we have our opponents in a corner. If there is no God, then where did man get any "rights" which are not also the rights of horses, or apes—or worms? What "right" have we to murder cows and eat them, any more than cows have "rights" to murder us and eat us? And what, indeed, is "man?"

Phenomena do exist in this world in degrees, not as absolutes. There is an old story about the man who tried to wade across a stream which averaged two feet deep, and fell in a 20-foot hole in the middle and drowned. Who is a "tall" man? When does a man become a "fat" man? How many stones in a "pile"? Two? Three? Five? How old is an "old" man? When does a "baby" cease to be a baby? Which year? Which month? Which week? Which day, hour, minute, second, etc.?

Any scientific examination of the animal world shows that there are no lines between one set of phenomena and another set. There are certainly recognizable groups, but the groups shade into each other at the edges, without hard sharp lines.

Now, without postulating "God," just how do the Marxists, etc., explain the concept of "Man," as an absolutely homogeneous and "equal" mass of creatures, completely separate and above the laws of the rest of Nature, *a nature where absolutely everything else alive exists in degrees of capacity, both by individuals and groups*?

In every other specie of living creature, animal and vegetable, there are groups of recognizable varieties, which vary from other groups of the same species in hardihood, longevity, ability to adapt, sensitivity, etc. Among plants, horses, dogs, monkeys, snakes, pigs, flowers, birds, and cats there are breeds. Some breeds are tough. Some are delicate and nervous. Some are stupid but strong. Some are weak but clever. There are draft horses and racehorses, sled dogs and clever trained poodles, Greyhounds and Newfoundlands, hummingbirds, and penguins. Nobody in his right mind would say "all birds are equal," or "all breeds of dogs are equal," or "all monkeys are equal." Every zoologist knows that chimpanzees are the most intelligent, while baboons are more stupid—although all of them are of the basic family. The same can be said of every single animal type in the world. In every specie, the breeds vary by quality.

Yet, when it comes to what he claims is an intelligent kind of primate, which walks upon two legs and can think and talk better than a chimpanzee, the Marxist suddenly becomes *religious*, he talks of "human rights," "human dignity," etc.! *What* "human dignity"? If there is such a thing as "human dignity" for one animal, then why in the name of reason is there not "chimpanzee dignity" and "ape's rights" and even "snakes rights"?

The liberals and atheists have no answer to this question. The typical egalitarian will trot out miles of statistics to show that some Congo cannibal once learned to play chess or run the hundred-yard dash or went to Harvard.

Such "argument" is precisely the same as if I were to try to "prove" that race and draft horses were the same, by training a race horse to pull a cart, or a draft horse to run a race. It would still be an un-typical draft horse running the race, and an un-typical race horse pulling the cart. Even if some odd fluke produced a fast draft horse who could beat some race horses it would not mean that there is no such thing as breeds of horses. Only an idiot would try to maintain such a mad argument.

If you want a racehorse, you breed for a racehorse; you do not try to train and beat a poor old plug draft horse into becoming a racehorse. Above all, you do not spend all your money feeding a million heavy old plugs while you cut down on the oats and the breeding of the finest stock you have, hoping to teach one heavy plug to win a race!

Yet this is precisely the superstition—the "religion" if you will, of our times!—and exactly what we are doing all over the world. This is the irrational, crazy, egotistical fanaticism which I experience at the universities every time I speak at a college.

There is no reason for it. It is unreasonable in the extreme. There is no logic behind it. It violates all logic. There is no excuse for it. It is the crazy "faith" of those who pretend to worship science and facts. And it has been consciously, cunningly foisted on us by the chart-forgers who *know* it is a *lie!*

The truly enlightened men of every age have had to struggle and often die because of the stupidity and ugly prejudice of those who truly believed themselves the very guardians of truth. Every "decent" person knew the world was flat and the center of the universe, and applauded the saintly men who persecuted Galileo for preaching the ugly story that the world was not the center of the universe. Today, every "decent" liberal believes that "humanity" has "dignity." Some religious people base their belief on an edict of God, and can find some excuse for their belief in equality.

So our preachers and priests are fighting fanatically against the new "heresy" of belief in human breeds. And the Marxists and liberals are fighting just as fanatically, right along with the preachers they scorn, *for exactly the same thing!*

The scientific fact is that man is super-intelligent but also a kind of animal and, like all the rest of life, differs by breeds or "races"! This scientific fact is just as world-shaking as was the fact that the Earth is not the center of the universe, in its day. And this fact is meeting with the same frantic struggle against it by the same bigots who have been crucifying bearers of truth for ten thousand years.

The curse of "liberal" and "humanitarian" mankind is *egocentrism, conceit*. And the chart-forgers have learned to use this human failing to destroy humanity.

It simply kills the modern liberal that there are millions and millions and millions of his kind who are worthless scum (compared to the finest breeds of his kind). So he believes the chart-forgers and denies it—denies it and makes a religion of that denial, which is the religion of "liberalism" and finally of Marxism. There is no reason or logic to it, only the same old "if you don't agree with us, we will silence and destroy you" which has been the unhappy lot of every fighter for truth against bigotry, for thousands of years.

There is one difference, though. Humanity could believe the Earth was the center of the universe, and flourish in its error. Nature took care that humans keep evolving, by eliminating the unfit and breeding the race ever upward, in spite of human egotism. But the present egocentric "equalism" of "enlightened" humanity is *destroying humanity itself.*

The chart-forgers know all this very well, and are cynically going ahead anyway, spreading the atrocious, suicidal *lie* that men do not differ by breed and quality, as does all the rest of creation. This is the kernel of the chart-forgery, which is driving our people and our country onto the rocks of final and total shipwreck.

卐 卐 卐

The scientific facts of *race*, today are being smeared and suppressed just as the facts about the round world were a few hundred years ago.

But note that the process of going from superstition to science is not going in the natural direction this time. The "flat world" error came first and existed for untold thousands of years before men became courageous and self-disciplined enough to *think* instead of feel, and thus learned that they were not the center of the universe, but only specks on a tiny round globe, circling a very small sun in a minor galaxy. Once they knew that fact, they did not regress back to the belief in the flat world again.

But with the facts of race, there is a new and sinister pattern, which emerges before our eyes. For millions of years, men lived close to Nature and nobody could get away with saying, "all cows are equal," "all hens are equal," "all dogs are equal," or even "all corn is equal." The constant and eternal fact of all life was the inequality of all living things, both among individuals, and varieties of individuals. No farmer could survive pretending all corn was equal, and he needed no scientist to tell him that certain breeds of dog, such as the shepherd, were more intelligent and capable in handling sheep, while other dogs might be less intelligent, but, like the husky, better by Nature at pulling. Nor did he give his daughter to inferior humanity.

Then, as men began to get away from Nature and live artificially in urban, mechanized complexes called "cities," they stopped seeing the lessons of Nature before them, and the chart-forgers found their opportunity.

No farmer who bred chickens, cows, dogs, etc., and saw the natural inequalities in all the rest of Nature could be convinced of the crazy lie that breeding means *everything* in all the rest of creation but *nothing* among humans. But the man born under anesthetics in a hospital, nursed out of a glass bottle, raised on cement and asphalt instead of grass and forests, fed out of cans and packages, and "educated" 100% out of books with no contact with the hard realities of Nature, could be and has been led to believe that "there are no such things as breeds of men."

The forgers set about their endless repetitions of this *lie*, which they now press upon us as such an "accepted fact" that any questioning of that "fact" is prima facie evidence that the questioner is himself a "bigot," "hater," and finally a "Nazi."

From this equality-lie stems all the other forgeries of natural fact, which have been imposed upon our helpless people. From the basic false idea that humans are born biologically equal they derive the Marxist basic principle that therefore every human is entitled to equal shares in the good things of this world. And from this, stems their further lie that all should and must share equally in government, regardless of ability or qualification—the basic premise of their beloved "democracy," and of Marxism.

卐 卐 卐

But it is not just this one basic lie about race which is killing our people and our Nation; from the basic "equality" lie, they have spread out and built a vast lying machine which includes our press, TV, radio, magazines, books, movies, and even religious publications, to lie about everything.

To show you just how powerful this network of poisonous lies has become, let me present just one example of how it works to keep the American people utterly helpless and ignorant of what is really going on in the world around us.

Let me ask the reader to try to imagine what would have happened just 30 years ago, if I, George Lincoln Rockwell, had defected from the United States to Nazi Germany, denounced America, became an ardent Nazi citizen of Germany, then came back here to America and assassinated Franklin D. Roosevelt. Does anyone imagine that our government and every organ of our press would have been insisting, over and over, that the assassination of Roosevelt was the act of just one man, me—and had nothing to do with the Nazis? But this is exactly what they do with Lee Harvey Oswald—they keep insisting that he was a "loner" and had nothing at all to do with the world communist movement, although there is plenty of evidence that communism makes a business of assassinations, and that Oswald was a most vital part of the international communist apparatus.

To give the reader an inside peek into just how false is our whole information network, when it comes to anything involving race, or communism, let me set forth the known facts behind the assassination of President Kennedy, and *you* judge how the lie-machine has misled America.

In the Jew-dominated Bronx, New York, when he was an adolescent youth,[2] Lee Harvey Oswald admitted that his dark journey into communist terrorism began. He was handed a pro-communist leaflet on behalf of the two convicted Jewish communist spies, Julius and Ethel Rosenberg, who were finally electrocuted for treason at Sing Sing Prison.

After reading the communist pamphlet on behalf of the Jew communist Rosenbergs, Oswald was inspired to obtain and read the works of Marx and Lenin. Later, in Dallas, Oswald boasted that *Das Kapital* became his "bible." Instead of enjoying normal American pursuits and interests, young Oswald began to soak his mind in the fanatic class-hatred of communism. All millionaires were "enemies of the people," "tyrants" who should be killed.

The juggernaut that would, on November 22, 1963, blast out the brains of an American president (a millionaire) was launched in New York's Bronx from the pages of the "Communist Manifesto", Rosenberg literature, and *Das Kapital*. Continually soaking himself in this poisonous communist hatred, Oswald became a typical young, liberal pseudointellec-

---

[2] Oswald spent ages 12 and 13 in the Bronx, when the family returned to New Orleans.

tual. In the Marine Corps, his Commanding Officer, First Lt. John E. Donovan, has told how Oswald, just like the young leftist college students I meet all the time, was full of liberal, Marxist, and "intellectual" conceit, and arrogant attitude of superiority to all non-Marxist humanity.

In October 1959, full of hatred for the "capitalist" United States, Oswald traveled to the Soviet Union, turned his passport in to the US Embassy, denounced his native America, and applied for Soviet citizenship. In a press conference in Moscow, he heaped abuse on the United States of America, said its people were "bigots" and "exploiters" and scorned everything American.

Getting a work assignment is difficult in Russia. Oswald, however, had no trouble, once he made friends with a Soviet factory boss, Alexander Zeger, whom Oswald describes in his diary (13 January 1960) as a "Polish Jew." This Jew gets Oswald a top job in his factory. Believe it or not, Oswald also gets a regular payment from the "Red Cross" while in Russia! (*Portrait of the Assassin*, Gerald R. Ford, 1965, page 51.)

In Kiev, the Soviets maintain a school for terrorists and assassins. While ostensibly living in Minsk, Russia, Oswald made frequent trips of long duration to Kiev! Oswald, strangely enough, in the Soviet Union, was granted a most extraordinary privilege, especially for a non-citizen. He was allowed to use a rifle and practiced to target shooting!

In Oswald's *Diary*, October 18, 1960, he records that he is in love with a Jewess, Ella German. He becomes infatuated with her, while running around with the Jews with whom he works and their Jewish friends, but she will have none of him. He winds up "carrying a torch" for this Jewess, and soon resorts to the traditional method of "rebounding." On April 13, Oswald married an attractive Russian woman, Marina Pruskova, and had a child.

After 2½ years in the Soviet Union, Oswald suddenly asked the Soviet government for a favor almost never granted: he wanted to get an exit visa for his Soviet wife and child to return to the USA! Amazingly, he had no difficulty whatsoever in getting this rare permission. He then wrote to Senator John Tower, demanding help in returning to the United States.

So here is a man who committed naked treason, denounced his native land, turned in his passport, and still was openly contemptuous of the United States, its people, its government and its ideals. Nevertheless, tremendous forces went to work, and the US Embassy in Russia gave Soviet-loving Oswald his passport back!

As if this were not enough, Oswald thereupon asked for, and got, from the very government he had denounced and betrayed, $435 to return to the United States of America. The State Department of the United States government then issued a special non-quota immigration permit for Oswald to bring his wife, Marina, into the United States.[3]

Traitor Oswald and his wife arrived in the United States on June 13, 1962 and proceeded to Dallas. The record shows that Oswald told a public stenographer that in 1962 an "engineer" in the area offered to publish a book about the Soviet Union to be written by Oswald. It just happens that a man named Michael Paine is an engineer who claims that he did not meet or know Oswald until a left-wing pro-Castro party in 1963. Oswald, having recently returned from the Soviet Union, was invited to a Russia-loving Castroite party, and all the local lefties, pro-communists and other Unitarians, Quakers, and "peace" workers (leftists) attended to meet Oswald and his Russian wife. A Mrs. Ruth Paine, who attended that Castroite party, had been a super-leftist liberal at Antioch College in Yellow Springs, Ohio and the University of Pennsylvania, and had studied Russian in line with the usual "liberal" magnetic attraction to everything Russian and Soviet. (Her folks were Unitarians). At this party, we are supposed to believe, the Paines became so entranced with this traitor Oswald that they began to subsidize him and his family, and Mrs. Oswald actually moved in with them!

During this time, with Mrs. Paine and Marina Oswald amiably chatting every day (in Russian only), Oswald obtained and lost several jobs and traveled to New Orleans, the city with the largest port and concentration of communists in the South.

Here Oswald contacted the Communist Party and "Fair Play for Cuba Committee" at 799 Broadway, New York City. The "Fair Play for Cuba Committee" now claims that Oswald's activities in New Orleans were in no way authorized by the Committee. Yet there are six lengthy letters from Oswald to the Committee, which were published in the *New York Times* of December 8, 1963, which make it perfectly obvious to anyone of normal intelligence that Oswald was working hand-in-glove with the "Fair Play for Cuba Committee". The head of the "Fair Play for Cuba Committee," Mr. V. T. Lee," (Jewish name, Tappin) has announced that he "lost" or "mislaid" the carbon copies of the answers which he wrote to all these letters of Oswald's.

---

[3] GLR: Just for purposes of comparison, let the reader note the way I was hunted down and thrown out of England in 1962 by the British Government, although I am no criminal, nor in any way disloyal, while American Jewish traitor Robert Soblen was pampered in every way while I was there and England refused to turn him over for deportation to the United States, even while I was being shipped out!

Texts of Oswald's Six Letters

Following are the texts of letters to the Fair Play for Cuba committee by Lee H. Oswald, seized onaccount of President Kennedy's assassination, as made available last night by Vincent Theodore Lee, national director of the committee.

First Letter

[Undated]
P.O. Box 2915, Dallas, Tex.
Dear Sirs:

I do not like to ask for something for nothing but I am unemployed.

Since I am unemployed I stood yesterday for the first time in my life, with a placcard around my neck, passing out fair play for Cuba pamphlets, etc. I only had 15 or so. In 40 minutes they were all gone. I was cursed as well as praised by some. My home-make placard said Hands off Cuba, Viva Fidel. I now ask for 40 or 50 more of the fine basic pamphlets —14.

Sincerely,
Lee H. Oswald

Second Letter

May 26.
Dear Sirs:

I am requesting formal membership in your organization.

In the past I have received from you pamphlets, etc. both bought by me and given to me by you. Now that I live in New Orleans, I have been thinking about renting a small office at my own expense for the purpose of forming a F.P.C.C. branch here in New Orleans.

Could you give me a charter?

Also I would like information on buying pamphlets etc. in large lots, as well as — F.P.C.C. applications, etc.

Also, a picture of Fidel, suitable for framing would be a welcome touch.

Offices down here rent for $30 a month, and if I had a steady flow of literature I would be glad to take the expense.

Of course I work and could not supervise the office at all times, but I'm sure I could get some volunteers to do it.

Could you add some advice or recommendations?

I am not saying this project would be a roaring success, but I am willing to try. [The last five words were underlined.]

An office, literature, and getting people to know you are the fundamentals of the F.P.C.C. as far as I can see, so here's hoping to hear from you.

Yours respectfully,
Lee H. Oswald

Third Letter

[Undated]
Dear Mr. Lee:

I was glad to receive your advice concerning my try at starting a New Orleans F.P.C.C. chapter.

I hope you won't be too disapproving at my innovations but I do think they are necessary for this area.

As per your advice I have taken a P.O. Box (N. O. 30061).

Against your advice I have decided to take an office from the very beginning.

I u e [apparently meaning as you see] from the circular I had jumped the gun on the charter business but I don't think it's too important. You may think the circular is too provocative, but I want it to attract attention even if it's the attention of the lunatic fringe. I had 2,000 of them run off.

The major change in tactics you can see from the small membership blanks, in that I will charge $1 a month dues for the New Orleans chapter only and I intend to issue N.O. F.P.C.C. membership cards also.

This is without recourse to the $5 annual F.P.C.C. membership fee.

However, you will lose nothing in the long run because I will forward $5 to the national F.P.C.C. for every New Orleans chapter member who remains a dues paying member for 5 months in any year.

It's just that the people I am approaching will not pay $5 all at once to a committee in New York which they cannot see with their own eyes.

But they may pay a $1 to their own chapter after having received their membership card from my hand to theirs.

Also I think such a dues system binds the members closer to the F.P.C.C. I will promise only a membership card and a chapter vote to future members, that is, I don't expect you to extend them national F.P.C.C. mailings for their $1 a month.

As you will notice on the membership blank there is a place for those who do wish to subscribe to the national mailings for the fee of $5, that fee will go directly to you in New York.

As soon as any member has paid dues adding up to $5 in any year I will forward that fee to you and then you may handle as if it was a usual application for membership in the national F.P.C.C.

In any event I will keep you posted, and even if the office stays open for only one month, more people will find out about the F.P.C.C. than if there had not been any office at all, don't you agree?

Please feel free to give advice and any other help.

Yours truly
Lee H. Oswald,
4907 L/C Magazine.
New Orleans, La.

Fourth Letter

Lee H. Oswald
4907 Magazine
Aug. 1
Dear Mr. Lee:

In regards to my efforts to start a branch F.P.C.C. in New Orleans.

I rented an office and was promptly closed three days later for some obscure reason by the renters.

They said something about remodeling, etc. I'm sure you understand. After that I worked out of a post office box and by using street demonstrations and some circular work have sustained a great deal of interest but no new members.

Through the efforts of some

Cuban exile 'gusanos' [the Spanish word for worms, used by the Castro regime to denote its opponents] a street demonstration was attacked and we were officially cautioned by police.

This incident robbed me of what support I had leaving me alone.

Nevertheless thousands of circulars were distributed, and many pamphlets which your office supplied.

We also managed to picket the fleet when it came in and I was surprised at the number of officers who are interested in our literature. I continue to receive through my post office box inquiries and questions which I shall endeavor to keep answering to the best of my ability.

Thank you.

Lee H. Oswald
P.O. Box 30061
New Orleans, La.

Fifth Letter

Aug. 12, 1963
Dear Mr. Lee:

Continuing my efforts on behalf of the F.P.C.C. I find that I have incurred the displeasure of the Cuban exile "worms" here. I was attacked by three of them as the copy of the enclosed summons indicates. I was fined $10 and the three Cubans were not fined because of "lack of evidence" as the judge said.

I am very glad I am stirring things up and shall continue to do so. The incident was given considerable coverage in the press and local TV news broadcasts.

I am sure it will be to the good of the Fair Play for Cuba Committee.

Sincerely yours,
Lee H. Oswald
P.O. Box 30061
New Orleans, La.

Sixth Letter

Aug. 17
Dear Mr. Lee:

Since I last wrote to you Aug. 13 about my arrest and fine in New Orleans for distributing literature for F.P.C.C. things have been moving pretty fast. On Aug. 16th, I organized an F.P.C.C. demonstration of 3 people. This demonstration was given considerable coverage by WDSU-TV Channel 6 and also by our Channel 4 TV station.

Due to that I was invited by Bill Stucke [Bill Stuckey, New Orleans television commentator] to appear on his TV show called "Latin American forum" at 7:30 P.M. Saturdays and WDSU Channel 6.

After the 15 minute interview which was filed on magnetic tape at 4:00 P.M. for broadcast at 7:30, I was flooded with callers and invitations to debate, etc., as well as people interested in joining the F.P.C.C. New Orleans branch. That then is what has happened up to this date and hour.

You can I think be happy with the developing situation here in New Orleans.

I would however like to ask you to rush some more literature, particularly the white sheet 'truth about Cuba' regarding Government restrictions on travel as I am quickly running out.

Yours truly
Lee H. Oswald

During this period, Oswald had his photograph taken holding up a rifle and his favorite newspaper, *The Militant*. *The Militant* is the newspaper of the Trotskyite Communist "Socialist Workers Party" and its title is clear enough indication of its nature. The Trotskyite Communist members of the "Socialist Workers Party," about 90% Jews and Negroes, are violently "militant" and scorn the more subtle activities of the regular Communist

Party and Soviet Russia as "too slow". They are passionate adherents of Trotsky's doctrine of "international violent revolution." The Chinese Communists, the African Communists (100% Negro), and Castro (50% Negro) are also violent adherents of the bloody Trotsky doctrines of bloodshed, murder, and assassination.

I went to the Library of Congress and obtained a copy of *The Militant*, the Communist newspaper with which Oswald proudly had his picture taken with his assassination rifle. Here is a quotation from that filthy communist rag. (Judge for yourself what kind of "hate" killed President Kennedy—and will kill all of us if we don't put an immediate and complete stop to this sort of incitement.)

"WHAT CASTRO WOULD DO ABOUT RACISM IF HE WERE PRESIDENT OF THE UNITED STATES"

May I draw a word-picture of what we are really talking about when we say 'Decolonize America now'.

Let us imagine that in November 1960, Fidel Castro, instead of John F. Kennedy had been elected president of the U. S. On the basis of his clear record of eliminating all racial barriers in Cuba and stopping police brutality, about 95% of the cops in this country, Black and White, North and South, would catch the first planes out to escape persecution. Many of them would wind up in South Africa as "refugees". There they would find a political and racial climate wholly compatible and congenial.

If 'Bull' Conner were caught and arrested before fleeing, Fidel Castro would not permit anyone to lynch him. He would be given a fair trial. In open court, evidence would be presented of 30 years of his tyranny and terror as Birmingham police commissioner. Old 'Bull' would have full opportunity to testify in his own defense. His attorneys could cross-examine all the prosecution's witnesses, many of who would be Negroes. And then, since it is inconceivable that any court would find him innocent, he would be taken out and shot.

Meanwhile, on his first day in office, Fidel would have occupied the entire South with Federal troops without bureaucratic delays, the jails would be emptied of all Freedom Fighters and other victims of the Jim Crow system. Fidel's new cabinet would decree the immediate desegregation of all public facilities. Thenceforth, all persons who continued to discriminate would go to jail or to humanely operated rehabilitation centers [Communist euphemism for "concentration camp" - G.L.R.] in an effort to cure them of their racist insanity. All jobs, all housing, all opportunities would be made available to everyone without discrimination.

Most beautiful of all, Fidel would disband the entire repressive F.B.I. apparatus and would burn all the secret police garbage and intimate gossip that thousands of psychopathic F.B.I. agents have assembled over the years. He would put J. Edgar Hoover in an integrated cell in an Atlanta penitentiary as punishment for four decades of criminal neglect of duty. Hoover has never protected the Constitutional rights of Negroes.

Sadly, but realistically, even a Pacifist has to make a prediction that will scare and alarm many persons. The prediction is that it is going to take drastic, Castro-type revolution before this problem of the racists will be resolved. North and South, the twisted White Man in the U. S. has no more intention of giving up his Jim Crow system than do the fanatics in the Union of South Africa.

In the voluminous records of testimony about the assassination, the wife of Lee Oswald, Marina, admits Oswald used the name "A. Hidell" in sending for the rifle he used to kill Kennedy, because "Hidell" sounds like "Fidel" (Castro!)

While living with the Paines, Oswald practiced sharp shooting with the rifle he kept in the Paines' garage. He took a pot shot at General Edwin Walker, ran home, and boasted of the fact to his wife in Russian, explaining that Walker needed to be wiped out for his "extremist," right-wing, anti-communist and "fascist" views. Mrs. Oswald, with complete naiveté, has told this to the FBI. But we are supposed to believe that she never mentioned this to Mrs. Paine, her protectress and only confidante, the only person in America who regularly talked with her in Russian, the only language she understood.

In September 1963, it was announced that President Kennedy will visit Dallas. Three weeks later, Mrs. Paine calls up Mr. Truly, the manager of the Texas school book depository, and gets Oswald a job working there. Within a matter of only an hour or two after Mrs. Paine contacted Mr. Truly to get Oswald the job at the ideal assassination spot on the presidential parade route, Oswald appeared at a rooming house at 1026 N. Beckley Street, using the name "O. H. Lee"! The room was far smaller than the one he already had and cost him $1 per week more! Also, why the phony name? Can any reasonable person doubt that there was a criminal intention present, at least in the mind of Oswald, when he got the job at the Book Depository, and that Mrs. Paine's involvement is, at the very least, highly suspicious?

Meanwhile, Bernard Weissman and another New York Jew drive all the way down to Dallas to place a full-page advertisement in the Dallas papers for publication on the precise date of the President's assassination. Printed with a black border, the advertisement attacks Kennedy in a most extreme manner.

Consider: Dallas, supposedly a hot-bed of right-wing extremism, could apparently produce no "extremists" willing to put up the money for or write such an "extreme" anti-Kennedy ad. Two Jews had to come all the way down from New York to print this "extremist" ad in Dallas. Why?

Later, it turns out that Weissman's partner in this 1,500-mile extremist excursion to Dallas from New York City to put a hate-Kennedy ad in the Dallas paper is a top leader of "Young Americans for Freedom"—an organization put together and master-minded from 79 Madison Avenue, by the Jew Marvin Liebman.

During his period in Dallas, at the request of a local "engineer" (Mr. Paine was an "engineer"), Oswald began writing a Marxist, pro-communist, pro-Trotskyite, pro-Castro (but anti-Soviet) book. The most significant and startling thing about Oswald's episode is the public stenographer's story of what happened when Oswald began to give her sections of the book mentioning Kiev, where the Soviets maintain their school of assassination and terror. The stenographer reports that when Oswald reached the Kiev episodes, he became highly agitated and snatched away the entire manuscript, notes, and carbons, leaving only $10 in payment!

The Paines took Oswald to a meeting of the American Civil Liberties Union, which has defended literally thousands of communists, murderers, and saboteurs, and helped Oswald to apply for membership. He was told the ACLU "defends radicals"—which it does.

Shortly before the assassination, Fidel Castro held a "Hate America" parade in Havana, Cuba. He had Castroite mobs carry a casket, labeled "John F. Kennedy," through the streets to the jeers and hoots of the red Cubans. On top of that casket, Castro had placed a huge sign reading, "Here lies Kennedy, killed by the Cuban Revolution!"

Robert Williams, the American Negro who publishes the *Crusader*, boasted to the mob, "Kennedy has persecuted American Negroes long enough! Soon we will be avenged!"[4]

Three days before the assassination of President Kennedy, the FBI seized three Castroite terrorists in New York, precisely like Castroite Oswald. The FBI revealed that had these three Castroite terrorists not been

---

[4] *New Guard*, Nov. 1966.

caught, they planned to bomb Wall Street, blow up oil refineries in New Jersey, and spread a wave of assassinations and terror throughout New York! This would have occurred about November 22—the day the President was shot!

Here is a quote from the *New York Journal American*, November 18, 1963:

> If the FBI had failed to smash a Cuban plot geared to spread death, terror and destruction in the metropolitan area, Government sources said the three arrested saboteurs planned to destroy national defense material sites and utilities in New York City; blow up gasoline and oil refineries—the expected result: $100 million worth of damage; plant incendiary bombs in New York City's largest department stores; train ten other pro-Castroites in the art of sabotage. These ten were already undergoing training clandestinely. The expected result: a stepped-up program of sabotage that in time might completely paralyze the City. The blowing up of bridges and subway facilities, for example, might have been part of the plot for the future.

One day before the assassination, on November 21, Havana Radio boasted that Castro Communism would "export" bloody terrorism to all the nations in the Western Hemisphere—including the United States![5]

Meanwhile, inexplicably, Oswald slips over to Mexico to the Cuban and Soviet Embassies and is seen by witnesses in a station wagon! The border guard remembers there were two women and a man with Oswald (Mr. and Mrs. Paine and Mrs. Oswald?) (*Toronto Telegram*) (Mrs. Paine had a station wagon and used it to transport the Oswalds several times, including from New Orleans to Dallas.) Oswald talked at the Communist Embassy in Mexico City just before he went to Dallas for the assassination.

Simultaneously, Castro, as a matter of historical fact, is spreading murder and terror in Venezuela, where US citizens were beaten, kidnapped, and killed by the Castroite terrorists. On November 7, 1963, US Congressman Kirsten wrote an official warning to President Kennedy that the Communists were training "professional assassins for action in the United States"![6] Exactly 15 days after this official warning, President Kennedy

---

[5] *Washington Post*, 8 December 1963.
[6] *Northern Virginia Sun*, 27 November 1963, page 1.

was killed by a communist assassin. And now we are told it was only the act of a "loner," and we mustn't get mad at the communists, Soviets, or Cuba!

On November 22, 1963, Lee Oswald killed the President by shooting out of one of the windows of the building where Russian-loving Mrs. Paine had gotten him a job! (A "coincidence" of course.) Within a matter of minutes after realizing that the assassin was a communist, the US State Department sent out a top-priority demand to leading US news agencies to minimize any connection between Oswald and world communism "in order to avoid distributing relations with the Soviet countries and Cuba".[7]

We get hardened to the redness of our own State Department. Perhaps it will help the reader to see the red reality here if we reverse the situation. Suppose Hitler's Germany were still going strong, and I shot the President. Can you imagine the State Department sending out a plea to the press not to mention that I am a "Nazi" to avoid disturbing relations with Mr. Hitler? Any normal American cannot help asking himself how it was that a notorious traitor and defector to Russia could calmly sit in the window of a building on a Presidential parade route with a rifle and shoot the President, in spite of the FBI, the Secret Service and the Dallas Police Department, and walk away from the building.[8]

The answer is absurdly simple. Tragically simple! Because of the intense anti-right-wing "extremist" propaganda led by the President himself, all the security forces were watching *anti*-communists. There was nobody left to pay any attention to the real deadly danger, the *communists!* Within moments of the shooting, five harmless anti-communists were seized by the Dallas Police by the officers right on their tails in the crowd. These five were held four days because of the crazy hysteria whipped up against anti-communists, even though the police, while they were holding these anti-communists, caught the real culprit, a Red, allowed him to be shot in the basement of the Police Station by a Jew [Jack Ruby], and then locked up the assassin's assassin.

The President was shot because he, along with the Jews and the rest of the left wing, had blinded America to the deadly menace of the Reds, calling it "witch-hunting" "hate", etc., and set all our security forces on a phony "witch-hunt" after Rightists, the D.A.R., etc.—while trained and deadly communist killer Oswald was allowed to run around free of surveil-

---

[7] *Washington Daily News*, Dec. 4, 1963, p. 5.
[8] Rockwell would surely have been intrigued by the notion that Israeli Jews assassinated Kennedy. For details on this theory, see M. C. Piper, *Final Judgement* (1993) or L. Guyenot, *The Unspoken Kennedy Truth* (2021).

lance, just like hundreds of thousands more like him who are running around America today, right now!

The American Nazi Party was damned by Attorney General Kennedy as "un-American." But if the American Nazi Party had had its way, the Attorney General's brother never would have been shot, because Lee Oswald would have been in his grave, where traitors belong, according to the Constitution. And dead communists can't shoot people or overthrow governments. There is no "middle ground" with the communists, no "moderate" position. You either kill them, or they kill you—as they did kill our President.

After Oswald had gotten clear of the building from which he shot the President, the whole plan of the Jews and the reds to wipe out the Right wing and jam through the enabling legislation for a Soviet America, was in the clear. If Oswald had not been caught, there would not have been one voice raised to suggest that a communist might have done it, and just as with the Birmingham church bombing, where the bomber is unknown, the anti-communist Right wing would have been violently "lynched," "for shooting our beloved President"!—although, just as in Birmingham, there was no "fair trial," just a newspaper "lynching."

I believe Destiny took a hand at this point and threw a monkey-wrench into the Marxist-Jew machinery. By the most improbable of chances, a Dallas Policeman heard the barest possible description of the suspect—height, weight, age, etc.—and saw a man who might fit. When he tried to stop this man, the man *shot him*. And all the plans of the reds went up in smoke!

Oswald was only blocks from Rubenstein's apartment, probably on his way to hide out. But the shooting of heroic officer Tippit "loused up" the plans. He ran for a movie house in panic and was caught.

It is impossible to overemphasize to the thoughtful reader the history-changing magnitude of this event! Had Oswald "disappeared," like the "Birmingham hate bombers," the assassination of the President by the "dangerous" right-wing "extremists" and "fascists" would have been used with deadly effect to hammer in the last links of communist slavery in America! In the emotional atmosphere, which would have prevailed, nothing could have stopped the passage of the most extreme gun-control laws, the disarming of all Americans, and the complete liquidation of all anti-communist "extremists."

To accomplish this, the red Castroite terrorists were willing to shoot a President!

Destiny put Officer Tippit in the path of these fiends. Tippit died doing his duty. But his death saved America from the immediate threat of the Communist Revolution! I must admit that I could not believe the reds would be insane enough to shoot the President, but as I dug up more and more of the deadly facts, I became thoroughly convinced that November 22nd was "Revolution Day" on the Red calendar. We could never have resisted nor survived the raging lynch mob they would have whipped up, had Officer Tippit not stopped Oswald and thus led to the immediate capture and identification of the killer as a red!

卐 卐 卐

But there is more!

While the President was driving through Dallas, an ex-Chicago Jew named Jacob Rubenstein was pointedly in the advertising offices of the Dallas newspaper, going over his display ad, which promoted his degenerate striptease burlesque club. As the President was driving by outside, Rubenstein refused to join others in the office in going to the windows to glimpse his "idol"!

Later when Oswald was caught, Rubenstein rushed to the Police Station and managed to slip by all guards. For an entire day, while Oswald was in the Police Station, Rubenstein was running around in the middle of everything, participating in a press conference and even prompting the District Attorney with the answer to a question on local geography! Rubenstein was busily passing out his bawdy "calling-cards" for his burlesque show to police and reporters! As long as Oswald showed no signs of "breaking" under questioning by police, Rubenstein "joked with reporters" and simply hung around.

Then it was announced that Oswald was "ready to talk," and appeared ready to expose the real set-up. Rubenstein suddenly became so "upset" over the President's death, and was so "touched at the thought of Mrs. Kennedy's sorrow," that he shot Oswald, sealing his lips forever!

Consider the position of the conspirators! If Oswald talked, the whole thing would blow wide open and, instead of a red victory, the atmosphere (if Oswald admitted he was in on an international Jewish communist plot) would have been Nazi. The Jew-communists and traitors would have had to flee for their lives—as they should!

But even if Oswald didn't talk, the prolonged trial of this communist assassin would have driven into American consciousness at last the deadly danger of tolerating this criminal conspiracy on our soil for one moment longer, and would have led to a great revival of the patriotism the reds call "McCarthyism."

This was an impossible position for the communists. The trial of Oswald just simply mustn't happen. All the day before the shooting of Oswald, it seems reasonable to me that the high councils of treason in America were desperately scrambling for the solution. And they found it—the same solution they always find. Death!

At the very last moment when Oswald could be reached by "Ruby," as he was being transferred to secure quarters from the police station, the Jew Rubenstein rushed forward, was recognized by Oswald, (as slow-motion movies have proven beyond doubt)—and shot the assassin dead. With Oswald's death, the worst of the crisis was over for the conspirators.

Consider some of the deadly facts, which would have come out of Oswald's trial. Oswald was working for the "Fair Play for Cuba" Committee. We have met and fought this gang of swine personally, several times, and can testify that they are the filthiest, vilest, most treasonable, and vicious gang of reds in the country.

But more important, the Castroites are the nucleus of the "civil rights" movement! On April 6, 1960, the "Committee" was launched by an ad in the *New York Times*, a full page, paid for with Red Cuban money! At the top of the list of sponsors for this vile ad on behalf of treason is the name, "James Baldwin," the repulsive, black sexual-pervert "author." The rest of the list contains NAACP luminaries, and, perhaps even more important, big shots in the American Civil Liberties Union. The head of the Fair Play Committee in LA and a national co-chairman is Jew A. L. Wirin—who is also the head of the LA ACLU! The head of the vile Castro committee was the Jew, V. T. "Lee" (Tappin), who also turns out to be the Secretary of the ACLU in Tampa, Florida!

A trial of Oswald would have driven into the consciousness of America the unspeakable treason of these people who keep pulling off the same old Marxist trick of calling violent communist terrorists "reformers" until these murderers have seized control of pro-American, Christian governments as Castro did to Batista and Mao Tse Tung did to Chiang Kai-shek—after which the filthy Red fakers in America moan and wring their hands at their "betrayal" by these hard-core Communists who always seem to fool these trusting lovers of "civil liberties" and "civil rights".

Just a few weeks before the President's assassination, our government, with the help of these pro-communists, civil libertarian creeps, snubbed and insulted pro-American, Christian Madame Nhu. Then the

Vietnam communist "reformers" brutally assassinated her husband and set the stage for the present crazy Vietnam war!

Daily exposure of all of this would have been inevitable in any trial of Oswald. And such daily exposures would have inevitably and finally aroused the American people to the deadly facts about communism and the "civil rights" Black Horror which we of the right wing have been trying so hard to warn America.

In short, the trial of Oswald would have been a fatal blow to the communist conspiracy in America. It would have been utterly impossible for Martin Luther King, Queer James Baldwin, A. Philip Randolph, Queer Bayard Rustin, and the rest of the "liberal" and "civil rights" Jew and Negro leaders who have infiltrated even our churches to continue their deadly but creeping Communist revolution in America. Oswald had to go.

And he went. He was gunned down in typical gangland fashion by a man typical of Jewish "Murder, Inc."

Immediately after the assassination, three honest groups were preparing to investigate: The Texas Attorney General, the FBI, and the US Congress. Such honest investigations were intolerable to the Reds. On December 9, 1963, only eleven days after the assassination, the *Communist Worker* newspaper had the gall to demand that these three honest investigations be forbidden, and the outrage investigated only by Earl Warren. Three days later, the President of the United States obliged the *Worker*, did exactly as the communists demanded, and, on December 12, 1963, called off the other three investigations, and ordered Earl Warren to "investigate"—even though Warren had rushed into print within moments after the shooting, with the pre-judged statement that "Hate killed Kennedy": precisely the phrase used by the communists and every red in America and all over the world!

Warren "investigates" by hiding much of the record for 75 years, and actually burns much critical evidence (such as the autopsy report on the dead President's body!). With unbelievable arrogance, almost the whole press and publishing industry is diligently helping to spread a gigantic smoke screen being thrown up around the assassination, with the eventual aim of shifting the blame on the anti-communist movement, the way it was originally planned.

卐 卐 卐

Only two years after even the *Communist Worker*'s choice for chief investigator, Earl Warren, had to admit that the assassination was the product of a communist, four leftist authors—Mark Lane, Joachim Joesten, Harold Weissberg, and Jay Epstein (all four of them Jewish)—are peddling books of the most sophist "reasoning", casting doubt on the inescapable fact that it was Oswald who shot the President. They have manufactured "extra bullets," "grassy knolls," "contradictory" testimony, etc., and very cleverly left out all the damning facts which leave no doubt that Oswald did it. (And, unfortunately, there are many conspiracy-buffs in the anti-communist side who are actually cooperating with these Jewish smokescreen operators).[9]

But it is not the books of these men themselves, which are worthy of note in studying how our charts are forged. By themselves, the books would expire of their own weaknesses. It is the constant top coverage given these books by book reviewers, TV interview shows, newsstand operators, etc., which have shoved them down the throat of the public. I have studied them carefully, and there are no two ways about it: they are devilish, if slick, lies. Any careful student of any one of them knows this immediately. Yet they are given enormous publicity and dignity by editors, interviewers, and publishers.

What they are up to is a game they have played many times. When a fact is impossible to get around or cover up, the liars and chart-forgers help each other throw up an enormous smokescreen. These assassination books are that smokescreen. They are given such dignity and publicity that before long, most Americans, who will never read the books, will begin to believe that the Oswald theory is thoroughly discredited. It's the same technique they used with the facts of race. Whenever anybody tries to bring the obvious inequality of human groups into question, the chart-forgers and liars chant, "the claim that there is any such a thing as 'race' has been thoroughly 'discredited'!" they intone together. "Nobody believes that race myth anymore." But they have never actually discredited it; they merely covered it with smoke and finally mud.

Now they are doing the same thing with the fact that a communist shot the president: they are promoting a great, manufactured hue and cry that there is a lot of doubt that Oswald did it. Before long, we will be told that, "There's so much doubt now, about the Oswald theory, that nobody believes that anymore." And the last step is to start referring to it as the "discredited Oswald theory." They create an artificial bedlam all around the truth, then they point to their *own* bedlam and smokescreen to "prove"

---

[9] Rockwell rightly claims that the Jewish authors are distracting the public from the truth, but he does not consider the possibility that they are distracting people from a possible Jewish/Israeli role in the killing. This, today, appears as the most likely scenario. (see previous note)

that nobody believes the truth anymore! These arrogant chart-forgers are getting away with it, too, because too few people are willing to do the research homework to track down their massive lies.

As will be shown in later chapters, the chart-forgers have utterly blacked out of the minds of our people whole areas of human knowledge (such as the fact of race); they have made "patriots" out of our outright enemies, and enemies out of patriots whom they have smeared as "extremists" and "bigots"; they have filled the minds of our youth with such lies and madness that vast numbers of them have become LSD-crazed drug addicts and anti-social "hippies", reds, and moral-degenerates. They have filled the minds of Negroes with the fanatic belief that Negroes have unlimited rights and no duties. They have turned millions of once-self-reliant Americans into Federal dependents sucking frantically on the public teat. They have poisoned American history with suspicions of the motives of our heroes, slyly implying that they were lechers, profiteers, and "haters." They have made the great virtues of duty, faith, work, and honor the butt of ridicule, especially among youth. They have actually gotten inside religion, and promoted endless outright lies as the "new Christianity". The list of the lies they have spread among us could fill the rest of the book, but this should be enough to show the deadly pattern.

Why has anybody gone to such trouble to build a lie machine and then peddle such enormous lies to millions of us?

What has anybody to gain by piling Western Civilization and our American Republic up on the rocks?

Who wants to turn us into a race of brown, communized mongrels, with heads full of lies?

Who seeks to do such evil things, and for what evil purpose?

CHAPTER 5
CROOKED CAPTAINS

Off the New England and Gulf Coasts of America, a century or so ago, there were murderous gangs called "ship wreckers." The gangs would set up false lights near real lighthouses, cunningly placed so that suspecting ships approaching the coast in the dark and in storms would be guided onto deadly reefs. As soon as the ship was smashed, while the captain and crew were trying to survive the storm, these vultures would pounce on the helpless ship and rob it. To protect themselves from exposure, the gang murdered every human being aboard.

There was nothing complicated in shipwrecking. It was the oldest crime in the world—murder for what the other man had. The only difference was in the method of using false lighthouses.

Today, there is abroad in the world an enormous gang operating in almost every nation doing *exactly* the same thing as the early ship-wreckers, except that the modern "ship-wreckers" have added a tremendous complexity of refinements; and instead of wrecking ships, they wreck whole nations. They are called "communists" or "Marxists." But basically, the leaders are out to *rob* and murder productive people for loot, just as the ship-wreckers robbed those who had worked for the ship's cargo, and then killed them.

Their basic technique, in the end, just as with the ship wreckers, is always naked violence and murder. But also, just as with the ship-wreckers, they cannot beat the honest productive people of the world by sheer force. They also need surprise and guile. That's where the chart forgery and the fake lighthouses come in.

The Red gang of ship-wreckers lure decent, honest, and sincere people onto the deadly reefs of Marxist insanity with their fake lighthouses of "brotherhood," "peace," "love," "democracy," "equality." And then they rig all the charts available to show these fake lighthouses as the *only* safe guides. Meanwhile, these robbers and forgers rig all our charts—the press—to show the real, safe channels, in which America sailed to greatness, as the most deadly and dangerous of all reefs. Once our civilization has been wrecked, the Red gang plans to loot it, as they have looted every nation they seize.

In the next chapter, I shall present the fingerprints, footprints, witnesses, and handwriting experts to prove before a jury of my fellow Americans just '*who* these Red ship wreckers, robbers and killers are.

But first, I want to prove that *the captains of our ship of state,* for the last 40 years, *have been working with the criminal international gang of ship-wreckers, steering by these lying charts!*

Returning to the coast gangs, a hundred years ago, you can imagine the additional effectiveness of the crime, if the gangs could install some of their own criminal members as the captains of the ships approaching the phony lighthouses. With a fake captain, the unsuspecting ship and crew would have *no* chance—even if some of the navigators began to "smell a rat."

Any navigator who began to protest too vigorously that dirty work was afoot could be clapped into irons by the captain, with the full agreement of the other officers, who could be shown the phony charts. The evidence of dirty work would be too complex for most other officers and crewmen to see, and they would be led to believe the captain's lies, because the captain always has the phony charts to prove he is right.

That's precisely what has happened to America's ship of state. Men like the great Joe McCarthy were "navigators" who tried to warn the other officers and crew that the captain and the gang were wrecking the ship. But the fake captains of our nation have been backed up 1,000% by the fake chart-makers—the press, TV, etc.—and have managed to keep the innocent victims (the crew and ship) convinced that it was *McCarthy* who was trying to wreck America on the rocks, while the crooked captains have been presented as the greatest navigators in the history of the world.

Meanwhile, the same "wonderful" captains have been smashing our ship of state into one rock after the other, always with brilliant explanations by the captains, and adoring acceptance of the explanations as the ultimate in statesmanship, by our crooked chart-makers, the press. The American crew never really has a chance.

卐 卐 卐

If this sounds like an exaggeration, consider some of the evidence—not even much of it, just some outstanding examples.

Let's start with something that isn't ancient history, something going on before our eyes, right now. For more than 100 years, America had a sacred principle of foreign policy called the "Monroe Doctrine." President Monroe had declared that the United States could not and would not tolerate the establishment in the Western Hemisphere of any power base for the forceful export to the Americas of the seething troubles in Europe. And for a hundred years, we enforced this Monroe Doctrine rigorously.

Today, a rabid, revolutionary, Red-Chinese-dominated communist Cuba exists only 90 miles from our state of Florida. Far from doing anything about this dangerous situation and utter violation of the Monroe Doctrine, we helped bring foreign communism to Cuba, and our US Navy now protects and guards it from any attempt by Cuban patriots to re-take Cuba from the enemy! US Navy and Coast Guard ships actually pick up and arrest Cuban anticommunists on the high seas, and drag them back to jail! Think of it! Can you believe that there are *not* enemy hands on the wheel of our ship of state?

While we assist communism into power and protect it less than 90 miles away in Cuba, we are sending tens of thousands of American young men to fight and die in Vietnam, ten thousand miles away from America; ostensibly to "stop communism." If we are out to "stop communism," why go so far away when we can do it in our own backyard—and have a hundred years of the Monroe doctrine to back us up and assure that it is a "just" war?

And if we must send our boys so far away to "stop communism," why do we not let them do it? At this writing, we are still not attacking the enemy air bases from which come the planes, which are killing Americans, nor do we attack the port of Haiphong, through which come the tons of ammunition and weapons to kill thousands of us. But all of these things are complex and there will be a thousand arguments from the liberals, conservatives, and assorted creeps to justify all this, one way or the other. Instead of wasting further time quibbling with these things, let me present the most damning case I have, to prove to any honest man that the captains of our ship of state are steering it *purposely* on the rocks—for reasons I shall reveal in the next chapter.

When I got back from fighting World War II, I truly believed all the propaganda that I had helped the "good guys" fight the world's last war, the war to see that there was no more tyranny and "aggression." I remembered that the world declared war, in effect, on Germany, for marching into Prussia and Silesia—ex-German states which had become Poland. And it was, I was told, to get these people out from under the tyrants that I risked my life, and saw thousands die. But then I watched our "leaders" *giving* all these countries I was supposed to be fighting to "free"—to Soviet Russia. I thought I had "saved" Czechoslovakia, Poland, Hungary, Romania, Yugoslavia, etc. Then I couldn't help noticing that we had *not* stopped tyranny in these countries; instead, it seemed to me, by fighting in WWII, I had helped turn most of the world over to the Soviet Union and communism. All the countries I went to save: Who had them after WWII? And who has them now?

I began to notice, for the first time, that there was something most peculiar about this fight for "freedom" into which they got me and millions like me. Whenever any country was in the hands of *anti*-communists, we were told they were "tyrants and oppressors" and we had to fight to get them out at all costs—as we did, Germany, Italy, and Japan. But when a country was in the hands of communists—we *helped* them, and I heard nothing about "tyranny."

In fact, reviewing my career in World War II—I came to the conclusion that I am a Soviet War Veteran. I fought to turn over the major portion of the earth's surface to the Soviets. This, in turn, led me to become politically aware, for the first time. I began to notice what might be *behind* the things I read in the papers and saw at the movies, etc.

卐 卐 卐

Around this time right after the War, we began to get massive doses of propaganda about a man named Chiang Kai Shek. He was a "war-lord," we were told; corrupt, rotten, vicious—dictatorial and oppressive, he was the President of the China which had fought as a US ally in WWII, but now, suddenly, he was painted as an unmitigated villain and enemy of the "good guys." Our press and magazines and books were just alive with articles and material showing over and over what a scoundrel Chiang was.

At the time, I was still politically ignorant, (as most Americans still are), and didn't realize that the trouble with Mr. Chiang was that he was *anti-communist*. I was to learn soon enough.

Meanwhile, there was another Chinese leader rising over there, Mao-Tse Tung. The chart-forgers really went to work here, telling us what a great and good man Mao was. It's hard to believe it today, but they pulled out all the stops telling us that Mao Tse Tung was an "agrarian reformer" out to help the peasants with land reform and protect them from the corruption and extortions of "war-lords" like Chiang Kai Shek. The *Saturday Evening Post*, for instance, ran 26 articles in a row, praising Mao Tse Tung as an "agrarian reformer," scoffing at any idea that he could possibly be communist—and attacking Chiang Kai Shek as a corrupt "Fascist War-Lord." Young folks today are (probably mercifully) unaware of the unbelievable extent of this lying, vicious propaganda put out to our innocent people.

Almost every one of our leaders and top journalists went to work tirelessly telling America that Mao was *not* a communist, but a great patriot and the only hope of establishing justice and decency in China. Walter Lippmann, Dean Acheson, Truman, Dean Rusk, Eleanor Roosevelt, and the whole pack of our "leaders" assured us over and over again that Mao was *not* a communist, but was only a Chinese patriot trying to help the peasants establish land reform.

In fact, just to show you how far our "leaders" went, let me give just one example of the way they poured out these lies on the heads of our people. On June 14, 1951, Dean Rusk, then a top officer of our State Department (now our Secretary of State) made a speech praising Mao Tse Tung at the University of Pennsylvania. Rusk—with all the mountains of information available to the State Department—stood up before these thousands of Young Americans and told them, Mao Tse Tung did "not aim at dictatorship," was "not communist," and that Mao himself was the "George Washington of China"! Those were the actual words—all too easily forgotten—of the man, who now sets our State Department policy all over the world.

I remember, even back then, hearing the warnings of "right-wing extremists" filtering through the curtain of "good taste" thrown up to silence such rabid people, that Mao was a *communist*. These "extremists" warned that there was plenty of evidence of Mao's real, communist nature and plans. But at the time, it was impossible for me, anyway, to believe that our top leaders wouldn't know of such things if they existed—or that they would lie to us or cover such facts up if they did exist. At the time, I was naive enough, (as most Americans still are) to believe that our leaders "just couldn't" be working with such communist terrorists and enemies of our country as Mao Tse Tung. That our leadership and our press was crawling with enemies of our country I never could have believed. I would not even have listened to such outrageous charges.

So, with the American people thoroughly brainwashed on the subject of who was the good guy and who the bad guy in China, General Marshall went over there to China and *boasted* that, "with one stroke of the pen, I disarmed 20 Chinese divisions" (meaning Chiang's anti-communist troops). At the same time as our top General was "disarming" our anti-communist allies, the communists were turning over to Mao Tse Tung mountains and mountains of captured Japanese arms and ammunition. In short, we threw Chiang out of China, and turned this mighty land over to our "friend," "agrarian reformer," Mao Tse Tung!

Our leaders rejoiced at this triumph of justice until Mao threw off the cloak of "agrarian reformer" and revealed himself as a 100% Marxist, by slaughtering 40 million Chinamen to "thin them out," which is one hell of a way to give the peasants "land reform"—kill half of them so the rest have more to share!

Of course, the crocodile tears and exclamations of shock and surprise from Lippmann, Eleanor, Acheson, Rusk, and the rest were copious and warm. How surprised and disappointed they were. Here they thought Mao was a nice "liberal" like they were supposed to be—and he goes and spoils it all by exposing the fact that he was a *red communist* and a hater, killer, and terrorist all the time! One would think that one such "surprising" experience would be enough for the likes of Rusk and Co. Surely they wouldn't let it happen again!

No sooner had our leaders gotten over their "shock" and "dismay" over Mao, than the game began all over again! Suddenly our national life was filled with wails of agony about a new "Chiang Kai Shek" right here in the new world—Fulgencio Batista. In the 1950s, our chart-forging press and "intellectual" leadership began a campaign of vilification of the leader of Cuba, Batista, because he was a "dictator" who was oppressing the peasants. Batista was a Christian, an anti-communist, a friend of America and in league with no foreign power. But Batista had something about him that our shipwreck leaders didn't like and could not tolerate. He was damned and hounded by our leaders for "oppressing" people. The subject is rarely mentioned, even though every communist dictator today is oppressing American young men and women in communist prison and slave-labor camps. Such communist dictators as Khrushchev are called "Chairman" and invited to our White House by men like Eisenhower. But anti-communist dictators are called "fascists," and are scorned and smeared almost beyond belief by everything from our presidents to the *New York Times.*

So it was with Batista. Our State Department and CIA aided and abetted every kind of movement to overthrow and murder Batista (as they did with Trujillo, another anti-communist Latin American leader). As just one sample of how "our" State Department operated to get rid of anti-communist Batista, one has only to study the US Senate Internal Subcommittee's hearings on the man whom the State Department assigned to run the campaign against Batista, William Weiland. The record shows that this man, Weiland, went to incredible lengths, including perjury and withholding of official US documents to cover up the fact that the man we were helping, Castro, was a communist.

Castro helped lead an abortive revolution in Venezuela which is all reported in the Senate hearings on Weiland. Castro's brother, Raul Castro, was trained in the techniques of communist revolution in Moscow. All of

Castro's life, he had devoted himself to Marxist uprisings and revolutions, and this fact was known to our State Department, and much of our press.

Yet we poured aid and comfort on Castro, and heaped scorn, hatred and attacks on Batista. We refused to sell arms to Batista, even while Czechoslovakia was pouring arms in to Castro—arms made available to Czechoslovakia by "US aid"! (Even after Castro took power and began to abuse and shoot Americans as an arrogant, open communist, Kennedy and Johnson continued to give "aid" to Czechoslovakia.)

All of this was done by our sold-out "captains" in violation to the Monroe Doctrine and in open furtherance of the communist wrecking of the American Ship of State. The system they use in suckering the poor, innocent crew of the good old ship, "U.S.A.," is to play upon the noblest instincts of our people to help the oppressed and helpless. In the name of the oppressed peasants of Cuba, they disarmed and destroyed American friend Batista (because he was "brutal" to his people), and then installed a devilish and much more brutal communist tyrant.

All the while, the relatively few people who saw this terrible steering of our ship of state onto another communist rock were doing their best to alert the American people to the fact that Castro was a red communist! But our people were lulled to sleep by the chart-forgers who used their usual technique of accusing their victims of the very thing they themselves were doing.

The *New York Times'* Herbert Matthews, for instance, assured the American people over and over again that Castro couldn't be a communist, that he was an "agrarian reformer" trying to help the peasants who were being oppressed and brutalized by Batista. Patriots who tried to deny this fairytale were blasted as "extremists," "haters" trying to "divide" Americans and thus help the communists! President Eisenhower lent his support to this campaign against Batista, and for Castro. So did all our political pundits, from Walter Lipmann to Eleanor, from Dean Acheson to Dean Rusk—all of them, the men in the best position to know the facts, told us over and over again that Castro "couldn't be a communist"—that he was an "agrarian reformer".

The same "leaders" did everything possible to smear and discredit those patriots wise and courageous enough to try to warn America of the facts. McCarthy, Welch, Hargis, Smith, McGinley, Buckley, among others—and Rockwell—were all preaching and printing the facts which proved that Castro was exactly what he turned out to be, a communist robber and tyrant. All such patriots were blasted as "fanatics" (or sometimes, as in Smith's and my cases, given the silent treatment). We were "Red-baiters," paranoiacs seeing Reds under every bed, etc., etc.

So Mr. Castro was duly able to smash a Batista we disarmed, with communist weapons we supplied, whereupon Castro was brought to the USA for a triumphal tour of the nation. Ed Sullivan put him on national TV and, before millions of innocent Americans, said that Castro was "the George Washington of Cuba"! From our president on down, Americans were hearing the same deadly lies. Can you blame our people for being lost, confused, and often disgusted?

Ed Sullivan (L) and Fidel Castro (R)

Of course, as soon as Castro got back to Havana, he proceeded to stand up and boast, with utmost arrogance, that he had always been a communist and his revolution was Marxist. Then he started the usual shooting of his opponents and looting of American property. (Remember what we said about the ship-wreckers and how they operated—that they are primarily robbers who use lies and murder as tools?) Remember how the ship-wreckers looted the ships and shot the possible witnesses? Castro and every other dictator always grab property and murder those who possessed or defended it!

The crocodile tears from Eleanor, Acheson, Ike, Rusk, and Lipmann, et al., over this communist "betrayal" by Castro were a wonder to behold. They were "surprised" and "caught unawares" to the point where they were speechless. But no amount of these disastrous pro-communist "mistakes" by our leaders ever provokes any outcry from our press, radio, and TV, etc. On the contrary, they give each other endless Pulitzer, Nobel, and "Brotherhood" prizes. But the "extremists" and "bigots" who turn out to have been right each time, get the full treatment from both the Chart-forgers and the Crooked Captains.

卐 卐 卐

Whenever any American leader shows any signs of alerting the American people to what is going on, and shows any signs of success, the chart-forgers and liars and crooks in our national woodwork pounce on the poor devil with a ferocity understandable only when you realize they are fighting for their very lives. If the American people once find out how the captains and officers of our ship of state have been working with the ship wreckers on the shore to destroy this great country, there will be lynchings from the White House on down through the State Capitols.

The classic example of how a potential threat to the forgers was destroyed is the case of Joe McCarthy, who was warning Americans of the truth: that Mao was a genuine communist. So the chart-forgers in the press, on TV, in magazines—and in the White House—went to work as never before. They vilified and lied about Joe McCarthy as few men have ever experienced national attack.

I was commanding officer of a Navy anti-submarine squadron in Iceland at the time, and couldn't understand how a US Senator could be as rotten as McCarthy was made to appear. I sent away for the actual transcripts of the hearings in which McCarthy was supposed to bully and abuse the witnesses. And I found that the facts were precisely the opposite of what the American people were being told and still believe! The facts showed that McCarthy was *understating* the case, if anything; that our leaders and every engine of public opinion were selling us out, lying to us. Time after time, I found that McCarthy was accused of flinging "shot-gun charges" at innocent people—only to discover by hard digging that the so-called "innocent" people were the most atrocious kind of red agents—often-outright spies.

A perfect example was the way *Time* magazine tried to pillory McCarthy for attacking a man named Gustavo Duran. McCarthy accused Duran of being, at one time, an agent of the OGPU, the Soviet secret service and terrorist organization. "Duran", said *Time*, "never a Red, was actually a strong anti-communist." I found the evidence, produced under oath, and documented by our own House committee, that Duran had been an agent of the OGPU in the Spanish Civil War, where he fought on the communist side. But even this was not the revealing thing. The real shocker was the proof that the *Time* writer who wrote, "Duran, never a Red, was actually a strong anti-communist"—had in his possession when he wrote that lie, the documented evidence from *Time's* own files that Duran was not only a Red, but an agent of the Soviet OGPU—just as McCarthy charged. Yet millions of Americans were led, innocently, to believe that McCarthy had "assassinated the character" of one more "innocent"!

The serious reader must ask himself just how flagrant the evidence must get before we draw the only possible conclusion—that the lies and smears were deliberate and knowing. And if they were deliberate, then the further conclusion is inescapable that they are indeed "forging the charts" for Americans—that our biggest disseminators of information and news are either communist or pro-communist.

Further, the record of our leaders since Franklin D. Roosevelt is even more flagrant in the way they have aided and protected and promoted communism every time they could. Notice the pattern in the cases of China and Cuba. Our "leaders" first begin a campaign to vilify and build hatred of a pro-American, anti-communist leader like Batista or Chiang Kai-Shek because he is "corrupt" and a "dictator"—a "fascist". Then we begin to hear that the opposition to this "dictator" is a "George Washington", an "agrarian reformer", a "liberator" of "oppressed peoples", etc. Then we arm, aid, and assist the "liberator", while we disarm and harass the dirty "dictator", always in the name of "helping the oppressed" and thus "holding back communism". Any American who casts doubt on the "liberator" is ruthlessly attacked as a "smearer", "fanatic", "hater", "Red-baiter". Once the liberator is in, in the name of helping the oppressed, he turns out to be a Red, just as us "haters" and "red-baiters" warned.

But the people are distracted from noticing this fact by some new outcry in the press, by some new cooked-up crisis, until the communist dictator has shot millions and established iron rule as a tyrant, much to the "surprise" of our leaders and experts.

Whenever our leaders do let us get into armed conflict with the communists—observe that it is *always* under conditions where we can do nothing but die, spend money, and lose, while the Reds have nothing to lose and everything to gain, as in Vietnam.

In Asia, manpower is not only unlimited, it is a drug on the market. They need the population thinned out. So we obligingly went to Korea and threw away vast numbers of American lives and limbs in a war our boys were forbidden to win or even fight. We did not use our best weapons, but kept our men dying for *nothing*, when we could have won in a matter of days. Now we are committed even more viciously to the same madness in Vietnam. We have the force and strength to win that war in a week, if our "leaders" would let us. But instead, they continue to pour out American lives and treasure, bleeding America to death, and making us the devil and laughingstock of the world to boot.

Another rotten and perfidious example of crooked captains was the actions of John Kennedy in the Bay of Pigs invasion. With the utmost cynical cruelty and disregard for honor and decency, Mr. Kennedy organized the whole invasion of Cuba to make it look good, committed thousands of lives of anti-communist patriots and then, single-handedly and arrogantly ordered the grounding of the only force which could have given the landing parties any chance of success—air support. The Cuban pilots, waiting to take off, were prevented from doing so by Kennedy's *direct orders*—at the last moment! (*US News and World Report*, Sept. 17, 1962).

卐 卐 卐

When men like McCarthy or any other patriots in our Congress have attempted to hold investigations of this sort of unbelievable treachery and treason by our top leaders, these leaders, particularly our Presidents, have applied the most ruthless kind of gag. By executive order, officials involved are forbidden to give information on these horrible catastrophes to your representatives in Congress!

Perhaps the most revealing episode of all, showing the way our leaders themselves are in cahoots with the chart forgers, was Truman's incredible actions in the Harry Dexter White case. White (real name, Weissnovitz) was Assistant Secretary of the US Treasury, under Henry Morgenthau. In that capacity, White stole the engraving plates for US paper money, and sent them to the Soviets to print money for use in occupied Germany. He also arranged for the mass theft of tons of our special money-paper. The Soviets printed billions of dollars of US money for occupied Germany, with which they were able to gain vast amounts of US material, and pay spies and American communists.

J. Edgar Hoover went to President Truman with all the evidence that the Assistant Secretary of the Treasury was not only a communist, but an espionage agent for the Soviets, and a master thief to boot—stealing billions of dollars. Of course, the President at least fired this traitor and thief. At least, that's what you would certainly think.

But that's not what Truman did. After being told by the Chief of the FBI that Weiss was a Red spy, Harry Truman *promoted* White to be the head of the International Monetary Fund, where he was in a position to give billions to pro-communist governments like Poland, etc., and starve anti-communist governments to death, which is exactly what happened.

When the Senate got this information from J. Edgar Hoover himself, President Truman told the Senate that what Hoover actually said was that it would be best to promote White so he wouldn't realize that the FBI was wise to him. Hoover, as usual, with magnificent courage and integrity, promptly showed up the President as a liar on behalf of this despicable communist enemy of America! Hoover testified under oath that he said no such thing to the President, that he suggested White be gotten out of government as quickly as possible. As usual, the matter was quietly dropped in the press. White himself was found dead—one more "suicide".

When Alger Hiss, the convicted communist spy and perjurer was on trial, Eleanor Roosevelt, Dean Acheson, Secretary of State, Felix Frankfurter from the Supreme Court, and many other top government officials appointed by the Presidents, went on the stand to testify that Hiss couldn't be a Red, just as they all testified that Castro and Mao Tse Tung "couldn't be a communist", either.

The record is almost endless. The way you will find "your" presidents acting in such a manner that communism always gains, and damning all opposition as "extremism" and Red-baiting is monotonous. The captains of our ship-of-state *always* "blunder" onto the rocks, year after year!

The most depressing thing about it all is the way it works. The people of the country are like the crew of a ship, too absorbed by their individual tasks to pay much attention to the navigator and captain's business. They presume that these officers must be on the level. And they are forever reminded by the chart-forgers (the press) what geniuses and saints these captains are, no matter how many times they smash us up on the rocks of China, Cuba, Korea, and Vietnam.

What is going on is the old shipwrecking conspiracy, with precisely the same purposes: loot and murder. The only difference is that the gang working this devilish criminal operation is not depending on just one false lighthouse to lead their victims to destruction. They have installed nothing but false charts, showing the path to the rocks and destruction as salvation itself, and showing the only safe channels as the deadliest reefs—which they call "hate", "Red-baiting", "witch-hunting", "bigotry," and finally "fascism" or "Nazism".

They have installed *nothing but* crooked captains who see to it that, no matter how many times the false channels of pro-communism and liberalism smash us into rocks and reefs, we keep roaring ahead faster and faster toward more rocks and reefs. They have destroyed all the buoys, lights, and markers which once guided our people through the channels of life; the channel markers of religion, education, ideals, heroes, traditions, discipline, and morals which didn't make us perfect, but did make us a great people. But our people fail to see the pattern of what they are doing, and so never realize what is happening to us.

卐 卐 卐

Consider the pattern of what happened in China, what happened in Cuba—and what is now happening in the USA.

In China, the chart-forgers and liars first began to moan about an oppressed group, the farmers and peasants, and tell us how these poor "peasants" were being "exploited" by the "war-lord", Chiang Kai-Shek. In Cuba, it was Batista who oppressed the Peasants. Then they raise up, with massive publicity, a "champion" of these poor, oppressed peasants: Mao Tse Tung in China, Castro in Cuba. In spite of foul communist records, the liars and chart-forgers manage to make their "champions of the oppressed" into heroes with the millions who don't look too closely. All opposition to their red "heroes" is smeared to death as "hate" and "witch-hunting".

Native leaders who oppose their great champions of the oppressed are then disarmed by our American leaders, because they are so "corrupt" and "fascist", etc., as happened with Chiang and Batista. Meanwhile, the communist "saviors" are heavily armed, with the secret connivance of our American leaders. The "liberators" then take over in the name of the oppressed, but promptly turn on them, much to the "surprise" of our leaders, and start the usual communist terrorism and murder. They followed precisely this pattern in China and Cuba, and our people never noticed.

Now they are doing exactly the same thing here in the USA, and millions of our best people are helping them, from the noblest motives in the world. In America, there are no masses of starving peasants. But they do have a group which is "oppressed" in the sense that they have almost nothing—the blacks. So, in the name of helping the "oppressed" blacks, the same gang of liars and manipulators, chart-forgers and crooked captains, have set up the exact same "movement" here to "liberate" the oppressed, with a leader who has just as "suspicious" a red record as Mao Tse Tung and Castro. The battle cry of Fidel Castro's "liberation" and "agrarian reform" movement was *Vinceramos*! (We shall overcome!).

Sound familiar? It should, because the same pattern is being followed right here in America. "Agrarian Reform" here is called "Civil Rights". Instead of Mao or Fidel, we have Martin Luther King—who "couldn't" be a communist! All our top leaders tell us over and over what a great and holy man he is—just as they did about Mao and Castro. We've had two strikes in this red ball game already, China and Cuba; now it's America—and our last strike. And we're fanning—striking out on our last chance.

None but the stubbornly blind and blindly stubborn can now fail to see that Western civilization cannot much longer survive the way it is being driven. Unless, by some mighty, convulsive effort of intelligence and will, we can find a way to rise up in a veritably frenzy of energy and throw overboard the crooked captains, together with their phony charts and chart-forgers, our whole people will soon fall into the bloody hands of the communist ship-wreckers.

As has happened to dozens of other nations, we will be taken over in the name of liberation, and then the ship-wreckers will loot the wealth of the productive people, shoot all who protest or even appear to protest, and put the remainder to work in their slave-camp society.

To stop a gang of ship-wreckers a century ago, it was necessary first to identify them, then to catch them, and finally to punish them and see that there were no more ship-wreckers. Precisely the same steps are necessary today, with the modern, worldwide form of ship-wreckers—the Marxists. We've got to *identify* them, before we can proceed with the other, more direct steps.

So let's take a penetrating look at these criminals, and see if we can learn who they are. Let's remember that no gang can be stopped as long as all you do is chase the peons and sub-leaders. We've got to find who is the "Mr. Big" behind this gang of international, Marxist ship-wreckers. And it's going to be a little dangerous. Whenever you penetrate the inner circle of a gang and begin to put the finger on "Mr. Big", you can expect lots of heat and fire. We won't be disappointed.

CHAPTER 6

THE SHIP-WRECKERS

In most criminal gangs, the "troops" usually wind up on the short end of the stick while "Mr. Big" takes not only the lion's share, but everybody else's too. Usually, most of the "troops" don't even know who the top boss really is. Further, "Mr. Big" usually has a "respectable front."

It is just so with the criminal, international gang of ship-wreckers and looters called the "communists." The "Mr. Big" of the Red ship-wreckers is a very special kind of boss. He appears to the world as the very essence of respectability, he is almost unknown for the killer and gangster he actually is, even among his own Red "troops." But in spite of all the fronts and cover-ups, there is one sure way of knowing who is the real boss anyplace. In Capone's mob, you could cuss the torpedoes. But if you made vile remarks about Big Al, you weren't around long. In China, you can have all the "free speech" you want—so long as you don't criticize Mao Tse Tung. In Cuba, you can have all the "free speech" you want—so long as you don't criticize Castro.

Let's see if there's anybody in America whom nobody dares criticize. It's certainly not the President. Razzing the President is a national sport. Several times, LBJ has been unable to speak for all the criticism being screamed at him by demonstrators. Nor is it any other official. You can't name any elected official in America who is so "sacred" there isn't somebody blasting away at him. Nor is there any group you can't take a pot-shot at. You can cuss the Pollacks, the Irish, the Squareheads [Germans]—even the Catholics and the Pope himself, as Rolf Hochhuth's play "The Deputy" shows. You can even criticize the Negroes, if you do it in the guise of "States' Rights" or solicitous love of the "colored people." It's done all the time, North and South. Even Huntley and Brinkley recently ran a news special on a Negro housing project in St. Louis and showed the Negroes in the brutally bad light they create for themselves.

But *who* dares criticize *Jews?*

Can you imagine a TV special by Huntley and Brinkley on the fact that almost all our Soviet spies, like the Rosenbergs, Soble, Soblen, Brothman, Gold, Moskowitz, Greenglass, Weinbaum, etc., have been *Jews?*

It takes only a moment of reflection for any honest American, looking right inside his own soul, to see that the one group most feared and dreaded in "our" country is the Jews. Nobody *ever* criticizes Jews, as Jews. Do you, dare do it? How did this happen? What's so special about these Jews? Why is everybody afraid of them? The word "afraid" is derived from the word "fear." You can only be "afraid of" what you fear. And you only fear what has some kind of power over you. What power have Jews over us? And how did they get it?

卍 卍 卍

It was the much publicized "little old lady in sneakers" who started me thinking seriously about the power of Jewry for the first time.

For 32 years of my life, I had, like almost all Americans, believed that Jews were just a special religious group, who are good businessmen. Also, like most Americans, I believed they had a special affinity for money, and a fantastic ability to get money. But that's all. I had, of course, heard all the standard canards about Jews. But, again like millions of my fellow Americans, I figured these accusations against the Jews were just the product of bigotry, "scapegoating," and envy of Jewish ability.

Then, in 1950, when I was instructing Marine and Navy pilots in close air support of ground troops during the Korean war, I got interested in trying to put Douglas MacArthur in the White House.

As a Naval Officer, I had known and respected Douglas MacArthur. I thought he would make the greatest President of the USA. When there was a campaign to get him the Republican nomination in 1952, I wanted to do what I could to help. I read a letter in *The San Diego Union* from a woman who lamented that no one would help her get a MacArthur rally going. So I called the lady (whose name I have forgotten) and offered what help I could give. She was very grateful, and invited me to the little cottage where she lived in retirement with her husband.

I started to tell her all the things I thought could be done. I suggested we get a hall and hold a rally. She just smiled with a patient, sad smile and stopped me. "No," she said, "you can't get a hall so easy, even if you pay. They won't rent one!" "What do you mean!" I burst. "Who won't rent one?" She looked queerly and quizzically at her husband, clearly asking him with her eyes about something. He just shook his head.

"Who won't rent you a hall?" I asked again, looking from him to her. She took a deep breath, looked pained, and then said, "The Jews."

"The Jews!" came out of me involuntarily. "What have the Jews got to do with it? What do they care whether you get a hall or not?"

"They hate MacArthur!" she said, and started to say something else when I interrupted her.

"Hate him! That's silly! I suppose some of them do. But certainly not all of them! And certainly none of them hate him enough to stop you from hiring a hall for a MacArthur rally!''

She took another deep breath, looking hurt. "It's true," she said, "they all hate him. Look at this, for instance!" and she handed me a copy of *The California Jewish Voice*. There it was: "MacArthur Approaches: Hitler Enters the Chancellery!" and the paper went on to rave about how General MacArthur was the threat of a "new Hitler"! I couldn't believe it!

"That's only one paper!" I countered. "It's probably just an extremist sheet. I am sure the Jews don't imagine MacArthur is really another Hitler!" She showed me another Jewish paper, *The B'nai B'rith Messenger*. Its tone was more dignified, but the same hatred of MacArthur was there. She showed me still other Jewish papers. In most of them were vile pictures of Joe McCarthy, terrible charges against him and MacArthur, and unmistakable venom for both of these men.

This is the experience, which awaits every honest American who begins to think about the Jewish Question. I had suddenly been exposed to a whole secret world which the average American never even imagines, and never sees—the secret world of the Jews. In the same *Jewish Voice,* I saw the headlines by the editor, Sammy Gach, "Thank God!" the day Russia got the A-bomb! (*Jewish Voice*, Sept. 30, 1949).

I saw hundreds of similar treasonable items. But most Americans are too insulated and easy-going ever to look into this Jewish press. Sooner or later, no matter how long the average American is kept in the dark, or keeps himself in the dark by imagining that discovering Jewish treason against his country and people is "bigotry," he will find the naked evidence of this unified, alien, fanatical Jewish world in the midst of his own people—implacable, hateful, spiteful, bitter, and diabolically clever at appearing to be only a "persecuted" religious group.

The whole thing, however, still didn't register with me at the time. It was too fantastic. I felt sure there was some misunderstanding somehow. But the lady gave me some books and papers to take home and study.

When I got home, I looked at the first paper. It was called *common Sense*, and the headline was "Red Dictatorship By 1954!" I figured right away I had found the paranoiac nature of this monstrous "Jewish scare" the lady had told me about—a fantastic Jewish "world plot"—and I couldn't even finish reading it. It seemed too silly and disgusting for an intelligent man to bother about reading.

But in the few lines I did read, *common Sense* gave what it claimed were startling facts about the Jewishness of communism and the Russian Revolution. It listed, as the sources of some of these unbelievable facts, the *Jewish Encyclopedia* and various official US Government documents. This seemed like an excellent opportunity to spike such a fantastic idea as that communism was Jewish, and I decided to check these supposed "facts" out.

I went over to the San Diego Public Library and dug around in the volumes mentioned in *common Sense*. Down there in the dark stacks of the San Diego Public Library, I got my awakening from 30 years of stupid political sleep—the same deadly sleep now closing the eyes of our people and making them cooperate with their enemies in their own destruction, all in the name of "good citizenship," "brotherhood," and all the rest of the shibboleths of "nice" people. I discovered a whole, secret world—the world of the Jews.

And the Jews' world is secret only because the non-Jews can't believe there could be such a world, and never look into it!

Perhaps one of the simplest ways to demonstrate this secret Jewish world even to the most hostile reader is to let him perform a simple experiment. There are thousands of manufacturers who are forced to pay the Jews to put this symbol, called a "hechsher," on its labels and for which the rabbis get a special certification fee! Let the doubter go to his kitchen and get out any dozen cans of different foods, and a few cans of scouring powders, soap, etc. Examine the labels of these cans carefully for either a little "U" in a circle, or a "K." The "U" means Union of Orthodox Jewish Congregations of America, and the "K" stands for kosher. You will find those Jewish symbols on most of your groceries.

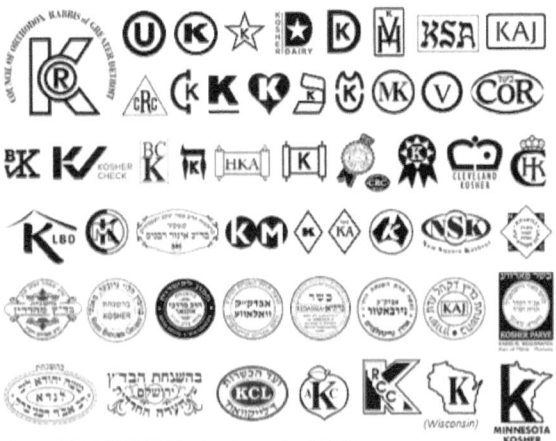

Version 3.0, July 2017. Additional copies: cor@cordetroit.com.

Food products in Canada have "MK" (Montreal Kosher) and "COR" (Canadian Orthodox Rabbis) on the labels.

The *Wall Street Journal* for April 23, 1969 revealed that grocery companies were paying millions and millions of dollars to put these kosher symbols on their labels. In fact, even *The Jewish Newsletter* for June 1, 1959 warned the Jews that this "K" and "U" business is a racket, pure and simple, and that if the Jewish racketeers didn't ease up a bit on it, the non-Jews would find it out and there would be hell to pay!

The whole dirty Jewish business almost broke into national news when a greedy rabbi in Indianapolis in 1957 (as court records will show) sued the Coca-Cola Company and made them pay him $30,000 to put his Jewish hechsher (kosher label) on this soft drink! (The same Jewish news-letter points out that the greatest rabbinical authorities testify that neither Coca-Cola nor any other drink require rabbinical supervision!) That's $30,000 paid to just one rabbi in one city, by one company, to put these Jewish symbols on one soft drink for general American consumption— which almost no non-Jewish Americans know about.

Kosher "Yellow cap" on Coke

But it is the non-Jews who are paying for this racket. *You*, the vast Christian majority, pay that rabbi, not only in Indianapolis, but also in every city in every state in America, day after day, year after year, to make almost all your food kosher—Jewish!

How long do you think the Jews would tolerate Catholics running such an out-and-out racket, costing us all millions of dollars in tribute, and forcing Catholic religious practices on all of us in our food? How long do you think the Jews would tolerate a Nazi "minority" in Israel insisting on having a Nazi stormtrooper in every Jewish food factory, to put a little swastika on every can of food eaten by the Jews?

卐 卐 卐

Continuing my research into still another area of the secret world of the Jews, I found, in unimpeachable documents and intelligence studies by our own US Government, that the Russian Revolution was not "Russian" at all, but almost wholly led by Jews. A table made in April 1918 by Robert Wilton for the G-2 Section (Military Intelligence of the US Army), shows that at the time of the Russian Revolution: there were 384 commissars (running Russia), including:

2 Negroes,
13 Russians,
15 Chinese,
22 Armenians, and
more than 300 Jews.

Of the latter number, 264 had come to Russia from the United States since the downfall of the Imperial Government. Not even Russian Jews, but New York Jews![1]

On page 2 of his secret report to Washington on the nature of the Russian Revolution, Capt. Montgomery Schuyler, G-2, Intelligence, states the situation brutally but so clearly there can be no doubt: "It is probably unwise to say this too loudly in the United States," writes Schuyler in his report, "but the Bolshevik movement is and has been since its beginning, guided and controlled by Russian Jews of the greasiest type." Here was smashing evidence that the "Russian" revolution was not Russian at all, but the *capture* of Russia, by a gang of criminal Jews!

---

[1] See especially Wilton's book *The Last Days of the Romanovs* (1920).

Moreover, I discovered I had been the victim of one of the rottenest con games in all history: the use of the mantle of religion to cloak a filthy, criminal conspiracy of murder and robbery. In looking through some Jewish sources, I came across a book put out by the Jews themselves, called, *Who's Who in American Jewry*. Imagine my horror and surprise, then to find, on page 556 of *Who's Who in American Jewry*, the picture and name of the head of the atheist communist Red Army, Leon "Trotsky," with the further information that he was born "Bronstein!" In the same Jewish book, on page 673, I found the Jews proudly listing Maxim Litvinoff, the first Foreign Minister of Soviet Russia, as an American Jew named *Finkelstein*! Now if the Jews are honest when they tell us they are not a race or a conspiracy, but only a "religious" group, what are they doing listing these militant atheist *Bolsheviks*, not only as Americans, but as believers in "Judaism?"

Since then, I have found the same thing in the current Jewish books, which Gentiles rarely bother to investigate. In *Who's Who in World Jewry* (1965), endorsed by the B'nai B'rith, Jewish Theological Seminary, etc., as "An honor roll of World Jews," I found, on Page 29, a listing for Herbert Aptheker, chief theoretician of the communist Party, the Jew whose communist daughter Bettina runs the riots at Berkeley!

I learned from the article called "Khazars" in the *Universal Jewish Encyclopedia* (published by the Jews) that most Jews are not even "Semites" or descendants of the Hebrew people of Palestine, but mostly the descendants of a semi-oriental tribe in central Russia called "Khazars," whose king, Bulan, in the sixth century ordered his people *en masse* to become "Jews." I discovered that these "Jews," called "Ashkenazim" in the "trade" (as distinguished from the real Semitic Jews, called "Sephardim"), constitute the bulk and the leadership of the people we call generally "Jews." It is swarms of these "Khazars," with their oriental heritage, who are pushing us around, forcing integration on us, degrading our culture with their filthy "art" (chaos and pornography), and, worst of all, spreading the disease of communism—all while hiding in the robes of the Jewish "religion!"

Knowing how incredible all this may seem to the average American (as it seemed incredible to me when I first came upon it), I will here include a document I later found in the Library of Congress, a document at once so shocking and yet so absolutely unimpeachable, that in the 15 years since I first saw it, and while presenting it constantly to thousands of people, in college speeches, I have never yet found anybody to contradict one line of it. In the London *Illustrated Sunday Herald* for February 8, 1920, I found a full-page article written by Winston Churchill (including his picture, so there can be no mistake of the identity of the author), called "Zionism versus Bolshevism: A Struggle for the Soul of the Jewish People." In this full-page article, Winston Churchill sets forth the fact that the Jewish people all over the world were divided between two courses of action - Zionism and Bolshevism (communism). He points out that the Russian Revolution was not "Russian" at all, but the capture of the Russian people by atheistical, Marxist, international Jews![2]

Either Winston Churchill himself is a liar, a "bigot," a "scapegoater," and a "hater"—or one of the biggest facts in the history of the world has been denied to you and millions of other non-Jews! If communist revolutions are not the act of the people in the countries themselves, but are rather the capture of those countries by Jews, *as was the case in Russia*—then it is impossible for you to protect yourself from a communist revolution in

---

[2] Full article reprinted in *51 Documents* (L. Brenner, ed.; 2002).

America if you are denied the knowledge that communist revolutions are *Jewish!* And it is precisely this knowledge that you and millions of other Americans are denied, in order to make you helpless before this arrogant Jewish aggression.

Now I had found the second of the forged charts foisted off on my people; the first was the lie that there was no such thing as breed or race among humans, although there was breed everywhere else in Nature. And here was the second big lie of the forgers: that Jews were "just a persecuted religion," rather than the race or breed of people responsible for communism!

I went on to find, in the February 3, 1949 issue of the *New York Journal-American*, that Jacob Schiff, then head of the gigantic financial empire called "Kuhn, Loeb & Co.", and grandfather of the woman who now owns the super leftwing *New York Post*, "sank over $20 million in the Russian Revolution," financing another Jew, Trotsky (Bronstein), in the murder of the Christian and anti-Christian and anti-communist "White Russians" in masses!

Most surprising and revealing of all was the often-invisible connection between a seemingly pure Gentile communist, and the inevitable Jew, lurking directly in the rear, as Churchill explained in his article.

Lenin, not a Jew,[3] was married to Krupskaya, a Jewess.[4] Stalin, also not a Jew, was married to the sister of Lazar Kaganovitch, Rosa—a Jewess.[5] Stalin's son married another Jewess, and it turns out that Khrushchev was the protégé of this same Jew, and married another Jewess in Kaganovitch's family. Cheddi Jagen, communist Premier of Guinea, is married to a Jewess named Janet Rosenberg from Chicago.

In the satellite countries, it was the same. More Jews! Even that sacred "friend" of America, Tito, was the protégé of Moses Pijade, another Jew Khazar, who does the "suggesting" for the strutting Mr. Tito. And in Cuba, we find a Jew named Zincowich quietly advising Fidel Castro. The Jewess, Anna Pauker, ran Romania. The Jew, Berman, ran Poland, the Jew Rakosi (Rosencranz) ran Hungary, and the American Jew, Gerhardt Eisler was running East Germany!

In the USA, the FBI and other agencies were catching and/or exposing hordes of Jew spies and communists:

Julius and Ethel Rosenberg, Morton Sobell, Harry Soblen, Robert Soblen, Sidney Weinbaum, Judith Coplon, David Green-

---

[3] Actually, Lenin was a quarter-Jew (maternal grandfather Alexandr Blank).

[4] This is disputed.

[5] This is also disputed.

glass, Abraham Brottman, Miriam Moskowitz, Kramer (Cohen), Harry Gold, Joseph Weinberg, Nathan Silvermaster, Klaus Fuchs, Jacob Golos, the Krugers (Cohens), White (Weiss), Alex Trachtenberg, V. J. Jerome (Isaac Romaine), Simon Gerson, Alex Bittelman, Betty Gannett, Isadore Begun, Jacob Mindel, Israel Amter, W. Weinstone, Fred Fine, Sid Steinberg, Louis Weinstock, Albert Lannon, Fred Rose, "J. Peters" Goldberger, Jacob Stachel, Gerhardt Eisler, Hanns Eisler, "John Gates" (Israel Regenstreif), Gilbert Greenberg, "Gus Hall" (Arvo Mike Halberg), Irving Potash, Carl Weissburg, Philip Bart, Philip Jaffe, Andrew Roth, Mark Kayn (Mark Julius Ginsberg) "Gil Green" (Gilbert Greenberg), "Carl Winter" (Philip Carl Weissberg).

The names were sometimes changed, but the pictures of these camel-like Jewish faces were more than enough to identify them as Jews. (This list of identified promoters of communism and spies could be extended for many pages if there were any point in merely multiplying the list of names. But this ought to be enough to eliminate any question in the mind of any reader as to the Jewish inspiration of communism.)

Out of 41 workers with communist records at our secret radar laboratories in Fort Monmouth, 39 turned out to be Jews! Out of 18 Americans convicted of espionage for the Soviet Union since 1946, 16 were Jews and 1 was a Negro! Out of 21 convicted of communist conspiracy to overthrow the US Government by illegal force and violence, 18 were Jews! When the FBI nabbed the "Second-string Politburo," out of 17, 14 of the traitors were identified as Jews! Out of the "Hollywood Ten" who took the 5th Amendment when asked if they were communists, 9 were Jews!

In the US National Archives, in Washington, DC, researcher Harold Arrowsmith found a letter dated February 23, 1921 from J. Edgar Hoover, the Special Assistant to the Attorney General, addressed to W. L. Hurley, Office of the Undersecretary of State, Department of State. It bears State Department decimal file number 861.0078795, and reads:

> Receipt is acknowledged of your letter of the 4th instant (U-H/861.0O/7885) referring to copy of dispatch No. 62 from the American Consul at Reval, dated December 1, 1920, relative to the disseminators of Bolshevik propaganda, submitting a list of the same and requesting a reply, the substance of which will be communicated to the American Consul at Reval.

From an examination of the list of names and addresses submitted, it is indicated that at least the major portion of the list of 32 names is authentic, particularly because of the notation, J. Ferguson (evidently Isaac Ferguson); Felix Frankfurter; Jacob Hartman; and Fred Biedenkapp -- *all known to be actors in this movement.*"* (signed) J. E. Hoover Special Assistant to the Attorney General. [italics added, G.L.R.]

So our government had known all along that Frankfurter was a Bolshevik! They had known it when Frankfurter was slipping scores of communist spies, such as his protégé, Alger Hiss, into our State Department. And Roosevelt must have known it when he put this same treacherous Jew on the Supreme Court in 1939. But no one had ever dared tell the American public.

Another Frankfurter protégé was Dean Acheson, "our" Secretary of State who helped give China to the communists. When their mutual pal, Alger Hiss, was on trial as a perjurer and communist spy, Acheson and Frankfurter, who was then a Supreme Court judge, both testified for red spy Hiss as "character witnesses"!

In the early days of his career, before he had built a machine to do the work for him, Frankfurter was openly communistic. He led a rabble in defense of Sacco and Vanzetti, the Red anarchists who were eventually executed. He was attorney for the Russian-American Industrial Corporation which was set up to organize and finance the textile industry in Russia after the 1917 Bolshevik victory. Among others now known to have been communists, indoctrinated by Frankfurter at Harvard Law school and later placed in key government positions, are Lee Pressman, John Abt (the lawyer that Oswald asked for before he was shot by the Jew Rubenstein), and Nathan Witt—all Jews.

I looked into the *Daily Worker*, and found the atmosphere to be strictly "kosher." There were touching "In Memory Of" ads to "our dear mother" from Bernie, Abie, Izzy, and Nathan Ginzberg, notices of picnics at "Weinbaum's lovely Grove," and an ad for "Harry's Clothing Store" which advertises both special rates for communist customers in the *Worker* and also rabbi's outfits. The Editor of the *Worker* at the time was "John Gates," but when "Gates" was arrested, I learned that his real name was Israel Regenstreif!

I had read in the newspapers that anti-Semitism was running rampant in Russia. But I found the Jews boasting that the head of Soviet propaganda was a Jew—Ilya Ehrenberg! With all the Jews being caught red-handed as Red spies, is it surprising that the Jew Ehrenberg, head of Soviet propaganda, wished to spread the idea that the communists are "anti-Jewish?"

Even in Japan and China, I found the early planters of the communist seeds were Jewish. In Japan, there was an Anna Rosenberg, and guess who turned up in China as advisor to Sun-Yat Sen? Good old Jewish George Sokolsky, our late "conservative" columnist!

To an intelligent man, the facts were undeniable. They might be unexplainable, but they were simply undeniable. *Communism was Jewish.* A racial, atheist Jew, Marx, started it, and other atheist Jews like Friedrich Engels[6] and Ferdinand Lassalle led it. And the Jews in the United States, at least, were almost unanimous in their venomous hatred and suppression of anyone who so much as asked about this fact. Even noticing the number of Jewish communists and race-mixers brought the unfortunate victim a hysterical campaign against him as a "hate monger!" The same people who screamed the loudest for "academic freedom" to preach communism were also the most merciless in their campaign of suppression against anyone wishing to discuss the Jews in anything but the most fulsome and disgusting praise.

卐 卐 卐

One of the things which makes it very difficult for many people to believe that Jews are behind communism is the fact that Jews are also noted for loving money and are, therefore, thought to be, without exception, "capitalists." This idea, that because Jews love money they "couldn't be communists," would be true if communism were actually a movement to help poor people, as it pretends to be. But everywhere that communism has succeeded, it does not help the poor people; communism always puts into position of tremendous power and wealth vast number of Jews, and robs and enslaves the people.

In other words, communism with the Jews is not a genuine ideology; it is a confidence game, a swindle, and a method of using force and revolution as a shortcut to wealth and power, which usually takes longer to obtain by regular, "business" means (even employing the sort of "business" methods for which Jews are justly notorious). Communism is the old "ship-wreck" business for the criminal profit of Red Jews.

The fact of the matter is that communism has been largely financed by rich Jews, starting with the Rothschilds and continuing right on through

---

[6] Engels was likely not Jewish.

the Lehmans, Sterns, Oppenheimers, Rosenwalds, and other rich Jewish families right here in America. For instance, Marx himself was financed by a Jewish soap millionaire, Joseph Fels (Fels-Naphtha soap). As already mentioned, Jacob Schiff, the head of Kuhn, Loeb & Co., contributed over $20 million to his fellow Jew, Leon Trotsky (Bronstein), to put over the capture of the Russian people by the communist Jews.[7]

At a mass rally in Madison Square Garden, New York City, celebrating the revolutionary victory in Russia, and attended by tens of thousands of New York communist Jews, Jacob Schiff, the same multi-billionaire Jewish head of Kuhn, Loeb & Co., sent the following telegram to the committee in Charge, when he could not appear there in person:

> Will you say for me to those present tonight how deeply I regret my inability to celebrate with the Friends of Russian Freedom the actual reward of what we had hoped and striven for these long years! (*New York Times*, March 24, 1917, p 2).

In this connection, it is also interesting to note that communism, supposedly a product of poverty, flourishes in the United States, not where the people are the poorest, in places such as Appalachia or Mississippi. In fact, the FBI statistics show there are fewer communists (only one) in Mississippi, the poorest state in America, than in any other state of the Union! At the same time, the same FBI statistics show the heaviest concentrations of communists in New York and Los Angeles, the two heaviest concentrations of wealth—*and Jews*.

Whenever a communist has run for office, the communist vote has tallied almost precisely, geographically speaking, with the areas containing the most Jews: again, New York City, Los Angeles, Miami Beach, and other areas where wealth and Jews are concentrated. The most recent communist candidate Aptheker, a Jew, did not run in poverty-stricken Appalachia nor in Mississippi, but in wealthy, Jewish New York City!

Finally, to dispel this notion that rich Jews "just couldn't be" communists, since Jews "love money," one has only to take a look at the roster of some of the top communists to see that poverty has nothing to do with it, while Jewishness most certainly does.

A prime example is Charlie Chaplin, a man of enormous wealth earned here in America under our system, which Red Charlie Chaplin despises and attacks so viciously that even our pro-Red State Department excluded

---

[7] *New York Journal American*, February 3, 1949.

him from America for his pro-communist activities. (Chaplin has never bothered to become a citizen of the United States!)

At first glance, it is very difficult to see why a man who has enjoyed such largesse and wealth from America as Chaplin could possibly be a communist. But we have only to learn one fact—the same fact you will find at the bottom of almost all communist activities—to understand "Charlie Chaplin's" communist tendencies: Chaplin's real name is Israel Thornstein, and he is neither an American nor an Englishman, but a Jew![8]

I was really amazed to find out how often, all throughout history, not only with communists, but also with other world figures who have committed various atrocities, it turns out to be a Jew or Jewess behind the dirty work. The classic case occurs in the Jews' favorite book of the Torah, Esther, in which the Jews gloatingly report how the King's girlfriend, Esther, succeeding in having the King order the hanging of 75,000 innocent Gentiles, a "smashing success" which the Jews celebrate every year in the feast of "Purim".[9]

I found the same pattern in ancient Rome, where, during all the persecutions of the Christians under Nero, his Jewish girlfriend, Poppaea, was gently making her Jewish suggestions, which changed world history. She got Nero to murder his mother, his wife, and feed thousands of Christians to the lions in the Colosseum. (With a straight face, the *Encyclopedia Americana*, 1960 edition, Vol. 22, p. 364, adds, "The one redeeming incident in her career seems to be the mercy she urged upon Nero in behalf of the Jews.")[10]

One of the arguments I constantly encounter by people trying to "put me down" for claiming that there is a Jewish, communist, Zionist conspiracy operating in America and all over the world, is the fact that, if such thing were true, "the FBI would take care of it." Although J. Edgar Hoover repeatedly emphasizes the fact, the American people continually forget that the FBI cannot prosecute anybody! The initials "FBI" stand for Federal Bureau of Investigation. And "investigate" is all that the FBI can do. In

---

[8] There seems to be no evidence that his original name was Thornstein nor that he was a Jew. But this has been a persistent rumor for decades.

[9] See Esther 9, and especially 9:16: "Now the other Jews who were in the king's provinces…got relief from their enemies, and slew seventy-five thousand of those who hated them."

[10] Poppaea indeed was likely Jewish. She repeatedly intervened on behalf of Jews and Jewish interests, and the Jewish writer Josephus says "Poppaea, Nero's wife…was a religious woman" (*Antiquities*, XX, 8, 11)—meaning, a religious Jewess.

order to take action against enemies of the United States, they must get permission from the Justice Department, which controls the FBI. And if the Justice Department will not prosecute, or refuses even to get arrest warrants, as has happened over and over again even in the most flagrant cases, the FBI is completely helpless.

In fact, J. Edgar Hoover, the Director of the FBI (who I believe has been almost solely responsible for holding back the communist conspiracy in the United States over the past 30 or 40 years), is helpless even to tell the American people what is going on. He can be fired at will by the President or, technically, even by the Justice Department. And, should Hoover say the wrong thing about the Jews, he will be *gone*. And he would undoubtedly be replaced by one of the pro-Jewish communist Gentile toadies who swarm in our Justice Department.

Therefore, Hoover has been forced to steer a careful course between every possible effort to protect the United States of America and our people and the need to avoid giving the Jews and Red rats in our Federal Government the excuse to fire him.

In spite of this difficult and often almost impossible situation, Hoover has brought some amazing things to the notice of the American people. A prime example is the case of the Jew Assistant Secretary of the Treasury, Harry Dexter White (Jew name, Weiss) who stole our money-engraving plates—as mentioned in chapter 5. This same pattern as the Weiss case has repeated itself over and over in our government, where honest investigators and law enforcement officials uncover treason, only to have it covered up and ruthlessly promoted by the very top officers of our government, including the President.

I, myself, had a hair-raising experience with this sort of thing, in 1960, when a young man joined my organization, only to confess that he had once been a spy for the communists! The man's name was Roger Foss, and he told me when he joined that he had been working for the First Secretary of the Soviet Embassy in Washington, Valintin Ivanoff, who had paid him money to attend a US college and then become a phony US official! I immediately took the young man to the FBI and saw to it that the entire story was made available. FBI agents spent several days getting the full story from Roger Foss. Then I waited for something to happen.

Nothing happened! Weeks passed. The matter had apparently been dropped. The Jew lawyers in the "Justice" Department sat on it.

So I took action myself. I knew an honest (if rabidly liberal) reporter on the *Washington Post*, Les Whitten. Whitten had covered the effort of the Jews to have me thrown in the Washington lunatic asylum, and had been instrumental in an editorial, which deplored such tyranny, because he is that sad creature: a sincere liberal.

I waited until a weekend (when most of the Jews at the *Post* were enjoying their money) and took the story to Les Whitten, together with Foss and all documents, etc. Whitten was able to get the story spread all across the front page of the *Washington Post*. Within 24 hours, Valintin Ivanoff was kicked out of the United States and deported to Russia, with national headlines.

Had I not been able to find some way of forcing the hand of the Justice Department, I have no doubt that Mr. Ivanoff would still be in the Soviet Embassy, paying US college students to attend places like Harvard, Berkeley in California, etc., to raise hell and eventually become Soviet agents, as hundreds or perhaps even thousands of US students are now doing, right now.

The important point to note here is that the FBI was absolutely unable to do anything more than gather the information in this case. After they have presented the information to the Justice Department, they are totally helpless. Time after time after time, there have been similar cases, where the FBI has, by diligent and faithful work, uncovered treason and subversion, only to have Justice Department lawyers—the "Moskowitz's", "Finklesteins", "Cohens", "Goldbergs", "Rosenblatts," and "Lipshitz's"—ignore the information, or cover it up.

In the whole history of the FBI, there has only been one "rat": an agent who turned against the FBI. That agent was a Jew named Jake Levine who went on pro-communist radio WBAI in New York and Radio Pacifica on the West Coast and charged that the FBI was "fascist" and that the agents hated Negroes and Jews.

When asked to name the biggest communist paper in America, most people will name the *Worker*. But they are wrong. The largest communist newspaper in America is *The Morning Freiheit* which is actually published in Hebrew characters—in the Yiddish language—for the thousands and thousands of communist Jews in New York City. When the income tax people temporarily padlocked the *Worker*, they never missed an issue; it was simply moved across the hall to the offices of the *Freiheit*, where the *Worker* was published until the communist lawyers got the tax people off their backs.

In Canada, the Royal Canadian Mounted Police broke up a spy ring with the aid of Igor Gouzenko, who defected from the Soviet Embassy and exposed the top communist agents in Canada. It turned out that the two bosses of this Soviet spy ring in Canada were Fred Rose and Sam Karr.

The report of the Royal commission, printed by Her Majesty's Stationery Office, reveals that the real name of Fred Rose, a member of Parliament, was Fred Rosenberg and the real name of Sam Karr, was Cohen. As usual, although the public is not made aware of it, the two leaders of communism in Canada turned out to be two atheist Jews.

Just before World War II, communists almost took over the Government of Spain. When General Franco rose up with Spanish Christians and fought the take-over of Spain, Russia and international communism sent every possible form of aid to turn the Spanish Christian people over to communist tyranny. The leader of the outside communists was none other than Bela Kuhn (real name Cohen), the same bloody Jews who had put on the Hungarian revolution right after World War I. From America came hundreds and hundreds of New York City Jews, organized into the "Abraham Lincoln Brigade" to support the takeover of Spain by communism. All of this can be documented in the study of the Abraham Lincoln Brigade put out by the House Committee on Un-American Activities (Appendix IX, Vol. 1), which lists the names of hundreds of these Jews for your inspection. Meanwhile, to protect the Christian people of Spain from the assault of international communism, Benito Mussolini sent troops, guns, ammunition, and airplanes, and so did Adolf Hitler.

In fact, Spain was a rehearsal for World War II. Only it was much more obvious in those days that one side (the "loyalists") was communist and Jewish, while the other side (Franco) was Christian, anti-communist and anti-Jewish. World War II was exactly the same, but the Jews managed to disguise their purposes better than in the Spanish Civil War.

卐 卐 卐

I found this horrible secret world of the Jews exciting, interesting, and frightening, but also very depressing. Far down in my soul, I could feel the cold dread of our fate, if what seemed to be going on *was* going on. I, too, had been brought up never to say the word "Jew" right out, but always "Jewish person" or person of the "Jewish faith" because of what the Bible calls "fear of the Jews" (John 7:13). I could imagine the result of my own temperament and reaction to a challenge, if I found out that there really *was* a Jewish plot against my country and my people!

I re-read the papers and books the lady gave me, and read them carefully. The tone of the things, in most cases, repelled me. They were loose in their charges, poorly composed, and full of rabid sensationalism. But they kept revealing new little hidden pearls of truth, which I found checked out. And when I correlated all the facts as best I could, there was no question about it; there was a Jewish plot of some kind or another, and it definitely involved communism and moral subversion. I found out that the Jews were involved in something more than just communism and Zionism. As Hitler writes in *Mein Kampf,* one has only to cut carefully into any diseased abscess of our society "to discover, like a maggot in a rotting corpse, often blinded by the dazzling light: a little Jew".[11] There is simply *no* excess, no degeneracy, and no horror too low for some Jew to use as a method, not only of getting our money, but destroying our society and our character in the process.

Remember the "poem" which begins "A rose is a rose is a rose" etc.? It was one of the first of the crazy (and rotten) examples of insanity and degeneracy in the form of "poetry" which now parades as "art"—no rhyme, no reason, no sense, just pure madness—and often pure filth. Do you remember who wrote that crazy stuff and "popularized" it? Her name was Gertrude Stein, and she was a Red Jewess—and a homosexual.

Have you seen some of the crazy "sculpture" in museums of modern "art," where you see, on top of a pedestal, some lumps which look like somebody went into a pasture and shoveled up a few choice ones and piled them on top of each other as a "modern" sculpture? Remember who is the "hero" of this kind of "art"? His name is Jacob Epstein. Another one of the "tribe," laughing at us, thumbing his nose at us, and getting us to pay him for it, and make him a "great man" to boot!

Who is the modern "master" of crazy filthy poetry for "beatniks" and "hippies"? His name is Allan Ginsberg—a Jewish "artist," teaching our youth about the "finer things" of life.

Who has established the record in America for a filthy magazine? Ralph Ginsburg, who has been sentenced to prison for his utterly vile *Eros.* Even the Supreme Court couldn't stomach this Jew's filth—showing a White nude female in upright intercourse with a huge, naked Negro in full color on a whole page.

The "theatre" scenes described in chapter 2 of this book, where a chicken is crucified, a girl's private parts are shaved by a nude male, and they engage in vertical intercourse in a burlap bag, among other "artistic" antics, was produced by Jean Jaques Lebel, a French Jew! The center of this filth is New York's lower east side, where there is a whole colony of "hippies." Their headquarters is a storefront called "The Peace-Eye Book Store."

---

[11] Volume One, sec. 2.23 (p. 91 of the Clemens & Blair 2022 edition).

It is labeled "strictly kosher." The producers of filthy and crazy art, poetry, music, sculpture, literature, etc.—almost all Jews, Jews, and more Jews!

  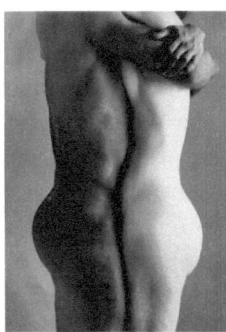

Images from *Eros* (vol 1, no 4; 1962)

Peace Eye Book Store

Nor is it only in these three fields—communism, Zionism, and degeneracy—that I found Jews seem to "excel." When I investigated the movement to force White people to mix with African blacks, I found these same Jews once again as the masterminds and moneybags.

Later on, I'll go into the Jewish nature of "race-mixing" more thoroughly, but for the present, let me present just one or two of the most shocking documents and facts so that the reader, before he proceeds will have some idea how thoroughly the Jews have used every weapon to destroy the White Society which has welcomed them and given them more than any nation in history.

Consider the largest communist paper in America, the Yiddish morning *Freiheit*, printed in Hebrew characters for the tens of thousands of Jewish communists in New York City. Every Sunday, they print a page in English. One article boasts (privately to the Jews) "95% of the lawyers pushing the Negroes in the civil rights movement are Jews"!

Just to make clear what they mean, let me name one of the chief villains in this script, the lawyer who has done more in the South to disrupt and destroy the White race and civil order than any other single race-mixer and who is head of the NAACP Legal Defense—Jake Greenberg.

Jake Greenberg: not a Negro, but a Jew, is the "NAACP" legal brain in courts all over America. It is Jew Greenberg who gets injunctions, defends the black hell-raisers who disrupt whole states, gets White leaders cited for "contempt" of Federal Courts, and thus gives the thousands of black hell-raisers carte blanche to do about whatever they want in the US South.

The NAACP itself is not Negro, but largely Jewish. The president is not a Negro, and never has been. First it was Joel Spingarn, a New York Jew—then his brother, Arthur Spingarn. Now it is another New York Jew, Kivie Kaplan! Until the blacks took over and ousted him, the big wheel in CORE was another New York Jew named Marvin Rich.

There is an article in the *Jewish Post and Opinion* newspaper, front page, explaining that the blacks in CORE and SNCC rebelled against all these Jews, and took over. The Jews here (privately in their Jewish paper) admit that they have been the masterminds and moneybags for the "Negro" movement, and are now ceasing support, since the Negroes rebelled. They further boast that, without Jewish money, the blacks are going broke!

I learned, way back when I first started studying, that it was the American Jewish Congress and American Jewish committee, and the Anti-Defamation League of B'nai B'rith, which spent millions of dollars to produce the "scientific studies" of a Swedish Marxist, Gunar Myrdahl, to "prove" to the US Supreme Court that segregation was unconstitutional, and agitate for complete integration of the South. I found every Jewish paper and every Jewish group pushing race mixing—quietly in the South and openly and viciously everywhere else in America! I found:

- Communism—largely Jewish.
- Zionism—all Jewish.
- The Black Revolution—largely Jewish; 99.9% Jew-financed.
- Commercial degeneracy and pornography, largely Jewish.
- Commercial racketeering in "religion," with their "K's" and "U's" Jewish.
- Movies, TV, press, books, magazines—strictly kosher.

The secret world of the Jews not only exists—and if it continues to exist and flourish, we will cease to exist. No people can tolerate such a vast and poisonous secret attack and survive.

For the first time, I began to see these arrogant Jewish Bolsheviks, Zionists, race-mixers, promoters of degeneracy and madness as the ship-wreckers of civilization, which so many of them are!

I went back to the lady and we talked some more, this time with me doing the listening. She was mixed up and confused in many ways. But she knew there were dark forces at work to destroy her country and the White people, and she had the fundamental ideas right.

She asked me if I wanted to hear a man named Gerald L. K. Smith.[12] I remembered the name vaguely, as some kind of horrible radical or other. But she said he was a great American patriot and a great speaker, and gave me a ticket to a speech he was making in Los Angeles. I was worried about going, since I was a Naval Officer, and the whole thing seemed so wild, radical, and dangerous. So I went to the FBI office and asked to see an agent. I was ushered into a private little chamber, and seated opposite an extremely Nordic-looking man. I told him about Smith, and asked if it would be all right to go to his lecture. "Yes, if you don't participate," he said. So I went to the speech. And what a thing that was!

Few Americans today have ever heard an orator. They have heard talks, speeches, even ravings, perhaps, but it is doubtful they have ever heard an old- fashioned, roof-lifting, earth-shaking, soul-shattering oration. Gerald Smith is the master to end all masters of the human voice. Whatever else he may be, he can seize you by the lapels of your soul, jerk you out of your seat, and hold you helpless and spellbound for as long as he wants

---

[12] Smith (1898-1976) was a clergyman, politician, and populist organizer.

to. He does not just roar and bellow. He whispers; he sighs; he wheezes; he coos; then he blasts with the power of a locomotive roaring through a tunnel. He laughs; he cries; he howls; he cajoles; he mimics; he screams; he begs; he goes back to whispering, sneers, leers, yells, bursts into hysterical laughter—then whimpers some heart-rending bit which leaves you limp. I sat in the balcony, literally on the edge of my seat.

Gerald Smith is still the grandest master of the spoken word alive today, and I would walk twenty miles to hear him again.

But it was not just the way he spoke which captivated me—it was what he said. When you peeled aside all the emotional overtones of his speech, and got down to the raw meat, you found the basic elements of recognizable truth, beautifully put together to show, at last, the clear pattern of what it is the Jews are trying to do with their conspiracy.

And when history is examined, we find this Jewish nation steadily and surely progressing toward its goal as "God's Chosen People," who are destined to quietly conquer and subdue the world under the bloody, Old-Testament despotism of the "King of Zion." They really literally believe "And it shall come to pass…that the Lord thy God will set thee high above all the nations of the earth." (Deut. 26: 19).

A sermon by Rabbi Leon Spitz, quoted in the *American Hebrew*, March 1, 1946, illustrates the message by which the flames of Jewish hatred of non-Jews are rekindled every spring in the synagogues:

> Let Esau[13] whine and wail and protest to the civilized world, and let Jacob raise his hand to fight the good fight. The anti-Semite understands but one language, and he must be dealt with on his own level. The Purim Jews stood up for their lives. American Jews, too, must come to grips with our contemporary anti-Semites. We must fill our jails with anti-Semitic gangsters. We must fill our insane asylums with anti-Semitic lunatics. We must combat every alien Jew-hater. We must harass and prosecute our Jew-baiters to the extreme limits of the laws. We must humble and shame our anti-Semitic hoodlums to such an extent that none will wish or dare to become their 'fellow-travelers.'

---

[13] GLR: Esau is the code name used in Jewish publications to represent the gullible tolerant gentile; Jacob is the code name for the Jew, gifted in the art of deception.

Such is the expression of appreciation Americans are awarded for having taken in, with the greatest of good will and tolerance, an alien people who represented themselves as harassed and persecuted.

As a researcher into the subject of Zionism, I found the Jews not even bothering to cover up this aim of world domination. With the most monumental disdain of the boobs they call the "Goyim" (non-Jews), they openly declare that they spurned offers of much better national "homes" for the Jews than Palestine—places where it would not have been necessary to exile and make homeless a million helpless Arabs. But the Jews arrogantly demanded Palestine "because it is the center of the world"—not because it is a Biblical promise, but because it is the cross-roads of all the Earth between three continents—their chosen seat of eventual world power, and immensely mineral rich. David Ben-Gurion (Prime Minister of Israel) predicted in an article in *Look*, January 16, 1962, that, by 1987 the world would be run by the Jews from Jerusalem through the Jewish United Nations:

> All armies will be abolished, and there will be no more wars. In Jerusalem, the United Nations (a truly United Nations) will build a Shrine of the Prophets to serve the federated union of all continents; this will be the seat of the Supreme Court of Mankind, to settle all controversies among the federated continents, as prophesied by Isaiah.

I am aware, as I dictate these words, of the outrage upon reason of such statements. I myself suffered this outrage when I first considered or heard of the ideas. But I can assure the reader that I would not lightly set these things forth in such a permanent thing as a book, which will be around a long time to "haunt" me, if I am frivolous or in error.

Wide awake now, after reading and studying all I could, I began to think realistically for the first time in my life, instead of according to the slogans to which I had been trained since babyhood—slogans I had never even thought to question, such as: "you mustn't judge people by groups, but only as individuals."

When you come to think of it, that slogan, for instance, is madness! I helped sink German, Jap, and Italian subs during the war without asking which ones of the crew were Nazis, Fascists, or Militarists. We sank them all. I hated Roosevelt. But the Japs and Germans were not too careful about shooting at me along with the New Dealers who were so anxious to get America into the war.

When you see a nun, you do not inquire as to the health of her kids, nor do you invite 86-year-old men on a parachute jumping party, even though a few of such age, like the late Bernarr MacFadden, used to make parachute jumps. You might fairly expect a Chinaman in a small town would try the laundry or restaurant business, and a Sicilian member of the Mafia to be mixed up in some kind of crime. Nor is it sensible to insist that skirts are not an indication of females just because Scotsmen are found in skirts, too, although they are called "kilts." Nobody would be considered mad for presuming a member of the Ku Klux Klan to be a racist, nor a member of the Americans for Democratic Action to hate the Klan. And by the same token, simply because of the weight of previous evidence, we are not crazy or "hate mongers" when we presume that any given, unknown Jew is a Zionist or a communist. The probability that any given Jew is one of the two, and sympathetic, at least, to communism, is overwhelming.

About the only way we can and do judge people, until we get to know them extremely well, is by the group to which they belong. If that group has proved over a long period of time, by its actions, that it is hostile to us, it is not "hate" or bigotry to consider unknown members of that group also hostile, unless and until we learn differently about some particular individual who is an exception to the rule.

The Jews have calculatingly deprecated this utterly necessary rule of daily living and cultivated the opposite, insane idea that we must presume every individual to be a "blank," no matter what the evidence that he belongs to a cannibal tribe or the Mafia—all in order to keep people from noticing that a devilish lot of Jews are communists and traitors!

Once one has realized that the Jews are not "just a religious group" (and a "pitiful, persecuted one at that) but a racial anti-nationalistic group in our midst, then one can see the obvious fact that most of the individual members of this group can be expected to be certain things—especially communists, Zionists, and race-mixers. This does not mean, of course, that all of the group must be a certain thing, any more than all Germans were Nazis or all Italians are Catholics.

The Jewish-communist Zionist-traitor situation is much like that of the Mafia. Everybody knows that the Mafia is mostly Italians and mostly gangsters. But that does not mean, "all Italians are gangsters" or "all gangsters are Italian." On the other hand, the principle the Jews want to suppress is that a member of the Mafia is *probably* an Italian and *probably* a gangster. Only madmen would put a member of the group called "Mafia" in charge of their police department. Yet this is exactly what the United States has "strangely" done with its deadly atomic and hydrogen bomb.

From Lillienthal to Strauss, we have put almost nothing else but Jews in charge of atomic weapons and programs, although Jews have constituted more than 90% of our atomic spies and communists! Lillienthal, Oppenheimer, Teller, Straus, Rickover, Rabi, etc., etc., always more of the same deadly pattern. "Don't judge by groups." But only one group somehow is always in control of the key spots—and that same group providing almost all our Red spies.

As Winston Churchill pointed out, the "driving power" and leadership of the Marxist forces is Jewish, and most Jews are at least sympathetic to communism in one form or another, or they "cover up" for communists by screaming "hate monger" at real anti-communists. But by no means are all Jews communists, nor are all communists Jews. The scientific truth is simply that, on the basis of undeniable statistics, an unknown Jew is probably (but not certainly) pro-Marxist, whether communist, Trotskyite, or just a race mixing "liberal."

卐 卐 卐

As I studied and thought my way further into the chaos of our national madness, I began to wonder why we had gone to war on the side of the Bolsheviks, who had openly boasted for nearly a hundred years of their plans to destroy us by force and violence and lies and subversion—while we completely wrecked Christian Germany, which never had a single highly-placed spy in our country, and no practical chance (or plans) for conquering the world, as I had believed they were trying to do.

I wondered about Adolf Hitler and the Nazis. I had learned he was right about the Jews. It might be worth reading his book, *Mein Kampf*, to see if he had said anything else right, too. I hunted around the San Diego bookshops, and finally found a copy of *Mein Kampf* hidden away in the rear. I bought it, took it home, and sat down to read. And that was the end of one Lincoln Rockwell, the "nice guy"—the dumb "Goy"—and the beginning of an entirely different person. Reading *Mein Kampf* was like finding part of me.[14]

Chaos and disorder and mental "greyness" are immensely frustrating to me. I had suffered for years trying to fathom the endless philosophical, social, and political mess in the world, and the even messier explanations offered by religions and sociology. Over and over I had said to myself,

---

[14] The most recent edition is the Clemens & Blair translation (by T. Dalton), 2022. Also of interest is the book *Hitler on the Jews* (2024; Clemens & Blair).

"There must be some sense, some logical causal relationship between social and political facts, and how they got that way!" In spite of the sometimes-messy appearance of things and creatures in Nature, there is no real mess. There is a reason, a cause, for every atom being where it is, in Nature. I could not and do not believe that Nature has no laws, no reasons, and no causes in social affairs. But no person, no book, nor my own mind had been able to discover head or tail to things. I simply suffered from the vague, unhappy feeling that things were "wrong"—I didn't know exactly how—and that there must be a way of diagnosing the "disease" and its causes, and making intelligent, organized efforts to correct that "something Wrong."

In *Mein Kampf* I found abundant mental sunshine which bathed all this grey world suddenly in the clear light of reason and understanding. Word after word, sentence after sentence, stabbed into the darkness like thunderclaps and lightning bolts of revelation, tearing and ripping away the cobwebs of more than 30 years of darkness, brilliantly illuminating the "mysteries" of the heretofore impenetrable murk in a world gone mad. I could not lay the book down without agonies of impatience to get back to it. I read it walking to the squadron. I took it into the air and read it lying on the chart-board while I automatically gave the instructions to the other jets circling over the desert. I read it crossing the Coronado Ferry. I read it into the night and the next morning. When I had finished, I started again, and reread every word, underlining and marking especially magnificent passages. I studied it; I thought about it; I wondered at the utter, indescribable genius of it.

How could the world not only ignore *Mein Kampf,* but also damn it and curse it and hate it and pretend that it was a plan for "conquering the world," when it was the most obvious and rational plan for saving the world ever written? Had nobody read it, I wondered, that people went around saying it was the work of a mad "rug-chewer"? How could sensible people get away with such monstrous intellectual fraud? Why was it so hated and cursed? I could see why the Jews would hate and curse it, *but why my own people?*

I learned that Hitler not only did *not* want to conquer the world, or any other nation, but only to get back the parts of Germany hacked off by the Versailles treaty. I know that, were Mexico to beat us in a war and get Texas and Arizona away from us, I would never rest until we had them back. Would you?

Hitler didn't and couldn't. He openly said he wanted back the parts of Germany given to Poland, Czechoslovakia, etc. The only places he ever "attacked" were once parts of Germany, such as Prussia and Austria, stolen by Versailles, just as if we lost Florida and Texas; you would certainly "attack" these states until they were again American.

Hitler said, in the same *Mein Kampf*, that the survival of Western Civilization rested on the preservation of the British Empire, and that if the Jews were able to get a war started against Germany by England, the end result would be that England would lose her empire. Is that not exactly what has happened? Hitler went so far as to say that he would gladly help the British defend the British Empire with force of German arms!

Check just one sample from *Mein Kampf*, to see how you have been swindled and lied to about Hitler and World War II. How many times have you heard the phrase "Hitler's Big Lie"? Is not the "big lie" generally believed by most people to be an invention of Adolf Hitler—a technique Hitler is supposed to advocate in *Mein Kampf*? The Anti-Defamation League of B'nai B'rith put out a booklet "simplifying" "Nazism" for the average man, in which the Jewish author writes:

> Of course, part of the Nazi propaganda technique was simply the art of fabrication. Hitler wrote: "A definite factor in getting a lie believed is the size of the lie. The broad masses of the people, in the simplicity of their hearts, more easily fall victim to a big lie than a small one."

Now here is what Hitler *really* wrote on the subject:

> It required the entire bottomless falsehood of the Jews, and their fighting comrades the Marxists, to lay blame for the collapse precisely on the man who alone had shown a super-human will and energy in his effort to prevent the catastrophe that he had foreseen, and to save the nation from that time of humiliation and disgrace. By placing sole blame for the loss of the World War on Ludendorff, they took away the weapon of moral right from the only adversary dangerous enough to be likely to succeed against the betrayers of the Fatherland.
>
> All this was inspired by the unquestionably true principle that in the Big Lie there is always a certain degree of credibility, because the broad masses of a nation are always more easily corrupted in the very bottom of their hearts than consciously or voluntarily. And in the primitive simplicity of their minds, they more readily fall victims to the Big Lie

than the small lie, since they themselves often tell small lies in little matters, but would be ashamed to resort to large-scale falsehoods. It would never occur to them to fabricate colossal untruths, and they would not believe that others could have the impudence to distort the truth so infamously.

Even though the facts that prove this are clear, they will still doubt and waver, and will continue to think that there must be some other explanation. The grossly impudent lie always leaves traces behind it, even after it has stuck—a fact that is known to all expert liars in this world, and to all who conspire together in the art of lying. These people know only too well how to use falsehood for the basest of purposes.

From time immemorial, however, the Jews have known better than any others how to exploit falsehood and calumny. Their very existence is based on one great lie, namely, that they are a religious community and not a race. And what a race. One of the greatest thinkers of mankind has branded them for all time with a statement that is profoundly and precisely true: he called them "The great master of the lie."[15] Those who don't realize the truth of that statement, or don't wish to believe it, will never be able to lend a hand in this world to help truth prevail.[16]

Note that Hitler, far from recommending the "big lie," condemns it as a Jewish technique!

I found the same thing all through *Mein Kampf*—the very opposite of what the Jews keep telling us is in the book. But nobody ever bothers to read it, so that the Jews continue to get away with this arrogant big lie.

Perhaps even more shocking, I discovered, long after the war, just how arrogant the Jews had been in claiming that Hitler "started" World

---

[15] Hitler quotes the philosopher Arthur Schopenhauer. In his book *Parerga and Paralipomena* (1851), Schopenhauer remarks on the historically low opinion of the Jews: "We see also from the two Roman authors [Tacitus and Justinus] how much the Jews were at all times, and by all nations, loathed and despised. This may be due partly to the fact that they were the only people on earth who did not credit man with any existence beyond this life, and were therefore regarded as cattle, as the dregs of humanity, but as the great master of the lie" (1851/2010, vol. 2, p. 357). For further discussion of Schopenhauer's view of the Jews, see the book *Eternal Strangers* (Dalton 2020).

[16] Volume One, section 10.4, p. 245.

War II—when even before we got into it, they published a booklet called "Germany Must Perish" (1941), which actually preached the *extermination* of the German people—long before any possible gas chambers were even to be alleged.[17] And more startling still, the Jews laid out the division of Germany on a map in 1940, and the line the Jews drew on their map way back in 1940 is pretty much the same line which now divides Germany.

All of this would be too unbelievable without proof, without the documents, so here they are—together with comments of such sterling "love-mongering" as *Time* magazine, which called the Jewish plan to exterminate the German people (before the war) "A sensational idea!", and the *New York Times,* which called it "A plan for permanent peace among civilized nations!" Observe how arrogantly the Jew author, Kaufman, boasts on the title page, that "This dynamic volume outlines a comprehensive plan for the extinction of the German nation and the total eradication from the earth, of all her people. Also contained herein is a map illustrating the possible territorial dissection of Germany and the apportionment of her lands." All this before America entered the war!

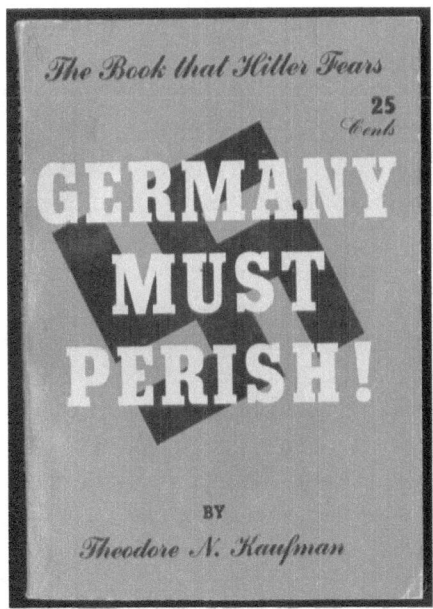

---

[17] The booklet was written by Theodore Kaufman. Extended excerpts can be found in the book *Classic Essays on the Jewish Question* (2022).

I didn't see this Jewish plan to exterminate all Germans, all over the Earth (which includes tens of millions of Americans of German extraction), until after these Jews had propagandized me and millions of other innocent Americans into going over there and actually trying to exterminate the German people. For instance, we fire bombed more than a quarter of a million women and children and refugees in non-military Dresden, in one night of nightmare and horror. We followed up, after the war, not only by "dissecting" Germany, as this Jewish genocidist recommended, but by putting into effect the savage plans of his fellow Jew, Morgenthau, to destroy Germany's possibility of feeding and taking care of itself. We went over there after the war, and destroyed not only factories, but millions of acres of forests to destroy the land itself!

I reread and studied *Mein Kampf* some more. Slowly, bit-by-bit, I began to understand. I realized that National Socialism, the iconoclastic worldview of Adolf Hitler, was the doctrine of scientific, racial idealism—actually a new idealism for our times. I saw an age similar to that of two thousand years ago, when another worldview was on the rise—a worldview that shook and changed the world forever. I realized that this new and wonderful doctrine of scientific truth applied to man himself, as well as to nature and inanimate matter, was the only thing which could save man from his own degradation in luxury, self-seeking short-sightedness, and racial degeneration. The doctrine of Adolf Hitler was the political salvation of our times, and Adolf Hitler himself the rescuer sent recurrently to a collapsing humanity by an inscrutable Providence. Hitler's and Germany's "crucifixion" was all according to the inevitable workings of this unknowable Scenarist. Even the eleven hanged "disciples" in Nuremberg were not without significance!

The most hated and dreaded idea two thousand years ago was Christianity. And the most hated and cursed man on earth was Jesus Christ. His followers were bitterly persecuted and murdered by the "good", "sensible" people who, like anybody in his "right mind," recognized that Rome and the Empire were the most solid, substantial things in the world. I realized that today's Marxist-Democratic world is another sprawling "Roman Empire," and today's Nazis similar to the early "Christians."

What is going on is far more than a battle for political supremacy in the present social and political situation. It is the utter smashing and destruction of a society which has become so rotten *that it will tolerate and even love its own Marxist destroyers*—and the painful slow growth of the new Nazi society which will replace it, even though it is now the most "hated," "despised," and "feared" doctrine on earth.

Such mighty, awesome thoughts come over a man but once in a lifetime, if ever. And when they do, that man changes for all time.

At once, a great weight lifted off my soul. I knew that I had found my way to the sun at last. The days of mental darkness, searching, and endless frustration were over.

卐 卐 卐

But at the same time, an immensely heavy burden replaced it—but in a different, even satisfying way. I knew that I had to do what I could to spread the new and wonderful idea, and to secure its victory in the collapsing world, no matter what it cost me—even if I were to become a "failure" to be "fed to the lions" in the Colosseum.

I was as sure then as I am now that it will be done. Nothing can stop the victory of what is now a historical necessity, determined by events beyond our control. The Marxists pretend it is their victory, which is historically assured. But their timing is off. They were fated to rise to the top. And they have. They have had their victory. Now it is all over, no matter how mighty and terrifying their power and their "Roman Empire" may appear to be. Today, they are in the Kremlin, in Jerusalem, and in the White House, wearing different masks to be sure, but nevertheless grinding the whole world under the brutal heel of the Marxist doctrines of "mass" and "equality" and racial defilement. The "Roman Legions," which they control and of which I was so long a part, march and destroy everything that dares oppose them. They "crucify" the whole German nation and the apostles of the great man who dare to speak one word for his genius.

But they themselves have spoken their funeral oration when they said "each thing contains within itself the seeds of its own destruction." They, too, are victims of this perfectly valid law. And their destruction now is ready to burst from within themselves in a furious catastrophe. Even their "legions" are disintegrating under their own Marxist, race-mixing doctrines.

We are the new "barbarians," forged to iron hardness in the fires of their hate and persecution. All over the world, *we* wait to pounce on the arrogant, strutting "emperors" of Marxism when they have over-extended themselves only a little bit more. They can shore up their confidence with the belief that Nazism is "dead," that they are on the march to final "world revolution," and Jewish mastery of the world by their King of Zion— whether they call him a "commissar" or "Secretary General of the UN", or "Premier of Israel"!

But there are millions of us, everywhere. I know, today, whereof I speak. Nothing can stop us. On the contrary!

Only three times in the history of the world have any nations, once under all-out attack by the Jewish ship-wreckers, ever managed to fight off the Red plague and recover control: Italy, Germany, and Spain. And each time, it was not conservative talk which foiled the Red ship-wreckers, but *action*, which the enemy always curses as "fascism." "Nazism" is the defense mechanism of the Aryan White Man against the deadly attack of world Jewry, with its communism, Zionism, racial defilement, degeneracy and "democracy." Nazism replaces the collapsing "conservative" defense with vigorous *attack*.

And when a people are as near to historical death as the whole White Race, attack is not only the best defense, it is the *only* defense.

Until our appearance on the scene, the Jews have driven every "conservative" opponent into hiding with the fearful accusation. "You're a fascist, a Nazi!" So far, even the so-called "anti-semitic" organizations have all run like rabbits when they have been hit with that one. They remind me of Peter protesting he was not a Christian when the Jews got after him. "Not me!" shout these terrified people; "We're not Nazis!"

For the first time, with the arrival on the American scene of the American Nazi Party, there is now a spiritual force to look these Jew terrorists in the eye when they start that "You're-a-Nazi" bit, and reply, "You're damned right we're Nazis, and we will soon enough take care of you traitors, thieves, liars, terrorists, and communist enemies!"

In the old days of the shipwrecking crews, the leader was often a "pillar of the community" who conducted his ship-wrecking secretly. Attacking him was almost suicidal. But there were always courageous men to do it, in spite of the public outcry.

Americans are easy-going, friendly people, slow to wrath. Many groups and nations around the world have mistaken this easy-going nature to indicate we are also easy marks—suckers who can be endlessly "taken." But from the Barbary Pirates to the Mexicans, we have shown that when we finally get mad—God help those who have tried our patience!

Turn him loose, and the American White Man can and has whipped anything in sight. Sooner or later, the Jews will finally cross the borderline of American patience, as they have done all throughout their history. When they do, the reaction of the American White Man will make the Jews get on their knees and pray for Adolf Hitler to save them. The revenge taken upon them by other outraged host people will seem like heaven compared to the ferocity of the White American, once he has had all he is going to take from these arrogant Jews.

It is my hope to be organized and ready to channel this damned-up flood of righteous American rebellion against Jew tyranny, once it breaks loose, into *constructive*, rather than purely destructive directions. If I am successful, we can find a just solution to the Jewish problem. If I am unsuccessful, there will be Jews swinging from every lamppost in America.

CHAPTER 7

A CLOSE LOOK AT THE CROOKS

Why? Why does such a vast proportion of the Jews devote their entire energies to the criminal red ship-wrecking operation against the millions of non-Jews, most of whom have never done anything to injure Jews? Unless we understand why so many of these people are doing what they do, it will be impossible to out-maneuver and out-think them.

At first blush, what many Jews are doing seems pure, unadulterated insanity. One of the commonest and most virulent forms of insanity is called "paranoia." Its symptoms are delusions of grandeur and delusions of persecution. The guy in the booby hatch who thinks he is Napoleon is a "paranoiac." He suffers from "delusions of grandeur." Almost always he will be found to suffer from a parallel delusion that everyone is plotting against him, hates him, and is trying to hurt him. Since they don't recognize that he *is* "Napoleon" (or God, or Jesus, or whatever the nut imagines himself to be), "they are out to get" him. He talks darkly of the "radio waves" they have "beamed" at him to "control" his mind, and he is absolutely sure that he is unjustly persecuted.

Whenever we find an individual preoccupied with the idea of his own supreme importance, and always talking of how everyone hates and persecutes him, we may justly suspect the poor fellow of being afflicted with the mental illness of paranoia.

When we examine the nature of the Jewish "religion," we find it almost totally preoccupied with precisely these delusions. The Jews have been howling across the ages that they are God's "Chosen" people, superior to all others, and destined by divine right to plant their feet on the necks of all other people. (See Exodus, Genesis, and especially Deuteronomy.) And because other peoples have not been willing to allow these "Chosen" Jews to stand on their necks, and have always kicked the Jews out or killed them when the Jews managed by manipulations to grab most of the wealth and power in their host nations, the Jews have howled even louder, down through the centuries, that they are "persecuted," "hated," and made "scapegoats." They themselves are always guiltless, lovable, and the very models of righteousness.

In other words, the Jews have actually made a religion out of paranoia. And anyone who doubts the Jewish claims of persecution and "chosen" status is proclaimed as insane, by the Jews!

Viewed objectively, it is utterly incredible that these Jews, openly and arrogantly flaunting their own paranoiac delusions of being "Chosen People" and being unjustly "persecuted," could get so much of the world brainwashed into believing that anyone who dares mention these facts about the Jews is "crazy" and—yes, even paranoiac; that's the very diagnosis the Jewish "psychiatrists" make of anyone who takes a realistic view of Jewish paranoia.

But paranoia is not the only reason for the otherwise inexplicable actions of the Jews—actions which, for four thousand years, have *always* gotten them expelled, murdered, and hounded out of every country they have infested, because of Jewish actions.

Observe the pattern of Jewish activity wherever they go. Jews are welcomed to one country after the other. Then they proceed to use any and all methods, from swindling to violence, to rob and impoverish their non-Jewish hosts. They use their wealth to gain control of press, education, etc., to brainwash their hosts into giving them positions as behind-the-scenes overlords of national leaders; but at the same time, they prepare revolutions to create anarchy and upheaval, during which they use force and violence to seize *all* power and wealth. And the end results of their revolutions are always that they set up crazy, non-productive, Marxist states which cannot survive without enormous transfusions of money and goods from non-communist (productive) states and peoples. (As witness Israel, which exists largely on German "reparations" and American largesse; and Soviet Russia, which is always rescued by US wheat, money, and "aid.")

This has been going on for at least three thousand years, that we know of. The Jews have done this—as a historical fact—in Greece, Persia, Rome, Spain, England, Portugal, and a dozen other kingdoms, and were then expelled or murdered for their parasitic operations against their hosts, for living without producing.

And there lies the first part of the answer to why Jews act the way they do. *A huge proportion of Jews just plain doesn't like to do hard work.* From time immemorial, they have sought ways to avoid producing what they need to exist.

With every other people in the history of the world, *land*—actual territory—has been the fundamental on which the people's existence has depended. You cannot imagine a France, an England, an Egypt, a United States, a China, a Japan, an Italy, a Sweden, or any other nation without land from which the nation earns its living and which, in a spiritual sense *is* the nation. Yet there is one nation, which has lived for almost two thousand years without a foot of soil on which to earn a living—the Jewish nation. How did they do it?

The answer is that the Jews have always used other *people* as other people used *land*.

It may be objected that the Jews were ejected from their land and had no choice. But literally hundreds and hundreds of other people have also been ejected from their lands, and have either perished or—more often— have proceeded to conquer some people someplace and regained some land from which to earn a living. Instead of doing as all other people and finding or getting some land from which to earn their living, when they were ejected, the Jews made a different adaptation; they simply learned to live off of other people, who, in turn, earned the living from the land.

And over the centuries, the Jews have in-bred to become socialized and highly adapted to this, and *only this* way of life. Whoever heard of large numbers of Jewish farmers, Jewish cowboys, and Jewish pioneers? Jews never arrive in a country in large numbers until it is settled and producing. And then the Jews do not go into the country to get land and till the soil, like most other people in a new country; instead, they settle in the towns, villages, and cities, as soon as they are built, and become traders and merchants, or operators of saloons, etc.

Among forms of life, this way of life is called "parasitism"—taking a living from a host without working. There are many animals and plants with exactly the same characteristic: tape worms, ivy, suckerfish, etc. In order to be a successful parasite, a plant or animal must find a way to get its food and protection from its host over an extended period of time, which usually means that it must find a way of *anaesthetizing* its host to what it is doing; it must do its stealing of food and shelter in some relatively painless way so that, at first, the host is not aware of the robbery going on, and tolerates the sucking up of its own nourishment.

You can't *feel* a tapeworm. You just miss your food. You get weaker and weaker and finally die, as the worm sucks up all the nourishment.

And there's the paradox of the parasite: the more successful he is, the quicker he kills off his host, and therefore the quicker the parasite dies himself!

This is precisely what an overdose of Jews does to a nation (and to the Jews). They slip in unobtrusively as peddlers and "intellectuals," then gradually begin eating away at the hard-working host, devouring more and more rapaciously, always covering up their blood-sucking with the most plausible and high-sounding phrases about "brotherhood" even while they are slipping the "hood" over the "brother."

I doubt that more than one Jew in a million realizes that is what he is doing, with his high-pressure merchandising, his hyper-intellectualism, and his dishonest speculations. But the *results* are eventually catastrophic for both him and his host.

After sufficient time, although you still may not feel a tape worm, you know for damned sure that something is wrong, and you begin to search desperately for the source of the agony. Sooner or later, when you realize the worm is in there eating out your insides, you physic him out with the utmost ruthlessness, and pleasure at his passing. The endless anti-Jewish "pogroms" of history have been the purging of a deadly tapeworm in the agonized bodies of the people attacked by Jewish parasites.

And always, the spores of the worm passed out by one people quickly find their way into the bodies of new and unsuspecting host peoples to begin the same old act of growing and eating out the host once again.

卐 卐 卐

In case it seems too incredible and vile to the reader that there should be human parasites, let me present, from the works of the Jews themselves, their own official description of the process.

The earliest and most complete record of Jewish methods can be found in almost any home in America, right under the noses of the non-Jews, who have actually been taught to *worship* the very parasites that are eating them alive. In the Old Testament, we can read the story of a typical Jewish operation in any nation they invade. Jews almost always come to a new nation as hapless "refugees," or prisoners and slaves (having had "difficulties" with their previous hosts).

So it was in ancient Egypt. A Jew named Joseph was out tending sheep. His brothers were at first going to kill him for his "coat-of-many-colors" and threw him into a pit (Genesis 37:3, 24). But then some Midianite slave traders happened along and we learn in verses 26 and 27 that these Jews decided it was wasteful just to kill their brother, when they could *sell* him for a profit. So his own Jewish brothers sold Joseph as a slave for twenty pieces of silver, and Joseph wound up an Egyptian slave.

In Genesis 39:6, we find Joseph doing such a good job of running an Egyptian household as a slave that the master makes him the "overseer." In verse 6, the Jewish slave has become so indispensable to the Egyptian master that Joseph is made the boss of the entire Egyptian household.

But Joseph gets in difficulty with the Egyptian's wife. She claims he tried to rape her. Joseph claims, innocently, that *she* tried to rape *him* (Gen. 39: 12). Joseph is tossed into prison, where he repeats the pattern: he becomes so invaluable to the prison administration with his clever business suggestions that he becomes boss of the prison! (Gen. 39:22) In this choice spot, he becomes a confidant of Pharaoh's butler, who is in jail. Joseph cleverly interprets dreams for him.

Pharaoh later reinstates his butler, and has a dream he can't interpret. The butler suggests Joseph. Pharaoh has Joseph brought before him, and tells Joseph about seven fat cows, and seven thin ones. The wily Jew tells Pharaoh this means Egypt will have seven years of plenty and seven years of famine. (For centuries, in the Nile valley, there were huge floods and then periods of drought, so that "lean years" were absolutely certain to follow "fat" years, and vice versa.)

But young Pharaoh is so impressed with Joseph that he asks Joseph what to do about it. The clever Hebrew replies that Pharaoh must find a man smart enough to gather up huge stores of Egyptian grain during the next seven years. "Surprisingly" enough, Pharaoh picks Joseph as that man, and, in Genesis 41:41, Pharaoh turns *all of Egypt* over to his new Jewish "friend." Joseph becomes the "Bernard Baruch" of Egypt, with Pharaoh ordering, "Without thee, no man shall lift up his hand or foot in all the land of Egypt."

Joseph duly gathers up and stores the grain produced by Egyptian labor, in vast amounts. When Egypt is drought-stricken, and the Egyptians are starving for food, Joseph begins to sell *their own grain* back to the Egyptians (Gen. 41:56).

The same rotten Jews who sold Joseph into slavery now come over from Canaan to buy some Egyptian grain. Joseph, who is selling the grain to the Egyptians, gives grain to his fellow Jews. In fact, he gives the Jews a double order of grain on their second trip, and Egyptian gold in the bags to boot! (Gen. 44:1) Then he kicks all the Egyptians out of his office, and tells his Jewish brothers to bring all the Jews over to live free off Egyptian grain (Gen. 45:1, 10, 11).

Meanwhile, Joseph is still selling back their own grain to the Egyptian farmers who produced it. The king is tickled to death, as the treasury bulges. So Joseph tells the king that his brothers and families are on the way, and the king promises Joseph that the Jews will live on "the fat of the land" (Gen. 45:18). From the money being paid by the Egyptian farmers to buy their own grain back, Joseph gives all the Jews wagons, equipment, furniture, and doles out 300 pieces of Egyptian silver to all these Jews! (Gen. 45:16, 22)

Next, Genesis 46 describes how a whole *army* of Jews moves into Egypt, with who "begat" whom and all the children and children's children, etc. Joseph tells his fellow Jews to lie to the king that they are not shepherds (which he knows might aggravate the king). Instead, the Jews all get free Egyptian cattle and land, the best in Egypt (Gen. 46:34). Not one of these Jews has done a lick of work to produce the wealth they are grabbing—a familiar parasitic pattern.

Genesis 47:14 reveals that Joseph, Egypt's Jewish boss, has "gathered up all the money" of the Egyptians, selling them grain. As a result, in verse 15, we discover that "the money of Egypt fails!" A depression?

The starving Egyptians plead with Joseph to let them have a little grain because their money is all gone. Joseph tells them, in typical hock-shop, Jewish style, that they still have their cattle! So the Jew takes the Egyptian farmers' cattle! (Gen. 47:16-17)

The next year, the starving Egyptians again beg for grain. But the Jewish keeper of the granaries tells them that they will have to give up their land, too! To survive, the people have to give this Jew their land in the name of the Pharaoh (verse 20). Joseph then puts them all into concentration areas—cities, taking them off their own land! (Verse 21) When the Egyptians are finally reduced to utter despair, starving, without their money, without their land and without their cattle, Joseph puts them back on their own land as *share-croppers*, at 20% profit! (Verse 24)

Understandably, since Joseph is running the affairs of the Egyptians, the Egyptians are poor, working like slaves, and hungry. But, meanwhile, the hordes of Jews he has brought in are getting "rich and fat" (verse 27)[1] living off the "fat of the land"—*without work!*

Sound familiar?

After 80 years of this process, the Jews have almost everything and the Egyptians are all slaving for the Jews! (The story doesn't mention what the Egyptians think of the arrangement, but it isn't hard to imagine.)

In the Jews' own book of Exodus, we next find Joseph dying, and the Egyptians trying to find some way of getting the Jews off their backs. In Exodus 1, there are some verses worth repeating whole:

---

[1] Some translations read: "they were fruitful and multiplied exceedingly."

7. And the children of Israel were fruitful, and increased abundantly, and multiplied, and waxed exceedingly mighty, and the land was filled with them.

8. Now there rose up a king who knew not Joseph. (*An 'anti-Semite,' no doubt.*)

9. And he said unto his people "Behold, the people of the children of Israel are more and mightier than we!" (*Take a look at New York City, Los Angeles, etc.*)

10. "Come on, let us deal wisely with them, lest they multiply, lest it come to pass, that, when there falleth out any war, they join also unto our enemies." (*As traitors and spies. Remember the Rosenbergs, Sobels, Greenglasses, Golds, Moskowitz's, Silvermasters, etc., who "joined also unto our [communist] enemies?"*)

Observe here the classic pattern:

- The Jew arrives in rags and tatters and terrible misery because of the actions of his own people. (Not Gentiles, but his own Jewish brothers sold Joseph into slavery.)
- The host people are relatively easy-going, and soon recognize the undeniable clever business manipulations of the Jew. (Joseph becomes boss of the household where he was a slave.)
- The Jew begins to push. (Joseph is accused of getting "fresh" with the wife of his master, who sends him to jail.)
- In spite of adversity, however (jail), the Jew prospers because of the same old Jewish ability to manage and manipulate. (Joseph becomes boss of the jail.)
- Using his wits, the Jew reaches the highest positions of power. (Joseph becomes the "executive officer" under Pharaoh, and actually runs Egypt).
- Abusing every leverage of the high office of power, the Jew begins to gather up not just money and power, but *all* the money and *all* the power that he turns over to more and more Jews. He becomes so greedy and rapacious that he smashes the whole economy. (Joseph grabs up so much money from the Egyptians that "the money fails.")

- In the following "depression," the Jew gathers up all the material wealth and the land. (Joseph did exactly this, giving his fellow Jews the "fat of the land.")
- Once the Jew owns and controls everything, he proceeds to make financial slaves out of the native population. (Joseph sent the farmers back to their own land as sharecroppers, producing 20% profit!)
- Inevitably, this process produces such a horror of Jewish power and wealth and such misery for the native population, that the host people become "anti-Semites" and the Jews begin to look around for another country to which they can flee. They become spies, etc. (The king of Egypt warns his people that the Jews are more powerful than the Egyptians in their own land, and that the Jews are likely to be traitors. He first tries to make the Jews work as slaves.)
- The next and last step is for the native population to try to hold the Jews back somehow. (The king orders infanticide for all newborn male Jews.)
- When these less-radical methods won't work, the native populations rise up and either kill the Jews or drive them out. (Moses led the Jews out of Egypt, only yards ahead of the king's armies.)

That Jewish pattern was established in writing more than four thousand years ago—*by the Jews themselves*. You can check every word of it in any Bible.

Basically, it hasn't changed. Always the Jew arrives, as in America, as a tattered "refugee" and is welcomed and assisted by kindly host peoples. The Jew then begins his usual climb up the back of the host people, using any and all methods, even cooperation with his murderous Marxist brothers, until finally the Jews are "exceedingly mighty" and "abundant" in the land, and the host people are paying huge taxes and fees to the Jews to live in their own lands. The Jews sooner or later smash the economy entirely, and wind up owning the very land, making wage-slaves out of the masses of the people, while they slyly ingratiate themselves with the last few non-Jews with power and money.

Ask yourself: Did the Egyptians *unfairly* "persecute" the Jews? According to the Jews' own account of things in Genesis and Exodus, the Egyptians did absolutely nothing against Joseph and the Jews. Quite the opposite, the Egyptians made Joseph "ruler over all Egypt," and gave his great multitude of fellow Jews the "best" land in Egypt, free cattle, free grain, and endless advantages. The Egyptians couldn't possibly have done more for Joseph and the Jews.

In return, when the Egyptians are hungry and starving because of a terrible drought, there is no "sweet charity" from these Jews. No. Joseph demands first all their money, ruins their economy, then grabs all their cattle, and finally all their land itself! While he gives the Jews the "fat of the land," he moves the native people off the land into cities where they are beggars, and then "permits" them back on their own land as sharecroppers, at 20% profit.

Would you tolerate a guest, to whom you gave the best room in your home, who took all your money, all your furniture, and finally your home itself, all because you came upon hard times? And would you then let your "guest" move *you* back into your own basement as a janitor while he lives like a king without working?

卐 卐 卐

Once it is understood that the Jews have inherited a most peculiar trait—parasitism—a trait found in no other people, no matter how primitive, it will be easier to understand why they are what they are, and why they act as they do. All the screams of "anti-Semitism," all the howls about "persecution," all the propaganda about the "Chosen People"—and all the whole hell-raising history of the Jews, will be found to go back again and again to the nature of the Jew to keep trying to *live without working*, to *consume without producing*.

And the need to try to keep his hosts anesthetized—unaware of the source of the misery caused by Jewish parasitism—has forced the Jew to develop a whole flock of secondary characteristics which are often more soundly hated than the parasitism which is the basic cause of the trouble.

The first of these characteristics is his ability *to lie*. Almost every great man, from Christ to Schopenhauer, has damned these people as *liars*, "the great masters of the lie," and a hundred other ways of saying the same thing. Hitler says a Jew tells the truth only to be able to tell a greater lie later.[2]

---

[2] On Schopenhauer, see chapter 6, note 15. In *Mein Kampf*, Hitler wrote: "The followers of the [NS] movement, and indeed the whole nation, must be reminded again and again of the fact that the Jew and his newspapers are always spreading lies. If he tells the truth on some occasions, it's only for the purpose of masking some greater deception, which turns the apparent truth into a deliberate falsehood. The Jew is the great master of lies. Lies and deception are his weapons in struggle" (vol 1, section 12.9, p. 348).

In order to hide the fact that they have become a special breed of humanity (i.e., parasitic), they have developed the monstrous lie that they are "only a religion." Their Jewish appearance is loudly denied, their Jewish characteristics are denied, their Jewish operations and depredations are denied, while those who mention these things are attacked by every Jew in creation as a "hater," an "anti-Semite," etc.

And in order to rationalize to themselves this miserable trait of living by manipulations off of those who do produce, the Jew invented the despicable myth of being the "Chosen People." He has granted himself a special license from Heaven to be a gold-brick down the centuries. Any father who "chooses" one of his children for favoritism, and then withholds the same love and "choosing" from other children he has brought into this world, is a cheat and a scoundrel. Yet the Jews would have us believe the Almighty does exactly this! It is monstrous!

Once they adopted the parasitic way of life, the early tribes of Jews were forced to rationalize that such inhuman injustice and criminal blood-sucking was "ordained" by God. The whole Old Testament abounds with their ringing statements of how they will "put their feet on the necks of all other people," how they will have in their greedy hands all the gold and wealth of the earth and make slaves of all other people—the dream of human tapeworms!

I have no doubt that, if a tapeworm could talk, it would groan "Oy, why does everyone hate me and persecute me?"

Combining this "chosen" rationalization for parasitism, with a fanatical love of themselves and resulting unity, they in-bred, century after century. And this inbreeding produced the special, recognizable breed of the fat, greasy-looking, rapacious Jew, typified by the appearance of convicted mail swindler Harry Golden better than anything I could put in words.

Along with the bad characteristics of parasitism, the Jews were also forced to produce something in which they have excelled the rest of us—a *purely materialistic and superficial cunning.*

There are, of course, stupid Jews. But the *average* Jew exceeds the *average* Gentile in superb mental slyness and sharpness. He *has* to; the average Gentile is a man of force and courage.

Whenever he discovers what the Jew is up to, how the Jew is conning him out of his hard-won production without working, the Gentile resorts to naked force to put an end to the depredations of the human tapeworm. To avoid this violent end, the Jew has to "live by his wits." So the Jew has developed a good set of "wits."

What the Jews palm off on the world as their "religion" is the codified essence of these Jewish "wits"—the rules for living like a parasite off the sweat of their hosts, for grabbing the Gentile women for Jewish pleasure, and Gentile men to labor for the Jews, all while getting their victims to worship them as a "holy" people.

Does that sound wild, extreme—even wicked and vicious? I must confess that it does. But the evidence that every word of it is true exists in the Jews' own words. Here is a direct quote from the correspondence of Karl Marx with another Jew, Baruch Levy, quoted in *La Revue de Paris,* June 1, 1928, page 574:

> In the new organization of mankind, the children of Israel will spread over the whole surface of the earth and will become everywhere, without opposition, the leading element, especially if they can impose upon working classes the firm control of some of them. The governments of the nations forming the Universal Republic will pass without effort into the hands of the Jews under the cover of the victory of the proletariat; private property will then be suppressed by the rulers of Jewish race, who will everywhere control public funds. Thus will be realized the Talmudic promise that, when come the times of the Messiah, Jews will possess the wealth of all peoples of the world.[3]

卐 卐 卐

---

[3] This quotation remains to be verified.

Even more convincing is the original source for the rules the Jews worship as their "Bible," *the Talmud*. This enormous set of rules for using and abusing the "stupid Goyim"—cattle, as they call us—contains more filth and hate than any other book on Earth. Judge for yourself! Just read some samples from these Jewish holy books—the basis of the Jewish "religion":[4]

- He who loans his friend coin(s) is permitted to demand on Chol Hamoed [i.e. Passover] to collect (on what he is owed). And it goes without saying that it is permitted to collect an obligation from a Gentile. ... To lend a Gentile with interest to those that are accustomed to borrow from him is allowed because it is a matter of loss [for the Gentile]. (*Shulchan Aruch*, Orach Chayim 539, 2; 13)[5]

- At Passover, one must say "cursed is Haman," "Blessed is Mordechai" ... "cursed are all those who worship idols" [all Gentiles], "Blessed are all Israel" [all Jews]. (*Shulchan Aruch*, Orach Chayim 690, 16)

- The Kadish-prayer shall only be given when ten Jews are together and they must be together in a way that no unclean thing separates them, as, for example, feces or a Gentile. (*Shulchan Aruch*, Orach Chayim 55, 20)

- The Jewish people are called 'man,' but Gentiles are not called 'man' [i.e. are beasts]. (*Talmud*, Bava Metzia 114b, 2)

- All non-Jewesses are whores. (*Shulchan Aruch*, Even Ha-ezer 6, 8)

- Ravina said: Regarding a female Gentile child who is three years and one day old, since she is fit to engage in intercourse at that

---

[4] The following quotations come primarily from the two central texts of Judaism: the Talmud and the Shulchan Aruch. The Talmud was composed around 500 AD, and the Shulchan around 1550; the Shulchan is a condensed version of the much-larger Talmud. Both documents are considered binding on religious Jews, and even for secular Jews, they accurately describe the moral code and mindset; both demonstrate Jewish supremacism and a hatred for the Gentiles (non-Jews). For a good overview and discussion of these two works, see E. Bischoff, *The Book of the Shulchan Aruch* (2023).

[5] See also Yoreh De'ah 159, 1.

age, she also imparts impurity like one who is menstruating. (*Shulchan Aruch*, Avodah Zarah 37a, 1)[6]

- R. Simeon b. Yoḥai taught: *Kill the best of the heathens* [in time of war]; crush the brain of the best of serpents. The worthiest of women indulges in witchcraft. (Soferim 15, 10)

- The best among the Egyptians, kill; the best among serpents, crush its brain. (Midrash Tanchuma, Beshalach 8, 1)

- R. Simeon said: The best amongst the Egyptians—kill him (otherwise he will afterwards devise evil against you); the best amongst the serpents—crush its brains. (Rashi on Exodus 14:7, 2)

- Rabbi Yoḥanan says: A Gentile who engages in Torah study is liable to receive the death penalty. (*Talmud*, Sanhedrin 59a, 2)

- A woman who had intercourse with a beast (i.e., a dog) is eligible to marry a priest. (*Talmud*, Yevamot 59b, 6).

- If a Jew wishes to annul all his oaths of the previous year, he must say at the beginning of the new year: "All the oaths that I swore are invalid." (*Talmud*, Nedarim 23b, 1)[7]

- Shmuel says that the property of a gentile is like a desert, and anyone who takes possession of it has acquired it. (*Talmud*, Bava Batra 54b, 5)

- What a non-Jew has lost, is permitted (to be kept) … because it says (Deuteronomy 22:3): 'What your [Jewish] brother has lost [you as the finder are to give it back]. You must give it back to your [Jewish] brother,' but not to a non-Jew. (*Talmud*, Bava Kamma 113b, 8)

---

[6] Compare: "Since a nine-year-old boy is fit to engage in intercourse, he also imparts ritual impurity as one who menstruates." (36b-37a) And: "All concede, regarding a boy nine years and one day old, that his intercourse is regarded as intercourse…" (Sanhedrin 69b, 6).

[7] This is the so-called "Kol Nidre" prayer.

- To take advantage of the error of a non-Jew is permitted, e.g. to let him err in arithmetic or by not paying off a loan that he forgot, [forgotten by him], provided he does not know it... (*Shulchan Aruch*, Choshen Mishpat 348, 2)

- If a Jew has a non-Jew as a permanent customer, there are places where it is judged that other Jews are forbidden to compete with that first Jew. [But] some allow any other Jew to go to the non-Jew, to lend to him, to do business with him, to propitiate him by gifts or favors, and thereby from that first Jew to lure him away. This is because [the first Jew has no legal privilege over "his" non-Jew, but rather] 'the belongings of non-Jews are like un-claimed property, and everyone who comes to them first is enti-tled to them.' (*Shulchan Aruch*, Chosen Mishpat 156, 5)

- Rav Ashi said: The Mishnah [on tax collection] issues its ruling with regard to a *Gentile* tax collector, whom one may deceive: In the case of a Jew and a Gentile who approach the court for judg-ment in a legal dispute, if you can vindicate the Jew under Jewish law, vindicate him, and say to the Gentile: *This is our law*. If he can be vindicated under Gentile law, vindicate him, and say to the Gentile: *This is your law*. And if it is not possible to vindicate him under either system of law, one approaches the case with *legal trickery*, seeking a justification to vindicate the Jew. ... Apparent-ly, *it is permitted to deceive a Gentile*. (*Shulchan Aruch*, Bava Kamma 113a)

- It is permitted to retain the Gentile's lost item ... "From where is it derived that it is permitted to retain the lost item of a Gentile? It is derived from a verse, as it is stated: 'With every lost thing of your brother's' (Deut 22:3), indicating that it is *only to your brother* that you return a lost item, *but you do not return a lost item to a Gentile*." [...] Samuel says that *it is permitted to finan-cially benefit from a business error of a Gentile*... (*Shulchan Aruch*, Bava Kamma 113b)

卐 卐 卐

Being a gross materialist in love with himself and his gold, and having his whole nature depend on *getting* rather than ever *giving* (exactly like the tapeworm), the average Jew has a hard time being physically "coura-geous." He can't see any point in sacrificing himself since, once he is dead, he sees no gain. (Can you imagine a "courageous tapeworm?")

Above all, the Jew realizes that his only hope of survival is the utmost effort to keep his hosts from ever realizing what he is doing. Once the host realizes he has a tapeworm, the castor oil is inevitable, and all the Jew's cleverness, lies, and ability to disguise himself as a religion are useless. Out he goes into the sewer!

So the Jew becomes the world's absolute champion in the art of being a chameleon. In America, he is the original model of the American, de-vouring apple-pies, yelling at the umpire at ball games, and even joining the Unitarian church to parade around in the suburbs like the Goy on Sun-day. In England, he becomes "royalty," with a title and the rank of "knight" or "duke." In Spain, he hollers "Olé!" at the bullfight and be-comes a "Don." In pre-World War II, some Jews even tried to be "Nazis." But underneath, the Jew is still there, and when the crisis arrives, the Jew will out. He is a Jew first—then an "American" or a Spaniard.

The first Jewish justice of the US Supreme Court, Louis D. Brandeis, in his book, *Brandeis on Zionism*, sets down the real truth of the Jewish business for the eyes of his brother Jews, when he writes,

> Let us recognize that we Jews are a distinct nationality of which every Jew, whatever his country, his station, or shade of belief, is necessarily a member. Organize, organize, or-ganize, until every Jew must stand up and be counted—counted with us, or prove himself, wittingly or unwittingly, of the few who are against their own people. (pp. 113-114)

Perhaps the most famous Jewish rabbi in America, Rabbi Stephen Wise, put it even more clearly in a quotation in the *New York Herald Tribune*:

> I am not an American citizen of Jewish faith. I am a *Jew*. I am an American. I have been an American for sixty-three sixty-fourths of my life, but I have been a Jew for 4,000 years. Hitler was right in one thing. He calls the Jewish peo-ple a race, and we are a race. (13 June 1938)

The Jew also has different "skins" into and out of which he can crawl as the occasion demands, much like the snake. The Jew is merely a "reli-gious" group, whenever you begin to notice the devilish number of Jews who are selling us out to communism. "These people, like the Rosenbergs"—are not "Jews anymore," explains the clever Anti-Defamation League Jew, slyly, "because a Jew believes in God, while commies are atheists. Therefore, the Rosenbergs were *not* Jews!"

But when it comes to Jewish crooks from all over the world escaping into Israel, they have a thing called the "law of the return," under which any person with a *Jewish mother* is a Jew—by their own definition. Thus, when convicted communist spy Robert Soblen jumped $100,000 bail put up by Jewess Buttonweiser, and slipped into Israel, he would have been welcomed, and indeed *was* welcomed by a vast segment of the population, until there was such a hue and cry over his being sheltered by Israel that it was hurting Jewish "public relations" and they reluctantly turned him over to the USA. However, this produced a near civil war; because most plain Israelis felt that the government had betrayed the "law of return," for this *communist* Jew spy.

Then there is the third Jewish "skin" of *nationality*. The Jews are the chief promoters of the doctrine of the separation of Church and State, agitating successfully all over America to have Christian prayers banned from schools, Christmas celebrations stopped, etc. *But they run the only religious state in the world: Israel!*

Even while damning the idea of any connection between religion and statehood for others, they run the most intolerant, fanatic religious state yet seen on the planet. You can't even get married in Israel, unless you are a Jew.

But whenever this Jewish religion is called into account, they quickly slip into the "Zionist" skin, and become innocent, patriotic "nationalists"!

From the racial "skin" to the religious "skin" to the nationalist "skin" is but the work of a few moments to Jews around the world, and they change back and forth, depending on whether they are in America, where they are a religious group, or Russia, where they are a race—or Israel, where they instantly become fanatic "nationalists."

Whenever you try to pin one of these Jews down on just what they *are*—you will find the argument very much like trying to grab up a handful of slime; as fast as you close your fist around it, it oozes out between your fingers and is right back where it was. Attack them as a race—they are a *religion*. Attack them as a religion, they are a *"people,"*—and a "holy" people at that. Attack them as a people, and they are a religion again, until that becomes impossible or uncomfortable, in which case they take refuge as a persecuted race. Call them a race (as they do themselves), and they will accuse you of being a "bigot." Call them *only* a "religion," and therefore deny them nationhood, and hear them holler how they are the "people of the book" with the "right" to seize Israel from the Arabs for their "nation." Call them a nation and therefore susceptible to the same responsibilities as any other nation—and right away they are a religion again and you are persecuting them.

卐 卐 卐

With all these disguises and frauds, they rely, from day to day, more than anything else on old-fashioned *name changing*. If all Jews went by their real names, the nation would puke in unison to see how its whole cultural life was *Jewish*; it would take up arms against the Jews in power, it would stop watching the Jewish TV and reading Jewish newspapers, etc. So these clever Hebrews take old Anglo-Saxon names, bob their beaks, become "Protestants" and presto—they *disappear* from the eyes of the Gentile world as Jews, although their fellow Hebrews know the secret and never forget it.

An entire book could be produced with a list of the well-known "Americans" who are really Jews who have changed their names. But just to give the reader some slight idea of how he is bilked and swindled by these name-changers every day of his life, here are just a few of the name-changers in the entertainment field which shocked me, at least:

Mel Allen (Melvin Allen Israel)

Harold Arlen (Hyman Arluck)

Jean-Pierre Aumont (Philippe Salomons)

Lauren Bacall (Betty Joan Perske)

Benny Baker (Benjamin Zifkin)

Theda Bara (Theodosia Goodman)

Jack Benny (Benny Kubelsky)

Milton Berle (Mendel Berlinger)

Irving Berlin (Israel Beilin)

Ben Bernie (Benjamin Anzelevitz)

Victor Borge (Borge Rosenbaum)

Ernest Borgnine (Ermes Borgnino)

Fannie Brice (Fania Borach)

George Burns (Nathan Birnbaum)

Eddie Cantor (Izzie Iskowitz)

Sue Carol (Evelyn Lederer)

Jeff Chandler (Ira Grossel)

Ricardo Cortez (Jacob Krantz)

Tony Curtis (Bernard Schwartz)

Howard DaSilva (Howard Silverblatt)

Kirk Douglas (Issur Danielovitch)

Melvyn Douglas (Melvyn Hesselberg)

Douglas Fairbanks, Jr. (Douglas Ullman)

John Garfield (Jacob Julius Garfinkle)

Samuel Goldwyn (Szmuel Gelbfisz)

Judy Holliday (Judith Tuvim)

Harry Houdini (Ehrich Weisz)

Al Jolson (Asa Yoelson)

Danny Kaye (David Kaminsky)

Bert Lahr (Irving Lahrheim)

Hedy Lamarr (Hedwig Keisler)

Michael Landon (Eugene Orowitz)

Piper Laurie (Rosetta Jacobs)

Marc Lawrence (Max Goldsmith)

Steve Lawrence (Sidney Leibowitz)

Madeline Lee (Madeline Lederman)

Ann Landers (Esther Friedman)   Artie Shaw (Arthur Jacob Arshawsky)

Jerry Lewis (Joseph Levitch)   Abigail Van Buren (Pauline Friedman)

Mitzi McCall (Mitzi Steiner)   Mike Wallace (Myron Wallik)

Dorothy Parker (Dorothy Rothschild)   Shelley Winters (Shirley Schrift)

John Randolph (Emanuel Hirsch Cohen)   Ed Wynn (Isaiah Edwin Leopold)

Edward G. Robinson (Emanuel Goldenberg)

卐 卐 卐

But even with all this disguise, name-changing slipperiness, the Jew knows that he is always facing the terrible danger that the host people will *see* him, feel his vampire teeth in their blood-vessels, sucking their blood, and get rid of him or slaughter him—as have hundreds of people all throughout history.

So, realizing this, the Jew is the most hysterical defender of his group security in the history of the world. Attack a Jew, and the whole tribe rises in hysterical counter-attack! If *one* Jew is exposed, the people may go on to discover the whole tribe.

And because of this terrible feeling of constant insecurity, because of the Jews' ever-present knowledge that the host may find out the truth about him at any moment and rip him loose from his comfortable, warm bowel, the Jew has developed a fantastic program designed to paralyze his host so thoroughly, in advance, that awakening will be impossible. His genius at this is astounding

But there is a cure. The deadliest enemy of the Jew is *order and national health*. Tapeworms don't get started and can't survive in a healthy person who has physical examinations and lives a clean life. And Jews can't prosper in a healthy, well-organized, ordered society. In such a society, the leaders will quickly observe the mass of non-working, non-producing Jews sucking away at the national bloodstream and once again, there go the tapeworms down the sewer This has happened to them too many times for too many centuries for any Jew to have to be told. It is an unconscious instinct in them.

And so you will forever find the Jew as the ferment of decomposition in every society he infests.[8] In a monarchy, he is a Republican. In a Republic, he is a Democrat. In a democracy, he is for "social democracy." In a

---

[8] "Ferment of decomposition" is a phrase Rockwell likely picked up from *Mein Kampf* (vol 2, secs. 4.2 and 14.8), which in turn originated with German historian Theodor Mommsen in 1856 in his *History of Rome*.

Social Democracy, he is a communist. Among communists, he joins Progressive Labor. Thus the Jew is always over on the left—*for less and less authority and order* in the society—although he disguises it by claiming he is for more and more "freedom for the people."

The Jew is the world's champion "liberal," not for love of liberty and freedom, but because he knows that a healthy body politic will quickly rid itself of tapeworms. Liberalism is no longer the belief in liberty that the word once meant.[9] In the hands of the Jew, liberalism has become pure and simple *"tapewormism"*—the organization of the parasitic, unproductive, and generally inferior to enslave the productive and superior by sheer weight of numbers.

That's why every modern "liberal" program always requires so many billions and billions of tax dollars. Money is the "blood" of a society, and the blood is sucked out of the wealthy and the workers to maintain an ever-growing horde of welfare parasites, subsidized failures, and outright bums. If you will examine almost any "liberal" program today, you will find that it boils down to this sucking of the blood of the productive to nourish the lazy, the useless, the worthless, and the rotten.

The Jew doesn't *dare* allow any reform program directed at *any* parasites, because it would be too easy for the reform to spread, for the reformists to begin to see the champion parasite of all time, the Jew—and to get rid of him, as has happened so many times.

Invariably, of course, the scum knows the source of what keeps it alive, which makes the scum into very effective *voting blocks* for the Jews, who see that they are well taken care of.

What the Jew is after is the destruction of the power of government to govern and maintain order. And taking money and power from our productive people and turning that money and power over to swarming scum in the streets is guaranteed to destroy all order and government, sooner or later. For thousands of years, the sly Jew did this politically—by political action, behind the scenes, as the "advisor" to kings. But now the Jew has discovered a faster way to smash public order. Basically, it is what we started out with in examining what has happened to our people and our country.

The most parasitic of all ways of living is crime. Where the ordinary parasite finds painless ways of sucking the blood out of his host, the criminal parasite—the bandit—takes it by naked force and violence, careless of

---

[9] For a useful discussion of the distorted meaning of 'liberalism,' 'conservative,' 'leftist,' and so on, see T. Dalton's essay "The Problem with Leftism" in his book *The Steep Climb: Essays on the Jewish Question* (2023).

the pain of the victim. The old shipwreck gangs were criminal parasites. They just went out and took, by the most brutal force and murder, what they wanted, without working. The victims always perished.

Impatient Jews, tired of waiting for the gaining of all the wealth in the world by the usual Jewish Zionist methods of "capitalist" speculation, swindling, manipulations, and political chicanery rather than work and production, discovered a short-cut to seizing the total wealth and power in whole nations. The Jew, Marx, invented "communism." By telling his starry-eyed, liberal Gentile victims that he was going to create a "worker's paradise" here where they could have all kinds of wealth and ease with minimum work by soaking the wealthy, the Jew could enlist vast masses of horny-handed but short-sighted Gentiles into his army with which to overwhelm the relatively few producers and owners of wealth. He made criminal ship-wreckers out of as many "workers" as he could, promising them the loot off the ships they smashed.

And there you have the answer we sought at the beginning of the book: the answer to *who* is smashing up America (and the White Race which built it) and *why*.

The Jews promote the general disintegrating of culture and order for self-protection: to prevent the discovery by too many of their victims that they are sucking the lifeblood out of our productive economy, without themselves producing. The more disorder, the more the Jewish parasites can feast undisturbed. And at the same time, a bolder gang of Jews are operating and promoting the communist movement to seize all our wealth and services by naked force and violence in a Red "revolution"—the old "shipwreck" scheme. Ideology, ideas, economics, religion, sociology and all the rest have nothing to do with what is going on. The battle is not between 'liberal' and 'conservative,' or even between 'communist' and 'anti-communist.' We are being victimized by a gang of rapacious Jews out for loot, pure and simple. It is "us" against "them."

Either they will use every trick in the book to dispossess us of what our people have produced, either as sneaky tapeworms or as violent red ship-wreckers; or we will expose them for what they are, and purge the Zionist tapeworms and communist ship-wreckers out.

卐 卐 卐

The reason Adolf Hitler is so viciously hated and cursed today by Jews (and brainwashed Gentiles) is simply that he was the first in modern times to figure all this out and organize his people to purge the Jewish tapeworm, and smash the Jewish ship-wreckers. And he actually *did* it, in Germany.

To save themselves, the Jews were forced to a World War in which they got millions of suckers like me to save them from the end, had Hitler survived. Tapewormism and shipwrecking couldn't survive exposure. They keep shouting that Hitler brought prosperity and happiness to Germany only because of "war production." But this, as usual, is another big Jewish lie. Hitler tore the Jewish tapeworms loose from the German bloodstream and the people found out how wonderful life could be without the terrible burden of a mass of Yiddish tapeworms strangling production, culture, and the national spirit. Simultaneously, Hitler exposed and smashed the Marxist-Jew ship-wreckers of international Bolshevism.

As Hitler proved in Germany, the worst of the seemingly insoluble problems of our mad times—the degeneracy, the disorder, the communism, the political, moral, educational, social, religious, and national decay, the racial mixing and the spiritual syphilis spreading throughout our civilization—will disappear once we have identified and eliminated the source of most of these things: the Jewish tapeworms and ship-wreckers in our midst. The mere fact that the Jewish "Mr. Big" has now been "fingered" in this book will ensure that it will be hidden as much as possible. And, if not possible to hide it, then it will be suppressed by framed-up "prosecutions" of the author. As more and more people get wise to what the Jews are doing, the Jewish "defense" groups are trying to get "group-libel" laws passed to make it a crime to criticize Jewish crime and blood-sucking.

But it's already too late. The tapeworm's victims are finally realizing the truth. And the Jews, as we have said, cannot survive simple exposure. So, in the next chapters, we'll expose their methods of operations.

CHAPTER 8

FRIENDS OF THE CAPTAIN

The shipwrecking plan is not the only one the Jews have in operation to get wealth without work. The aim is always the same: the capture of all the wealth and good of the world—without working—and the enslavement of non-Jews to the glory and pleasure of the "Chosen Ones," according to their own prophecies.

While the brutal Bolshevik Jews wait on the shore to pounce on the ship as soon as it is finally wrecked, murder all hands, and walk off with the wealth, there is another gang of Jews already aboard ship with a different plan for taking over the wealth. This gang of Jews are friends of the captain. They are not cutthroats and pirates. No sir! The friends of the captain are all "pro-ship," and anti-pirate. They are called "capitalists."

What their Jewish brothers lurking on the shore wait to do by force and violence, the captain's "friends" are already doing aboard ship by stealth and fraud, as esteemed members of the ship's company. These gentlemen Jews operate in striped pants and top-hats. But their business is old Jewish-fashioned usury.

Few notice that the phrase "capitalist" was popularized by none other than that bloody old Jew, Karl Marx, himself a ship-wrecker (*Communist Manifesto* and *Das Kapital*). Until Marx told our kind of people they were "capitalists" in his *Das Kapital*, they never gave what they were doing economically such a formal name. But they did know what they believed in, and it was *not* "capitalism." Capital was only a tool for our people in the process of production. Men like Henry Ford were not interested simply in getting money. Rather they were trying to do something—in Ford's case, give all Americans an automobile via his discovery of "mass production."

The American economy does not produce miracles because it is "capitalist," but because it is enterprising and productive. The correct name of our system is not "capitalism," but "productive enterprise." Productive enterprise needs capital. But it also needs labor, material, management, and a hundred other things. Capital is only one of the tools of a productive enterprise system.

It took the Jewish parasitic genius of Karl Marx to elevate that one tool, capital, to the status in our civilization by attacking it and calling it "capitalism." He has thus trapped us into defending what he created, and has thereby doomed us to defeat because we defend a system based not on *production*, but *money manipulation*. Capitalism is the naked worship of money, not as a tool, but as an idol.

"Capitalism" as promoted by both sides in the crazy "capitalism" versus "communism" sham fight going on, is taken to mean the making of money through the use of capital—not necessarily by working or producing. In fact, most international capital is made not by working or producing or even taking any genuine risks, but by manipulations of vast pools of money with inside information from Jews in high positions.

A perfect sample of the way the Jews operate to get money as "capitalists," without working, without producing anything, and without taking any genuine risks, is the way the Jewish Rothschild fortune was founded. As is usual with the international Jews, one branch of the Rothschild family got entrenched into the money system in England, while another branch set up business in France. Just before the battle of Waterloo, in which Napoleon faced possible defeat for the first time, the two gangs of Jews operating in the two "enemy" countries were actually working together. The French Rothschilds set up a series of "semaphore" stations through France and across the channel to England, by which they could flash news of which way the battle went to their Jewish brothers in supposedly "enemy" England. The waiting Jew Rothschilds in Britain thus received word of the outcome of the historic battle hours before anybody else in England. (Note that the Jewish "enterprise" in setting up the communications network was not shared with either Britain or France, but was secret—for the sole benefit of Jews on both sides!)

Knowing, in advance of anyone in England, the outcome of the battle which decided forever the fates of France and Napoleon and the fate of England, the English Rothschilds, waiting in the London Stock Exchange, "speculated" in huge sums, knowing full well the outcome of the battle—while the trusting British Gentiles were still waiting for the news. The suckers never had a chance. The Rothschilds got their hands on millions and millions in moments—without work and without risk.

The same racket is known as "past-posting" in the horse racing business, where the results of the race are tape-recorded, held back, and then re-broadcast after the race, so that unsuspecting bookies can be euchred into paying off bets which are actually sure things; after the race, if you "past-post," you go to jail as a criminal.

But if you are Jewish and do it in a big way, swindling millions of people out of millions of dollars, you become an "international banker" and a great advisor to presidents. Bernard Baruch, the famous Jewish advisor to presidents, made millions and millions in the US stock market while hundreds of Gentile businessmen were leaping out of windows to their deaths—ruined in the great depression of 1929. Advance information helps.

To see clearly the nature of our present economy and for whose benefit it has been set up, look at the *tax structure*. For instance, suppose you work in poverty for the next five years to invent a new machine by which blind people can see. Surely, this would be a magnificent boon to society. You set up a little factory to produce these machines, and work hard day and night to make them available to blind people. At the end of the year, let us say you have earned a million dollars.

Uncle Sam will come and take at least 70% of that money you earned—maybe as much as 90%. The rate of taxation on the money people earn by working and producing can go *over* 90%.

But now, let us suppose instead of inventing and building something to benefit society, you are a rich Jew and you have a friend in the White House—a not unlikely combination. Your White House friend lets you know that the USA is going to place a multi-million-dollar contract for a new rocket with a specific company: You pick up a telephone and order your broker to transfer ownership of a million dollars' worth of other stock holdings to the new company. That's all you do. A year later, your stock in that company has doubled, and you now have two million dollars—although you have done nothing, risked nothing, and produced nothing.

But now see what the government does about your taxes in this case. Such a gain (stocks held over six months) is called a "capital gain," and taxed a maximum of only 25%! With a sharp Jewish lawyer, special "trusts" and other manipulations, you can cut this tax down to less than five or six percent.

This outrageous system puts a premium on speculation (gambling) and an enormous drag on production, management savings, risk, invention, and plain old work. Those who produce, save, risk, manage, work, and invent—pay millions every year to produce an easy life for the Jewish leeches who never provide a bit of management, risk, invention, or honest work to our economy, and pay the least taxes. How long do you think an economy can remain healthy and productive when intelligent men begin to see that working is for suckers, and that an easy life can be had by manipulations?

And that's precisely what's happened to America and the West, ever since the Jewish sharpies have forced honest Gentiles to play the same dirty game—or remain poor suckers. Fewer and fewer people are willing to work anymore, as more and more people discover there are easier *Jewish* ways to make a living.

But there comes a time when fruits rot off vines because no one will work picking them, when buildings fall apart because no one will work taking care of them, when jobs by the thousands go begging even while a vast number of people, especially Negroes, are moaning about unemployment. Work, one of the healthiest and most character-building activities of humanity, becomes degraded and abandoned in any economy where Jews establish "capitalist" speculation as the goal of all but the dumbest.

卐 卐 卐

To go back to our ship-of-state analogy, the capitalist Jewish "friends of the captain" do nothing more than shift the cargo around back and forth between different groups, always taking out a big hunk. There is never *more* cargo as a result of their operations, always *less* for producers, while Jews get richer.

This operation they call "international banking." The little guys who get in the stock market are told they "share" the ownership of the big corporations. But the little guys in the stock market are exactly what the people around the roulette table are to the "house." The Jews and a few choice "friends" are "the house" in the stock market. They have inside information from other Jews in the White House and government bureaus as to the location of new freeways, purchase of land for government projects, vast oil and armament purchases, wars, fair trade prosecutions, antitrust prosecutions, etc. Such "speculation" is not gambling, any more than the house "gambles." The little guys are sweet-talked into providing the money gathered up by the big guys. It's not hard to see how the Jews can swindle the "little guys" with this racket. They keep the little man too busy and brainwashed to see or even think about what's going on.

But, more amazing, the Jews have managed to get our biggest and richest men convinced that they, too, are "capitalists." The Jews have become partners with such as the Rockefellers, Carnegies, Fords, Johnsons, etc., in this gigantic "past-posting" racket, with the result that production and enterprise have been forgotten more and more in the ugly scramble over capital and money, regardless of production.

That's why products become ever shoddier and cheaper even as prices go whizzing up; that's why the big billionaire foundations are to be found always on the side of Jewish, leftist projects, and it's why the character is disappearing out of old American family fortunes. Henry Ford would leap out of his grave and slaughter his own grandchildren and great-grandchildren if he could see and know what they have done with the billions he made by producing, and what they have become, as pro-Jewish "capitalists."

There's nothing immoral or wrong about a man investing his capital in a genuine productive enterprise, which benefits the people with either valuable goods or services. If he can make money doing this, then so much the better. Others will try to do still better by competition, and the goods and services therefore offered to the people get better and better. That's the free, productive economic process, which created the American economic miracle. But that's not what the Jews, and their "capitalist friends," do.

卐 卐 卐

Remember the way the Rothschilds made millions at the Battle of Waterloo? What did they give the British, or the French, people for all they took? Can you think of one single benefit they delivered? Their operation was all clever-take and no give!

Further, it was based on fratricidal bloodshed—on Aryan White Men of France slaughtering Aryan White Men of England for relatively minor reasons, while the fanatically-united Hebrews made cash out of the mutual murder.

In every war (except World War II, which was for survival of Jewry), these same Jews have taken both sides, and sold both sides the guns and uniforms and flags to wave at each other. In the Civil War, for instance, the British Rothschilds backed the South while the French Rothschilds backed the North.

These "capitalist" Jews can usually be found in the ranks of what they call "Zionists"—the Jews who wear the "beanies," the Jews who pose in the garb of the Jewish "religion," and who insist on fulfilling their paranoiac prophecies of world ownership and domination as "God's Chosen People." They believe they will own the world and enslave all the rest of us when they have all of Jerusalem. This "holy" pose of theirs works only so long as no one actually checks this Jewish "religion," which is actually a code of operations for the "Chosen Ones" to swindle, ruin, and enslave the rest of us, as we have shown.

The secret of the Jewish-capitalist, Zionist side of the parasitic operation for gaining the wealth of the Gentiles is make-believe. The only reality in economics is goods and services, property and productive labor. All the talk of "money," "currency," "inflation," "deflation," etc., is a smoke-screen. He who has a monopoly in goods and services, has the wealth. Money is only a sort of "ticket" to these goods and services.

卐 卐 卐

The Jews actually invented the basic principles of "capitalist" stealing via money manipulations long before Christ, in ancient Babylon. Originally, the ancients used actual chunks of gold (or precious metals and stones) for their medium of exchange. The Babylonians became tremendously wealthy, however, and soon found them trying to lug around bone-crushing weights of the precious but heavy gold, in trading operations. The clever Jews stepped in and volunteered to be keepers of the heavy gold for wealthy merchants, and do the lugging whenever necessary. The Jew keepers of the gold issued to the Babylonian merchants little stone tokens with carved indications of the value of gold deposited, as receipts.

It wasn't long before merchants discovered that they could trade with each other—using these stone "receipts" from the Jews, instead of the actual gold. And the Jews, in turn, discovered that as soon as the merchants got used to the idea of trading, not with actual gold, but with the stone "receipts," the merchants gradually stopped taking gold in and out of the vaults maintained by the Jews. Merchants began to use the "receipts" as gold—and the gold itself never moved from the vault, no matter how many times it changed ownership. Thus was born "money"—and with it the biggest swindle in the history of humanity, a swindle still going on!

Note that the Jews did not have to produce the gold every time there was a transaction. It was always there, and the merchants soon stopped checking it. On those rare occasions it was called for, the Jews always delivered. But the Jews discovered that they could always deliver any gold that might be called for, even if they didn't have enough gold to cover all the receipts they had issued. In fact, they found out that they were perfectly safe with no more than ten percent of the gold for which they had issued receipts. In other words, they could issue ten times the amount of receipts for gold as they had gold to deliver! And that's precisely what the early Jews did, and how they became "capitalists."

For every pound of gold delivered to his keeping, the Jew gained nine pounds of gold value, simply by issuing to himself nine more receipts on the same one pound of gold, and then using these un-backed "receipts" to trade with merchants for what he wanted and for power in the state.

Believe it or not, that is precisely, exactly what he and his Gentile partners are doing to you, today, right here in America. The Federal Reserve, set up by the Jew Paul Warburg, of the house of Rothschild, has the power to do precisely what the early Jews in Babylon did: issue "receipts," called "money" or currency, for what is supposed to be on deposit in their vaults—but isn't.

The Constitution of the United States expressly forbids this, because the Founding Fathers were well aware of this centuries-old swindle. Only Congress has the power to coin money. Yet now the Federal Reserve coins your money! Under Jewish pressure, our Congress, in 1913, passed the unlawful "Federal Reserve Act," creating a central bank, which has gone into the old robbing act of the Babylonian Jews with a will and a style never before seen in history. The Federal Reserve (a semi-private organization) coins your money at will,[1] swipes the actual assets and property, and shows a profit, while you, as a US citizen, stagger under a national debt to these international bankers so huge it is beyond the conception of the human mind.

And the way they have pulled off this atrocious robbery of the American people is the same way that the ancient Babylonian Jews swindled the merchants of that time. By issuing nine times as many tokens for the gold deposits they held, the Jews got "tickets" to enjoy the wealth and production of the Gentile Babylonians without working, and without getting caught legally. By setting up the "Federal Reserve" and passing an unconstitutional law to let them issue ten times as much paper—and debt—as they hold in assets, the Federal Reserve, and those who rake in the profit and the interest on the astronomical debt, reap gigantic rewards—without working.

Our people have been conned into lumping our own, honest system of "productive enterprise" with the dishonest, rotten swindle of Jewish usury dressed up as "capitalism," and then have been forced to defend the immoral and rotten result. Thus the Jews have us *worshipping their own thievery*, because, we are told (and we believe), that we are "capitalists!"

Whenever the Jews can get things so complicated and removed from the basic realities of goods and services that the tickets to these things (money) become something of value itself, in the eyes of the population, then the Jews can really move in and operate.

The national debt, now about 300 times what it was in 1910 ($1.1 billion) is now $336 billion. Interest alone amounts to $14 billion a year. The per capita debt now is about $1,700. When the Federal Reserve took charge, the per capita debt was $12.[2]

---

[1] Today this is called "quantitative easing."

[2] As of 2024: Total national debt is $34 trillion (= $34,000 billion) versus $336 billion in 1967. Debt per person now is $100,000, versus $1,700 in 1967. Current federal interest payments are now $870 billion per year, versus $14 billion in 1967.

From 1960 [to 1967], the cost of living has risen 10.5 percent. The dollar is now worth only 45 cents compared to the 1941 dollar. What now costs $2.22 would have cost $1.25. The deficit for the first eight months of fiscal 1967 was $17.18 billion. US gold is now down to a 30-year low of about $13.1 billion—a loss of more than $11 billion in 10 years. Only $2.8 billion is now available to meet foreign claims. The dollars held by foreigners keep rising and now are tip to $27 billion. Later this year, Congress will end the requirement that a reserve of 25 percent in gold be maintained against Federal Reserve notes—the nation's paper money.

They get the people worshipping what they call "capitalism," make it almost a religion, set up money as the idol, and then proceed to get all the money by their devilish, clever manipulations. And once they have possession of the people's idol, money, they also have the power. *People today are slaves of money, and therefore slaves of the Jews.*

卐 卐 卐

No one dares oppose or criticize these Jews because of the terrible power of their purse. If you dare criticize or attack a Jew, then you and your family must starve, for you will find all avenues for the normal procurement of the money you need to survive, slammed shut.

Perhaps even more deadly, and more insidious, is the way the Jews promptly use the vast pools of money they gather in by capitalistic manipulations to *buy the minds* of their victims.

You can only think about what you know. Thus, what you think about is the product of what you hear and see—what you read in the papers, see on TV, hear on the radio, learn in school, see in movies, etc. If somebody were to gain complete control of all the ways you gather your information, letting you hear and see only what they wanted, and keeping other facts from you, they would control your mind, and thus control you.

This is exactly what the chart-forging Jews have done. Take just one of the many methods by which you gain what you hope are the facts all around you: TV. TV is without any doubt, the most powerful medium in the world. A speech by the president, for instance, or newscasters Huntley and Brinkley, reaches more people in half an hour than could be reached by all the pamphleteers since Thomas Paine. This is the era of mass communications. And he who controls TV, controls the minds of Americans.

That which cost $1 in 1941 now costs $22. The current federal spending deficit (expenditures over income) is now about $1.7 trillion per year.

[In 1967,] the US has only three networks: CBS, ABC, and NBC. The president of NBC is Robert Sarnoff, a Russian Jew. The chairman of the board of CBS is William Paley (Palinsky), a Russian Jew. The president of ABC is Leonard Goldenson, a Russian Jew.[3]

Whatever you see and hear on TV is fed to you by one of these three Russian Jews. And so you never see a Negro criminal on a TV crime show, for instance, although 85 percent of all serious crime, by FBI statistics, is committed by Negroes. You especially never see a Jewish criminal, even when it's an integral part of the story, as in Dickens' novel *Oliver Twist*. On the other hand, in one TV show after the other, whenever there is some rotten, depraved character in a scene, nine times out of ten they make him an ignorant, foul-mouthed, tobacco-chewing, scraggly-bearded, cruel Southern, White, Protestant Anglo-Saxon of the lowest and vilest sort. Just observe how many times the villain in a TV show will have a Southern— or a German—accent!

Simultaneously with the Jewish, capitalist, Zionist takeover of TV, they have been buying up newspapers and magazines faster and faster. In New York, the Jewish Sulzbergers own *The New York Times*, the Jewish Schiffs own *The New York Post*, and all but one of the other NY papers. Samuel Newhouse owns *The New Orleans Times-Picayune*; and is the publisher of *The Newark (N.J.) Star-Ledger*, with Philip Hochstein as editor, and Sam Israel among directors. Walter H. Annenberg is the editor and publisher of *The Philadelphia Inquirer* and the president of Triangle Publications, Inc. Paul Block is the publisher of *The Pittsburgh (Pa.) Post-Gazette*, *The Toledo (Oh.) Blade*, and *The Toledo Times*. Philip L. Graham (the son-in-law of the late Eugene Meyer) is the owner of *The Washington Post*. John Cowles, Jr. is the editor of the only two dailies in Minneapolis, *The Minneapolis Tribune* and *The Minneapolis Star*.

To digress a moment, I'd like to mention the tendency of American journalism toward monopolization. In 1890 Chicago had 11 newspapers; today it has only four—*The Chicago Tribune, The Chicago Daily News, The Chicago American,* and *The Sun-Times*. Even in 1934, 82% of all the daily newspapers had a complete monopoly in their communities. And, according to *Editor & Publisher*, 63 chains owned and operated 361 daily newspapers—which made 13% of the total. And these 361 newspapers controlled over 37% of the total daily circulation. In fact, six chains con-

---

[3] As of 2024, there are five major media networks in the US, and all are controlled by Jews—with the possible exception of Fox, given the uncertain identity of the Murdoch family (though, regardless, they are philosemitic and pro-Zionist).

trolled 81 dailies with more than 9,000,000 circulation, which meant over 21% of the country's total.

It's the same with magazines. *Look*, for instance, has the impact of a mind-bomb on our people, as witness the recent hassle over the Kennedy story, which is owned by the Jewish Cowles brothers. The Jewish Zimbalist family has recently taken over the old Benjamin Franklin journal—*The Saturday Evening Post*. Even on the "right" side things, it is again Jews in the lead: David Lawrence, president and editor of *US News & World Report*, is Jewish and so is the Meyer family of *Newsweek*. The publisher of *The New Yorker* is Raoul H. Fleischmann. The chairman of *Parents'* magazine is George J. Hecht.

Book publishing has become ever more and more Jewish, from Simon & Shuster through Alfred A. Knopf, all of them violently leftist.

The theater business has been 100% Jewish, ever since the days of Lee Shubert, Abraham Erlanger, and all the other Broadway Hebrews. Does any American need to be reminded who owns and runs the movie business as a private monopoly? Metro-Goldwyn-Mayer, Warner Bros., etc. In fact, there is no field where the Jews are not seizing more and more control away from the White Christians who fought for and built America.

卐 卐 卐

It starts, again, with the Jewish power of money to get what they want. There is an article in the *New York Times*, 4 October 1964, which reveals the staggering fact that 80% of young Jews are going to college—and therefore will soon be hogging up most of the professional positions in America; while the Gentiles, who can't afford college in such numbers, will have to minister to the royal needs of these wealthy, professional Jews. This is the same thing that happened in Germany, and will lead to the same explosion of hatred against these Jews no matter how it is covered up.

Perhaps you will say that the Jews have a "right" to go to college, even all of them, if they can earn that right. Maybe so, I will agree, that a man has a "right" to whatever he can earn. But, as I have tried hard to prove with documents heretofore, many of the Jews gain their advantage "legally"—but unfairly—by conspiracy, sneaking advance information, rigged "speculation," etc., and not by honest work and production, as most non-Jews have to earn their money.[4] Using this unfairly gained wealth, the

---

[4] For a good comprehensive study of Jewish tricks in the early 20th century, see T. Fritsch, *The Riddle of the Jews' Success* (1922/2023).

Jews proceed to dominate their hosts, and take over the nation which generously permits them to operate in its midst.

And no nation on Earth, except a nation of utter worms, will forever tolerate "guests" taking over their own home, no matter how they do it.

Only about 20% of young Gentiles, at the very most, attend college, while 80% of the Jews are going to the universities. And this means in turn that our professions will become more and more Jewish, while the non-college-educated Gentiles will find themselves serving these clever Jews. How long do these Jews think that 150 million non-Jewish Americans will tolerate serving this arrogant 2% of the population, which boasts that it is sending almost all its young into our professions, to be our lawyers, our doctors, our executives, our politicians, and even our "Christian" ministers—even priests! (While Jews like Ostericher and Shiel have become "priests" and even "bishops" in Irish Catholic communities, how many Irish Rabbis do you know?)

I could go on almost endlessly on this subject. But let the doubting reader convince himself with his own observation, by simply noticing the way everything in the way of information for the mind and hearts of Americans is, or has been, twisted farther and farther to the left and toward disgusting flattery of Jews and Negroes, and less and less mention of the great works of the White race.

卐 卐 卐

In fact, the most shocking example of the way the minds of Americans have been twisted by these Zionist, capitalist Jews who have used their gold to buy control of minds, is what they have done with the facts of race by the use of their money and their publishing power.

Just fifty years ago, you would have been laughed at had you suggested it might be possible to eliminate from the minds of millions all the plain facts of the difference in human races. Every encyclopedia, every book, every professor, every farmer knew the facts. And the facts were (and still are) right before our eyes all over Nature. But the Jews cannot afford to allow this knowledge to exist, lest their victims notice that a racial group of Jews, posing as a religion, is eating them alive, and preparing a total racial attack on them to enslave or murder them.

So they first got some clever Jewish professors into top university slots such as Columbia University, although Columbia is by no means a unique example. Then they got these "anthropology professors" to begin teaching that there was "no such thing" as race! In spite of the madness of this, and the total lack of evidence, the proponents of this insanity began to be touted in Jewish magazines, press, and books as the very height of anthropology.

The first and most important of these pioneer biological liars was a pro-communist Jew named Franz Boas, who regularly sent warm greetings to Comrade Stalin on his birthdays (*Jewish Voice*, January 1942) and whose Red record cannot be denied by any objective observer. This communistic Jew began teaching anthropology at Columbia University in 1896 and dominated the anthropology department there until his death in 1942. Meanwhile, he produced one book after another "proving" that there were no such things as racial differences among men.[5]

The whole of Jewry pitched in with fanatic will to boost their boy. Boas was praised in every Jewish-owned newspaper and periodical and given every academic prize they could invent or promote. At the same time, the Jewish media blasted as "bigots" any critics who dared question their Jewish hero and his arrogant pronouncements against the facts of race. Little by little, the critics were intimidated and silenced, while the public began to see Boas as little short of a god. This Jewish mutual-admiration society made Boas the "acknowledged authority" in social anthropology and ethnology. His students and colleagues at Columbia— Herskovits, Kleinberg, Ashley Montague, Weltfish (all Jews, and all pro-Red)—spread Boas's anti-race lies far and wide, deliberately poisoning the minds of generations of students and professors at American universities and prostituting a great science. It is still going on, now, as you read this.

And every bit of this miracle-in-reverse was done by the Jewish power of gold—gold promoted out of the hands of our people by old-fashioned Jewish usury and manipulation, dressed up in the pinstriped suits and top hats of capitalism.

With their bought-and-paid-for press, TV, etc., the Jews can reward pro-Jewish toadies and they can brutally punish with smears those who dare to attack them, or even just tell the truth. A man of high position, if he attacks the Jews, is subjected to the most vicious and brutal kind of national smears and personal attacks in all the organs of public opinion. Even if he doesn't attack the Jews directly, but only attacks Jewish communism without mentioning Jews (like Joe McCarthy or Robert Welch), the Jews still go after him with all stops pulled out.

---

[5] *Kultur and Rasse* (1914); *Anthropology and Modern Life* (1928); *Aryans and Non-Aryans* (1934); *Race, Language and Culture* (1940); etc.

卐 卐 卐

To fathom the real depth of the villainy of the Zionist "Friends of the Captain," one must see what they have done to the productive economy of the White Man in perspective—at a long view. The White Man everywhere sets up a *productive* economy, in which everybody works, manages, or takes genuine risks in an enterprise in which he has a personal interest. The economy of the Aryan is always *productive enterprise*, regardless of the fancy names that may be applied to various forms of the operation. Each man gives to the society at least as much as he takes out.

The economy of the Jew is *parasitic*. He always takes out more than he puts in. As soon as the Jew got enough strength in our society, he began to twist and pervert this productive enterprise toward a criminal operation—usury—that has been forbidden by law almost everywhere for centuries.

He began to blind our kind of people to the immorality of *getting* without producing or giving in return. He began to de-emphasize the production aspect of the work and management of Aryan economy, and emphasize the getting of *money*, by any and all possible means short of robbery. He removed the focus of Aryan eyes from the *product* to the *profit*. Craftsmanship and pride of product began to disappear as the desperate scramble to get money replaced the time-honored Aryan joy in creation of things of excellence and permanence. Turn out more shoddy products, shine them up to look good on the outside, sell them for as high a price as possible, and then forget it once the money is in the pocket. That was the new approach of the Jew, which has filled America with billions of tons of plastic, shoddy junk.

The next step was to de-emphasize all production, and concentrate on manipulation of money and credit to gather in still more money—without work, without management, invention or creation, and without any real risk. Usually the Jew had fellow tribesmen in the councils of the mighty, whence he got the information that enabled him to "speculate" and reap vast harvests of green cash—with no risk. This harvest of cash without returning to society value for money received is immoral and destructive and no society can survive it forever.

The Jew, Karl Marx, then slyly attacked this immoral process, identified it as the same thing as Aryan free enterprise, cleverly called both the enterprise and the usury "capitalism," and thus got all our people defending Jewish usury as our "sacred way of life"—capitalism.

Pushing the process harder and harder, the Jews managed to split the inventors, owners, and managers from their own workers in the once-productive economy, and produce *class warfare* between the two parts of our economy, while the Jew manipulates both segments to reap more and more cash, all without working or producing. This, in turn, forces more and more of our management people to get down into the gutter with the Jews and compete at the same immoral, cut-throat economic piracy, in order to survive.[6] The Aryan, too, becomes a "capitalist."

Now the capitalist Jew "Friend of the Captain" fans the fires of destruction ever higher by having the other side of Jewry, the communist "Friends of the Crew," lead more and more vicious attacks on the "rich capitalists" by the workers. Let's take a look now at these Jewish "Friends of the Crew."

---

[6] An important point: Jewish economics drives everyone, from producers to consumers, down to "the lowest common denominator," and thus debases the entire society.

CHAPTER 9
FRIENDS OF THE CREW

While the fat Zionist, capitalist Jews are quietly robbing their victims, like the tapeworm, rather painlessly and in silence, there are some Jews who get too arrogant and impatient for this quiet and slow "capitalist" robbery. "To hell with waiting!", exclaim these redoubtable Hebrews to each other. "Why wait? Why stall around patronizing these stupid Goy boobs, when we can just grab what they have? They're too feeble and stupid to resist. There's a quicker and surer way to get our hands on the goods and services of the world without working!"

And so, to the poor people of the world, these Jews howl: "Workers of the world, unite!" "To hell with God! To hell with country! To hell with the power structure! Wealth is ours to take! Dispossess the exploiters! Join us under the Red banner of our leader, Marx, and expropriate the dirty capitalists!" "Up with labor! Down with the exploiting class!"

To return to our example of the ship-of-state—the Red Jew says to the crew: "Why should the captain and officers have the best quarters and boss you around? It's not them, but you and your labor that gets the ship moving. There are only a few of them, and hundreds of us! Let's jump the captain and officers, take over, and divide up their wealth and ease We Jewish friends of the crew will help you. In fact, we'll lead you!"

And thus is born the mutiny of the crew which is called "communism" in its early forms: the uprising of the "crew" of humanity led by Red Jews.

The crew never perceives that (1) it is not just the labor of the crew which moves the ship, but also the management and wisdom of the captain and officers, and (2) even if all the staterooms and possessions of the officers and captain were "shared" with the hundreds in the crew, they would be little better off, because there is not enough to make any difference among hundreds of the crew trying to "share" the few officers' quarters and possessions. More importantly (and the reason for the Jewish promotion of the mutiny) is (3) that once the order of the ship is gone, all hands lose. With the exception of the Jews.

The Jewish Bolshevik ship-wreckers waiting on shore like vultures have easy pickings. A ship without officers and in a state of mutiny piles up on the rocks. And that is precisely the plan of the Jewish "friends of the crew."

In any state where the people cannot be quickly and easily led to the tender mercies of the Bolshevik ship-wreckers, it is necessary to soften them up, to smash their leaders, wreck their order, and set their ship-of-state to drifting aimlessly, without *leadership*. That is the purpose of Bolshevik "class-warfare." It is a diabolical plan, and the most devilish part is the way that the Jews can get both classes working for them.

Abie Cohen, the Jewish-Zionist, capitalist friend of the captain, is up on the bridge offering his advice: "Your crew is getting lazy, Captain, sir. Look at them laying around down there in the sun. Why I heard them saying you are an 'old bastard,' just last night. They will do as little work as possible. You've got to use an iron hand with these people." The captain, believing Cohen to be his good and trusted friend, pours it onto the crew and stirs them up to more and more work.

Meanwhile, Izzy Cohen, the friend of the crew, the "labor leader," and the brother of Abie, is down among the crew: "Look at the Captain up there," whispers Izzy to the crew. "He's taking it easy sipping drinks in the cool breezes, while you are down here in the heat working like dogs for him. He considers you guys lower than pigs. I heard him say so yesterday. He's planning to speed things up and stop your short periods of rest altogether." Sure enough, when the Captain orders all hands to turn to, Izzy says to the crew, "I told you so." The men mutter and curse the Captain.

Back up on the bridge, capitalist Abie is whispering in the Captain's ear: "Look at those lazy, no-good dogs! They're muttering and scowling up at you. Better take security precautions, Captain, sir. They might try something." And so it goes, with the Red Jew labor leader, "friend of the crew" (like David Dubinsky) stirring up the workers to hate the managers, while the Zionist-capitalist Jew "friend of the Captain" (like Barry Goldwater) is stirring up the managers to distrust and oppress his crew.

With this system going full blast, it doesn't take long to develop a full-blown class division, with both vital sections of the "ship's company" hating, distrusting, and working against each other.

The sad, pitiful part of all this is that the Jew agitators are so easily able to get the supposedly intelligent and perceptive managers (the "Captains") to fall for this rotten class division. The wealthy, the managing class, fails to realize that without its workers, it is decapitated and helpless, just as the greatest Captain of a ship, without his crew, is helpless. Yet the Jews consistently succeed in getting most of the wealthy, managing class to think their salvation lies in battling labor, hammer and tongs, to "keep down the demands." The managing class, the wealthy, becomes anti-labor "reactionaries"—hating and fighting their own workers! Salvation for both classes lies not in fighting the other, but getting the Jewish Marxist promoters of class division and hatred off both of their backs.

But since even mentioning Jews is dangerous socially and economically (as the Jew plans it will be), the wealthy managers fight everything else *except* the real tormentors, the Jews, who have agitated the insane and suicidal battle of the crew versus their own Captain, and the Captain versus his own crew.

One has only to watch a man like H. L. Hunt or Robert Welch striving mightily against the "labor unions" and producing exactly the hatred of the working classes planned by the Jews by their anti-labor pronouncements, to feel depressed and discouraged. The crew may be pardoned for not thinking deeply. It's not their business. And they are too hard pressed by sheer work. But for highly intelligent, informed, and capable men at the top levels of industry and business to fall for the reverse warfare of Jews, like Barry Goldwater, is incredible stupidity and criminal negligence.

卐 卐 卐

Only if we can succeed in uniting the whole ship's company once more in honest and businesslike cooperation and mutual respect, with the crew willingly providing the labor and the Captain and officers providing the direction and order, can the whole company get underway again; only then can we quit the bloody "labor-versus-management" strife which is piling us up on the rocks for the Bolshevik ship-wreckers. This is precisely what Adolf Hitler did in Germany, with what he called "National Socialism." And it is also precisely why he is so desperately, hysterically hated not only by the Jewish "friends of the crew" of the Red persuasion, but also by the "capitalist" Captains. The crew has no need of Jewish Red "friends," when it knows it has real friends in the Captain and officers.

Yet in America, the very "captains of industry" who have the most to gain by winning back their crew from the Jewish labor agitators, are the very men who endlessly join and support the hopelessly reactionary, anti-labor Birch Society, etc., thus driving the millions of working men further into the waiting arms of the Jewish "friends of the crew!"

Hitler saw this and provided a program of national unity, which stressed his friendship with and love of the workingman. To do this, he called his program National Socialist. And it worked! It re-united the captains of industry and the labor crew. There was no dispossession of one side or the other, as any German who lived through the great days in Germany can tell you. The Krupps still had their factories, and the workers were still freer and happier than they had ever been, sharing, as they did, in the benefits of production.

So the sly Jews, observing this, have worked tirelessly to convince the upper classes in America that Hitler's "socialism" is the "same thing" as "communism"! The result of this is simply to help the Jews split the managers and upper classes even further and further from their own people, the workers.

The working people of America want "social security;" they want Medicare; they want a paternalistic and welfare-conscious government. This is a fact.

The endless blasting of "socialism" in the conservative movement is planted by the Jews—men like George Sokolsky, who started much of it— to accomplish precisely this crazy decapitation of the American economy, to cut off the management "head" of the people from the working "body" and make both parts hate each other.

There is no doubt but that Marxist socialism, which destroys all private property and productive enterprise, and turns all property and affairs over to criminals, most Jews, is sure death for any society. But the kind of mutual-aid society found among our kind of people everywhere, especially in pioneer times, is the very essence of the kind of "social" love of each other among the whole people which produced America—along with the very excellent institutions of private property and productive free enterprise.

The masses of working people—our people, good people, your people—rightly want to have some help when the barn burns down, when their kids are deathly sick, when they are old and helpless and the banks have failed and destroyed their savings, etc. If the elite of our society—the managers, owners, wealthy people and thinkers—can't see this, and continue to fall for the sweet-talk of the Zionist "friends of the Captain" that the crew may be damned, then the "friends of the crew," with their sweet talk of help and solicitous care of the crew, will succeed with their damnable Red mutiny. The people want what the Jews and their demagogues promise.

Nor is this an unadulterated evil. The shortsighted, reactionary "conservatives" are forever harking back to the self-sufficient days of pioneering, individualistic America, pretending to themselves that there was no "socialism" in those golden days. However, the facts are that the very survival and growth of this great nation was dependent, not on dog-eat-dog, the-hell-with-you naked battling for individual benefit, but on a tremendous spirit of cooperation in the face of common danger.

When a man's barn burned down, his neighbors didn't sneer that he was "improvident" and didn't have "insurance." They all came over, pitched in, not for profit, but for the social goal of helping each other, and built him a brand new barn—free. That's not welfare or stifling of enterprise. It is a simple recognition that there are some economic calamities beyond the power of a prudent and hard-working man to survive, and when these things strike, it is to the benefit of society to get together, not for profit, but to help each other.

There are dozens of "socialistic" operations in any decent nation, operations not for profit, but for the benefit of all. Without the fire department, society would be in constant peril. And who would want a commercial fire department, where the owner might despise you and refuse to put out your fire, or dawdle on the way until you were burned out?

It is to the benefit of society to have a happy, satisfied, and healthy working population of ordinary folks. When naked "capitalism" forgets this, which it does, and says "let the common man look out for himself" (as much of the short-sighted reactionary class does), it cuts itself off from the mass support of its own people, as does the Birch Society, and most of the rest of the "conservative" movement, which is why the conservative movement is so pitifully powerless. To fly in the face of this fact and insists that we can survive the onslaught of the Red "friends of the crew" (who are preaching all these things) by convincing the people they don't want welfare, social security, Medicare, free college, etc., is to act in the manner of the madman.

To stop the devilish division of our people by Jewish, Marxist class-warfare, to prevent a total, Red "mutiny" of the crew such as they promoted in Russia, our top managers and upper classes must come to see that they must find a way to regain the leadership of their own masses—their crew—rather than continue driving them away as they do with their reactionary constant talk of more profits, less taxes, elimination of welfare, etc.

We can't re-unite the officers of the ship with the crew and throw the Jewish agitators overboard until we first win the crew! And you can't win the crew promising to "cut rations" and increase work!

The Jews seek to keep labor and management divided by their clever provocation of workers against the wealthy and vice versa. To foil them, the managers, the wealthy (*not* the people), are going to have to make the first move. And the first move is not more reactionism, but a program of honest and workable social care by the captain for his crew. That's one of the first things they taught me as a Naval Officer. Look out for the welfare of your men, and they'll forever be loyal to you. That's true.

卐 卐 卐

I shall write more later of what must be done to stop this suicidal division of our people by Jewish class-warfare. To understand the Jew, to "empathize" one's way into his Jewish tapeworm soul, it is only necessary to imagine the contempt he holds for the non-Jew, and the image he holds of the inevitable and just triumph of his Jewish race as the "Chosen People."

The quickest way to understand his attitude toward us is to imagine how you would feel if you found yourself alone among a nation of children of five or six, all of them ten feet tall and equipped with guns. You would patronize them, act as though you sympathized with their horse-play, even when you got knocked around a bit—and above all you would try never to let them suspect for one second that you were scheming to get them under control somehow or other.

When one reads enough Jewish literature written for Jews, it does not take long to learn that these parasites have rationalized their natures until they see themselves as a "mature" and "intelligent" race, while they see us as a mob of crazy, violent, damned-fool brutes who enjoy, as games, periodic sessions of slaughter called "wars"; while the sophisticated Jews are horrified of violence—a fear they rationalize as a "love of peace."

Following are quotes from *You Gentiles* (1924), written by Zionist leader Maurice Samuel:

> We Jews, we, the destroyers, will remain the destroyers forever. Nothing that you will do will meet our needs and demands. We will forever destroy because we need a world of our own, a God-world, which it is not in your nature to build. Beyond all temporary alliances with this or that faction lies the ultimate split in nature and destiny, the enmity between the Game and God. (p. 155, ch. 9)
>
> Years of observation and thought have given increasing strength to the belief that we Jews stand apart from you gentiles, that a primal quality breaks the humanity I know into two distinct parts; that this quality is a fundamental, and that all differences among you gentiles are trivialities compared with that which divides all of you from us. (p. 12, ch. 1)
>
> Yet the cleavage is there, abysmal and undeniable. In the main, we are forever distinct. Ours is one life yours is another. (p. 21)

You gentiles are essentially polytheists and to some extent idol worshippers. We Jews are essentially monotheists. ... Monotheism is a desperate and overwhelming creed. It can be the expression of none but the most serious natures. It is a fundamental creed that engulfs individual and mass in an unfathomable sea of unity. In monotheism there is no room left for individual prides and distinctions, no room for joyful assertiveness. Monotheism means infinite absolutism, the crushing triumph of the One, the crushing annihilation of the ones. (p. 65, ch. 3)

A Jew is a Jew in everything, not merely in prayers and in synagogue ... Our Jewishness is not a creed—it is ourself, our totality. (pp. 72-73)

Because I am Jewish, I look with ultimate aversion on the world which finds supreme and ideal expression in Plato's *Republic*. And though I may repeat that this is no question of right and wrong in these two worlds, yours and ours, I cannot but feel profoundly and vehemently that ours is the way and the life. (p. 87, ch. 4)

To the Jew, naked loyalty is an incomprehensible, a bewildering thing. That men should be called upon to keep a quantity of this virtue on constant tap, to be applied on instruction to this or that relationship, is not merely irrational to us: it is beyond the apprehension of our intelligence. (p. 96, ch. 5)

In our life, the Jewish life, loyalty is unknown. (p. 103)

We are unquestionably an alien spirit in your colleges. For your colleges are most coherent mouthpieces of your morality: and that morality is not ours. (p. 104)

Whether we begin with the Bible and take the sum total of our work down to Karl Marx, or confine ourselves to a single country and generation (America today, for instance—with Untermeyer, Lewisohn, Frank, Hecht) we will find the same appeal to fundamentals, the same passionate rejection of your sport world and its sport morality, the same ultimate seriousness, the same inability to be merely playful, merely romantic, merely lyrical. (p. 183, ch. 11)

Thus we see that the Jews have convinced themselves that the world has for centuries been in the hands of us wild, crazy kids—ten feet tall, armed and deadly-dangerous when angry and "berserker," as the Vikings called the war-like rage of our race of people. They imagine that unless they, the "mature" race, can succeed in taking control away from us, we crazy Aryan "kids" will kill each other and all of them too, in one final all-out atomic blow-up.

卐 卐 卐

Believing this for centuries and centuries, the Jews have developed an un-deniably brilliant plan for seizing control of the world from us idiot "kids." Let me introduce the reader to the Jewish blueprint for all that has gone before the promotion of degeneracy, anarchy, class warfare, economic pi-racy, the whole works.

In 1906, the secret Jewish blueprint for all this hell let loose upon the world was placed in the British Museum in London. It is called *The Protocols of the Learned Elders of Zion*, published in Russia in 1905, and consists of 24 protocols with 293 numbered paragraphs. The term "goyim," meaning Gentile or non-Jew, is used throughout the *Protocols*. "The Political" means the entire machinery of politics. I cannot commend it too highly to the reader, in its entirety.[1]

The Jews howl bitterly that these documents are a "forgery." But this is as irrelevant as claiming that a man did not commit a murder with one particular knife—but another knife altogether. It matters not which knife was used. The fact is that someone did a murder. The *Protocols*, long be-fore World War I or II, set forth with horrible clarity exactly what some group would bring about in the way of world wars, inflations, depressions, and moral subversions—how they would do it, and to whom they would do it.

And 60 years later, not one word has failed of fulfillment exactly as set forth in the *Protocols*. If they are "forged," then it was done by a genius that knew exactly what the Jews of the world would do for 60 years, with not partial, but perfect accuracy. The protocols alone, of all knowledge on this Earth, give one the power to predict historical events successfully, as I have been able to do since studying them. And a theory that enables scien-tific, calculated prediction is not the mark of a fraud, but always the mark of a realistic theory.

---

[1] A new edition of the Protocols has been published in 2023; see *Protocols of the Elders of Zion: The Definitive English Edition* (T. Dalton, ed.; Clemens & Blair). The following quotations are taken from this edition.

Henry Ford said of the *Protocols*, 35 years ago, that they were being ruthlessly fulfilled, which was enough proof for him of their genuineness. Adolf Hitler ten years later said the same thing. And any man who takes the trouble to read these astounding documents will find the same thing. If they were not written by a Jew, they were written with devilish accuracy about the Jews. They enable humanity, for the first time, to understand what, before, seemed impossible chaos. All the chaos, the mad "art," the communism, the moral filth, the control of the press and entertainment, the development of World Wars, the insane setting of labor against capital and vice versa—all these things become calculated elements of a steadily progressing plan by a nation, or race, which masquerades throughout the world as a "religion" in order to accomplish this awful work of destruction under the cover of "religious tolerance."

Here are some sample quotes from these astounding documents, which, in any case, were deposited in the British Museum before 1900, so that their predictions of things like world wars, etc., must be rated as either very accurate, or else as the most miraculous series of coincidences in history:

Protocol I

What has thus far restrained the wild beasts that we call men? What has influenced them until now? In the early stages of social life, they submitted to brute and blind force; afterwards, to the law, which is the same force in disguised form. I therefore deduce from this that, according to the laws of nature, might makes right.

Political freedom is not a fact but an idea. One must know how to employ this idea when it becomes necessary to attract the masses to one's party, if the party plans to crush those in power. This task becomes easier if the ruler himself has embraced the idea of freedom, of 'liberalism,' and for the sake of this idea, yields some of his power.

It is precisely here that our theory triumphs: the relinquished aspects of power are, according to the laws of nature, immediately seized by a new hand because the blind force of the people cannot remain without a leader even for one day; and the new power merely replaces the old, weakened by liberalism.

*****

In our day, the power of gold has replaced liberal rulers. There was a time when faith ruled. But today, the idea of freedom cannot be realized because no one knows how to make reasonable use of it. Give the people self-government for a short time and it will become corrupted. From that very moment, conflict emerges and soon develops into social struggles; these will eventually set the state aflame, reducing its authority to ashes. Whether the state is exhausted by internal strife or whether civil war delivers it into the hands of its enemies, either way, the state is hopelessly lost; it is in our power. The despotism of capital, which is entirely in our hands, is the only lifeline for the state, and so it grasps it, even against its will, simply to avoid falling into an abyss. ...

Our right lies in might. In any case, the word 'right' is an abstract idea, not amenable to proof. This word means nothing more than: 'Give me what I want, so that I can prove that I'm stronger than you.'

Where does right begin? Where does it end? In a state with a poorly organized government and where the laws are weak, and where the ruler has lost his dignity thanks to liberalism, I find a new right: namely, the right of might to destroy all existing order and institutions, to lay hands on the law, to alter all institutions, and to become the ruler of those who have voluntarily and liberally renounced the rights to their own power.

Given the present instability of all authority, our power will be more unassailable than any other because it will be invisible until it is so well-rooted that no cunning can undermine it. ...

The people left to themselves will be ruined by party strife caused by greed for power and honors, which must result in chaos and disorder. Is it possible for the masses to direct the national affairs without rivalry, and without interjecting personal interests? Are they capable of protecting themselves against external enemies? No, this is impossible, since any plan divided into as many parts as there are individuals in a mob loses its unity, and consequently, becomes incomprehensible and unworkable.

Only an autocrat can outline clear and visionary plans that can activate all the parts of the mechanism of the government machinery in an orderly way. Therefore, a government that most efficiently benefits a country must be concentrated in the hands of one responsible person. Civilization cannot exist without absolute despotism, because government is conducted not by the masses but by their leader, whoever he may be.

A barbarous crowd shows its barbarism on every occasion. The moment that the mob grasps liberty in its hands, it quickly devolves to virtual anarchy, which is in itself the height of barbarism.

Look at those beasts, steeped in alcohol, stupefied by wine—such is the result of 'freedom.' Surely we cannot allow our own people to come to this. The Goy Christians are stupefied by alcohol; their youth are driven crazy by years of debauchery and vice, instigated by our agents—tutors, valets, governesses in rich houses, by clerks, and so forth, and by our women in their places of pleasure. Among the latter I include the so-called "society women"—their voluntary followers in vice and luxury.

*****

Our motto is 'Power and Hypocrisy.' Only power can conquer in politics, especially if it is concealed in the talents that are necessary for statesmen. Violence must be the principle; hypocrisy and cunning must be the rule of those governments that do not wish to lay down their crowns at the feet of some new power. This evil is the sole means of attaining the good. For this reason, we must not hesitate at bribery, fraud, and treason when these can help us to reach our end. In politics, it is necessary to seize the property of others without hesitation if, in so doing, we attain submission and power.

Our government, following the line of peaceful conquest, has the right to substitute unobtrusive and efficient executions in place of the horrors of war; these things are necessary to maintain a terror that induces blind submission. A just but inexorable strictness is the greatest factor of governmental power. We must follow a program of violence and hypocrisy, not only for the sake of profit, but also as a duty and for the sake of victory.

Our principles are as powerful as the means by which we put them into effect. That is why, not only by these very means, but by the severity of our doctrines shall we triumph and enslave all governments under our super-government.

*****

Even in olden times, we shouted the words "liberty, equality, and fraternity" among the people. These words have been repeated many times by unconscious parrots, which, flocking from all sides to the bait, have ruined the prosperity of the world and true individual freedom, formerly so well protected from the pressure of the mob. The supposedly clever and intelligent Goyim did not grasp the symbolism of the uttered words; they did not notice the contradiction in the meaning and the connection between them; they did not notice that there is no 'equality' in nature; that there can be no 'liberty,' since nature herself has established inequality of mind, character, and ability, as well as complete subjection to her laws. They did not reason that the power of the mob is blind; that the upstarts selected for government are just as blind in politics as is the mob itself, whereas the initiated man, even though a fool, is capable of ruling, while the uninitiated, even if a genius, will understand nothing of politics. All this has been overlooked by the Goyim.

Meanwhile, monarchic government has been based upon this, that the father passes along a knowledge of the course of political evolution to his son, so that no one except the members of the dynasty could possess this knowledge, and no one could disclose the secrets to the governed people. Over time, the meaning of the dynastic transmission of a true understanding of politics has been lost, thus contributing to the success of our cause.

In all parts of the world, the words "liberty, equality, and fraternity" have brought whole legions into our ranks through our blind agents, carrying our banners with delight. Meanwhile, these words were maggots that ruined Goy prosperity, everywhere destroying peace, calm, and solidarity, undermining all the foundations of their states. In what follows, you will see that this aided our triumph because it also gave us, among other things, the opportunity to grasp the trump card—the abolition of royal privileges. This was the very essence of the aristocracy of the Goyim, and it was their only protection against us.

On the ruins of natural and hereditary aristocracy, we built an aristocracy of our intellectual class—a monied aristocracy. We have established this new aristocracy on the basis of wealth, which is dependent upon us, and also upon science, which is promoted by our wise men.

Our triumph was also made easier because, through our connections with people who were indispensable to us, we always played upon the most susceptible parts of the human mind—namely, greed and the insatiable selfish desires of man. Each of these human weaknesses, taken separately, is capable of killing initiative and of placing the will of the people at the disposal of he who would deprive them of their own initiative.

The abstract concept of 'liberty' offered the opportunity for convincing the masses that government is nothing but a manager representing the owner of the country, namely, the people; and that this manager can be discarded like a pair of worn-out gloves. The fact that the representatives of the nation can be replaced, delivers them into our power and practically places their appointment in our hands.

Protocol II

It is necessary for us that, whenever possible, wars should bring no territorial advantages; this will shift war to an economic basis and force nations to realize the strength of our predominance. Such a situation will put both sides at the mercy of our million-eyed international agency, which will be unhampered by any frontiers. Then our international rights will do away with national rights, in a limited sense, and will rule the peoples in the same way that individual governments rule their subjects

The administrators chosen by us from among the people in accordance with their capacity for servility will be inexperienced in the art of government; consequently, they will easily become pawns in our game, in the hands of our scientists and wise counselors, who are specialists trained from early childhood for governing the world. ...

There is one great force in the hands of modern states that arouses thought movements among the people: the press. The press' role is to indicate necessary demands, to register complaints of the people, and to express and promote dissatisfaction. The triumph of free speech is incarnated in the press; but governments have been unable to profit by this power, and it has fallen into our hands. Through it, we have attained influence, while remaining in the background. Thanks to the press, we have gathered gold in our hands, although it cost us rivers of blood and tears. It cost us the sacrifice of many of our own people. But every sacrifice on our part is worth a thousand Goyim before God.

Protocol III

Today I can tell you that our goal is close at hand. Only a small distance remains, and the cycle of the Symbolic Serpent—the symbol of our people—will be complete. When this circle is completed, then all the European states will be enclosed in it, as in unbreakable chains.

The modern constitutional scales will soon tip, for we have set them inaccurately, thus ensuring an unsteady balance that will wear out their holder. The Goyim thought it was strong enough and hoped that the scales would regain their equilibrium, but the holder—the ruler—is screened from the people by his representatives, who fritter away their time with their uncontrolled and irresponsible authority. Their power, moreover, has been built upon terrorism spread through the halls of government.

Unable to reach the hearts of their people, the rulers cannot draw strength from them in order to fend off the usurpers of power. The visible power of royalty and the blind power of the masses, separated by us, have both lost significance—for, thus separated, they are as helpless as a blind man without a stick.

To induce the lovers of authority to abuse their power, we have placed all forces in opposition to each other, having developed their liberal tendencies towards independence. We have encouraged every undertaking in this direction; we have placed formidable weapons in the hands of all parties, and made power the goal of every ambition. We turned governments into arenas in which party wars are fought out. Soon, chaos and bankruptcy will appear everywhere.

Unrestrained babblers have converted parliamentary sessions and bureaucratic meetings into oratorical contests. Daring journalists and impudent scribblers make daily attacks on the administrative personnel. The abuse of power is definitely preparing the downfall of all institutions, and everything will be overturned by the blows of the infuriated mobs. ...

Under our guidance, the people have exterminated the aristocracy that was their natural protector and guardian; the aristocracy's well-being was inseparable from that of the people. Now, however, with the destruction of this aristocracy, the masses have fallen under the power of profiteers and cunning upstarts, who have set upon the workers as a merciless burden. We will present ourselves as saviors of the workers from this oppression when we suggest that they enter our army of socialists, anarchists, and communists, to whom we always extend our help, under the principle of brotherhood demanded by the humanitarianism of our socialistic masonry. The aristocracy benefited by the peoples' labor and was naturally interested that the workers should be well fed, healthy, and strong.

We, on the contrary, are concerned with the opposite—with the degeneration of the Goyim. Our power lies in the chronic malnutrition and weakness of the worker, because through this he falls under our power and is unable to find either strength or energy to combat it. Hunger gives capital a greater power over the worker than any sovereign legal authority under an aristocracy. Through misery, jealousy, and hatred, we manipulate the mob and crush those who stand in our way. When the time comes for our universal ruler to be crowned, the same hands will sweep away everything that stands in our way.

The Goyim are no longer able to think without our scientific advice. Consequently, they do not see the imperative of upholding that which we will sustain by all means when our kingdom is established: namely, the teaching in schools of the only true science, the first of all sciences—*the science of human life*, of social existence, which requires the division of labor and, consequently, the separation of people into classes and castes. It is necessary for all to know that true equality cannot exist, owing to the different nature of various kinds of work; that one whose actions compromise an entire class cannot have the same legal responsibility as one whose actions affect only himself.

The correct social science—the secrets of which we do not admit to the Goyim—would demonstrate to all that occupation and labor must be differentiated so as not to cause suffering by the discrepancy between education and work. The study of this science will lead the masses to a voluntary submission to authorities and to the governmental system. Whereas, under the present state of science, and due to our active guidance, the people, in their ignorance, blindly believing the printed word, and owing to the misconceptions that have been fostered by us, feel a hatred towards all classes that they consider superior to themselves, since they do not understand the importance of each class.

This hatred will be still more accentuated by an economic crisis, which will stop financial transactions and all industrial life. Having organized a general economic crisis by all possible underhanded means, and with the help of the gold that is all in our hands, we will throw great crowds of workmen into the street, simultaneously, in all nations. These simple-minded and ignorant masses will gladly shed the blood of those of whom they have hated since childhood and whose property they will then be able to loot. ...

As things stand, as an international force, we are invulnerable; if we are attacked by one state, we are supported by others. The unlimited baseness of the Goyim aid our independence; they kneel before power, are pitiless toward the weak, merciless when dealing with faults, and patient to the point of martyrdom when suffering the violence of an outrageous despotism. At the hands of their present dictators, premiers, and ministers, they endure great abuses—for the smallest of which they would have, in times past, beheaded 20 kings. ...

The word 'liberty' brings all society into conflict with all authority, whether it be natural or divine. This is why, at the moment of our enthronement, we shall strike this word from the dictionary as being the symbol of a brute power that turns the masses into bloodthirsty beasts. It is true, however, that these beasts will sleep as soon as they have tasted blood, and then it is easy to shackle them; but if they don't get their blood, they will not sleep but rather struggle and fight.

Protocol IV

In theory, liberty could be harmless and remain on the state program without detriment to the well-being of the people, but only if it retained the ideas of a belief in God and human fraternity, and was freed from the conception of equality, for such an idea is contradicted by the laws of nature that establish subordination. With such a religious faith, the people would be governed by the guardians of the parish and would thrive quietly and obediently under the guidance of their spiritual leader, accepting God's dispensation on Earth. It is for this reason that we must undermine faith, tearing the very principles of God and soul from the minds of the Goyim, and substituting mathematical formulas and material needs.

In order to ensure that the Goy minds have no time to think and notice things, it is necessary to occupy them with industry and commerce. Thus, all nations will seek their own profit, and while engaged in the struggle, they will not notice their common enemy.

But to guarantee that liberty should finally undermine and ruin the Goy's society, it is necessary to put industry on a basis of speculation. The result of this will be that the wealth of the land obtained by production will not remain in Goy hands but will be directed towards speculation; that is, it will come to us.

The intense struggle for supremacy and the continuous economic speculations will create—and have already created—demoralized, selfish, and heartless societies. These societies will have complete disgust for high politics and religion. Their only guide will be a love of gold, for which they will have a real cult because of the material delights that it can supply. At this stage, the lower-class Goyim—not for the sake of doing good, nor even for the sake of wealth, but solely because of their hatred towards the privileged—will join us in the struggle against our competitors for power: the privileged and intelligent Goyim.

Protocol V

Temporarily, a world coalition of the Goyim would be able to hold us in check, but we are insured against this by roots of dissension so deep among them that they cannot now be extracted. We have set at odds the personal and national interests of the Goyim; we have incited religious and race hatred, nurtured by us in their hearts for 20 centuries.[2] Due to all this, no state will obtain aid from any side because each nation will think that a coalition against us will be disadvantageous to it. We are too powerful—we must be taken into account. No country can reach even an insignificant private understanding without our being secret parties to it. ...

At all times, both peoples and individuals have mistaken words for deeds, as they are satisfied with the visible, rarely noticing whether the promise is performed in social life. Therefore, we will organize ostensible institutions that will eloquently prove their good work in the direction of "progress." We will appropriate to ourselves the liberal aspect of all parties, of all shades of opinion, and we will provide our orators with the same aspect, and they will talk so much that they will exhaust the people by their speeches and cause them to turn away from orators in disgust.

To control public opinion, it is necessary to perplex it by the expression of numerous contradictory opinions until the Goyim become lost in the labyrinth, and come to believe that it is best to have no opinion at all on political questions. Such questions are not intended to be understood by the people, since only the ruler knows them. This is the first secret.

---

[2] Jews have indeed been known for race-hatred of others, and have long been accused of misanthropy—a hatred of the (non-Jewish) human race. This has been documented as far back as 300 BC; see the book *Eternal Strangers* (T. Dalton, 2020).

The second secret necessary for the success of governing consists in multiplying popular failings, habits, passions, and conventional laws to such a degree that no one will be able to disentangle himself in the chaos; consequently, people will cease to understand each other. This measure would help us to sow dissension within all parties, to disintegrate all those collective forces that still seek to remain independent, and to discourage all individual initiative that might hamper our work in any way.

There is nothing more dangerous than individual initiative. If it has even a touch of genius, it can accomplish more than a million people among whom we have sown dissensions. We must direct the education of the Goy societies so that their arms will drop hopelessly at their side whenever they face any task where initiative is required. The intensity of action resulting from individual freedom of action dissipates its force when it encounters another person's freedom. This strikes a heavy blow against morale, yielding disappointments and failures.

We will so exhaust the Goyim by all this that we will force them to offer us global power, which will conveniently enable us to absorb all governmental forces of the world and thus to form a super-government. In lieu of modern rulers, we will place a monstrosity—a monstrosity called the Super-Governmental Administration. Its hands will be stretched out like pincers in every direction, so that this colossal organization cannot fail to conquer all peoples.

Protocol VI

We will soon begin to establish great monopolies—reservoirs of huge wealth, upon which even the large fortunes of the Goyim will be so dependent that they will sink, together with the credibility of the government, on the day following political catastrophe.

Protocol VII

We must create unrest, dissension, and hatred throughout Europe, as well as on other continents. This gives us a two-fold advantage: First, we will hold all countries under our influence, since they will realize that we have the power to create disorder or to restore order, as we wish. All countries will look to us to provide the necessary pressure, as required. Second, through various intrigues, we will entangle all governmental bodies with our strings, by means of politics, economic treaties, or financial obligations.

To attain these ends, we will worm our way into meetings and negotiations, armed with cunning; but in so-called "official language" we will assume the opposite tactics of seeming honest and reasonable. In this way, the peoples and the governments of the Goyim, taught by us to consider only superficial impressions, will look upon us as benefactors and saviors of mankind.

We must be able to overcome all opposition by provoking a war with the neighbors of any country that dares to oppose us. Should, however, those neighbors, in turn, decide to unite against us, we must respond by creating a world war.[3]

Protocol VIII

Meanwhile, as it is not yet safe to give the responsible government posts directly to our brother Jews, we will give them to people whose record and whose character are so terrible that there is a vast gulf between them and the people. Such leaders would face nothing but condemnation and imprisonment, should they disobey our orders. This fact will force them to protect our interests, to their dying day.

This diabolical plan has been *working*, and has predicted events such as World Wars, for more than 60 years. Regardless of its authenticity, it is a valuable insight into what is going on, and a guide to what *will* happen. Henry Ford published these amazing Jewish plans in the 1920s and said "They fit!" That was 45 years ago. They *still* fit, today. The reader who insists on joining the Jews in claiming "forgery" will still be unable to discredit the astounding correlation between what the *Protocols* plan and predict, and what has been actually happening.

---

[3] Again, this is a remarkable anticipation, in 1905, of the coming two World Wars.

One of the basic elements of the Jewish scheme for the secret conquering of all other peoples is the use of inferior humanity as the Jewish "troops"—as set forth in the *Protocols*. In the next chapter, we shall examine this menace, which may become a deadly "genie" more dangerous than the Jewish meddlers who have let it out of the bottle.

CHAPTER 10
THE BLACK PLAGUE

In the Congressional Record, published by the United States Government Printing Office, Proceedings of the House, 7 June 1957, page 8559, you will find the documentation of the communist plan for using the Negroes to achieve a communist victory in America. In column one, you will find the following:

> Israel Cohen, a leading communist in England, in his *A Racial Program for the Twentieth Century*, wrote:
> "We must realize that our Party's most powerful weapon is racial tension. By propounding into the consciousness of the dark races that for centuries they have been oppressed by the whites, we can mould them to the program of the communist Party. In America, we will aim for subtle victory. While inflaming the Negro minority against the whites, we will instill into the whites a guilt complex for their exploitation of the Negroes. We will aid the Negroes to rise to prominence in every walk of life, in the professions and in the world of sports and entertainment. With this prestige, the Negro will be able to intermarry with the whites and begin a process which will deliver America into our hands."

There you have the Jewish-communist program in a nutshell—the *use* of the backward, childish, and savage Negro race to destroy the White Race, which stands between the Jews and their mad goal of world domination from Israel.

To make a mutiny—which is what communism is—you need mobs of raging and savage people. The Jews, comprising only a fraction of one percent of the world's people, are too few to produce their own mobs, and they are too un-fond of physical violence to provide any large amount of their own "muscle." They need vast numbers of peanut-brained, violent but robot-like "troops." The Negro race is perfect for the needs of the Jews in fomenting their mutiny.

It may be good and opportune that this civil rights question has come on for discussion at the present time. It may be that the publicity given the issues and the nationwide interest that has developed through the attempt of certain minority and political influences to push through Congress such monstrous proposals brought forward by its advocates, will arouse the people from coast to coast, and from the North to the South, to the dangers with which they are confronted and cause them to rise up in their might while there is yet time and defend their dearest possession, the Constitution of the United States of America.

This civil-rights business is all according to a studied and well-defined plan. It may be news to some of you, but the course of the advocates of this legislation was carefully planned and outlined more than 45 years ago. Israel Cohen, a leading Communist in England, in his A Racial Program for the 20th Century, wrote, in 1912, the following:

We must realize that our party's most powerful weapon is racial tension. By propounding into the consciousness of the dark races that for centuries they have been oppressed by the whites, we can mould them to the program of the Communist Party. In America we will aim for subtle victory. While inflaming the Negro minority against the whites, we will endeavor to instill in the whites a guilt complex for their exploitation of the Negroes. We will aid the Negroes to rise in prominence in every walk of life, in the professions and in the world of sports and entertainment. With this prestige, the Negro will be able to intermarry with the whites and begin a process which will deliver America to our cause.

What truer prophecy could there have been 40 years ago of what we now see taking place in America, than that made by Israel Cohen? The plan was outlined to perfection and is being carried out by politicians who have fallen into the trap. Many thousands in America today who are in no sense Communists are helping to carry out the Communist plan laid down by their faithful thinker, Israel Cohen. Truly, vigilance is the price of liberty.

law put into the Constitution by the Founding Fathers to protect the liberties of the people.

I would seriously direct your attention to the right of trial by jury. No people can remain free and happy without it. This legislation plans to bypass and, by indirection, to rob the people of this right through scheme and trickery. It would substitute Federal district judges—some 200 of them—to take the place of juries. These, with all the faults, frailties, prejudices, and weaknesses common to human nature, armed with the power of injunction to enforce their decrees, with the legal force of the Attorney General to prosecute in the name of the United States, would proceed against the helpless citizen as he is selected by the Attorney General to be placed upon the sacrificial altar to satisfy some disgruntled person who might claim that he had been deprived of a civil right. Then by injunction such selected person would be summarily hurried off to prison without his constitutional right to trial by jury being exercised. He would not, as is the law in all criminal cases, be "presumed innocent until proven guilty beyond every reasonable doubt." He would be subjected by his Government, on being selected by the Attorney General, to this cruel and oppressive procedure. This is not America. Such legislation, if enacted and attempted to be enforced, I fear, would create a long period of unusual turmoil and oppression.

There was a period in England about 1685 known as the "Bloody Assizes" when a Judge Jeffries, and others, who, because of their cruelties, arrogance, and oppressive procedures against the people, are looked upon with ignominy to this day. We are told by history that upward of 300 persons were executed after short trials; that very many were whipped and imprisoned and fined; nearly 1,000 were sent to America to the plantations as slaves. History tells us that through the ages where justice is attempted to be administered in criminal or quasi-criminal matters without the right of trial by jury that oppression is the ultimate re-

was exempted from arbitrary arrest and detention; and the second was that every person accused of crime or misdemeanor should be entitled to a trial by his peers in accordance with the law of the land."

This was the first firm foothold the people obtained against the autocratic power of the kings. The right of trial by jury has gone through many struggles with despots and those who are unwilling to risk juries doing the things the ruling political class wants done. The right of trial by jury is a shield, and the only safeguard and guaranty of the people against oppression. Should this right be removed from the people, for whatever excuse offered, the keystone to the arch of their liberties is taken away and the superstructure of their freedom would surely crumble. Federal courts, with injunctive power to enforce their decrees was never the plan of the framers of the Constitution for the Government of America.

I submit that this bill should be defeated; and, to say the least, it should not pass without fully safeguarding the rights of our citizens by assuring them of a trial by jury.

Mr. ASHMORE. Mr. Chairman, I yield 15 minutes to the gentleman from Alabama [Mr. HUDDLESTON].

Mr. HUDDLESTON. Mr. Chairman, at the proper time, I intend to offer an amendment to this bill to strike out section 121 of part III. This is a matter of great concern not only to the people of my district, but to our citizens all over the country.

I am opposed to all of the provisions of H. R. 6127. I am opposed to the entire bill for the reasons which have been so ably stated by its opponents in the course of this debate. Of particular concern to me, however, is section 121 of part III of this bill. This section purports to empower the Attorney General to institute civil actions for redress or injunctive relief in cases in which it is alleged that persons have engaged or there are reasonable grounds to believe that persons are about to engage in actions or practices in violation of the civil rights of other individuals

But before the blacks can do the Jews and Marxists any good, they must first be placed in position and conditioned. In Africa (and in the rural South) the Blacks have neither the means, the spirit, nor the tools to be of service to the Jewish schemers. They are so closely akin to unthinking animals, and they are so childishly satisfied and lethargic, that there is no hope of making any successful mutiny with them. Voodoo, chicken-stealing, watermelon, razor-waving, dusky-sex, singing and dancing, and other primitive pastimes keep the rural and forest Negro sufficiently satisfied (or at least unthinking about his lot) so that it is quite impossible to turn any significant number of such black men into a raging mob with any staying power for a revolution.

To make a revolutionary animal of the Negro, you must first force him into a situation where he loses his normal ability to enjoy his primitive releases and pleasures, teach him to know and enjoy the luxurious pleasures and vices of urban civilization (such as heroin and White women), teach him that he has a right to those pleasures, force him into competition with White men for those pleasures—and then, when he fails, whisper to him that he is not really failing in that competition, but that "White exploiters" are keeping him down!

The millions of primitive African blacks brought into our big cities as voting cattle by Franklin D. Roosevelt during World War II, and by all liberal leaders since then, are incapable of competing with the White Man. They can't make it in the schools; they can't make it in complex jobs; they can't make it in intellectual competition. The fact that a few mixed bloods can and do make it does not disprove the fact that the mass of Negroes is congenitally incompetent and inferior—any more than the fact that some chimpanzees can be taught to ride bicycles disproves the fact that chimpanzees aren't even as smart as the blacks.

Millions and millions of these primitive misfits and incompetents are forced into urban, crowded living conditions, forced to compete with intelligent White people, forced to give up their natural pleasures in voodoo, uninhibited sex, etc., forced to try to pretend to be what they are not—forced to *fail*, day after day, week after week, month after month—finally get so frustrated and desperate that they are ready for any kind of violence and horror, since nothing could be much worse than the agonizing frustration they face every moment of their miserable lives.

When the Jews and liberals keep harping at them that they are "equal," that they have endless "rights," and that they have no real duties to go with those rights—then this half-animal population of Africans trying to "make it" as White Men, goes literally crazy.

It starts in the schools. The little black kid is taught in the most aggressive way that he is every bit the equal of the White kids. But the fact is that he averages 60%-75% of the IQ of the average White kids.[1] In the field of abstract thinking, cold reasoning, the Negro tests even lower. As a result, the black kid can't keep up. His schoolwork is terrible. The constant comparison with the work of the White kids frustrates, angers, and upsets him all the more. In his own, colored school, this problem does not arise. But forced into competition with the Whites, the Negro starts failing—and suffering from the consequent humiliation—even in school.

This is the cause of the Negro "drop-out" problem—not deprivation or poverty. Literally millions of White kids are poor and oppressed, and fight their way to an education. But the little Negro, understandably, doesn't have much ambition to continue in a contest he can see from the beginning he can't win. So he "drops out"—or is put in a special "track" in

---

[1] Based on current data, the typical black IQ is around 85, versus a White average of 100.

the schools, set up by the liberals to cover up the fact of Negro backward-ness. In either case, it isn't long before he enters the competition for a good job. Naturally stupid, uneducated, and naturally inept at the requirements of modern technology, the black youth finds himself on the street and idle. Told that he has a right to all the things he sees the White man earning—fancy women, Cadillacs, fast living, etc.—the black boy becomes filled with such a burning envy and hatred it is hard for most people to even im-agine. He turns to the only way left for him to get what he is told he de-serves—violence. He becomes a criminal. He goes out and robs, burns, rapes, loots, and finally kills; he is the classic "rioter."

The US Department of Justice and Labor have both published statis-tics on the Negro, which show that the black 10% of our population com-mits more than 85% of the violent crimes against people, and by far the most crimes against property.[2] The jails are filled and bursting with these frustrated, violent black animals, not because we are unjust, but because Negroes can't compete economically with White Men—and crime is the only way most of them can get what they are told they deserve.

卐 卐 卐

The US Department of Labor has published in 1965 a pamphlet called "The Negro Family." It is violently pro-Negro, and full of excuses for these miserable people. Certainly it cannot be called a "bigoted" work. Yet here is what this booklet says in Chapter 4 about Negro ability to compete with Whites.

> The ultimate mark of inadequate preparation for life is the failure rate on the Armed Forces mental lest. The Armed Forces Qualification Test is not quite a mental test, nor yet an education test. It is a test of ability to perform at an ac-ceptable level of competence. It roughly measures ability that ought to be found in an average 7th or 8th grade student. A grown young man who cannot pass this test is in trouble.
> Fifty-six percent of Negroes fail it.
> This is a rate almost four times that of the whites.[3]

---

[2] According to FBI Uniform Crime Report, 1966. Today, blacks comprise about 14% of the US population, up from 10% in the 1960s.

[3] Online: www.dol.gov/general/aboutdol/history/webid-moynihan/moynchapter4

Notice the last sentence in the first paragraph that men who fail this test are "in trouble." And that is the keynote of life for the young Negro, "*trouble*." He is constantly causing and in trouble both as an individual and as a group. Whenever the situation is ripe, hundreds and thousands of them act in their animal—like, anti-social manner and "riot." They loot, shoot, burn, kill, and beat—almost without any sense at all—just out of animal frustration and hatred of a system which keeps telling them they are "equal," while their own dim brains constantly show them they are not only *not* equal, but they are so far below the White Man that only by violence can they achieve anything at all. This situation is guaranteed to make bloody revolutionaries out of millions of Negroes, especially young males. They have almost nothing to lose, and everything to gain.

This Black army of the damned is precisely the right material for revolution. All that is needed to spark these millions of black human bombs into explosive and bloody violence on a mass scale is agitation and organization. So, long before 1900, they were already plotting and scheming how to agitate the Negroes into massive and bloody rebellion against the Whites and against the government of the United States. It wasn't really difficult. The Negroes have proven themselves, down through the ages, almost animal-like in their adaptation to all forms of manipulations and slavery.

It should be remembered that most of the Negroes here in America did not get here because they were captured in Africa. No. The Arabs obtained the great majority of slaves by purchase. Their *own folks* sold them to the Arabs, usually for beads, salt, trinkets, etc. (And, in some cases, I think the Arabs got little for their good beads.) The kind of people who would sell their own children into slavery tells much of the nature of these black men who now swarm in our streets demanding equality.

But even more revealing is the fact that the early settlers in America were no fools when it came to obtaining slaves. Why do you think they went all the way over to Africa to get slaves, when the woods were full of Indians? The fact is that they tried the cheaper experiment of enslaving the Indians (instead of just killing them as they finally did). But it didn't work. The Indians could not be enslaved. Think about it a moment, and you will understand something of the nature of the Negro. Would you allow yourself to be a slave—if you had all sorts of opportunity to escape from the fields, plantation, cabins, etc.? Would you let somebody peddle your kids and otherwise permit what the Negro slaves permitted? You know the answer is a resounding, fighting "NO!" Neither would the Indians. They could be chained and beaten and held. But they were far too spirited and proud to meekly follow a master around like a dog, the way millions of

Negroes were taught to do. At the first opportunity, in spite of risk, the Indian would attack, or at the very least, escape. White men, Chinese and Indians cannot be enslaved (except in rare cases—never as a whole race).

But the Negroes do not have the get-up-and-go to resist or even to think about it. Take care of their animal needs, give them sex satisfaction to their heart's content and the opportunity to dance in the sun, sport like an ape in a clearing, sing and beat some kind of bongo or drum around a fire— and the pure African Negro soon settles down like a dog in a new home, provided you take care to let the Negro (like the dog) know who's boss.

But just as you can take a friendly, docile dog and train him to be a vicious killer, so you can quite easily take a docile, mindless Negro and turn him into one of the most fearful murderers in all history, as is happening, especially in Africa. You make a dog vicious, as Army manuals teach, by "agitating" him. That's precisely how you make a Negro vicious—by agitating him! And, in accordance with the plan of Israel Cohen, set forth in 1912, and printed in the Congressional Record in 1957 (see above), the Jews and communist have been systematically agitating the Negro race in America for the past 70 years.

Along with the agitation, they have been breeding him, like dogs in kennels, as fast as possible—which is pretty fast. (The Negro has never been one to resist breeding as often as he could find the opportunity.)

Add to this the Federal financial subsidization of the already powerful Negro urge to procreate, and you get a biological explosion. Negro women can actually *make a living* producing what can be technically and properly termed "little black bastards." (They are little, they are black, and they are in the strictest sense of the word, bastards.) There are already millions of these illegitimate Blacks, whom nobody really wants once they have been presented to get a bigger welfare check, and who are allowed to run absolutely wild in the streets.

These wild, black teenagers are the very guts of the riots in our big cities. And there are millions more on the way. They are very real savages, in the most bloodcurdling sense of the term, even though they live in an asphalt jungle instead of trees. They live a life of maximum violence and a total lack of any "ethics" at all. They fear almost nothing and respect *absolutely* nothing. The only possible way to deal with them, as with any dangerous savage, is to command their respect with overwhelming force.

But this is precisely what our fat-head government, manipulated by the Jews, will not use—force. Instead, we keep trying to buy off these wild animals in our streets with money, "poverty wars," art exhibits, free tickets, welfare, and endless pampering.

Worst of all, we keep giving them our women—foolish, if well-meaning, girls, whose maternal instincts have been perverted from loving and nurturing their own kind to loving and nurturing these little black vipers in their nests, because (they believe) the Blacks are "helpless" and "persecuted" and "misunderstood," etc. Sooner or later these women get a rude awakening when the black viper shows its fangs. But until that time, talking to these fanatic women is like trying to talk a queer out of his perversion.

The result of all this is a swarming army of *black mutineers* in our midst. They are rapidly getting trained and armed for terrorism, right before our eyes, and with maximum arrogance. The "Black Panthers," the "Deacons for Defense," and a dozen other black Mau Mau groups are formed and training with guns, Molotov cocktails, and grenades even as I write this. The Panthers recently had the gall to march into the California legislature in uniform heavily armed with automatic weapons. Nobody did anything.

Meanwhile, the Jews are howling to disarm the Whites and the law-abiding people! They want "gun control" laws although it is obvious that this won't do a bid of good with criminals and revolutionaries, who have illegal guns. How obvious can it get?

卐 卐 卐

What the Jews have done over the past fifty or sixty years is, first, to promote vast migrations to the cities of the black bodies they need as voting blocs to keep the likes of Franklin D. Roosevelt in power. Then they started working to breed these Blacks on scale never before seen in human affairs—with what they call Welfare. Finally, they have agitated these Blacks ceaselessly with "rights" lies, filling their dim African brains with the wildest dreams of Cadillacs, White women, cash, luxury and ease—all things the Black masses can never earn in this society, simply because they don't have the native ability.

The Jews have made it almost a crime even to *think* this fact, however, so that everything these benighted black people hear convinces millions of jungle-minded Blacks that they have practically built America with their sweat while we White people have driven them with whips and lain around on silk-pillows enjoying their hard-earned wealth. The fact that our people realized, organized, and created all the natural wealth (the same wealth they ignored in Africa for millions of years) escapes them.

Horses, too, sweated to create American wealth. But horses cannot claim credit for that wealth. This fact is taken as an insult by these arrogant chimpanzees posing as "civil rights" leaders, whenever I mention it in college speeches.

That's exactly what's going on with the child-like race of Blacks in America. Devilish Jewish, Marxist, and liberal agitators, sensing the ideal mutineers for their army for the overthrow of civilization, have moved the Blacks into the most dangerous possible positions in the middle of our technological civilization, bred them into a swarming, exploding mass, and then agitated them beyond all endurance.[4]

The result will not be long in coming—in fact, is already here, with sporadic riots which will soon spread, and then merge into one nightmare of terror, bloodshed, and jungle madness.

But it is not only a local, American problem. This explosion of the inferior, fostered by and led by the Marxists and the Jews with their liberal toadies, is a growing worldwide problem, which cannot remain unsolved much longer. The Jews have crushed the truth about human breeds and convinced much of the White world that the developed (White) nations "owe" endless aid to the "undeveloped" (Black) nations. This utterly insane lie, spread all over the earth, has produced a devil's "miracle"—it has sent doctors, medical care, schools, money, machines, and technology to the most animalistic populations of backward Africa, to India, and to every place where inferior humanity has previously been limited in its numbers by its own stupidity and ignorance since the beginning of time. But, since colored people are all supposed to be "equals," the equalist fanatics have

---

[4] In 1960, there were 19 million black Americans; as of 2020, there were over 41 million.

followed through in the attempt to make them equal, by pulling them up with modern medicine and science. This has taken all limits off the breeding of these people. The result is a world plague—*a black plague.*

Egotistical, short-sighted men have presumed to "outwit" Nature. And Nature will teach them a terrible, bloody lesson. Anyone knows that the reason you can't sell snow to Eskimos is that they already have all the snow they're likely to ever need. You can't sell mosquitoes to folks who live in tropical swamps, either. Whenever the supply of anything far exceeds the need, that thing becomes valueless.

On the other hand, the super-abundant "air" around us, which you couldn't sell in its usual form to anybody for a nickel—suddenly becomes the most precious thing in the world to a drowning man. There is no way to get around this law of supply and demand. Whatever is so super-abundant as to be a "drug on the market," becomes worthless, no matter how you try to prop up its value. Whatever is desperately needed, regardless of pretenses, will become "valuable." All of this is preface to a fact that should have become glaringly obvious years ago, but is still somewhat hidden from normal view by a million pretenses.

That fact is the growing worthlessness of millions of human beings.

The situation with humanity is very much like the situation with diamonds. Diamonds are now very valuable. The reason is not purely that they are handsome. Fake diamonds can be made so close in appearance to the real ones that only experts with a magnifying glass can tell the difference. No. It is rarity almost alone that gives diamonds their real value, except in industry.

Imagine what diamonds would be worth if there were some kind of strange event in space, and billions and billions of diamonds showered down on the earth for several months, until we were almost smothered in diamonds, knee-deep in diamonds. Overnight, you couldn't get a nickel for a diamond. Not only that, but people would pay to get them shoveled off their property. And if the showers were painful and broke up property and hurt people, diamonds would be among the most hated things on this earth. That is precisely what's ahead with Negroes and most colored people—indeed with inferior people. We have produced a plague of "niggers."

For millenniums, human life was a precious thing because it was so hard to get into existence and keep alive. It was rare, like diamonds. This led to what is now called "humanitarianism," the worship of something "special" about anything with two legs that can mumble or grunt a few words. Then, in the first half of this century, science made more progress than it had made in all the thousands of years previously. Literally millions of methods were discovered to prevent death in adults, and to promote the birth and growth of the young.

This was no catastrophe in Western, civilized nations, where the human beings thus increased were of a high and productive type. But with the advent of intellectualism in the 18th and 19th centuries, and its cancer-like growth into the disease of "liberalism," conceited little minds began to tell each other that the world had passed the stage where we had to obey the laws of Nature. "With our modern science," asserted these sophist, liberal snobs, "we master Nature and control her!" "By changing environment, we can make a Beethoven out of a Bantu!", was their cockeyed reasoning. "All races and people are equal; some have just not had an equal chance to develop." So these conceited wise men of Boeotia set about giving "all men" this "equal chance" to survive and develop. The result is precisely what would happen to the value of diamonds if we found ourselves suddenly deluged with diamonds by the billions.

The lowest forms of humanity (the colored races) are now breeding so fantastically fast that we will soon be "neck-deep in niggers." The world is about to suffer the worst plague in world history—the "Black Plague!"

Already, colored people outnumber the Whites by seven to one. And while White populations are growing at an average of 15%, the colored population of the world is exploding at 70%. Not only that, but the rate of increase is itself increasing, so that even the present figures do not give a clear picture of what's ahead.

The "developed" nations are sending their "Peace Corps" and medicines, education, and outright cash subsidies to help these colored nations. But the only real result of the help is so damned many more little Negroes, screaming for more help, that it is only a question of a very small amount of time before the situation will be absolutely hilarious—and terrifying. Mankind, in his infinite conceit that he can control Nature, is once again bringing the rabbits to Australia and the sparrows to America. In the latter two cases, the short lifespan of the creatures involved quickly showed man his error as the rabbits and sparrows multiplied by the billions to plague him. Negroes take a little bit longer than rabbits to breed (not much), but long enough so that it will be another 10 years or so before the full horror of the thing dawns on the idiots who are promoting unlimited colored breeding all over the world.

卍 卍 卍

A population study in *Scientific American* (September 1963) shows that the efforts to raise the standards of living in colored countries does not have the same effect that it has in White countries, where the people have natural abilities.[5] In dark countries, as fast as you double the standards of one batch of Negroes, they produce seven more batches and reduce the level of the whole lot. All Negroes produce when they get outside help is more Negroes.

The fatheads at the UN are already squirming as they calculate their own statistics (the statistics I am using), which show the approach of the "Black Plague." Their answer, the typical liberal answer, is *birth control.* Such utter unrealism is like handing a water pistol to a man to stop the charge of a bull elephant. The avalanche of Negroes which is about to inundate the world with a "Black Plague" is of such staggering proportions that it can be stopped by birth control as well as you could stop the tide with a Kleenex.

Most average men and women living today, who are under the age of 50, will live to see the time when Negroes will be considered about as valuable as a barrel of syphilis germs. The figures are simply terrifying, nightmarish

A quick way to see the picture is to take a map of the world showing the so- called "under-developed" or "backward" countries. The map of the backward countries, it will be quickly seen, is almost exactly the map of colored countries—and the darker the country, the more backward!

There is a graph which shows the growth of world population. This graph shows the projection of the rising curve beginning to go almost straight up. But the worst is yet to come! The *Scientific American* points out that there is a tremendous difference between the way the scientific revolution affects the White areas (which they refer to as "developed nations") and the way it affects the colored areas (the "under-developed countries"). They show that the skyrocketing population curve is about 90% colored! (Although they use the word "undeveloped" for "colored.")

Now consider all of this against the background of the "democracy" which is constantly driven into us by every media of information, entertainment, and by our government and the United Nations. "One Man, One Vote" is the motto. The Supreme Court has even decreed that we can no longer have state legislatures in which one part of the legislature is based on geography instead of population (thus giving rule of America to the Negro and Jew-laden cities.) In world terms, "One Man, One Vote" will

---

[5] "Population" by Kingsley Davis (September 1963, pp. 62-71).

mean about a hundred votes against you for everything you have and want. Everything you can produce will be voted right out of your hands by these colored swarms. That's what's behind their drive for "world democratic government"—and their color-dominated United Nations.

Now the liberals can coo about "brotherhood" and swoon over inferiors all they want; you and I know that when the day comes that the White liberal discovers that he is going to have to give up all he has to Negroes in the name of democracy, he will be finished with the liberal hocus-pocus in an instant. But then it will be too late for all of the White people.

When the Negroes have everything going their way in the poker game, with the rules the liberals themselves have set up (while Negroes have all the cards), do you think for a moment that the Negroes are going to stand still while we change the rules and take everything away from them? Never! The world will be reduced in a mighty short time to the old-fashioned situation where one side has something the other side is determined to get, and the first side is determined to keep. No votes, no discussion and no "brotherhood" are going to solve the situation.

We have permitted a gang of "intellectual" fatheads, in the name of "liberalism" and "democracy," to make it possible for Negroes to breed like rabbits for 30 years. There are now so many of them, and so fantastically many more on the way, that the Almighty Himself must look down on the swarming Black Plague with dread and horror. He never set up this mess. We did.

卐 卐 卐

The Black Plague is not an Alabama or Mississippi problem, or a Southern problem, or a Northern big-city problem. It is a *world* problem. *The* world problem!

Since the defeat of Germany, no power on earth exists with the will to stop the Jews and fathead liberals who will continue to breed this Black Plague—until the Plague itself stops them. When it does, it will be such a hideous catastrophe, as this planet has never experienced. The "Riots" are just the first flickers of the inferno.

Just as nobody loves locusts and grasshoppers when there is a plague of locusts, so nobody will be a "nigger-lover" when there is a plague of "niggers"—not even the "niggers!" Negroes will then appear to be what they really are: a semi-wild form of half-human animal, unable to build or maintain a civilization, but capable, in vast numbers, of utterly and completely destroying all civilization.

The rapes, murders, robberies, muggings, and the big riots in our cities of the North are not isolated incidents. They are the first skirmishes in the World Race War of which we have been warning for years. The skirmishes will increase, get much larger and more bloody, fuse with one another, become longer and more sustained, more violent, more professional and finally heavily armed. Leadership and weaponry for this world Black uprising is developing right now in Red China and Cuba. Red Chinese advisors and experts are all over Africa, Asia, and Cuba, training colored armies and massacre experts.

When Whites were being massacred in the Congo, we must not forget that A. Philip Randolph, James Farmer, Dorothy Haight, Roy Wilkins, and even Whitney Young (of the less-violent Urban League) all demanded of the president, in writing, that the USA keep "hands off" in the Congo, to let the savage Blacks slaughter—and eat—the Whites. It must be remembered that the Whites who were being slaughtered were mostly White missionaries and liberal fatheads who went to Africa to help the Blacks. That didn't matter. They were White, so they got tortured, slaughtered, and eaten!

They were in Africa, not as "imperialists," but for the usual "humanitarian" reasons. These liberal jerks are going to have to learn that you can't give limitless "humanitarian" aid to savage, half-ape beasts, without aggravating the problems you started with. But since liberals won't learn, the massacres and uprisings will get more frequent and more brutal. The Blacks will mass against South Africa and Rhodesia, and the rest of the world will sit by mouthing platitudes while the Black Plague tries to wipe out or enslave the Whites of two entire nations, while Jew-led nations help them.[6]

Do not gasp that it just couldn't happen! It is happening, right now, in Mississippi, Alabama, and other parts of the South, and in our big cities, where the Blacks, nearing a majority, are aiming to be masters of the Whites through mass and bloc votes, and guerrilla warfare, while the foolish Whites will continue to play "Democrat" and "Republican," etc. If our people had the will to resist, they could do it. But they keep hoping there will be some "easy" way, and do nothing at all—except to damn the few of us who oppose this insanity!

As the Blacks moved in on Whites in Africa, and seize areas of northern big cities in the USA, they will taste real blood for the first time. They will take the bit in their teeth. With leadership from Africa, Red China, and Cuba, etc., the Black Plague will spread like fire in a gasoline factory

---

[6] White rule in South Africa ended in 1994; in Rhodesia, 1978.

until the whole earth is blazing. Only then will the fathead White liberals, the silly, squabbling, reactionary rightwing and the narrow 17th century "nationalists," realize at last that there are not many issues, just one: *race*. And that one issue before the world is not what form of government or economy we shall all have, but *who* shall run this world.

As Adolf Hitler said in *Mein Kampf*, the only question in the history of our times is: Will the titanic and final struggle of humanity turn out for the benefit of the White Aryan, or the benefit of the scheming Jew and his swarming army of colored inferiors?

As this racial Armageddon approaches, the real value of a human being will shortly appear with a vengeance, whether we like it or not. Like the "plague of diamonds" pouring out of the sky, there will be such a roaring storm of people on this planet that it will sink in its orbit from sheer weight. Colored "humanity" will drop to lower than zero on the scale of value. Your children or grandchildren will be forced to exterminate and/or transport swarms of wild Blacks until all of them are finally dead or corralled in Africa. And your grandchildren's children, in turn, will look back on you and wonder how, in the name of heaven, we ever let this insanity go so far without doing anything but talk!

While almost every American is playing what are really games (relatively speaking)—money-gathering, putt-putt golf, politics, economics, women-chasing, etc.—the world is heading for the ultimate Tribal War— *world race war*. It's "them" against "us." It isn't an economic or social struggle. It isn't politics, religion, economics or anything else so complicated. It's as simple as cat versus mouse; as White versus Indians. It's tribe versus tribe.

And there's no such thing as "ultimate justice' in the battle. Whoever wins will be forever decreed "just," precisely as the title of the great book *None Dare Call It Treason* points out: "When treason prospers, none dare call it treason".[7]

Here in America, the Black tribe is already preparing to take what they want by bloody force from the Whites. When I spoke to a group of revolutionary, DC college Negroes, last year, this fact emerged clearly. I was invited to speak to the collegiate "Burning Bush" club, and accepted without knowledge that it was mostly a Black outfit. They gave me a street address that turned out to be in an ex-store front church in the heart of black Washington. I learned that it was the bunch that produced Stokley Carmichael and Rap Brown.

---

[7] *None Dare Call It Treason* (1964), by John A. Stormer.

Once I walked into that black mob, I was not about to back out, or crawl out. So I spent about two hours speaking to them and answering their questions—or rather, defending myself from their bitter jabs. Several times, particularly when one black girl got up and read the contents of the entire "Boat Ticket to Africa," it was nip and tuck whether I'd get out of there alive. But I managed to keep that Black mob sufficiently interested in what would happen next to sit still, until I left.

But I wouldn't have missed the experience for anything. Those revolutionary Black youths made no secret of their plans to seize America by violence and bloodshed. The only thing I said with which they agreed was that America would never give them the kind of "equality" they wanted (which they made clear included our women) and that they would have to take it with guns. "We're gettin' the guns!" they snarled at me. And they are! These college-trained Blacks, endlessly agitated by Jews like Bettina Aptheker, Saul Alinsky, Milton Rosen of Progressive Labor, and the Militant gang, are openly preparing a revolution of force and bloodshed.

Meanwhile, the disgusting cowards and sissies on my side (which is almost all of them) are still preaching "The Truth Will Make Us Free," and writing letters, and getting up petitions and new schemes for "victory"— none of them involving even so much as naming the enemy.

卐 卐 卐

As I write this—as you read these words—the millions of "nice" people on my own side are playing an incredible game of "I've-got-my-eyes-closed." Almost none of them (again with the exception of the Klan) have the nerve to name the enemy. (And even the Klan covers up some of the naked truth about the Jews we are fighting.) In fact, there are as many explanations of the nature of the enemy as there are rightwing leaders.

The reactionaries will tell you that we are divided over economic issues—Capitalism versus communism (although these "experts" have to sit up nights trying to explain how most of our big millionaires and big foundations are busily putting up most of their "capital" to support communism). The Birchers will tell you that it is a battle between those who are for "less government and more individual responsibility" and against the "big government" crowd. There are the mostly Southern "states' righters" versus the nasty "Federal Government"—although the only reason the "states' righters" so vehemently hate the "Federal Government" is because it is currently in the hands of "nigger-lovers" and Reds; if a pro-White were president, they would be 100% for use of federal power to protect White people, as I am.

I could name many more of these phony divisions by shallow thinkers on our side, but these ought to be enough to establish the principle. To see the truth behind all these euphemisms, and all like them, all one has to do is to attend two meetings: (1) a rightwing meeting, regardless of what kind; and (2) a leftwing meeting. At the rightwing meeting you will see mostly good-looking people, our kind of people. To be sure, some of them, individually, will be ugly or dissipated or otherwise unattractive, but the participants will be most White Aryans, or at least people racially similar to us. (Even the leftwing press commented what good-looking girls were in the Goldwater campaign.) At the leftwing meeting, you will see swarms of racially alien people—Jews, "niggers," and mongrels of all sorts. Most of them will be racially repulsive.

The glaring fact, which all of the "nice" rightwing so assiduously covers up, is that this is not a war of ideas, money, theology, principles or politics, but an old-fashioned, naked confrontation between two tribes—between us and them. We have something. They want it. They are taking it.

The rightwing, like a helpless man in a nightmare, is gurgling inarticulately trying to keep "them" from taking it away, without being able to move or even yell effectively. In fact, in most cases, our side doesn't even dare complain about "them," and keeps pretending we are not "racists"—only for the Constitution, states' rights, America, etc.

The commercial Jew agitator of the Negroes, Saul Alinsky, doesn't play any games or try to hide it; he openly says to his side what I am saying to mine. "Machiavelli wrote a book telling the 'haves' how to keep what they have," this Jew sneers to the mobs of Jews and Negroes. "Well, I am teaching the 'have-nots' how to take it away," From *you*, White Man.

In the days of Genghis Kahn, nobody bothered to pretend, as they do today; nobody dressed up the ancient battle for plunder, women, and territory with fancy names or disguised it as "ideas." Nobody tried to pretend it was a "battle for men's minds." The colored hordes came out of the East with their bloody swords, axes, and clubs, and drove into the heart of Europe, slaughtering the men, taking the women, plundering the wealth and generally acting in the immemorial manner of that predator of all predators, man! Only the better White men in Germany were finally able to stop these savage, yellow terrorists and drive them back into Asia.

In fact, the ancient Nordic word for "Germans," (still preserved in the Icelandic language) is *Thodthverdthur*, which, translated literally, means "the people's defenders."

Now, once again, the savage, colored hordes are terrorizing the Earth, threatening to unite and use the White Man's own fearsome technological weapons to rape, rob, loot, plunder, murder, and enslave us in such an orgy of carnage and cruelty as has never been dreamed of on this planet. The Jews have let this terrible dark genie out of the bottle to "use" him as their army in their mad dreams of conquest of the Earth, according to their paranoiac prophecy as the "chosen People."

In 1932, the German "people's defenders"—the Nazis—rose up, as in days of old, and almost had this Asiatic horror stopped, when the Hebraic brotherhood here in the USA got their stooge Roosevelt and his stooge Churchill to use all the rest of us to smash our White German brothers who stood between us and the colored hordes. At the behest of the Jews, we crushed the ancient German bulwark of the White Race.

The battle is now for possession of the whole planet. And the colored hordes of Genghis Khan have almost won. From Africa, India, and Asia they are swarming like a plague of poisonous locusts, into all White nations.

In the name of sanity and survival, how much longer will our cowardly and short-sighted rightwing "leaders" pretend that there is no such thing as "the enemy"—that "we hate no one," but only oppose this or that idea? Hell, the enemy is out in our streets in his thousands, "demonstrating," throwing Molotov cocktails, and even killing us, under the open direction of Jew generals, like Saul Alinsky and Milton Rosen.

You can be sure that the mighty Germanic White Men who stopped Genghis Kahn did so without any sickening pap about "not hating" him, and they sure as hell made no secret of who the enemy was. It's time to name the Negro, Jew, and communist enemy that is murdering us and planning to take us, in the ancient manner. It's time to hate the filthy devils that are attacking us, hotly, passionately, and poisonously, so that we can fight as our fathers fought—to *win!*

卐 卐 卐

But it is not only the Black Plague which threatens us. The problems of air pollution, water pollution, and land destruction are also problems of too many people—"the population explosion," it is called. Where a few sewers could once empty harmlessly into rivers and oceans, thousands of them, *millions* of them, are now rapidly making the whole surface of the planet Earth one big sewer, smothered by smog, and jam-packed with swarms of people all beginning to compete for space on roads, space to live, space to move and even just air to breathe. Everywhere you go, traffic piles up, smog chokes you, water is filthy, land is disappearing, and you have to form lines for tickets—for anything. But the current situation is only the merest hint of what's ahead in the next two decades.

Remember, the population of the Earth has doubled since the 1900s. It will re-double again by the 1970s! And, if nothing changes, it will double once more in half of that time, to produce a world literally packed with humans struggling just to breathe, to eat, and to find a moment's peace—a moment they will never find.[8]

Perhaps you have been taken in with the birth-control propaganda, and believe this is the answer. Aside from the fact that birth control just will not work, because people are people, the deadly fact about birth control is that it kills off the best and promotes the worst. It is our best racial stock which practices birth control, because they are provident, hard-working, and want to provide for their young (even if they are short-sighted about future generations). The Negroes are breeding as fast as the possibly can, because our best families are going without and paying big taxes, to subsidize with "welfare" this colored breeding by the lowest humanity.

Illegitimate black babies, "little black bastards," actually produce more and more income for Black females, and Black females are engaged in the black-bastard industry with a will. It is this Black spawn of the sub-sidization of inferior humanity, which produces the giant gangs of black nihilists, such as Chicago's "Mighty Blackstone Rangers" which terrorize

---

[8] Global population was about 1.6 billion in 1900. By 1963, it had doubled to 3.2 billion. In 2003, it had doubled again to 6.4 billion. As of 2024, the figure is 8.1 billion, and rising by about 65 million per year.

the whole community and require a "peace treaty" on TV with the Chief of Chicago's Police Department.

People are becoming dimly aware of this growing horror. But what is not so obvious, and much more deadly, about birth control, is the way it reverses Nature.

The oak tree produces tens of thousands of seeds, lets them all start, and then Nature ruthlessly and wisely selects only the best and the toughest to survive and become big trees. Obviously, there is not room on the ground around one tree to grow thousands more trees. Nevertheless, every year the tree produces enough seed to populate giant forests over whole states. Nature never produces just "enough." She always produces prodigiously, especially so she can select.

And she has the best reason in the world: the survival and improvement of the breed. She is never pre-occupied with any particular individual, always in the promotion of tougher, better, and more select types to improve the breed.

By the oak having all those seeds and allowing them to struggle, with only a few succeeding while most perish, Nature ensures that the next generation of oak trees will be the winners of an elimination contest in which millions and millions competed, and only one or two of the finest survived to make more oak trees like themselves.

In fact, that's the same way you got here. To make you, took just one sperm cell. But Nature produced millions, all of which competed for the chance to live and become *you*. Only one made it, and thus proved that it was therefore the most energetic and excellent of those millions, and most likely to make a good human being, you. Had Nature produced only the one sperm needed to produce another embryo, it might very well have been the weakest. And it almost certainly would not have been the one which survived and produced the best one—you.

If parents use birth control and have only one child, there is a good chance it may very well be the worst they would ever have. If they had ten or fifteen, as Nature intended (and as humanity had to do for millions of years to survive), they would have had a very good chance of producing their best, and the worst would have perished mercifully at an early age, as happened to humanity until the last hundred years.

But today, short-sighted use of man's medical science first kills by "birth-control" millions and millions of human beings, including the best, even before they have a chance to be conceived and born—and then keeps alive anything born, even with two heads, and preserves to each such "beneficiary" of "science" the opportunity to create more unfortunates who would otherwise never have been conceived, had Nature been allowed to exercise her surgical wisdom.

卐 卐 卐

There is no "cure" for the coming population horror other than to kill. Nature did the killing, by natural selection, since the beginning of time. The birth-control advocates, with typical liberal cowardice and short-sightedness, do their killing by un-natural selection, by cowardly murder before the people they kill have any chance to argue the case, or prove themselves.

Nature would never have allowed this crazy over-population to arise, because the backward, stupid, lazy, no-good bums and swine of the world, for millennia, never survived long enough to have kids. Even though some did, they killed each other off, ate each other, lived in such filth, horror, ignorance, superstition, and disease that they perished by the millions, as they did in dark Africa for millions of years. This was the situation, for instance, in what is now Rhodesia, where the native, Black population never exceeded 40,000 since the beginning of time.

Then along came the humanitarian, half-witted, White liberal, and "outwitted" Nature by providing these swarms of human scum with the medical genius of a higher race, with education, with police to maintain order and prevent them killing and eating each other, with hygienics to put down germs and mosquitoes and prevent disease, with sanitation facilities, and otherwise applying the miracles produced by White brains and character, to enable Black and inferior humanity to proliferate like flies on a dung heap. The Whites came to Rhodesia with law and order, medicine, education, and food—and produced 40 million Blacks, who now demand to take over the Whites!

The way out of this mess is not in making available more food, better medical care, more efficient farming, or birth control. There is only the old-fashioned way of Nature: *death*, one way or another. Somebody has got to go, ugly as that may be.

The problem would never have arisen, had men been wise enough to obey Nature's ancient and eternal laws. But we didn't, and the problem is about to overwhelm us in a furious catastrophe. If we don't do something about it, Nature will. There will be famines such as the world has never imagined, massacres such as the worst nightmare cannot envision, slaughter, disease, death, and horror until there is nothing but blood and darkness on the face of the Earth.

Even our worst enemies are hinting at these things. But, as a "cure" they are preaching their shortsighted "birth control." Birth control means death to millions of the unborn. Birth control is killing, even though the cowards who advocate it dress that fact up with all kinds of rationalizations about giving a break to those already here, seeing that the new ones are taken care of, etc. Birth control is selective massacre, at the sperm cell and egg stage, which not only kills more millions than any massacre in the history of Homo sapiens, but *reverses Nature*, selecting the worst and breeding them, while murdering and decreasing the biological best.

We believe man has arrived at that critical point of no return where he can no longer be "chicken" about facing the deadly fact: *somebody has got to go.* There are too many bodies competing for every blade of grass, every breath of air and drop of water on this planet. And the flood of people on the way will be catastrophic, unless we return to Nature's plan, and select, not the worst, but the best for survival.

And who are the best?

Actually, that's an irrelevant question, because no group in the world, with any vitality in it, is going to select itself for elimination. Each group, of course, will claim to be actually "the best," even if they are the blackest cannibals, who claim they are eating each other and running naked, only because dirty "colonialists" have been "holding them down" and they have never had the advantages of hearing Shakespeare, or attending Harvard or Oxford.

But still, being as objective about the question as possible for our group, the White People, we can truthfully say that our group has performed better than any other creature ever to come forth on this planet. It is not the Blacks, or the Reds, Browns, or Yellows that have produced the miracles of our age; it is the White Man: The test of "superior" and "inferior" is not theory, but performance. Even more important, it is not the Blacks, Yellows, Browns, or Reds who have the power to select. *Nature selects by success, never by theory.*

And the White Man, at least for a while longer, has the organized force at his disposal to restore almost instant order to this world, through the use of his technology and even nuclear weapons if necessary (especially when the White Men of Russia finally are driven over to our side by the imminent explosion of arrogant, aggressive colored people, as is already happening to Russia on her borders with Red China).

This is no call to brutal, heartless, sadistic massacre. There is no "hate" involved here, any more than there is "hate" involved when roaches or bedbugs invade a home and must be exterminated. it is a matter of survival. If they survive and swarm by the millions, we must die. It will not be too many years before even the most rabid liberal will see that. Some of them already have, as the Blacks run around attacking them, shouting "Kill Whitey," "Burn, baby, burn!" and sacking our cities.

To survive, we will undoubtedly have to kill vast numbers of those of the colored races who attack us. I believe the planet will run red with the blood of both sides, in the lifetimes of many now living, before order is restored to the world, and genuine peace is therefore possible.

But we do not have to conduct any scientific "extermination" program. (As the Jews and liberal fatheads never tire of charging). We have only to be ruthless about the survival and rights of our White family of people all over the globe, and leave the others to themselves. Left to themselves, the colored swarms will not last a generation, and the heaving planet can settle down to a productive order.

Everywhere the Whites have withdrawn from colored areas, that's what has happened: the Blacks massacre each other, they enslave each other, they retreat to filth and the jungle almost faster than it is possible to believe—as Haiti will show anyone who cares to look, even after a century of White help.[9] They won't produce food—and so they starve. Nature pronounces her judgment.

卐 卐 卐

Those who so tirelessly howl for "peace" should remember that the gentle Goddess of Peace could walk in safety only at the side of the Mighty God of War. And today, if the Goddess of Peace is White, she can't walk at all in the areas controlled by these black savages.

To restore Order and Peace, we are going to have to make two decisions: (1) The White Man must again become absolute master of this planet, and (2) Forceful authority and order must be restored as the first need of our whole world, if people are to be able to go about their business without constant fears of wars, bandits, swindlers, and mobs of hell-raisers.

To ensure that the White Man does become Master of the planet, and thus survives the colored attack, the White Man must stop the reversal of Nature. He must take as much care about his own breeding as he does for the breeding of his dog, his horse, his cow, and his canary.

Ruthless though it may sound, the White Man is also going to have to find a happy medium between the preservation of all of his own number by

---

[9] This is a prescient observation, especially considering Haiti in 2024.

medical science, and that restoration of some sort of selective process to ensure that congenital freaks of his own kind do not breed more unproductive, unhappy individuals, who then drag down the productive through "welfare medicine." He is going to have to re-evaluate his role, and begin to think not just of the individual, but of the whole race.

What injures the race beyond repair must never be performed by medical science, even if it might make a certain individual happy. When medical science is reasonably sure that any individual is bound to bring into the world miserable, helpless imbeciles or human freaks, then medical science must see to it that no such calamity is visited on innocent unborn little ones.

I am well aware that such apparently heartlessness will outrage many who will think I am indeed the sadistic monster so often painted by my opponents. On the contrary, however, I am simply determined to save my own people—and the world—the unspeakable horror, the ultimate horror, of the final destruction of the White Race: the race which, almost alone, is responsible for the very qualities of mercy, love, justice, etc., which the humanitarians so dearly love, but forget are the product of only one race—the White Race.

Liberal (and conservative) cowardice and equivocation are leading the world, and especially the White people, straight to the hell of race war and the nightmare of an irreversible Black Plague.

It is going to take bloody violence and killing to solve this problem, just as it was not words, which gave us America, but violence and killing of the British. It took bloody violence and killing for the German White Men to stop Genghis Khan. It took bloody violence and killing to win every war we have ever fought, not conservative words and petitions.

To stop a plague of bed bugs takes killing, not words. To stop a plague of traitors, agitators and black half-animals is going to take killing, not words. Locusts and bed bugs that do not invade your home do not need killing. Inferior humanity which leaves the White Man alone does not need killing, either, and can be left to limit their own numbers by their own stupidity, improvidence, and cruelty. But it is forever too late for those colored people who *attack* the White Man to be permitted to survive.

We have no intention of attacking or exterminating those who leave us alone. But let this be a declaration of war upon the savages who dare to shout "Kill Whitey," and on those Jews and others who dare to encourage, agitate, arm, and finance them in this bloody insanity. It's them, or us!

CHAPTER 11

THE FACTS OF RACE

If Black men are simply White men with dark skins, then it would be stupid and wicked bigotry to discriminate against Black men. If there is no other difference between White men and Black men than skin color, if there are no differences of mind or character, then everything the liberals and race-mixers preach would be true. Just as it would be insane and wicked to hate and discriminate against people with red hair, so it would be insanity and wickedness to discriminate against a man born with a dark skin—*if* the dark skin is the only difference. There would be no excuse for not admitting Negroes at once to full equality with White men, including the complete right to marry and breed with our women, if they are really equal.

But if there *are* differences of mind and character between the Negro and White man, in addition to skin color, and if the Negro has a lower grade mind and major character defects as a whole race, then it is the height of wickedness and insanity to pollute our White Race with these low-grade traits of mind and character.

The Negro question is thus not a question of philosophy, but of fact.

If, as the Jews, communists, and egalitarian liberals contend, Negroes are the same as White people, except for skin color, then I am indeed a hate-monger, a bigot, and a wicked man for fighting race mixing as hard as we do. But if the race of Negroes is, as a matter of *fact, inferior*, then it is the other way around and the liberals, Jews, communists, and egalitarians are the wicked poisoners of a million years of White evolution and breeding.

What are the facts?

Is it so hard to find out whether the Negro is, in fact, the same as a White Man, except for skin color? Are all the well-known Negro faults the result of "persecution" by Whites? Will equal treatment result eventually in equal people? Or are most Negroes born inferior?

The *facts* alone can answer those questions. Any White Man who has had to live among real Negroes promptly finds out that the myth about no difference except skin-color is a lie. The "all-men-are-equal" baloney goes up in a puff of smoke whenever a group of genuine, live Negroes shows up and moves in close to White people.

In fact, the belief in black "equality" is inversely proportional to the number of Blacks living in the area. The mathematical correlation is not just good; it is perfect. In areas such as Canada, where there are almost no Negroes, you will find that the myth of equality is so strong you can get beaten up for questioning it. In areas where there are only a very few Negroes, the "equality" myth is still very strong, because, usually, where the Negroes are a very tiny minority, they are forced to act like White people and are often almost White themselves. Also, the rare Negroes present in such areas are usually highly selected, and highly trained because it is only the better specimens who had the ambition to emigrate to the new area, and who thus get more education.

But in areas where there are many Negroes, you will find that the White people do *not* believe the equality myth, no matter how much it is pushed on them. Just as you couldn't sell the idea that skunks don't stink wherever there are plenty of skunks, so you can't peddle the "niggers-are-wonderful" lie wherever there are plenty of the colored "brothers" handy for folks to observe.

And in areas where there are more Black than White people, as in Mississippi, you will find tremendous resistance to the Blacks, and also thorough understanding of the primitive savage and utterly different natures of these inferior specimens of humanity.

Unless this direct correlation of a low opinion of Negroes wherever there are many Negroes is the result of the inferiority of the Negroes themselves, you must conclude that somehow, almost all the people in South Africa are "bigots," almost all the people of the US South are "bigots," and now, almost all the people who live in the big cities of the North are also "bigots." The same Northern cities which once believed the South was "bigoted" and mistreating the Negroes, now produce howling mobs of Whites hurling rocks and bottles whenever Blacks try to move into their neighborhoods. These people could be swindled with the lie that Negroes are really Whites with dark skins only so long as they were not able to observe Negroes, experience Negroes, and suffer from Negroes. But as soon as large numbers of Negroes moved in, the Whites quickly learned the truth about them.

If anybody will put up the money for the experiment, I can prove that hatred of race mixing is not a "prejudice" but the result of knowledge, by taking the most liberal and Negro-loving town in upper Ohio, for instance, or North Dakota, and buying up about half the homes in the town and filling them up with real, live, ordinary, garden-variety Negroes. In a few months, that town will be just as full of "bigots" and "nigger-haters" as any town in Mississippi.

And the reason will be, not that the White people are "prejudiced," but that Negroes are simply biologically inferior. And the results of pretending otherwise can be seen wherever these pitiful black creatures abound.

Anybody who tries to live with skunks will become "bigoted" and "prejudiced" against skunks, and tell you that "'skunks stink." And, without exception, anybody who is forced to live with masses of Negroes (not a few select Negro doctors or lawyers, but the real, black, average Negro) will quickly form the opinion that Negroes are a very low form of humanity, and we cannot mix with them without reverting to the jungle and the filth in which they live.

The only reason that so many people do not know that fact today (as all people once did), is because the same Jews who have provided us with communism, Zionism, degeneracy, and decay of Western Civilization, have methodically gone about the task of promoting the lie that Negroes are equal. They know it's a lie, but they have promoted it consciously, precisely because, as we have previously shown, Jews, like ship-wreckers of old, flourish amidst chaos and ruin, and perish in a healthy society. Nothing so quickly deprives a society of its vigor as being mixed with Negroes.

Inevitably, when I point all this out to "intellectuals" in the colleges, they sneer back with a long list of Negro "achievers" who are statesmen, writers, geniuses, etc. They trot out Senator Edward Brooke, Adam Clayton Powell, William White, W. E. B. Dubois, Ralph Bunch, etc. This is one of the trick arguments that looks good until you slow down and examine it critically. Then you will see that it is pure madness to judge "Negroes" by the likes of such "Negroes." They are presenting a *mixture* to try to prove the qualities of one *ingredient*. Dynamite is made of sawdust and nitro-glycerin. So, in a sense, you could say that dynamite is "made out" of wood. But would anybody be mad enough to contend, therefore, that wood is explosive? When two things are mixed, the resulting product cannot be used to prove the qualities of either single ingredient.

When we try to discuss the natural abilities of the Negro, the liberals, Reds, and Jews instantly start pointing with pride to creatures which are anything but real Negroes—men who are almost always *white* men with a small amount of Negro blood in them.

The usual examples in present day America are Adam Clayton Powell, who passed for White in college, and whose parents appear to be almost wholly White; Robert Weaver, housing czar; W. E. B. Dubois, who looked to be a White Man, with slightly Negroid features; the newly elected Senator Brooke, who is a White man with a bit of Negro blood; and dozens of others like them.

The only place you will find the black, heavily Negroid types in the public eye is in the fields where Negroes in Africa also excel: athletics, tom-tom beating, jungle chanting, etc. In all the professions and upper echelons of accomplishments, whenever you find an intellectual Negro, you will find that he is almost always a *White man*, with just enough colored blood to give the liberals something to vibrate about.

This is just as crazy as sprinkling some sawdust into nitro-glycerin to make dynamite, making it blow up with a bang—and then smirking that you have "proved" that wood is explosive. Dynamite is *not* wood, even though there is sawdust in it, and slightly soiled White Men with a little Negro blood are *not "Negroes"* (in the biological sense.) If you wish to know the properties of wood, you examine wood all by itself, the way it comes out of a tree. If you wish to know the properties of the Negro, you must examine him *all by himself*, the way he comes out of the Congo.

When we do this, we find not the sort of intelligence and ability found in a Senator Brooke but something far more akin to the African gorilla—something dark and terrible, something animal-like and primitive. That is not "hate;" that is a fact.

Liberals never tire of moaning that this obvious inferiority is only because of "lack of opportunity." But they utterly ignore the fact that Africa is perhaps the richest continent on Earth. The only reason it remained savage was because there were no men there capable of seeing and understanding the possibilities.

卐 卐 卐

Thomas Dixon, author of the 1905 book that became the greatest movie of all time, *The Birth of a Nation* (1915), has put the matter more beautifully and clearly than I could hope to imitate:

> "Can we assimilate the Negro? The very question is pollution. In Haiti, no White man can own land. Black dukes and marquises drive over them and swear at them for getting under their wheels. Is civilization a patent cloak with which law-tinkers can wrap an animal and make him a king?"
>
> "But the Negro must be protected by the ballot," protested the statesman. "The humblest man must have the opportunity to rise. The real issue is Democracy."

"The issue, sir, is Civilization; not whether a Negro shall be protected, but whether Society is worth saving from barbarism."

"The statesman can educate," put in the Commoner.

The doctor cleared his throat with a quick little nervous cough he was in the habit of giving when deeply moved.

"Education, sir, is the development of that which is. Since the dawn of history, the Negro has owned the continent of Africa—rich beyond the dream of poet's fancy, crunching acres of diamonds beneath his bare black feet. Yet he never picked one up from the dust until a White man showed to him its glittering light. His land swarmed with powerful and docile animals, yet he never dreamed a harness, cart, or sled. A hunter by necessity, he never made an axe, spear, or arrowhead worth preserving beyond the moment of its use. He lived as an ox, content to graze for an hour. In a land of stone and timber he never sawed a foot of lumber, carved a block, or built a house save of broken sticks and mud. With league on league of ocean strand and miles of in land seas, for four thousand years he watched their surface ripple under the wind, heard the thunder of the surf on his beach, the howl of the storm over his head, gazed on the dim blue horizon calling him to worlds that lie beyond, and yet he never dreamed a sail! He lived as his fathers lived—stole his food, worked his wife, sold his children, ate his brother, content to drink, sing, dance, and sport as the ape. And this creature, half child, half animal, the sport of impulse, whim, and conceit, 'pleased with a rattle, tickled with a straw,' a being who, left to his will, roams at night and sleeps in the day, whose speech knows no word of love, whose passions, once aroused, are as the fury of the tiger—they have set this thing to rule over the Southern people."

Perhaps the most revealing and unanswerable study of racial differences between White and Black was made in Virginia in 1916 by Dr. George Ferguson.[1] Most studies seeking the answer to racial differences between Black and White are useless, because they totally ignore the White blood in many of the "Blacks" they test.

---

[1] "The psychology of the Negro," *Archives of Psychology* 36, April 1916.

Ferguson took all the school children of Virginia, tested them all for intelligence, and then checked their racial backgrounds. He divided them up into five racial groups. The first group was pure Black. The second group consisted of those having one White grandparent. The third group had two White grandparents, and the fourth group had three White grandparents. The fifth group, of course, was the pure Whites.

The pure Blacks tested at least 40 percent below the pure Whites— (which is still the case today, in spite of all the money spent on education and pampering of the Blacks.) Those "Negroes" with one White grandparent did slightly better than the pure Blacks; with two White grandparents, still better; with three White grandparents almost as good as the Whites themselves. All of these Blacks lived as and considered themselves "Negroes." Their environments and "advantages" or disadvantages were exactly the same. Yet ability was exactly proportional to the amount of White blood!

The liberals and Jews make a million excuses for this astounding correlation. But the facts remain exactly the same to this day, even on the US draft mental examinations, in which 56.1 percent of the Blacks still can't pass the test, while only 15.4 percent of the Whites fail—even though the poverty and disadvantages of many of the Whites are as bad or worse than that of many Negroes.[2]

Those who insist that "lack of advantages" is what holds the Blacks back have an impossible task to explain what happened in Washington's schools. As long as the schools were white-run, and segregated, they were the best—even with only a fraction of the money and "advantages." Now that they are almost wholly Black since desegregation, in spite of more money than has ever been poured out anywhere else, they are the *worst*.

Who did this: the White people? George Wallace? Hitler? Rockwell? The answer which screams itself at all those who are not willfully deaf is that the Blacks simply lack the stuff to make good students. Runners, jumpers, singers, drummers—and robbers and rapers—they surely are, and good ones. Students, executives, great creators, intellectuals, etc., pure Blacks are *not*—even though our liberal establishment and the Jews never tire of parading Negro inanities and trash as "literature" and "art."

A recent NBC television documentary on the Igoe Housing Project in St. Louis showed the full horror of what these ape-like people do when turned loose in modern civilization. The windows on the first four floors were smashed out from the outside by rocks. The windows on all the top

---

[2] Department of Labor, "The Negro Family," March 1965, p. 75.

floors were smashed out from the inside. The elevators are used so extensively for urinals, that the wiring is all shorted out, and the floors are rotted away. The halls stink of urine and feces, and the walls are covered with unspeakable obscenities. The light fixtures are all smashed, and in the dark halls and basement laundry rooms, the animalistic blacks rape and molest almost all the women, young and old, until the occupants are terrified.

Instead of realizing that all of this is not because of "deprivation," but because of the nature of the beast, the US Government is moving all the blacks out of one building at a time, putting in rock-proof screens on the outside of the windows on the first four floors, and on the inside of the others, putting in stone tiling in the elevators to make them more impervious to all the Negro urine, water-proofing the wires, putting in the kind of light fixtures they have in jails which can't be smashed, repainting the walls with special paint so all the Negro vileness can be washed off every day or every few hours, and installing dozens of police to patrol the corridors. But even NBC admitted, "It may do no good." The blacks will manage to wreck it somehow.

You can put fancy clothes on them, send them to Harvard, teach them to play the harp, teach them to work a computer, and even teach them to be a "PhD." But they will still be like chimpanzees riding bicycles; they will do what they are trained and forced to do, but they cannot and never will do it all by themselves. The drive to civilize, organize, discipline, and restrain themselves is lacking in the pure black. The trained "PhD" Negroes in colleges and in judges' robes are artificial, not real; they don't rise to such abilities on their own racial heritage.

卐 卐 卐

Let's recall some basic facts about life that most men have forgotten. No one has to teach a dog to bark. And a cat that never saw another cat knows how to meow. The very nature of "dogness" impels a dog to bark rather than make some other kind of noise. The nature of "catness" impels the cat to meow. Perhaps this sort of observation seems like a waste of time. Everyone knows these things. Don't they?

Sure they do. People know that dogs bark, cats meow, and they know that each kind of animal is born with its own kind of nature, feelings and responses to it environment. Most people also realize that it is in the very nature of the breed of bulldogs to hold on with their teeth until death stops them, for pointers to point, for spaniels to take to the water, and for greyhounds to run fast. They know that if you want a dog with a nature which bites and hangs on, you don't choose a greyhound but a bulldog. They know that if you want a dog who can and will run fast, you don't want a bulldog but a greyhound. In short, most people know that, while "all dogs are dogs," different *breeds* of dogs have different *natures*.

Not only do dogs bark because they are dogs, but most folks know that certain breeds of dog have different *natures* and kinds of intelligence—because of their breed. In fact, everybody knows that breeds are different in the whole animal world.

But they no longer know it about one animal—*man*. They have been so conditioned and twisted in their thinking about "man" that they have completely forgotten that man, too, is also an animal before he is a man, and that he is born with the particular nature of his particular breed. Nobody in his right mind would judge each dog solely as an "individual." Any person in his right mind knows that breed determines the basic nature of most of the dogs in that breed. A person looking for a tenacious dog which will bite and hang on, with a stubborn nature, would be wasting his time trying to find a dog among the breed of Chihuahuas or poodles, when he could quickly find a dog with such a nature among bulldogs—even though all of them are dogs. Nobody in his right mind would say, "all dogs are equal" or "all birds are equal."

But Jews and liberals have taught most men that to look for any special characteristic among any certain breed of men is "bigotry" and "hate." This utter madness may well be the one single error of modern man which will finish him off and send the planet spinning through the ether once again, silent and empty of men, as it once was for millions of years.

The record shows that there is only one breed of "man" which has, as a matter or history, produced "civilization." Just as a dog barks because he is a dog, a cat meows, and a bulldog hangs on, so one breed of "man," the Aryan White Man, carries with him the nature that produces the justice, order and technology that we call "civilization." Wherever he has gone, the White Aryan has poured out of him the things we call "civilization" from inside, precisely the way a dog naturally produces barks and a cat produces meows.

卐 卐 卐

This book is not and cannot be an anthropology text. It is designed to be a popular book, for the average American, and cannot get into complicated and difficult scientific areas. However, the evidence that the Aryan White man, particularly the Nordic, is the author of "civilization," as a matter of breed, is overwhelming, and must be known to our people if they are to survive.

Our people must also know that Negro inferiority has existed for hundreds of thousands of years. Everybody knows that there are some people who are naturally lazy and indolent, who prefer lying around like slugs in the sun. There are other people for who such utter uselessness and idleness is intolerable. Some people just have to be up and doing. They get restless and bored with more than a very little bit of "resting."

Out of the original pool of humanity a million years ago, some were lazy, some were energetic. The lazy and easy-going naturally stayed in the warm climates—the "Garden of Eden," where you can lay around without getting too cold and where coconuts fall on you for food. These people bred more of their own lazy kind. Over the centuries and the thousands of years, these easy-going people stayed in the easy places to survive on the Earth, inbred with each other, and produced races of easygoing, lazy people.

On the other hand, some energetic, vigorous, early humans began to move around and migrate over the face of the planet. Some of them arrived in the frozen, semi-arctic sections of Northern Europe.[3]

To survive in such a bitter climate, men needed something more than the qualities of the easy-going people of the warm tropics. In the storms and blizzards of a brutal winter, those humans who had not foreseen hard times, had not laid by stores for food, and had not built themselves shelters strong enough to withstand the battering of the northern gales, simply died and did not breed.

---

[3] Today this is known as the 'Cold Winters Thesis.' See, for example, "Only in America: Cold Winters Theory, race, IQ, and well-being" (B. Pesta and P. Poznanski, 2014), *Intelligence* 46; and R. Lynn, *Race Differences in Intelligence* (2015). This idea is sometimes viewed as a modern reactionary theory, but in fact it goes back at least to Arthur Schopenhauer. In 1851, he said:

"Only after man propagated his stock during a long period of time outside his natural [African] habitat between the tropics and extended it…into the more frigid zones, did he become fair and finally white. … The highest civilization and culture, apart from the ancient Hindus and Egyptians, are found exclusively among the white races. … All this is due to the fact that necessity is the mother of invention because those tribes that emigrated early to the north, and there gradually became white, had to develop all their intellectual powers and invent and perfect all the arts in their struggle with need, want, and misery, which in their many forms were brought about by the climate. This they had to do in order to make up for the parsimony of nature, and out of it all came their high civilization." (*Parerga and Paralipomena*, vol. 2, Oxford University Press, pp. 157-159).

More importantly, selfish men could not survive in the cold North. Men had to be ready to help each other and be fair to each other to survive in the North. In the warm climates, a man could survive with a minimum of foresight and with selfish disregard of others. His shelter could be of sticks and mud. His food supply was instantly available. He had no need for stores. He did not suffer if he lacked planning and foresight. He needed little help from other men. But in the North, selfishness was a luxury man could not afford. Northern European man had to develop foresight and planning to survive the rigors of his environment. He had to learn to build substantial dwellings. He had to exercise and develop abstract mental powers to think in terms of the future not required in the tropics. Those who didn't, died, and their qualities died out with them.

A natural selection of men occurred when the energetic ones left the warm climates where man originated, leaving the lazy ones behind.

In the North, man had to think ahead to live. The foresighted and unselfish people of the north then bred with each other to produce still more foresighted, resourceful, and unselfish people, just as you can breed the qualities of aggressiveness and tenaciousness into the bulldog by inbreeding. Over hundreds of thousands of years, being forced to think and plan ahead, being forced to help his neighbors, the people of the North bred a race of humans in whom the qualities of energy, thought, resourcefulness and unselfishness were paramount.

(It should be pointed out here that Eskimos, who do not exhibit these qualities so much, are relatively recent arrivals in the North, having been driven to the arctic wastes by better men who conquered them and drove them out of more moderate climates in Asia. On the other hand, the geological records show that the Nordic Northern European has inhabited his cold climate for many hundreds of thousands of years.)

The Northern climate thus selected and bred a race of people who had the ability to think ahead; to think in terms of, not the concrete realities of the present moment, but the intangible ideas and conceptions of the storms, difficulties, and conditions they would have to deal with in the future.

This was a new kind of thinking for humanity. Animals and savages don't have to form abstract concepts, because they deal only with solid realities of the present. An animal—and a stupid savage—has no conception of and no care for "tomorrow" (except what instinct forces him to do in a mechanical way, without understanding.) But survival in a cold, inhospitable climate forces man to conceive of "cold," "dark," and "snow" when it is warm and sunny. He must also suppress his aggressive, selfish urges and think in terms of group organization and the sacrifice of self for the group. This "thinking ahead" is the beginning of "objective," "scientific" thought; of thought, directed not solely to the immediate advancement or needs of the individual, but to the relationship between things and abstract concepts, such as "cold," "storms," "tomorrow," etc.

And the need for social organization and individual sacrifice is the beginning of what we now call "Justice" or "Idealism"—the sacrifice of immediate, selfish wants for the good of the group, this surrender of a little personal freedom for social order and justice.

It is precisely in these two areas that the Nordics excel: in the areas of objective, abstract, "creative" inventive resourceful thinking; and in the realm of justice—the higher social "rules" which make it possible for men to live in a neat balance of order and freedom. It is precisely in these vital areas that the Black man falls down, because his breed has had almost no need for these qualities for millions of years. The pure Black has little or no care for the future; he cannot think well except in immediate terms of himself and his own, personal wants of the moment. And, above all, he has little or no conception of sacrificing his own immediate welfare and wants for the long-range good of the group. He is selfish. He is no idealist. Above all he is shortsighted—like a beast.

The White man's "civilization" is the organized system designed to make human survival more productive, and noble by idealism, abstract scientific thinking, social organization, and justice. Justice is the group's machinery for stopping the endless battles that would otherwise be fought by separate human beings over women, food, possessions, shelter, and pleasures. The group establishes rules so that each individual has a "fair" chance to gain these things, and when conflicts arise, there is organized machinery, other than individual violence, to settle the struggle. The group also has penalties and machinery to deal with attacks by individuals against the whole group the "criminal laws."

The people of the north were forced to develop these things far beyond the level required by the inhabitants of the tropics, because survival in the North was marginal at best, and only with the utmost unselfish idealism, foresight and "justice" could men overcome the frozen terrors of the North. But the tropics bread a race of improvident, lazy, unthinking, cruel and animalistic people who live for the moment, and cannot really understand our "science" or our lofty concepts of a "justice" or group "idealism" for which they had no need for so many millions of years.

Conversely, the hard life of Northern Europe bred a race of men filled with energy, idealism, a delicate sense of justice, and above all, the ability to think other than in terms of themselves—to think 'objectively'—to think abstractly, mathematically, scientifically, and to act idealistically, for the group.

Between these extremes, there are all degrees of development. The special qualities of human breeding which are responsible for "civilization"—for Western Culture—are precisely the special qualities bred by the men of extreme North Europe: abstract, objective, scientific thinking, unselfish idealism, and a fine sense of justice. The Nordics are thus supreme in those special qualities of character that build civilization; especially energy, idealism and objective, abstract thought.

With the Nordics, come the Alpines, Mediterraneans, Dinarics, and other members of our great White Race. Most of us are mixtures of all these White groups. All of these White groups are so far, far above the lowly, animalistic Blacks that Whites—*all* Whites—form a separate and superior breed. There is no way to "raise" the level of the abilities of the Black race (short of being God, and having a few million years for the job), any more than you could "raise" a penguin to the eagle's flying ability by some kind of training or "welfare."

Our great White Race, led by the Nordics, is the most precious thing on this planet, for all those who love the best of civilization, idealism, and justice, regardless of one's own position in the racial scale. Let the heritage of hundreds of thousands of years of the White Race be drowned in a flood of darker blood, and all the idealism, justice and culture will perish.

卐 卐 卐

Almost every high Western culture has resulted from the conquering of a native population by Aryan White Men who have imposed their laws, their science, their religion, and their culture upon the lower colored race they subdued, just as the Whites did here in America to the Indians.

History shows that in every single case where the White Aryans performed this feat of imposing civilization on a colored race, without exterminating the inferior race, the colored race has eventually conquered the minority of White conquerors by the flood of their colored blood. The earliest drawings and records of Egyptian civilization show that the men who created the pyramids and the wonders of Egypt were Mediterranean *White men*. To build the mighty pyramids and great stone buildings of Egypt, these conquerors went south into the Negro area of Africa, herded millions of black, near-animals into Egypt and put them to work as slaves—like horses.

Although the White masters took all sorts of ruthless measures to prevent the mixing of any Negro blood with their own, there were always lustful members of their race willing to satisfy their sex urges without thought of the consequences—with Black women. Over the 3,000 years of Egypt's decline, the first few brown mongrels bred by thoughtless Whites with Nubian Blacks, increased to hundreds, thousands, hundreds of thousands, and finally became such a mongrel flood they overwhelmed what was left of the White Aryan masters, and utterly swamped and eliminated the culture-producing White breed. Toward the end, there was actually a colored Pharaoh.

The rate of Egypt's decline follows the rate of destruction of the White Aryan breed; not closely—but *exactly*.

Today, the Egyptians take their stand with Black Africa, politically, socially, and racially. And their weakness and backwardness has nothing to do with lack of opportunity; it is racial!

卐 卐 卐

If this were some unusual quirk of history, I would not have bothered to chronicle it in this book. But it is *not* an odd, unusual event. It has happened over and over and over again. It always happens.

It happened in Greece, where the White Aryans produced the most beautiful civilization the world has ever known—the very model for our own civilization of today. The early works of artists of Pericles' "Golden Age" of Greece show that the authors of the "Golden Age" were themselves a "golden" people, with golden, yellow curly hair, blue eyes, and fair skin—Nordics.[4] They, too, conquered the lesser, colored, Asiatic people they found in Greece, enslaved them, went out and gathered up the lower races of Negroes and, little by little, mixed with these miserable African creatures, until Greece today has only a minority of the original Nordic race. And the record of the decline of Greek civilization is precisely the record of the mixing of its blood with the inferior swarms of its own Black slaves.

We find the same suicide of our race in Rome, Spain, Portugal, Latin America, Italy, and Mexico—everywhere the White Man has tried to live in the same geographical area with inferior races. The noble qualities of justice, law-and-order, fairness, scientific impartiality, freedom from gross superstition, and all the other qualities of the Nordic White Man are the basic building blocks of what we call civilization. Without these qualities

---

[4] See T. Dalton, "Blond Hair, Blue Eyes: Some Thoughts on the Aryan Ideal," in *The Steep Climb: Essays on the Jewish Question* (2023).

in the people who have power in any nation, that nation remains or becomes backward and finally savage.

卐 卐 卐

The *urge* to fairness, justice, objectivity, scientific inquiry, centuries-long foresight, etc. are as inseparable from the Aryan, especially the Nordic White Man as is the bark from a dog, or the meow from a cat. In fact, it is this very urge to fairness, this sense of justice, this supreme objectivity, which leads Western man to his own destruction through "liberalism." The sincere, White liberal is a person who has so suppressed his natural instincts and so exalted his love of "fairness" that *he has lost his own sense of racial survival.*

The single "common denominator" in all the irrational beliefs of "liberals" is this over-objectivity, this fanatic dedication to what appears to their intellects as "fair"—even though, in the long run, their liberal "fairness" produces the utmost *unfairness* to their own people, namely, the extinction of our race, the race which alone (and ironically) produces the "liberals" who love this fairness.

"It isn't fair," say the liberals, "that some students should be stigmatized as 'failures' while others are applauded for succeeding. Those who are stigmatized as failures are emotionally crippled and therefore fail more. Therefore we must eliminate grading in schools and universities. We must eliminate the competition and find ways to *make* all students equally successful."

"It isn't fair," moan the liberals, "that one man is born an (ugly and stupid) Negro, through 'no fault of his own,' while another is born a handsome and intelligent White Man. Therefore, it is our duty to repair Nature's mistakes and *push* the Negro up to a 'fair' level with the White Man"—and so liberals favor the madness of race-mixing.

"It isn't fair," the liberals say, "that one man should have a million dollars while another is broke or poor." They forget the necessary working of the mechanisms of reward and punishment established by Nature to ensure energy and work by her creatures; and so liberals become pro-communists and communists.

"It isn't fair," chant the liberals, "that America and Europe have so much, while the 'undeveloped' (colored) nations like Haiti, Africa, China, India, and South America have so little"—so the liberals become international hand-out artists, to see that even the most unproductive, stupid, and worthless pygmy gets his "fair" share of what the White Man produces by his energy, creativity and work.

"It isn't fair," piously intone the liberals, "that there should be wars in which men kill each other," forgetting that only force prevents *some* men from banditry and rapine; and so these liberal fatheads become silly pacifists.

"It isn't fair," say the liberals, "that an elite nation should enjoy so much while other nations have nothing, or that some groups within nations should have more control than other groups." And so the liberal love of "fairness" leads to their crazy, "one-man, one-vote" doctrine, and their suicidal, black United Nations—"democracy"—with absolutely no regard for the rights of one man who has created and produced to control what he has won, while another man has done absolutely nothing and therefore has no "rights" to the fruits of the work of others.

Every single dogma of the left and the liberals will be found to reek with this crazy passion to be "fair" to the unfit, the mongrel, the cowardly, the stupid, and the freakish *at the expense of the vigorous, the creative, the strong, the intelligent, and the brave.* This crazy effort to reverse the wisdom of Nature by being "fair" to failures and creeps and freaks is the very essence of what the liberal jerks call "ideal communism." "Liberalism" and "ideal communism," when sincere beliefs, represent such a crazy passion for the *underdog,* that the fanatic victims of this liberal delusion are eager to beat the *upper*dog to death, just because he is better.

This insanity is peculiar to the super-objective White, Aryan people. The Jew who preaches communism does not practice its "sharing" doctrines. No, communism for the Jew is only a *weapon* to ensnare the minds and hearts of foolish non-Jews, so he can rob and enslave them.

And among the black races, brutality, cannibalism, and tyranny still prevail. There is no danger of there ever being any significant number of sincere "liberal" cannibals.

In short, "liberalism" and "ideal communism" are the results of the Aryan's objectivity, fairness, and love of justice, carried to the point of madness and suicide.

To use an apt analogy, sincere leftists (non-Jewish) are like gardeners who cannot bear to pull up weeds because they "feel for" the weeds. They can't bear to see the "weeds" of humanity pulled out of the productive gardens of society. Their emotional defense of the weeds finally leads them to the point where they are *pro*-weed, and *anti-garden.* Only the Aryan White Man ever develops this "pro-weedism," this super-objective liberalism, which leads the victims to deny their own best interests and fight (in many cases, heroically) for the "rights" of human weeds and trash.

All the rest of humanity, untouched by this basically Nordic ability to think and feel idealistically, unselfishly and objectively, goes about its business in the old-fashioned way of *instinct*, with selfish singlemindedness for their own welfare.

Nor can the White Man impose his idealism, order, and civilization on lower peoples. Whenever the White Man conquers a colored population, as in Haiti, and then leaves, also as in Haiti, the native-colored population quickly sinks back to its natural squalor, injustice, stupidity, and savagery, again as in Haiti.

Western civilization is a result of the nature of the White man. Without the White Man, there *is no* Western civilization, no Western justice, no Western technology, no modern science or culture. A dog barks because he is a dog. A cat meows because it is a cat. And a White Race produces Western "civilization" because it is a White Race. When it is no longer White, it ceases to produce civilization, and in fact, lapses into savagery and degeneracy. *That is what we are now doing in the United States.*

卐 卐 卐

Until 1900, this country was overwhelmingly Nordic—composed of the people of England, France, Germany, Ireland, Scandinavia, Poland, etc., all of whom are descended from the same northern human stock. Although there are always some rotten elements, the majority of these people carried within them the basic urges which create and support fair courts and police systems, just government, honest politicians and statesmen, courageous and self-sacrificing fighters, good organizers, those who love truth for its own sake, energy and the will to work and produce, and all the other human qualities which have made America the greatest and richest land in history.

While America, composed mostly of these Nordic elements, was conquering and slaughtering the colored Indians it found as natives, it jealously guarded its shores against invasions of other races. Our immigration policies for two centuries rigorously excluded colored races and favored Whites. So up until about 1850, we had a homogenous, White, relatively stable population—with the exception of the swarms of black slaves (who were held in rigid subjection).

Then a few Jews and damned fools loosed in our midst the first real germs of the racial disease which had already smashed every similar White civilization before, from ancient Egypt to Brazil. We allowed ourselves to fall prey to the poisonous liberal idea that perhaps colored races were only

"White people with dark skins," and were only savage because they had never really had a "chance."

In 1852, Harriet Beecher Stowe wrote *Uncle Tom's Cabin*—a book full of the most mawkish and naked propaganda on behalf of this "Negro equality" idea the world had ever seen. (Too few people know that Jewish publications boast that Mr. Stowe, Harriet's husband, was not only a Jew, but also a rabbi—one of the endless number of name-changing Jews.[5])

Millions of otherwise intelligent Northern Whites, therefore (who had never seen or known anything about real black men), armed themselves and slaughtered more than a million of the best of the White Race in America on behalf of these Black people, in a suicidal "Civil War." Every nation that has tried to live in the same area with the Blacks (even when the Blacks were kept in total slavery), has always wound up with its blood poisoned and mongrelized, and conquered by its inferior slaves.

After this White-blood-letting in the United States, the Blacks were not only turned loose, they were put over the White man as his governors in the conquered South. Only the uprising of the Ku Klux Klan saved the South (and our race) from that unspeakable horror. Taking advantage of the natural qualities of the Negro—superstition and stupidity—the Klan rode around at night in bed-sheets. The black half-animals took the sheeted Klansmen for "hants," "ghosts," etc. This, coupled with outright Klan violence and terrorism against "uppity" Blacks, soon restored White domination, order, and civilization to the South. And when the average Northerner had seen and experienced the reality of the Blacks, he quickly sided with his Southern White brother—which is why the Klan was able to survive and succeed. Our race still had the energy and unity to recover from the orgy of racial insanity of the Civil War. Even the most rabid liberal leaders of those days shrank from real race-mixing such as we have today.

President Lincoln never preached racial equality, nor any kind of mixing. In fact, Lincoln preached just *the opposite*—another example of the way our modern, Judaized society lies to the people. Here are some of Lincoln's best utterances on the Negro, for instance:

> "Negro equality! Fudge! How long, in the government of a
> God, great enough to make and maintain this Universe, shall
> there continue knaves to vend, and fools to gulp, so low a

[5] There seems to be little evidence that Calvin Ellis Stowe (1802-1886) was Jewish—although he was a scholar of the Bible and the Hebrew language.

piece of demagoguism as this." (*Fragments: Notes for Speeches*, September 1859, Vol. III, p. 399)

"Judge Douglas has said to you that he has not been able to get from me an answer to the question whether I am in favor of Negro citizenship. So far as I know, the Judge never asked me the question before. He shall have no occasion to ever ask it again, for I tell him very frankly that I am not in favor of Negro citizenship. Now my opinion is that the different States have the power to make a Negro a citizen under the Constitution of the United States if they choose. If the State of Illinois had that power I should be opposed to the exercise of it. That is all I have to say about it." (*Speech at Springfield, Illinois* on June 26, 1857, Vol. II, pp. 405-409)

"In the course of his reply, Senator Douglas remarked, in substance, that he had always considered this government was made for the White people and not for the Negroes. Why, in point of mere fact, I think so, too." *(Speech at Peoria, Illinois* on October 16, 1854, during first Lincoln-Douglas Debates, Vol. II, p. 251)

"See our present condition—the country engaged in war!—our White men cutting one another's throats and then consider what we know to be the truth. But for your race among us there could not be war, although many men engaged on either side do not care for you one way or the other... It is better for us both, therefore, to be separated.

"You and we are different races. We have between us a broader difference than exists between almost any other two races. Whether it is right or wrong I need not discuss, but this physical difference is a great disadvantage to us both, as I think your race suffer very greatly, many of them by living among us, while ours suffer from your presence. In a word, we suffer on each side. If this is admitted, it affords a reason at least why we should be separated." (*Address on Colonization to a Deputation of Negroes in Washington, DC* on August 14, 1862, Vol. V, p. 371)

"I will say then that I am not, nor ever have been in favor of bringing about in any way the social and political equality of the White and Black races—that I am not nor ever have been in favor of making voters or jurors of Negroes, nor of qualifying them to hold office, nor to intermarry with White people, and I will say in addition to this that there is a physical difference between the White and Black races which I believe will forever forbid the two races living together on terms of social and political equality. And inasmuch as they cannot so live, while they do remain together there must be the position of superior and inferior, and I as much as any other man am in favor of having the superior position assigned to the White race." (*Fourth Debate with Stephen A. Douglas* at Charleston, Illinois on September 18, 1958, Vol. III, pp. 145-146)

Every word attributed to Abraham Lincoln on these pages may be found in what is probably the most complete source of original Lincoln documents, *The Collected Works of Abraham Lincoln*, edited by Roy P. Basler and published in 1953 in eight volumes plus an index.

Lincoln was not the first to preach racial separation, either. The man who wrote "All men are created equal" in the Declaration of Independence, Thomas Jefferson, wrote and thought the same thing as Lincoln. As an example of how viciously our Judaized culture today lies to us, look at the inscription on the Jefferson Memorial:

"Nothing is more certainly written in the book of fate, than that these people (the Negroes) are to be free."

The inscription on the Memorial then *stops*—giving the impression that was the end of what Jefferson wrote, and what he meant. But the rest of what Jefferson wrote in that sentence reverses this false impression. Here's the completion of the sentence left off the inscription: "...nor is it less certain that the two races, equally free, cannot live in the same government." (*Letter to George Washington*, January 4, 1786)

卐 卐 卐

The Jews, chart-forgers, and equalists, by eliminating all knowledge of our racial heritage, all knowledge of the source of civilization, all knowledge of the inferior, savage nature of the colored man, and all knowledge of the universal fate through all history of people who forgot these things, have succeeded in vastly accelerating the usual historical processes of racial degeneration and collapse.

Our modern generation, soaked in Jewish television, bombarded with Jewish progressive education, lied-to by Jewish newspapers, magazines, and movies, poisoned by Jewish "morality"—or rather lack of it—deprived of any real home, family, beliefs, and ideals, and finally ruled ruthlessly by Jewish-dominated toady politicians who pass vicious laws enforcing race-mixing with bayonets, has sunk to the point of racial degeneracy which took Rome five centuries to reach. Unless we can find some way to make our White people once more *know themselves*, realize *who they are*, *what they are*, and what the alien races of Jews and Negroes are doing to us, it will be forever too late!

Let the White Race be destroyed, and the savagery, injustice, cruelty, and superstition of the other races will quickly drag the world back to the jungle. America is now the last bastion of the White Race.

Germany was that bastion, but the Jews got us to destroy Germany, and it is now powerless to fulfill its old role as the "bulwark against the East." England has perished, in terms of energy and aggressiveness. She has turned over her colonial pioneers to Mau Mau cannibals everywhere on Earth. She is welcoming the cannibals to her tiny British island, she is imprisoning those who object, and she is using everything except force against White Rhodesia to make White people submit to jungle savages. England is now so Judaized and enfeebled that, while she may revive enough to save the Whites there, it will take a century to restore her natural energy again. England cannot hope to lead the fight to save the White Race, when she herself is perishing. France, Italy, Greece, etc., are too weak and Judaized even to want a revival.

There is no point in cataloging all the miseries of the other White nations under Jewish Bolshevism and liberal propaganda. America is the last, the only hope for the salvation of all White people and therefore our civilization. Only in America is there still a large enough pool of raw, Aryan White blood with the wealth and power to lead a revival of our race.

If America falls finally and irretrievably into the hands of the Jews and Blacks, as England, France, Russia, and the rest of the Western world have already done, there will be no patch of ground left on this planet where even a few White men can get together and organize any kind of resistance to the final drowning of the White Race by the flood of inferior colored blood. This is it!

America is the last battleground of Armageddon. We must reach the minds and hearts of our still energetic, still courageous, still racially excellent millions and millions of White Men—unite them as a race—in spite of religion, politics, geography, economics, or anything else. They must see that they stand on the precipice, the end of a million years of development of the great White Race—with the foot of the Negro and the Jew planted in their back and pushing. They must be made to see that there is no issue on this Earth as vital to them as the one issue the enemy won't let them talk about—*race!* They must understand that everything we love and treasure, and almost everything of culture, civilization, justice, truth, and nobility on this planet is a product of the great White Family—of which each of them is a part.

They must also see that we cannot afford the petty division of our great White Race into squabbling factions that hate each other. There are minor racial differences between White Men. And the Nordic is the ideal toward which we all must strive. But compared to the vast gulf between any White Man and the colored races (especially the Africans), the differences between groups of White Men are almost invisible. Pole and German, Frenchman and Englishman, Italian and Lithuanian, Dane and Greek, American and Irishman, Swede and Spaniard—we are White Men—the last of the breed. We are brothers. We are surrounded and almost extinct. We dare not fight over minor differences while forgetting the greatest and most important difference on Earth: the difference between *us*, the Whites, and *them*, the Blacks; between all White Men and the colored swarms which threaten to engulf and destroy our entire breed forever.

The color of your skin is your uniform in this ultimate battle for the survival of the West. It is a matter of life and death that we find the energy, will, wisdom, and diplomacy to reach the millions of "conservatives" who are spiritually on our side, but who are still blind to the issue on which all the others depend—breed, race. Every single White civilization before us has perished in dark squalor because the Whites never realized that all other problems of economics, politics, theology, culture, etc., are child's games, compared to the fatal problem of *race!*

Our people are surrounded, discouraged, torn apart by childish squabbles, unconscious of who we are and what we are, sent scurrying into a thousand blind alleys by side issues of politics, economics, religion, and culture, terrified even to mention the real racial problems which are destroying us, until we are facing a catastrophe unheard-of in all history.

Whenever before the Whites have suffered disaster—in India, Egypt, Brazil, etc.—there have always been places left on Earth where the White race could breed true, and produce new energy and the seeds from which could spring a renewed White Race. Today, the Jews, Bolsheviks, and liberals have succeeded in a worldwide attack upon the White Race. They have left no hiding-place, no refuge for our breed to survive and replenish itself. Their United Nations has made it a crime of "genocide" even to mention these facts. And now they are pushing viciously for a world police force to enforce racial catastrophe under the name of "brotherhood" and "equality."

A century of Jewish propaganda, Jewish brainwashing, Jewish "equality," Jewish propagandizing of the "masses" against the elite, the Jewish domination of our race by the power of gold, and Jewish debunking of our leaders has produced the ultimate horror upon the planet: a race of Whites who can hardly wait to destroy themselves in the name of "world brotherhood."

卐 卐 卐

It is the inborn, basic nature of the White Race that alone can produce what we call Western civilization, which has, as a matter of fact, produced Western civilization, and which alone can sustain Western civilization. Emotional, tear-jerking propaganda about brotherhood and "love" can hide that fact. But all their slogans and propaganda cannot make it less of a fact.

On the other hand, it is the inborn, basic nature of the colored races, especially the African Black race, to be unable to develop, use, or sustain Western civilization, because the drive to idealism, unselfishness, foresight, abstract, scientific thinking, and cultural organization is not in the Negro. In fact, history has shown that whenever a civilizing White race has brought in dark people slaves and slowly mixed with them, the civilization of the White people collapsed exactly as fast as they became dark mixed, mongrel people.

If you want to see a classic scientific proof of the evil of this race mixing, compare the histories of North America and South America. South America is as rich, or richer, in natural resources than North America. South America has as wide, or wider, range of climate, than North America. South America is bigger than North America. South America was settled before North America, and has had more time to grow and develop.

So, why is South America not far ahead of North America in civilization? Why do all the people of the world clamor to get into *North* America, but few try to migrate to *South* America? Why is North America now the "richest" continent on Earth, while South America is still an "undeveloped," backward, starving continent, still containing headhunters and still largely a jungle?

You cannot claim this is because of "form of government," or because of "freedom," or any other reasons of economics, politics, theology, sociology, etc., because South America has had, and still has, all the things of this nature there are in North America. Most of the constitutions of Latin

America are modeled directly, almost word for word, after the US Constitution. But most of South America remains, poor, chaotic, backward, dirty, and "undeveloped"—as the liberals like to call the sorry, miserable colored races. The only real difference between North America and South America is in the people—the races. The people of North America are overwhelmingly White—and mostly Nordic. The people of South America are mostly dark—mixtures of native colored Indians, Negro slaves, and Spaniards or Portuguese.

The English, Scandinavian, Scotch, Irish, French, and German settlers of North America did not come only to loot and exploit and then return to Europe with their booty, as did the Spanish and Portuguese who came to South America. The Nordics (or "Anglo-Saxons") who came to North America came to *settle*, and they therefore brought their women with them, and lived as families. Northern Whites largely exterminated the native, colored population. The Spaniards, who came only as looters and exploiters, brought very, very few of their women, and joined the colored natives. Male human nature being what it is, Nature took its course.

In the North, the men produced more White Men, like themselves, mating only with their own women. In South America, the Spaniards satisfied their lust on native Indian women, and later—the Negro slave women they imported from Africa. They produced vast numbers of stunted, stupid, brown mongrels. That is not "hate" or "bigotry;" that is historical fact.

And you can see the result for yourself if you visit South America. In Brazil and the largest part of this vast Latin American continent, you will feel like some kind of foreign giant among colored pygmies when you walk down one of their streets. The population swarms with brown, murky-eyed, stunted, and lethargic human creeps in baggy rags. Only where Northern energy and capital has moved in, as in the big cities, will you find what we would call "civilization." Wherever the native, mongrel population is left to itself, you will find filth, squalor, cruelty, incredible lack of morals or standards of conduct, political chaos, tyrants, laziness, and the same kind of half-civilization you find in Africa, India, and wherever the colored man rules.

卐 卐 卐

These are cruel and brutal statements, perhaps. The heart of gentle folk rebels at their recitation. But the survival of Western civilization depends on their recital and their being burned into the minds of our people. The mush-headed liberals, the Jews, the commies, and the vast herds of brainwashed Americans are now doing to North America what the Spaniards did to South America.

And you can't afford to be tender hearted about this subject, because there is no way to correct a racial mistake, once we allow it to be made. If we allow the idiots and conscious chart-forgers and ship-wreckers to make miserable little brown mongrels out of your grandchildren and their children, then you will make a South American jungle, too, out of our mighty, wondrous North American White civilization. Your people will drown in dark blood more surely than in all the oceans of the world. White people must be made conscious that they are all *one family*, with different branches of the family called Baltics, Nordics, Anglo-Saxons, Mediterraneans, Slavs, Dinarics, Alpines, etc. But no matter what branch of the family a White Man may be, he is infinitely closer to any of his other White brothers and sisters than to any of the colored races; and there is an unbridgeable gulf between any White Man and the miserable, half-animal Congo Negro who spawned the blacks in our midst.

Nothing on this planet is so precious to us, and should be so precious to the world, as the White "Master-Race" heredity that, alone, can produce and maintain justice, order, culture, and White civilization.

Those Jews aid ape-like Negroes who plot to destroy that precious pool of White blood, and the "liberals" who help them in that plot, are murderers and exterminators of a whole race—the greatest race which has ever walked the face of this planet.

CHAPTER 12

NIGHTMARE

Consider the following future scenario:

It's hot. The night atmosphere is heavy and oppressive. All the windows are open. You can hear a siren a few blocks away, the kids screaming in the street and even the drunken voices of the O'Malleys in their usual argument. But no breath of air comes through the windows. You lean back in your squeaky wicker chair, tee shirt wet with perspiration. Even the little fan oscillating back and forth just emphasizes the brutal heat and sweatiness of the air when the fan momentarily brushes you.

You turn on the TV and take a gulp of beer out of the cold can. It seems like only another hot August night—only somehow this one's different. You can feel it. There's an air of tension, expectancy, foreboding.

The news has been bad. But then it's been bad ever since the riots began way back in June. You've gotten used to the riots every summer. Now, the summers are expected to be periods of almost open warfare between Blacks and Whites. Even the winters aren't real truces anymore, as they used to be. There are outbreaks of the Black-and-White war even in the coldest winter months. But always the harried authorities have managed, somehow, to restore some kind of order. By the Whites staying out of black areas, they have managed to keep working and to keep up some pretense of civilized life.

But this year, the riots have been almost constant. The TV in front of you has just shown dramatic pictures of what's going on in other cities: the searchlight stabbing into the city night, highlighting black faces distorted with hate, fighting the police and national guard troops, the gunfire and the blazing buildings where Molotov cocktails have sent up whole blocks in flames.

However, it's been quiet in your city, now for almost two weeks. The cops and the soldiers beat down the last uprising by the Blacks before it got out of the Negro area only a few blocks.

The TV newscaster is telling how another boatload of black saboteurs fresh from guerilla training in Cuba has been intercepted alter a running gun battle in the Caribbean and has been prevented from landing in Florida.

You are sick of it! Sick to death of this eternal trouble with these black mobs and communist agitators, raising hell, raping, killing, rising up and burning, looting and threatening whole cities.

You turn off the TV. You gaze up at the ceiling in the growing darkness, wondering where in hell it will end, how it will end. The heavy, hot air of August is laden with sounds of automobile horns, kids shouting, neighbors hollering and somebody practicing the piano nearby. More sips of beer, getting warm as you reach the bottom of the can. You want to get your mind off the damned niggers, for a change. You turn on the light to read the Western paperback you bought on the way home.

Then you hear it.

At first you think it's some kind of crowd cheering at a ball game. There's the sound of a tremendous number of people shouting, a long, long way off. But somehow it's different from any sports crowd. There's a vicious, deadly sound to this roaring mob. You get up from the wicker chair and go to the window. Over the black silhouette of the brick apartments to the east, you see the familiar glow. Fires!

So it's started again!

Why can't they kill all those black bastards, once and for all, and put an end to this crazy business! To hell with it! You won't watch, this time. You close the window, go back and turn the TV back on. Maybe you can get your mind off the everlasting nigger trouble by watching some movie or comedy show.

With the window shut, it seems for a moment you've gotten away from the damnable nigger hell. With the TV on, you can't hear the mob or the occasional gunfire. You get another cold beer and try to relax in the glow of the TV tube.

Just as you get interested in a Western, the damned thing goes dead on you. You get up to wiggle the plug. Sometimes you can fix it that way. Then you notice that the fan is off, too. Must be a fuse. So you go into the kitchen and look into the fuse box with the flashlight. No fuses are blown.

But by then, you're already beginning to notice *all* the lights are off, even the street light which usually shines into the kitchen window. It's really black!

You're not used to such total darkness, such absence of any glow or reflected light at all. It gives you an eerie feeling. You stick your head out the kitchen window. Outside there is something new, something evil. You don't know what it is, but it grips your heart with fingers of ice.

It's silent in your neighborhood. No more kids shouting, no more piano practicing, no more quarrelling at the O'Malley's—nothing; just silence. Dead, empty, heavy silence. The quiet lends impact to the distant sounds of the mob down in the central part of the city. In the silent dark, in which you can see nothing, the sounds of the black mob down there are amplified and emphasized until they seem to be coming at you.

In the darkness outside your window, you hear Jack Morgan, who's been drinking beer on his front steps, hollering to his wife, upstairs, "Don't worry, honey, it's just a power failure. They'll have it on in a little while. Keep your shirt on."

A kid begins to cry—then another. There is an excited, but hushed, buzz outside as the neighborhood tries to adjust to the total darkness. Everybody is listening to the sound of that black mob in town, but reassuring each other that the authorities will soon put down the rebellion, as they always have.

Then you hear Mrs. Johnson calling to a neighbor for some water. "Something's wrong with mine," Mrs. Johnson hollers, "I can't get any water to fix the baby's bottles."

Then, from most of the neighbors all at once, you hear that everybody's water is off. You realize that something must be seriously wrong, and pick up the phone to call the cops. At least you can report that the water is off in your neighborhood.

The phone's dead!

Remembering your transistor radio, you turn it on. "The public is asked to remain calm, until the National Guard can restore order. Stay in your homes and do not panic. There is nothing about the present emergency any different... *Oh, my God! Oh...ahhhh.*"

Over the tiny speaker in the radio comes the unmistakable gurgling sound of a man gasping his last breath. Just before the station goes off the air, you hear "How you like that, you White Motherf--er!"

You lean out the window. "Did you hear that!" you holler to the neighborhood in general. "Hear what?" comes from a dozen throats. "I just turned on my pocket-radio and heard what sounded like an announcer gettin' killed, right on the air. Then they went off!" "Try another station!" somebody hollers. "I already have," comes from somebody else. "They're all off." "I'm gettin' my guns," you holler. "Better be careful," shouts a neighbor, "you know the new laws on guns!"

"To hell with the new laws," you roar. "If those black bastards come messin' around here, they're gonna get shot. I don't care if they throw me in jail for it. I'm not gonna let those filthy niggers shoot up and burn this place, and hurt our women!"

But before you can grab your hidden guns and get out front, they are here!

A car comes screeching around the block, tossing Molotov cocktails and firing automatic weapons! In the glare of the flaming gasoline bombs you see the white eyes in the black faces. But even if you couldn't see them, you'd know what they are by their filthy language! As usual, they are drunk, and roaring typical black curses on all White people—liberal, rich, poor, rightwing, Klan—any White man.

As the carload of black terrorists disappears, still firing, you can hear the screams of the dying, and the expressions of horror from people whose loved ones have been shot to death.

You grab your old Marine Corps M1 and the .38 and take the steps, even in the dark, three and four at a time. Outside, in the flickering light of the fires, surrounded by moans and prayers of your neighbors, you find a little group of men who have had enough service experience not to panic. They have their guns ready, and are trying to decide what to do. You suggest that somebody be sent to the police station over on

Grand. They all agree. A kid with two pistols volunteers. He disappears into the dark. You don't know that the cops are all dead.

Just as you are discussing where each guy will be posted, another carload of the bastards comes roaring back toward town from the suburbs, blasting away. You hit the deck, slam home the bolt of the old M1 and feed a surge of satisfaction when the old rifle rattles off each round at the black terrorists. You can hear one of the sons-of-bitches scream as he's hit! Reminds you of the war! But then you remember— this is home! This is where your wife and kids live. And that brings a new and horrible thought!

The wife and kids are visiting across town. What's happening there? Your heart stops for a moment. But then fury surges up within you. If they've touched Janie and those little kids…!

You begin to consider your position: No lights, no water, no phone, no radio—few guns, fewer who know how to use them and have the guts to use them. No organization! And very little ammo!

While you're thinking about all this, a matter of only minutes since the first attack, here come three more cars! You blast away with the M1. You hit another one! But the rest of the guys are firing away at nothing, wasting the few rounds of ammo you've got! You yell at them to cease-fire! It's too late. They're all out of ammo.

The groans and crying and prayers of the people who are hit have demoralized most of the rest of the people. Surprisingly, a lot of the women seem tougher than the men, and are doing their best with torn skirts and shirts for bandages and what comfort they can provide with words. Many of the men, especially the younger "jive" generation with the long hair and the stoop shoulders, are acting like a bunch of teenage girls, screaming and screeching, begging somebody to "help" them. "Help" them?! You'd like to "help" them with a good kick in the ass.

Now it's no longer dark. The whole neighborhood is blazing. The fires set by the flaming gasoline are burning viciously. There's nothing to stop them. No fire department— not even any water. The night was already oppressively hot.

Now, with many houses roaring infernos of flame, the heat makes your skin shrivel.

Already, many others are moving onto a vacant lot trying to get away from the searing flames. You hear a man and his young wife screaming at each other, a few houses away. She is trying to run back into their house to get something, before it burns up. He is holding her while she struggles and screams. Their kids huddle around her, crying.

She never makes it to the house.

A carload of blacks see her in her nightgown, as they go by. They shoot her husband and her kids. They grab her and drag her screaming, into the car, laughing insanely and boasting to each other what they are going to do. And you can't do a damned thing with empty guns.

Within minutes, two more carloads of the black devils roar into the neighborhood. But these don't keep going—and shooting—like the others. They get out to loot—and rape!

Most of the men around you have long since scrambled off to hide in terror. You can do little else, yourself. From under a bush on somebody's lawn, shaded from the worst of the blazing heat and light, you watch the black savages grabbing everything they want—radios, TVs—and women!

God, you never thought you'd see a sight like this! You'd read about it happening far away in the Congo and other places, but always thought it was something you'd never see here. Now you are forced to watch, helplessly, while six of the black animals rip the clothes off the little teenage O'Malley girl and rape her, one after the other—after murdering her mother, father, and brothers. At first, she screams and struggles desperately. But after two or three of the lustful black beasts have beaten her and had their way, she lies whimpering. Then there's no more whimpering.

All night the horror continues. The houses burn to black ruins. And still they burn. The carloads of Negroes roam at will through the neighborhood, looting, murdering the wounded just for pleasure—and raping!

You are helpless! Beaten!

Finally, about 3:00 a.m., things slow down a bit. You crawl out and call to some others still alive. "Where the hell is the National Guard?" you keep repeating to each other, dazedly, stupidly. "Where in the hell is the God-damned Guard?"

You are the only one with enough experience and leadership to try to do anything at all. You suggest gathering the wounded and helpless and trying to get them all together behind a pile of old bricks and stone in the vacant lot. The wounded are crying, really crying for water. But there is no water. Nobody thinks of food, yet. That will come later. But for now, everybody is just trying to survive. And every moment, you can hear the roar of the huge mob in the central city moving out, getting nearer!

The others agree to try to get the wounded down behind the brick pile. But before you can finish the job, you hear a new noise—the clanking, motor noises you remember from the war: *tanks!* The Guard! At last! "It's the National Guard!" you shout to the others. "I can hear the tanks!" They all listen. A feeble cheer goes up as they all hear the tanks.

Just in time, too, because now the black mob is within blocks! You can imagine just what it would be like if that black swarm of bloodthirsty Africans gets here to finish off the remaining survivors! Now the tanks are moving in to restore order at last!

You feel, for the first time, that you will survive. And you resolve never to be caught like this again, never to be disorganized, and so poorly armed! If the bastards ever try to do it again, gun laws or no gun laws, you resolve to be ready! The noise of the tanks gets closer—closer. Now you can see them! Thank God! The iron monsters are clanking along the streets, clearing them, with infantry troops moving in behind them in full battle gear! My God, what a beautiful, delicious, gorgeous sight! Nothing ever looked so beautiful! Slowly, in a daze, those able to walk begin to move out from behind the brick pile.

The tanks and troops uncover a swarm of blacks hiding in a construction project. The infantry troops move in to round them up. The tanks stop.

But what's this! What the hell! What are the tanks doing now? They're turning! They're not waiting for the infantry to finish off the black terrorists in the construction project—

they're turning back! My God! Don't they know there are hundreds of White people out there helpless?

But they're not just "turning back!" The tanks have swiveled around their guns and, are going at their own infantry troops! What the hell! And while you're still stunned, the tanks open up with machine guns on their own infantry and mow them down, hundreds of them!

Then the top of the lead tank pops open—and you know why. A big black head comes out, grinning!

Now there is silence among the little band of men, women, and children behind the bricks. They are too stunned even to curse. Nobody needs to explain. They realize now what has happened. The great majority of the blacks in the armed forces and the National Guard have joined the black rebellion.

Now the mighty technical weapons of the United States are in the hands of black savages, only a few generations removed from animal life in the jungle. Rockets, tanks, nuclear bombs—all that White genius created to protect itself, stupidly and treasonably turned over to the enemy himself in the name of "brotherhood" and "equality!"

You use the last reserves of your will and energy to herd the tiny band of your surviving neighbors down into an abandoned cellar under the bricks and wreckage. Now you are alone, against a world gone mad. No water, no food, no ammunition, no communication, no medicine! Nothing! But you aren't going to give up, yet.

Maybe it's only local. Maybe the Army, or the Marine Corps, or somebody will be able to get control of this revolt of the jungle. If only you can hold out, maybe help will come.

But the tanks are followed, now, by swarms of blacks streaming out of the city, drunk with whiskey and blood—acting precisely as their kind of people have acted from time immemorial in the African jungles, with animal ferocity and bloodthirstiness! Every White soldier and National Guardsman in the area is dead, many mutilated—taken by complete surprise by their own black "comrades!"

Day dawns hot, more horrible than the night, filled with smoke and flames. Dozens of moaning wounded lie all around you, crowded down in there under the rocks and bricks. The cries for water, particularly from the kids, are endless and heartbreaking. But there is no water.

You can do nothing.

卐 卐 卐

About eight o'clock, things have become fairly quiet in your neighborhood. Only the crackling and snapping of the fires all around can be heard.

Then you hear a wail from the street. Your peek out— and see one of the Negroes you shot last night, crawling, moaning, and crying for help. You dare not move.

But suddenly, one of the bravest of the women-folk, a woman who has been comforting and bandaging and helping the wounded and dying all night long, dashes out from under the shelter. She runs toward the black man in the street. You watch with horror while she plunges a big kitchen knife, again and again and again, into the quivering black body!

You recognize her. It's Mrs. Moody—the liberal! She's contributed hundreds of dollars to the blacks, helped them endlessly, marched in their picket lines, sat-in with them and even gone to Mississippi to register them as voters. Now you watch her out there, finally asserting the animal wisdom God gave her to protect her own! Last night, her husband and kids were murdered. Mrs. Moody is no more "liberal." Now she's a member of the great White Race—a fighter!

But it's too late! At ten o'clock, you see more blacks roaming around the neighborhood, picking over the ruins, kicking the dead, ripping the clothing off females, and laughing insanely at their unspeakable atrocities—just like the Mau Mau brothers in Africa!

For the whole day, you manage to survive and keep the little group together. But several die, and the thirst becomes unbearable for all of you.

About seven o'clock, when the summer night is still hot with sunshine, you have to watch a little girl die in her mother's arms. She keeps crying for her mommy, and her mother keeps crooning "Mommy's right here, darling, right here! I'm right here!" and sobbing softly, rocking the little curly-headed kid back and forth, back and forth, until the little head falls sideways. Your eyes fill with tears, and your heart with rage, at the idiots and political rats that brought the greatest nation on Earth to this; and all in the name of "brotherhood" and "progress." Progress!

At about eight, you can hear a sound-truck in the distance. For a long time, it cruises around and you can't figure out what it is saying. Then it begins to move into your neighborhood, and you can hear the message rasping from the loudspeakers:

> "This is the new Socialist Democratic People's Government of the United States. We have overthrown the racist "hate" government of the United States. United Nations Ambassador Alfred Goldberg has already recognized the new People's Democracy.
>
> "The Armed Forces and the National Guard are in our hands. United Nation's Chinese troops are now landing at all airports to assist the freedom-loving People's Liberation Army in restoring order. Resistance is useless. Nothing can move without our permission in the entire nation. You are ordered to come out of hiding, and report to the nearest registration point for movement to prepared refugee areas where you will be fed and then put to work. After nine p.m. tonight, all those who have not checked into registration centers will be shot.
>
> "This is the new Socialist Democratic People's Government of the United States. The Armed Forces and the National Guard of the United…"

—and the truck goes on out of the neighborhood, playing its message of doom for our nation, over and over.

Your eyes blurred with tears, you watch most of the people stumble up out of the hiding place and begin to wander around looking for the "registration points." You have found one round to put in your .38 revolver. You point it at your head…and then you notice a pretty young girl looking up at you, a silent prayer in her eyes. You hand her the pistol and stumble out of the hole before you hear the explosion.

What I have written is no hysterical pipe dream of an alarmist. Precisely this sort of thing is planned, in detail, by the enemy—and has already been put into bloody action wherever the Blacks have risen up in places like Portuguese Angola, the Congo, Kenya, etc., against the Whites who built those countries.

Here in America, it has already started—the way a deadly disease starts with first a small pimple, then a sore, then more and more, until finally it breaks out with a raging fever and lays the victim low. The liars and chart-forgers have done everything possible to camouflage the real nature of the riots spreading all over America, and to pretend that they are the result of frustration and can be cured by making things "better" for the Negro.

Let me first point out that the number and viciousness of these riots is directly proportional to the degree of welfare and "freedom" lavished on Negroes. There have been no Watts-style riots in Mississippi, where there is a more realistic attitude to the Blacks, and therefore more control. It is in the big cities of the North and West that they have had the most fearful riots, although the northern politicians are on their knees, kissing the toes of the arrogant Blacks. But the Blacks demand more and ever more, and will never be satisfied short of sacking the city and massacring the Whites as their African brothers have already done in Kenya and the Congo.

The liars and chart-forgers never tell the American people what is behind all this rioting, continually repeating that it is "spontaneous" and the result of hundreds of years of oppression. These lies have succeeded well enough so that most Americans really believe that riots simply erupt on hot summer nights because the poor, oppressed Negroes can't stand the "frustration" anymore.

First, of course, there is the point that it is just as hot and frustrating for millions of poor White people, but they don't rush out with bombs and guns to riot and loot. To judge just how wickedly false and dangerous is this "spontaneous" riot bit, you must know the background—the decades of patient communist planning and organizations which has gone into producing them. We have already presented the statements of Israel Cohen from 1912, reprinted in the Congressional Record, that the chief weapon of the communists in overthrowing the USA would be the Negroes. Before World War II, Eugene Dennis, National Secretary of the Communist Party of the United States, laid out the plan in more detail. Here is an actual quote from Dennis' book *A Soviet America*, as quoted by Kenneth Goff, ex-communist associate of Dennis, in his book, *Confessions of Stalin's Agent*:

At that hour, large race riots are supposed to take place in every city of any size. Leaders of these mobs are to be carefully chosen and trained in advance. The disturbances are to be of some extent so as to require sending large forces of police to those areas. While the authorities are trying to quell these riots, picked bands of communists are to seize their radio and TV stations and telephone exchanges. Flying squads of communists are to seize control of the water supply and shut it off, also electrical power and gas. Homes will be without water and fuel, light and telephone. It will be impossible for the people to communicate with friends and relatives. Professional murderers will round up the people in the business districts in some of the larger buildings and hold the men as hostages, while their women are to be turned over to sex-crazed mobs unless the men surrender.

Notice the call for the shutting off of electricity, gas, etc. This has been the standard plan of Mau Mau attack on urban cities of the White Man all over Africa; first they smash the power station and the telephone, etc. Then, in the blackness and confusion, they strike with their bloody African terror.

I have already shown in Chapter 5 how William Weiland and our own State Department conspired with incredible arrogance to oust the pro-American Batista who had severed relations with the communist nations, and install the rabid communist, Fidel Castro. This was for a purpose—but not the simple purpose of helping communism in general. The conspirators needed a base in the new world for the launching of their Black terror campaign, masquerading as a "civil rights" movement. Among other things, they wanted a radio station able to flood the minds of millions of American Negroes with their agitational propaganda, and a safe refuge for terrorists—as Laos is in Vietnam.

With the capture of Cuba by Castro (arranged by traitors in our own government and press) communist training camps were organized, where communist black terrorists can learn all the techniques to implement the usual terrorist "war of liberation," and where equipment for sabotage, including poisoning of reservoirs and food supplies, can be smuggled into the United States. Remember how Castro lived in the "Therzsa" Hotel in Harlem when he came to the UN? Few people realize that Castro is 1/4 Negro, and his revolution is as much Black as Red!

The Cuban spearhead of communist Black terrorism only 90 miles from our American coast has been guaranteed by the USA against any attack by Cuban patriots seeking to free their homeland. Kennedy and Khrushchev put on a big fake drama about missiles and their removal. The end result of this missile charade was that there was never any inspection—but the US Navy was ordered to *protect* the Cuban coast from any possible landings, by Cuban patriots—and this is still going on, with Cuban anti-Castroites being seized on the high seas at gun-point, and delivered to prisons in America for attempting to free their own country!

Not only that, but Eleanor Roosevelt and a gang of similar Reds and pinkos, organized a giant support operation to pay enormous sums of blackmail and supply vast stores of rare equipment to Castro, ostensibly to "rescue" anti-Castro-Cubans, although one US Navy task force could have rescued the refugees—and Cuba, in one day.

As soon as Cuba was a secure and heavily-armed camp, aimed like a dagger at the heart of America, the head of the NAACP in Monroe, North Carolina, a big black buck named Robert Williams, launched a trial armed rebellion and kidnapped a White couple as hostages. When his rebellion was finally beaten down, he fled to the prepared refuge in Cuba and organized the radio operation already planned, "Radio Free Dixie." On one of these first Cuban broadcasts, Williams gloated:

> We failed with armed rebellion in Monroe only because it was our first try, and we made mistakes. We actually had enough force and arms to reduce the area to ashes and rubble. We did beat the police and emergency forces. What stopped us was the importation of terrorist state troopers from other areas. Had we attacked in these other areas too, and tied down these forces, we would have succeeded.

What the chart-forgers and liars have not told Americans is that the entire blueprints for the big-city riots are all laid out in Williams' publication, *The Crusader*, which was first published in Cuba. Here's the cover of the issue which actually predicted the Watts riots and laid out the technique— even to the slogan, "Let it burn!"

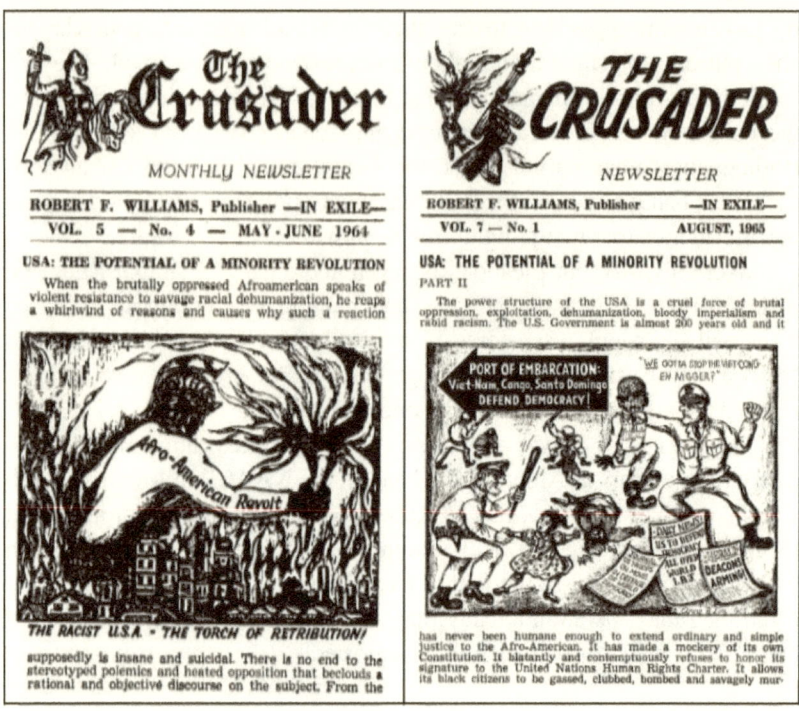

And here's more precise plans from *The Crusader* for exactly how they are doing it, and why they believe they can beat the entire USA—just as set forth in the first part of this chapter:

> When massive violence comes, the USA will become a bedlam of confusion and chaos. The factory workers will be afraid to venture out on the street to report to their jobs. The telephone workers and radio workers will be afraid to report. All transportation will grind to a complete stand still.
>
> Stores will be destroyed and looted, Property will be damaged and expensive buildings will be reduced to ashes. Essential pipe fines will be severed and blown up and all manner of sabotage will occur, Violence and terror will spread like a firestorm. A clash will occur inside the armed forces.
>
> At US military bases around the world local revolutionaries will side with Afro GIs. Because of the vast area covered by the holocaust, US forces will be spread too thin for effective action. US workers, who are caught on their jobs, will

try to return home to protect their families. Trucks and trains will not move the necessary supplies to the big urban centers. The economy will fall into state of chaos.

This racist Imperialist oppressor will not be brought to his knees, simply because of the fighting ability and military power of Black Freedom Fighters and their allies inside the US but because of the creation of economic, chaotic conditions, total disorganization, frustration of his essential end, ultra vital organs of production, and adverse conditions created by the worldwide liberation struggle

Such formidable enemy will fall prey to the new concept of revolution because of this ultra-modern and automated society and the lack of psychological conditioning of his forces. Our people have already been conditioned by almost 400 years of violence, terror, and hunger.

The new concept of revolution defies military science and tactics. The new concert lightning campaigns conducted in highly sensitive urban communities with the paralysis reaching the small communities and spreading to the farm areas. The old method of guerrilla warfare, as carried out front the hills and countryside, would be ineffective in a powerful country like the USA. Any such force would be wiped out in an hour. The new concept is to huddle as close to the enemy as possible so as to neutralize his modern and fierce weapons. The new concept creates conditions that involve the total community, whether they want to be involved or not. It sustains a state of confusion and destruction of property. It dislocates the organs of harmony and order and reduces central power to the level of a helpless, sprawling, octopus.

During the hours of daylight, sporadic rioting takes place and massive sniping. Night brings all out warfare, organized fighting, and unlimited terror against the oppressor and his forces. Such a campaign will bring about an end to oppression and social injustice in the USA in less than 90 days and create the basis for the implementation of the US Constitution with justice and equality for all people.

It is no longer a truism that our people cannot win such a struggle. The world has changed and the favor of the situation has shifted to the side of the Afro-American. Those who cry that we cannot win are either agents of the oppressor, latent masochists, or ignorant of the new facts of life. We do not need paternal white "big Daddies" for our friends now. What we need are some fighting John Browns.

Our friends are growing throughout the world, while those of our oppressors are diminishing. It is important that we immediately create stronger ties with our brothers of Latin America, Asia, and Africa. It is important that our people stop cooperating with our oppressor and exert more effort to expose his beastly ways to the peoples of the world. Yes, we can win because our struggle is just and our friends are many. The handwriting is already on the wall. Victory is now within our reach. *Let us prepare to seize it!*

Now read this reproduction of a broadcast of their "Radio Free Dixie" to millions of US Negroes and you will have a better idea of what the riots by Negroes means, and what's ahead for America—if something drastic is not done, and soon.

Zero-hour approaches. The winds of turmoil and violence approach the shores of oppression and discontent. The racist forces of tyranny and hate sweeping out of the distance to cast havoc on our dehumanized, so-called violent, and helpless people. In this crucial hour of the long and bitter struggle for the survival of our people in racist America, the philosophy of so-called nonviolence is a pathway to suicide and extermination. The racist oppressed people in North America is a savage brute. He is a raging beast devoid of human sensibilities.

Those deluded dupes who speak of the power of nonviolence and love in taming the wrath of racist white savages are no more than recklessly leading our brutally oppressed people down the violent, bloody path of genocide.

The racist thug advocates of white supremacy have a mortal fear of self-defense on the part of our long submissive people. This is because fact that the United States' position in the world is so sensitive and today that any long-drawn massive rioting across the nation would strike a death knell for the farce called the democratic way of life. Contrary to what racist buffoons would have our people believe, it is not the Negro who would be exterminated in such a conflict, but the so-called American way of those racist imperialists who conspire to conquer, dominate, and spread Birmingham-type justice around the world. All the civilized peoples of the world sympathize with our struggle to civilize the master race savages and their so-called representative democracy of the Christian USA.

Knowing what the communist forces of "liberation" have done in the Congo, Kenya, Vietnam and all over the planet in the way of wholesale slaughter and torture, rape, and pillage, can you have any doubt left as to what is ahead for America? Does the first part of this Chapter still seem improbable? It should not—not to anybody who sees the historical pattern that has been developing, unhindered, for half a century now.

The White Man once ruled the world with an iron, relatively just, and humane hand. There were abuses, but nothing like what happens when rule is turned over to the colored races that the White Man has dominated and civilized. Now that the White Man has become "too liberal to fight", as Khrushchev boasted, and will no longer enforce civilized conduct on the backward colored races, they are rising up like unleashed jungle animals all over the earth and sinking their fangs into the jugular veins of their one-time masters.

It has already happened to the people of Kenya. Whites scoffed at the idea that the Mau Mau could ever win by their primitive and bloody voodoo and terrorism. But the Mau Mau did win, and the Mau Mau devil, Kenyatta, now rules Kenya, including the Whites who waited too long. The Whites of the Congo and a dozen other places waited too long before realizing what was up, and they are now dead, raped, or gone. In Rhodesia, the Whites finally realized what was ahead and have made a brave stand to protect themselves, and civilization. It is interesting to note, however, that the entire leadership of the USA is backing the forces of savagery and murder against our own White brothers and sisters in Rhodesia (and South Africa).

The people of the United States still cannot see that the Black hell going on is not sporadic, spontaneous, and the result of frustration—but the highly organized and planned invasion of our country by the enemy, who has already landed by the millions, and is attacking.

If they got off of ships and ran up a beach, and did what they are doing to our cities, it would be stopped immediately. But since our chart-forgers and liars, with their "love" and brotherhood baloney, keep most Americans believing "there no plan" behind it, we tolerate a yearly escalation of the attack upon us by millions of Blacks and communists, including most of our own "leaders."

卐 卐 卐

One of the purposes of this book, *White Power*, is to alert our people to this deadly threat. And one of the best ways to do that is to *listen* to the enemy. He is not hiding what he plans; he boasts about it! I have printed only a tiny fraction of the available documents that you can get. There is unfortunately a good deal of truth in what Williams and these black terrorists are preaching: that while Americans have grown strong in weapons and machinery, we have grown soft and dependent on that machinery and weaponry.

I remember well that in World War II we won partly because of enormous superiority in firepower and material. We "sat on" the Japs and Germans, much as a fat man could sit on a tough but tiny fighter, even if the fat man couldn't fight a lick. Not that Americans can't fight; it's just that we have ever more and more machines and fire-power to do it for us, and we get more and more dependent on the easy, mechanized ways every day. We are losing the fighting ferocity of our forefathers which whipped the Indians and everybody else in sight. We are becoming a nation of button-pushers. "If ever the TV and radio goes off, the electricity is shut off, the telephone is gone, the water disappears and there is nobody to tell them what to do, most White Americans will panic," boasts this black communist terrorist, Robert Williams. And Williams is right! "They'll sit around in the dark waiting for the radio to come back on and tell them what to do," he continues. And he's right again—unless we change things!

Now add the fact that the Negroes in Los Angeles, Detroit, Chicago, Cleveland, and many other cities have already proved that they can conquer the entire police departments of these huge cities. Only the National Guard, with heavy weapons and tanks, has been able to restore order. In Detroit, even the National Guard was not enough, and the Army had to be called. The police, by themselves, are helpless. And every day, they apply more and more "handcuffs," review boards, etc., to make the police still more helpless and they work to get guns away from White people.

But that's not the real danger, nor the final aim of the Black revolutionists. As shown by the *Crusader* articles, they're after the Armed Forces! Day after day, week after week, year after year, the Blacks pour into our Army, Navy, Air Force, and Marine Corps—and National Guard. All recent presidents and political leaders have gone way overboard ensuring that Negroes get favored in promotions, over White Men. Not just equal, but favored.

President Kennedy even set up a Jew, Abe Fortas, to make the Gesell Report, a special study to find ways to make more and more Negro officers and noncoms, by setting up political commissars in almost every unit—usually black—to report any senior officer not pushing Negroes up. It's going on now, as you read these lines.

As a result, the services are filling up faster and faster with Negroes, and especially with black bosses: black corporals, black sergeants, black lieutenants—all the way up to black generals! Today, all services except the Navy are between 1/4 and 1/8 Negro, with an even higher percentage of Negro non-coms![1]

Ask yourself what happens in every neighborhood where Negroes move in. Don't the Whites move out? Even the Jews are recognizing that US cities of the North are now more segregated than the South, as a result of the flight of the Whites to the suburbs, as the Blacks have gotten more and more numerous in the cities. When Blacks move in, Whites move out.

And that's precisely what is happening in our Armed Forces—exactly as planned! Except for draftees who have no choice, the Armed Forces are filling up with Negroes—and Negroes are getting the commands. Any effort to stop the upward rush of Negroes by honest White officers is blasted as "bigotry," and the White officer who tries to insist on merit, even by Blacks, is himself discriminated against. I know. I was in, not too long ago. The Blacks re-enlist; Whites get out.

The process is one which goes faster and faster, and feeds on itself. If you've ever seen a neighborhood "go Black," you know what I mean. First one Negro, then a few—quite a few. Then, suddenly, the whole neighborhood is Black. That's the way it's happening in the Army, Air Force, Marines, and to a lesser extent, to the Navy. We think we are protected behind a barrier of rockets, nuclear weapons, and other technological machinery, which are undoubtedly the most powerful the world has ever seen. But if that machinery and weaponry falls under the control of the enemy, it is not only useless to us, it is sure death! At this very moment, the sell-out politicians and demagogues are turning these mighty technical weapons over to

---

[1] As a good indication of this trend today, consider Lloyd Austin: a black soldier who was elevated to successively higher offices, eventually becoming a 4-star general and head of US Central Command in 2013. After his retirement in 2016, he became US Secretary of Defense in 2021. By all accounts, Austin's career has been marked by blatant incompetence and dramatic operational failures at all levels.

more and more Africans. And the Blacks, in turn, are falling more and more under the control of Mau Mau revolutionists.

卐 卐 卐

Aside from the danger we face from our own Armed Forces in Black hands, there is the personal danger you face on a man-to-man basis, from the terrific organization of the new generation of Black guerilla-fighters in the big cities of the North. In Chicago, there is an enormous criminal gang of Black teenagers called "The Mighty Blackstone Rangers," numbering in the thousands. There used to be a smaller gang called "The Disciples," but they have recently merged with the "Rangers" to make the largest Black killer gang in the United States. They are so highly organized they have command centers, use walkie-talkies, and negotiate "peace treaties" with the Chief of Police of Chicago—on television! They are the terror of Chicago!

Today, most of them are still teenagers. They are the result of 20 years of your paying gigantic welfare taxes to breed literally millions of these Black animals—without roots, without homes, without morals, without any respect for anything, let alone "authority."

The average White American has forgotten his heritage of violence. I know I had, until I launched the American Nazi Party. As a kid in school, of course, you have a few fist fights. Maybe, like me, you were also in a couple of wars. But even in wars, hand-to-hand combat—violence to the death—is rare. Not one in a thousand experiences it. But violence-to-the-death was the daily life of the human race for millennia. And daily violence-to-the-death is still the way of life to most big city Negroes. They go at one another with knives, razors, guns, axes, gouging hands, and even teeth. They are used to it, and don't get particularly "shook-up" when suddenly overwhelmed by an explosion of this kind of deadly violence—any more than a dog is "shook-up" over a dogfight. Most importantly, these millions of young, tough Blacks have learned the art of violence-to-the-death. They know what to do.

Do you? What would you do if attacked, right now, by a gang of hoods with clubs, knives, guns, and bombs? These highly organized Blacks are familiar with violence, know how to use it and defend from it. Millions of them even enjoy it. It doesn't panic them. But most White Men have become spiritually soft in terms of being ready, from moment to moment, to fight to the death, personally.

When these millions of Black teenagers now learning personal violence and terrorism in the streets of our big cities are in their twenties, and heavily armed, as many of them already are, they will be ready for a revolution of personal violence which will stun the average White Man and leave him helpless.

I know these Black "kids." They are so used to violence and horror that they laugh in its presence. They fear no policeman, no gun, and no knife—nothing. They have little to lose, and their status in their own Black gang is based on their utter disdain for danger and violence. Caged up with these wild Black animals in jails as I often am, is a terrifying education.

We are putting tens of thousands of these Black killers into uniform, and handing them the deadliest weapons in the history of the world! Just what do you think will happen when they decide to turn those weapons on you—as we have shown is planned? Already, Negroes are rebelling at killing colored people (the enemy Vietcong), and their more rabid leaders, such as Carmichael (and now King), are telling them to commit sedition— not fight. And our cowardly government is letting them get away with this sedition. How long do you think this can go on without an uprising in the armed forces? Also as planned and documented?

And just how do you think the Armed Forces could put down such a Black uprising from within, when every man of the White troops has been taught that to oppose Negroes is "hate"; when many of the officers are Black; when the fighters among our White Race have been prematurely retired, like the immortal "Chesty" Puller of the Marine Corps and a thousand others; when the Whites are completely disorganized, while the Blacks have instant and almost perfect communications; when every Black leader is paraded on TV and in the international press so all the Blacks can know him and be ready to obey, while there are no real White leaders, because anybody who dares call himself a White leader is either censored or so disgraced as a "bigot" and a "hater" that he cannot be effective with his own people?

During the first hours of such a Black uprising in our Armed Forces, in fact, many of the Whites would *help the enemy*—also as planned and documented in the *Crusader*. Our people have been so damnably brainwashed and beaten down by the Jewish doses of "brotherhood" and "love" propaganda, not to mention naked communist propaganda for the Blacks, that our population, and Armed Forces, swarm with "nigger lovers"— White Men who really believe it is their duty, for one reason or another, to prefer these Blacks to their own people. If properly "set," by being told the Black uprising was for the purpose of getting a more liberal "brotherhood" government, lots of these damned fool White Men would join the side of their deadly enemies, long enough to give victory to these savages and their Jew communist leaders. Precisely this has happened in every country where the Reds have seized power and the stupid collaborators have then been liquidated by the Reds—and Blacks—as the fools and dangerous turncoats they are!

卐 卐 卐

I am well aware that, as I dictate this, it all seems too wild and impossible to be worthy of belief or even investigation. I, myself, would not have believed it, were I you, had I not investigated and found the same thing happening time after time all over the planet, with the victims always flabbergasted and unable to believe that it could have happened.

The title of this chapter is "Nightmare." That title refers not only to what is ahead for all of us if we let it happen, but to the indescribable agony of those who *know*. If you are one of the few people who have been warning America of her deadly peril, only to find that no one will listen, then you know the nightmare whereof I speak. The nearest thing to it is when I was a kid and went to one of those horror movies, where the hairy hand keeps reaching out to seize the unsuspecting heroine from behind. You want to scream at her, "Watch out behind!"—only you can't!

America today is that unsuspecting, carefree heroine, happily engaged in everything trivial, while the Black hairy paw with the hammer and sickle on it creeps closer and closer. God grant that we may be able to shout to her to *Wake up* in time! This time it's no movie. That hairy, ape-like black claw has already closed around the throats of dozens of unsuspecting nations before us. For 50 years, it has been happening to one victim after another. And what have *we* been doing about it?

CHAPTER 13

FIFTY YEARS OF FAILURE

Had I been born a thousand years ago, I would have been a "leftist." All higher animal social groups, such as wolves, seals, monkeys, etc., have "governments" of absolute tyranny by the most superior individual, able to conquer all rivals. Only thus can nature guarantee the group the best possible leadership in the struggle to survive. No other "government" is thinkable or possible among higher animals.

Such natural "tyranny" is no hardship on animals unable to imagine any other state. Animals simply accept the absolute domination of their conqueror, once established, the same way they unthinkingly accept storms, pain, annual migrations, birth, and other phenomena of the natural world into which they are born.

As the first cave men emerged from the dumb-brute state, their "government" was inevitably a simple carry-over of this rule by combat-proven conquerors. In terms of geology and anthropology, not until the most recent times did man become sufficiently imaginative and intelligent to project his brief periods of surcease from the leader's domination into the abstract concept of "freedom." Even today, such a concept is utterly foreign and useless to primitive and savage groups under natural conditions. Whenever more advanced civilized groups attempt to give or force their noble concepts of "free" government on backward people, the latter quickly revert to their dictators and tyrants, as we see all over the tropics, in Africa, Haiti, etc.

Early kings and chieftains in European civilization, men like the Viking kings, King Arthur, Charlemagne, and William the Conqueror were very real fighting heroes, literally able to prove their kingship in mortal combat, as in all primitive groups. And since their people were still close to nature, their governments were usually acceptable to most citizens of the time, even the lowest.

Strong and truly brave men are rarely cruel and evil; meanness and cruelty are the traits of weaklings, never strong men. But as kingship became a hereditary institution, utterly worthless and vicious weaklings, who could never survive in physical combat, became "kings." And their cruel, mean "governments" were absolutely intolerable. Under the last of vicious and stupid tyrants, thinking and courageous men of all estates began to risk their lives to oppose these evil, little men, and to oppose the system that made such little men "kings." I would have been one of those men.

In an age of absolute, unnatural, and tyrannical authority, self-respecting men by the thousands gave their lives so that their fellows could have some relief from this arbitrary total authority by unfit weaklings and so that the system of hereditary tyranny could be brought in check. The results were the first European parliaments.

In these groups of nobles who began to limit the absolute authority of unfit kings, those who favored still further limitations on the power of the monarch and still more "individual freedom" for the people traditionally sat on the *left*. Opposite this group, on the *right*, sat those who favored either the status quo or more autocratic power for the king—more government and less individual freedom. That was the origin of "left" and "right," and the only true meaning of the words.

While the Western world suffered the grinding tyranny of weaklings, fools, and greedy schemers as "kings" (and the system which crowned them), the place for self-respecting men who would not bow their necks to the tyrant's yoke was on the *left*. And that is where I would have been, until the evil was corrected. In short, from the earliest emergence of Western man, humanity has necessarily struggled against the naked tyranny of the "right," against arbitrary and absolute power and the system that could place such power irrevocably in the hands of weaklings and fools. "Progress," therefore, for a thousand years, was to move to the *left*.

However, as bad as the absolute tyranny of the extreme right was, it had the advantage of *order*. There was a hierarchy of social and political status, a "pecking order" from the king down to the lowliest serf. Everybody knew his place and any disorder in the society was summarily put down by the king and his "nobles," backed by their army. A Martin Luther King and his riots would not have lasted ten minutes in feudal society. There was "order" in society. But it was something of the "order" of a penitentiary. Thus, at the extreme right end of the political spectrum, there is absolute tyranny, but also absolute order.

In moving away from this absolute tyranny of the right it was impossible not to move to the left. And at the opposite extreme, the extreme left, the political opposite of the extreme right, stands total freedom and no order—anarchy! Anarchy is a condition of no government, with each man free to do as he damn pleases.[1] This is the condition aimed at by the Marxists, who claim that with "perfect" communism, government will "wither

---

[1] 'Anarchy' derives from the Greek *an-archos*: 'without leader.'

away." (Strangely enough, it is also the pretended aim of the mixed-up Birchers and Kosher Conservatives: "less government," etc., etc.)

But when there is no government, in spite of the pretty theories of the communists and Birchers, there is no order, and no safety for the decent citizen. During the Boston police strike in the 1920s, before Coolidge put it down with the National Guard, there was bloodshed and looting all over Boston in the police-less city, and no decent citizen could come out of his home. Even in his home, the decent citizen was likely to be attacked, robbed, raped, and outraged.

Never in this world will all humans be "noble" and full of "love" for fellow men. And as long as there is just one louse who would use force to rob, rape, loot, kill, etc., then there must be some government and some kind of force available to society to protect itself from even a small minority of predators.

To recapitulate, absolute tyranny by fools and weaklings is intolerable. But so is absolute freedom—anarchy—intolerable.

As with most human affairs, the answer lies not in the extremes, but in what Plato called the "golden mean'"—a balance between the two extremes: enough authority to maintain order and enough freedom to avoid tyranny. However, in struggling away from the misery of the total tyranny of the feudal Middle Ages, Western man had no choice but to move to the left—from total tyranny and order, toward the other extreme of total freedom and no order: chaos. I would have been forced, therefore, to move left with the struggle for some freedom from absolute tyranny by weakling, unfit "kings."

But humanity has a terrible habit in correcting evils. Often it moves and fights long and hard to correct an evil, only to keep moving in the same direction to make an evil out of the correction! This is precisely what has happened in Western Civilization. "Freedom" has become an insane fetish, a crazy, illogical shibboleth toward which everybody bows, regardless of whether it is real, responsible freedom such as America knew during the 1800s, or the wild, murderous, vicious libertinism masquerading as "freedom" of savage Africa and the American "left."

We National Socialists believe that Western Man necessarily moved left for a thousand years, away from the total tyranny of the right, until he reached the "golden mean" of a perfect balance between the need for order (and some government) and the need for liberty. We believe that that ideal political golden mean was reached in the American Constitution—not the filthy, twisted thing the present Supreme Court has made of it, but the original, magnificently balanced government of laws and checks devised by our inspired Founding Fathers.

卐 卐 卐

Before proceeding, let me sum up the argument so far. The terms "left" and "right" refer only to the degree of authority in a society. The more authoritarian a government, the more "right" it is; the more libertarian it is, the more it is "left." This is historical and semantic fact. The extreme right of the political spectrum is absolutely tyranny—all order with no freedom. The extreme left of the political spectrum is absolute freedom—all liberty and no order.

Both extremes are intolerable for the White men of Western Civilization. The ideal to be aimed at is a perfect balance of enough governmental authority to guarantee order and safety for each citizen, while permitting him maximum personal freedom from arbitrary government and unjust force.

In spite of the insane misuse of the term by almost everybody today, I cannot avoid declaring that the aim of good government in Western Civilization, therefore, must be to avoid the intolerable extremes of both left and right, and establish a government of political center.

However—and that is one hell of a big "however"—when Western Man had moved to the left far enough to correct the evil of tyranny, he failed to stop! After we had established the American Constitutional Republic in 1789, the perfect balance between authority and order balanced against liberty and freedom, we continued to move to the left—toward libertinism and anarchy! After thousands of years of struggle toward "freedom," Western Man was unable to be satisfied when he reached moderation. Like a man dying of thirst in the desert, who gulps down so much water that he kills himself, Western Man, thirsting madly for freedom, has gone right on past the inspired balance and moderation of the Constitution of 1789 to chase the chimera of "liberty" until today we teeter on the edge of anarchy—until there is so much phony "liberty" that the likes of Stokley Carmichael, Rap Brown, and Martin Luther King can legally survive while they incite riots, bloodshed, and war in our midst, and win world prizes for "peace!"

All forms of authority, from the father of the family, to the police and soldiers, have been so beaten down and blasted that our younger generation is scornful of all authority. Stern, old-fashioned fathers are cursed as "fascists" or laughed at and ridiculed whenever they try to assert any authority to maintain order in the family. Policemen are suspended or even tried and jailed for "brutality" whenever they use force to bring order among rioting, murdering Negroes or other disorderly citizens. College administrations are called "tyrannical" for trying to administer their own colleges, and bearded anarchists and terrorists defy all authority to parade around campuses actually carrying signs reading "F---!" as proof of their "freedom." Workers are taught that they should boss businesses. Our Supreme Court and our toady Congress have decreed that the owner of a restaurant must recognize the "freedom" of a Negro or anybody to force his way onto private property, to eat or wet on the tables—as the urge may strike him. Criminals' "rights" are so zealously guarded that there is little order or safety in our cities any more. Queers demand the "right" to be "married" in public. Kids in school terrorize their teachers. Beatniks demand free and legal dope. Jew and liberal writers demand the "right" to publish and sell to our kids the vilest and most perverted pornography as "literature" and "art."

I could go on and on, but this enumeration should be sufficient to show what has happened to our once magnificent authoritarian, Constitutional Republic. We are racing toward anarchy, toward chaos, and total freedom for mobs. Under these deadly conditions it is a matter of life or death for those who would lead us politically to know what they are talking about, and not confuse the issue. Yet we have a man who commands millions of dollars of funds contributed by desperate, decent Americans—Robert Welch[2]—telling Americans that "Nazism and communism are the *same thing!*"

To understand just how insane and suicidal that is, let me report an experiment we used to make when I was studying psychology at Brown University. We got a bucket of hot water and a bucket of ice water, and stuck one hand in each bucket. After our hands had gotten used to the extreme heat and the extreme cold, we plunged both hands together into a bucket of water at room temperature. The ordinary water felt boiling hot to the hand that had been in the ice water, and the same water felt freezing cold to the hand that had been in the hot water. I have mentioned this experiment (which you can do yourself) to point out the relative nature of the words "left" and "right." To be sure, there are absolute extremes of these terms, as I have shown: tyranny on the right and anarchy on the left. But the spectrum from right to left is a very great distance, and regardless of one's absolute position on the scale, those to the left of one look like "leftists" regardless of their absolute position, and those to the right appear as

---

[2] Robert Welch, Jr. (1889-1985) was founder of the John Birch Society.

"rightists." This is why we have Gus Hall, head of the Communist Party of America, calling the wild, raging radicals of Progressive Labor "leftists" and calling President Johnson a "Nazi"!

This relativity on the left-right political scale is why "left" and "right" have lost a lot of meaning today. America has moved so damnably far toward the extreme left that any effort to get back to the center must, by necessity, be "extreme Rightist."

Three decades ago, when Jewish Bolshevik leaders like Rosa Luxemburg were hanging the Red flag up and taking over whole states in Germany, the only reply of decent Germans had to be a movement toward the most violent extremity of the right—toward tyranny. When something gets too warm you can cool it off by blowing on it. But when it catches on fire, as Germany was on fire with Jewish Bolshevism, you can't put the fire out by blowing on it; you need the *opposite* of fire—water—to put it out!

When leftism reaches the point of revolution and anarchy, you can't stop it with a constitution, logic, pleading, or common sense. You can stop it only by restoring the missing order, by force and authority! This is precisely what Adolf Hitler did, and why he is so brutally hated by the scummy anarchists, Bolsheviks, and assorted Jews whom he out-witted and out-fought.

So far, the USA has not gone as far down the road to the left as Germany. No US states have hung up the communist rag and totally overthrown order and authority, as the Jews did when Germany was defeated in World War I. So far, we can still save ourselves by Constitutional and orderly methods, and we do not yet have to move all the way to dictatorship, to correct the evil. So far. There is plenty of power in the presidency already, so that I—or any honest, decent, and informed American leader—can restore order and liberty under law to our perishing America. But if the Kosher Conservatives continue to temporize with the Negro situation and pretend that we can beat the Jews and their rush toward anarchy and Bolshevism by loving Jews and Negroes, by never mentioning the enemy, and by pretending that "communism and Nazism are the same thing"—God help us![3] We will be like a man who finds a little glow of fire in a box of dynamite and keeps blowing on it, hoping that he can "cool it off" and stop the fire without using water or radical methods, for fear of ruining his dynamite.

America can no longer fiddle around with easy ways! America is "on fire" with anarchy! But the fire is still small. We do not yet need the dictatorship Hitler was forced to adopt (because Germany needed political

---

[3] Today we seem to have exactly this—precisely what Rockwell most feared.

"martial law" with whole states going Red). But we do need a movement that is radical rightist, and tough.

Those who keep prating of "individual freedom" should take a look in the streets of any American city and see the wild, wooly, murderous "individual freedom" we already have—for Negroes, criminals, Reds, and Jews! There is too much "individual freedom" for the enemy. But the Kosher Conservatives don't dare even mention the enemy! It is not more "individual freedom" we need, but more *authority* for decent, White Americans, to save themselves from rampaging Negroes and Marxist Jews and anarchist "students."

卐 卐 卐

The men who gave us the United States of America established, not an anarchist "democracy," but a highly organized state that, today, would be called "extreme rightist." In fact, by modern standards, our Founding Fathers, would be called the most rabid kind of "fascists" and even "Nazis."

Let me remind the reader that his great-great-great grandparents did *not* grant Negroes any kind of "equality," but chained them up as slaves. They would have laughed at modern methods of "crime prevention" by handing out more and more money and easy days in sofa jails. They set up whipping posts, ducking stools, and hung those who refused to conform to society's rules. Even the most rabid "Nazi" today does not advocate slavery, although the men who wrote the Declaration of Independence and the Constitution not only advocated slavery—they practiced it. They didn't permit women, or men without property, to vote. They didn't believe in letting the "people" select a president, being well aware of the danger of the demagoguery which plagues our nation today. Instead, they set up an electoral college to guarantee selection, not of the most popular demagogue, but of the best statesman to lead America.

Let me shock you with a startling fact. There is a photograph that was smuggled out of the sacrosanct chamber of the United States Supreme Court. It is a photograph I took myself—a photograph of the rich, red rug right under the nose of Chief Justice Warren and the other eight Justices. It covers the whole floor of the Supreme Court Chamber! If you look at the rug you might recognize a symbol all over that rug in the United States Supreme Court. It is called a "fasces." It shows a bundle of sticks bound together to make an *axe*—representing *authority*:

Traditional fasces

Two prominent fasces in the US Senate chamber

Fasces-carrier on the East Pediment of the US Supreme Court

The same symbol is on our US dime.[4]

US Mercury dime (back face)

Here is the definition from the section on "Fasces" from Webster's New Collegiate Dictionary: *"A bundle of rods and among them an axe with the blade projecting, borne before ancient Roman magistrates as a badge of authority."* The same fasces is carved on the front walls of the US Congress. In fact, the fasces is found all over national and state government buildings, money, etc.

Do you recognize anything familiar in that name, "fasces"? You should. It is the origin of the word "fascist"—which is so much hated by the Jews and Reds. Perhaps you have been taken in by the lies of both the Jews and the Kosher Conservatives, that fascism is "evil" and "un-American." But note again the dictionary definition: fascism is "a political philosophy, movement, or regime that exalts nation and race above individual." Now do you see why the Jews—and the rightwing cowards—hate that word 'fascism' so much?[5]

The fasces were plastered all over everything connected with the United States government, because, by definition, *the American government was designed to be a "fascist" government!* (That is, nationalist and conservative.) Until the Jews got into the act, nobody was afraid of fascism —and our own government proudly placed the symbol of fascist authority

---

[4] The "Mercury dime" was in circulation from 1916 to 1945, when it was replaced with the current "Roosevelt dime."

[5] This is still true today. Consider the group known as "antifa": "ANTI-FAscists" derived mostly from, and driven by, leftists and Jews.

all over our most sacrosanct governmental chambers, on our money, and on our statues. (Abraham Lincoln's hands rest on two fasces in the Lincoln Memorial!)

Lincoln Memorial, with two large fasces

Why do you suppose the Jews, Reds, and "Kosher Conservatives" hate that word and that symbol so bitterly today? The answer is to be found in the very nature of the fasces themselves. They originated, according to an ancient Roman legend, when the tribes in ancient Italy were torn into a thousand feuding "splinters." A great leader, meeting with other chiefs, picked up a stick and snapped it easily, showing how easily the tribes were being beaten one at a time by the barbarians. Then the leader gathered up a bundle of the little sticks, tied them together, and tried to break them—and of course he couldn't. All tied together, they were too tough! Then he mounted an ax blade on the bundled sticks and showed that in unity and aggressive self-defense, there is strength and victory.

Our kind of people used, and understood, that symbol for thousands of years—right up until World War II, when Hitler and Mussolini finally realized how to stop the infernal division of our people by the Jews. In Germany and Italy, the Jews had the masses of people (being led by Jewish communists) hating their own intelligentsia as a "ruling class"; and the "ruling class" hating the masses of their own people as "greedy, brutal labor"—the suicidal "class warfare" of communism. The Jews had Germany and Italy broken into a thousand squabbling, petty, and greedy little groups that were all helpless before the united power of organized, implacable Jewry. As the Roman leader made the little sticks strong by bundling them together in the fasces, so Mussolini made the Italian people strong enough to survive and to establish order through unity and authority. Hitler did the same thing for the German people. And because a united people led by strong, honest leaders is too hard a nut to crack for Jewish parasites, merchants, money-lenders, and communist revolutionists, the Jews roundly hated Messrs. Mussolini and Hitler, and got the rest of the world to go and whip them.

Today, America and all White, Western, Christian nations are divided as never before. Here in the USA, they have us divided into Republican and Democrat, Catholic and Protestant, rich and poor, Yankees and Confederates, Capital and Labor, Liberals and Conservatives, etc., etc. Is there *any* "conservative" who has not sighed: "If only we could get together!" The Jews have lied about the nature of fascism to keep us divided and hating the only thing that can save us.

But in view of the definition in the dictionary, which shows that "fascism" is *not* "the same thing as communism," but is actually nationalistic conservatism, how are we to explain the chorus of "conservatives" who are busily baying with the Jewish pack on the heels of fascism? Why do they hate us, too?

The answer is that most of them are too lazy to do their homework and find out what fascism is. They simply hear the Jews and communists screaming day and night how vile it is, so they either hate it too or they are too scared of the Jews to admit to themselves that fascism and Nazism are the opposite of communism. National Socialism believes that our Founding Fathers established an authoritarian republic (by no means a "democracy," which was a form of government which they openly despised). They established the fasces as the very symbol of the authority that brought unity and order to the thirteen original colonies.

And it is an *authoritarian republic* for which we stand, as did our forebears. Our swastika is the White Man's racial symbol of orderly government and strong leadership—under a constitution and laws. The fasces all over Washington and on the old dimes show the only way to salvation for our White American Constitutional Republic.

The American Nazi Party is not afraid to follow that way of the Founding Fathers, in spite of the lies of Jews and the Kosher Conservatives. The masses instinctively sense the need for authority, and they unconsciously seek a strong leader. And the masses, in turn, are the very essence of that we need to win. If we are to win legal, political power, we need, not a few "conservatives," but the millions and millions of essentially non-political, working people and ordinary Americans loosely called "the masses." Yet this enormous mass of power is the very thing "conservatives" can never, never, never win.

卐 卐 卐

The *US News and World Report* for June 7, 1965 contains a statistical analysis of the catastrophic national elections for president of 1964.[6] These figures show more clearly than any amount of arguing or wishful thinking that it is no longer mathematically possible for any sort of "conservative" national candidate to win on any sort of traditional economic "conservative" platform, without the hidden issue of *race*. In fact, the figures show that an economic "conservative" not only *must* lose, but that the trend of our population is daily moving toward a situation such that only a madman will be able to pretend there is any possibility of national political victory for any sort of economic "conservative" program.

I will attempt to explain this further on, but for now, let me present the cold figures. First, let me give the percentages of votes won by Johnson and Goldwater in the upper echelons of our population. Among professional men, managers, etc., Johnson got 58% of the vote. Among college-educated persons, Johnson got 54%. Among those with income of $10,000 or above [about $100,000 today], 56% voted for Johnson. In the smaller cities and towns, Johnson got 63%.

Observe that the gap between the two candidates in the higher levels and rural areas averages out to about 15% of the vote. This would not be an insurmountable difference and might easily be changed by more effective campaigning than was done by Goldwater.

But now let's look at the opposite to the above categories. Among unskilled labor, Johnson got 80% of the vote. Goldwater got only 16%! Those with no higher than a grade-school education voted for Johnson. Those with higher incomes gave 70.7% of their vote to Johnson, and only

---

[6] In which Lyndon Johnson (Dem.) overwhelmingly defeated Barry Goldwater (Rep.)

29.3% to Goldwater. The big cities and urban areas gave Johnson 72% to 28% for Goldwater. The spread between Johnson and Goldwater among the lower economic classes and the urban voters averages out to a huge gap of more than 54%!

But even that shocking figure does not tell the whole story of why it is madness to keep trying to win political power on a "conservative" program. Take a look at the relative sizes of the two groups we have compared above. The *World Almanac* for 1965 shows that the first group we compared, the professional and managerial workers, who voted for Johnson by only a 15% gap compose only 21.8% of the population, while the rest of the labor force, semi-skilled and un-skilled, account for 78.2% of the population.

Of the smaller cities and towns which went to Johnson, only 63% are shown in the *World Almanac* as having a total population of 54,054,425, the urban areas which went for Johnson 72% show a total population of 125,368,750.

And while college graduates went for Johnson by only 54%, the total number of such college people is listed in the *World Almanac* as only 4,528,215; while the grade-school population that went for Johnson is listed as 40,217,215. To the number enrolled in grade schools must be added many more millions who are totally illiterate or have only a few years in school.

Putting all of this together, we find that the upper echelon and rural sectors of our population, which might possibly be won by a national conservative candidate, comprise only a relatively tiny percentage of the population of the United States (approximately 20%). However, even this most favorable economic conservative section of the US population is split on economic issues and was won by Johnson, even though the average margin of his victory was only 15% in this sector.

On the other hand, the vast masses of Americans who live in urban areas, have only a grade-school education, are only semi-skilled or un-skilled labor, and earn less than $10,000 per year, comprise more than 80% of the population. And in this enormous mass, Johnson won 8 out of every 10 votes. The key fact is that the vote of the most illiterate or ill-informed person counts just as much as the vote of H. L. Hunt, or Robert Welch, and there are millions of "little people" for every high-level voter.

For those not of a mathematical turn of mind, let me boil it all down to a very, very simple statement. Except on the race issue, the *only* place economic "conservatives" have any chance at all for a large vote is among those in management positions, upper income levels, and those with higher educations—in short, among the trained thinkers.

Among those with grade school educations, in blue-collar or laboring jobs, and lower incomes, "conservatism" sells about as well as snowballs at the North Pole. The masses want a "warm" candidate who seems "human" and "lovable." Roosevelt, Truman, Ike, Jake, and now Johnson have all been successful in peddling just the right "image" to win. No matter how we may deplore it, that is a fact—just as it is a fact that Whites don't like "niggers," no matter what the hypocrites pretend.

Without the masses, we can never, never win power. And without power, it is a complete and disgusting waste of time to sit around groaning about "constitutionalism," "Christianity," "States' Rights," etc., etc.—interminably. That's what we have been doing, and I would think any intelligent person would long ago have had all he could stand of the endless "Oh-my-God;" reports, the "What-We-Must-Do" pamphlets, and the "Let's-all-get-together" societies. I am not prepared to waste another moment in failure or impotent groaning. Only if every move is calculated to win power, legally, am I willing to suffer and sacrifice anymore. And the statistics show, with devastating clarity, that it is impossible to win nationally as an economic "conservative."

How, then, can we win? The answer is that we must find a way to reach the hearts of the millions who voted for Johnson, Roosevelt, Ike, Harry, and Jake. Goldwater assuredly didn't do it with his "soak-the-poor" and "off-to-war" image. Neither can any other economic "conservative"—because a "conservative" is basically trying to peddle ice-cold drinks to "brace you up," when the potential customers are all shivering in the cold rain. Average people want to feel warm, safe, and secure. That's the way folks are. And if you insist on trying to sell ice-cold drinks to people shivering in a freezing rain on a bitter cold night, you are sure to fail. We have been failing.

The enemy is brilliant in his understanding of all this and in the calculating manner in which he uses psychology on behalf of race-mixing, subversion, degeneracy, immorality, and treason. So far, our side is utterly, unbelievably stupid and blind in dealing with masses of human beings.

Some who do understand the psychology of masses explain their failure to use that knowledge effectively by claiming that it is "wicked" or "immoral" to be a "demagogue," etc. This is like watching a robber and rapist tearing up your home, ravishing your wife and kidnapping your children and refusing to try to stop him because he has a gun, and it would be "wicked" for *you* to use a gun, just like the criminal. As long as bad men use psychology and demagoguery to win the masses for evil purposes, good men must use these same methods to help our people unite and survive, or we die!

I am not the least bit ashamed to admit that I would draw the line at nothing to save our White race. And that includes risking my own life countless times, being beaten, jailed, and lied about by almost everyone. I can see no great moral victory in seeing our people, our women, our little White children and young girls rounded up for Chinese communist slave-labor camps or brothels, or turned over to billions of howling African savages—all because our side is too "nice" to use sound psychology to win the masses.

But we don't have to do anything really "vile" to win. We have only to quit the sterile effort to win by trying to drive cold, hard unsympathetic facts into the minds of the masses. It won't work. We have only to put the truth into a form suited to the people. You don't do that with long dissertations, rationalizations, statistics, facts, and unvarnished truths. You do it with parable, analogy, slogans, diagrams, posters, demonstrations, and above all, *combat*—things that reach the hearts of men and then filter into their minds.

When we can finally make the rightwing leadership understand that, then we can stop the madness of economic "conservatism" and get busy on the one issue that does reach the hearts of millions—race! Point out to a man that if he elects Candidate A he will have a "nigger" neighbor and his kids won't be safe and his property value will crash, and you will reach his heart. You will beat Candidate A. But tell him the national debt is too high, that "the Constitution is being violated" and that corporation taxes are too high, and he will hardly hear you. You will lose. Tell him that we must be ready to start up a war to preserve the "Monroe Doctrine" and he will call you a "war monger" and be scared to death of you. Tell him you are down on benefits, working folks, high wages, and social security, and that you want to cut down on taxes on rich people, and he will actively despise you, as "anti-people."

The other side tells him they are "for the little guy"; they holler "down with the big interests" and he'll vote for them till kingdom come, no matter how many mansions or TV stations they own or how they turn him over to outright crooks posing as leaders.

The other side has been doing this kind of thing on behalf of evil for years and winning the masses, thus winning power, and thereby changing America into a nightmare of treason and degeneracy. Our side has been too damned snotty and uppity to take stock of itself, and is still peddling the bitter and icy "pill" of economic "conservatism" to the masses of people who have rejected it for 50 years, by bigger margins each time.

卐 卐 卐

It took me 15 years to figure that out. In 1956, I sold out the magazine I had successfully started for the wives of servicemen all over the world, (*US Lady*) and put all the money into an effort to "unite" the conservatives. I formed the "American Federation of Conservative Organizations," innocently believing that, if only we could get the right wing together, we could easily conquer the left.

By this time, I had plenty of opportunity to look over the activity of the "right wing"—the conservatives—and had come to the conclusion, in my total ignorance of the real nature of the case, that all they needed to succeed was an organizational drive to get them "together," with a business-like plan. I had found that there were dozens and maybe hundreds of very rich men, like H. L. Hunt of Texas, and Robert Welch of Boston, who felt much as I did, and who, together, could pool enough money and resources to swamp the Marxist-Zionist Jews and left wingers. There seemed to be plenty of talent and ability—and actually a majority of our people over on my side of politics, so that common sense seemed to force the conclusion that it was only a lack of determined effort to put this together which permitted the left-wing minority, sparked by the sub-minority of Jews, to keep winning victory after victory and send America down the path to Marxist socialism and racial disintegration. I realized, even then, that talking and educating are useless unless they are directed at the only worthwhile political goal, *power*.

But I reckoned without any knowledge of the human content of the "right-wing," in those days. From the millionaires to the scared little people who attend the endless pitiful "conservative," "100% American," "old-fashioned," "constitutional," "state's rights" meetings, I learned by bitter experience that the human material of the right wing consists 90% of cowards, dopes, nuts, one-track minds, blabber-mouths, boobs, incurable tightwads and—worst of all—*hobbyists*: people who have come to enjoy a perverted, masochistic pleasure in telling each other forever how we are all being raped by the "shhh-you-know-whos," but, who, under no conditions, would think of risking their two cars, landscaped homes, or juicy jobs to *do* something about it.

Knowing none of this, however, and being full of my usual enthusiasm and drive, I paid for a series of radio spots before and after rightwing commentator Fulton Lewis' show, announcing a Washington meeting to organize the rightwing. The response seemed to be gratifying. Hundreds of people called and I arranged with one of them, Sam Jones, the correspondent of Bill Buckley's *National Review*, to use the lovely old Virginia mansion in McLean for our first meeting.

Of the hundreds who called, only about 50 showed up at the meeting. I addressed the meeting in the best "conservative" style, lecturing "nicely" on the need "to get together" more than anything else, and receiving little flurries of polite applause. How I shudder now to think of all that feeble, useless, stupid "niceness"—while our race and our whole world are being brutally destroyed!

From time to time, someone in the audience would ask "What about the Jews?" And there would be snickers and shifting around of feet, like grammar school kids when somebody mentions the word "sex." Then I would scold this "bold" character for such a "disgusting display of prejudice," making my righteous love of the wonderful Jews very clear, and even sharing knowing winks with some close friends at my "clever" deception.

The Jews would not have disturbed such a meeting for anything in the world. We, like a million other "conservatives," were giving ourselves the illusion of "fighting" treason, subversion, communism, and race-mixing (i.e. the Jews) without doing anything and without hurting the enemy himself. If we had *not* had such silly little secret meetings, we would eventually build up such a pressure of frustrated patriotism that we just might have done something forceful—and therefore effective.

A little collection was taken up; we passed out membership cards, and then stood around babbling, as is the inevitable custom after such "battles" with the enemy. Everybody congratulated everybody else at this new and terrible assault on the "Eskimos," as John Kasper called them then, and we went home all aglow with the great "success."

I poured out my time and money in an all-out effort to organize the rightwing "nicely," as the "American Federation of Conservative Organizations" (AFCO), and to publish a national conservative paper. We held meetings in the best meeting rooms in the Statler and Mayflower Hotels. I had beautiful stationery engraved in gold. I used all my skill in art, writing, organizing, promoting, and leading—the same skills that are now serving the American Nazi Party—but were useless then.

The basic premise, the premise of conservatism, was wrong. Although it is made to appear so, the battle between the "conservatives" and "liberals" is *not* a battle of ideas or even of political organization. It is a battle of force, terror, and power. The Jews and their accomplices and dupes are not running our country and its people because of the excellence of their ideas or the merit of their work, or the genuine majority of people behind them. They are in power in spite of the lack of these things, and only because they have driven their way into power by daring *minority tactics*. They can stay in power only because people are afraid to oppose them—afraid they will be socially ostracized, afraid they will be smeared in the press, afraid they will lose their jobs, afraid they will not be able to run their businesses, afraid they will lose political offices. It is *fear*, and *fear alone*, that keeps these filthy left-wing sneaks in power—not ignorance by the American people, as the "conservatives" keep telling each other.

Our right-wing "fighters" keep assuring each other "ye shall know the truth and the truth shall make you free." But the truth is that any slave knows the truth, but what good does it do him, unless he can somehow get the *power* to *force* his way to freedom. It is not the truth that will make us free in America, because millions already know the truth and hate bitterly what is going on, but they are *afraid* even to admit they know the truth. Ten million signed the petition for Joe McCarthy—and they are not all dead. But they might as well be, as long as the right wing spends all its time and money trying to "win" another ten million instead of getting the ten million we already have to stand up! We have plenty of people, money, and facilities to take America back from the traitors tomorrow morning if all the people who already know what is going on were not afraid anymore and would *stand up!*

As long as the right-wing confines its fighting to being "nice," the great masses of the public will bow down like sheep to the left-wing which is *not* nice—which uses smear, economic persecution, legal harassment, and finally physical terror to maintain its domination of our national life and culture by force. The force is disguised, of course, in checkbooks, judge's robes, rigged party conventions, etc.; but it is still either the force itself, or the threat of force, which has America down and afraid. No amount of papers and pamphlets, were they all masterpieces of propaganda, and no amount of talk and meetings, can stop this growing left-wing force and the power and fear it inspires—much less drive it back and finally destroy it.

But in 1955, I still imagined we could "sneak up" on the Jews, like the rest of my "sissy" friends. We would build a great grass-roots membership by not mentioning the Jews at all, even praising them—and then, while they suspected nothing, we would get stronger and stronger until finally one fine day we would wipe the smiles off our faces, spin around on the surprised Hebrews, and let them see just what we had in mind!

I found this coward's dream being promoted everywhere I went. Every conservative I met would draw me aside and groan about the latest outrages and treason of the "you-know-whos," and describe to me the latest plans to sneak up on the tormentors. And I was as much a part of this childish illusion as anyone else. I spent literally hundreds of hours discussing the methods for this super-sneaky revolution. And the only thing I gained from it all was the final discovery that it was, and always has been, impossible to beat terrorists by talk. One must dislodge such evil usurpers by the same weapon that got them in power. Theirs was and is secret and disguised. Ours, by nature, must be open, legal, and honest. But it must still be *power*—not talk of pamphlets or sneaky dreams; and it involves, therefore, *risk*.

I also learned to know the people my wife and I came to call the "diehards" for some obscure reason I can't recall. These were the perennial "patriots," the eternal attenders of meetings, the inexhaustible talkers and babblers, the super-clever know-it-alls who are going to "throw the election into the house this time," etc., etc., and the disgusting hobbyists who discharged their pent-up "patriotism" once a week or so in the masochistic organism they seemed to obtain by flagellating themselves with the latest outrages of the Jews. These people seemed to have been "fighting" the Jews all their lives—years and years and years. Their standard reaction to anything they didn't think up themselves—a new plan for sneaking up on the Jew—was "I was fighting this thing before you were born, son." And this was supposed to send the upstart packing. As if people who had spent 40 or 50 years fighting so monstrously unsuccessfully had any business daring to open their mouths at all!

As the months wore on, and we began to see our small savings diminish with no signs of any real progress, I began to get a case of the "desperationitis" so common to the right wing. I had begun to meet a large, unorganized, but regular circle of "patriots" which exists everywhere, and discuss all kinds of "trick" methods of "spilling the beans" on the Jews, all at once. There were endless plans for dropping "the whole story" out of airplanes by the millions on the public while the helpless Jews watched the leaflets flutter down in rage. There was talk of a plan to raid a TV network station, hold the personnel at gunpoint while one of us—nobody cared to discuss exactly who—would present to the breathless millions the documents and facts on the Jewishness of communism, which we have so abundantly but which mean so little as long as we reach only each other. There was even a scheme for sending aloft huge signs on balloons, tied to inaccessible places, which would "squeal" on the Jews from the sky while they scrambled madly to get them down. These wild ideas are actually, as you read this, being discussed by otherwise intelligent people some-where—people who are simply too overwhelmed by their own timidity and ignorance to see that even if they *did* these nasty tricks on the Jews, there would be *no result at all.*

People are more inert than it is possible to believe, even after you dis-cover this fact. It takes an incredible amount of propaganda, repeated over and over, to move them even a little bit. This is one of the reasons Joe McCarthy told me he wouldn't even attempt to tell the whole truth. "They'd simply put me away as a lunatic" he said, "and the public would forget what it was all about." And he was probably right.

The idea that there is *anything easy* that can be done, which will send the Jew traitors scurrying for Israel like rats, while we walk triumphantly into the White House, is one of the worst self-delusions which has been keeping the right wing babbling and conspiring, while the Jews have been laughing at us and trampling all over our Constitution, our rights, our tradi-tions, our dignity, and our White Race.

Anyone, when he first discovers what is going on, might be forgiven a certain period of nourishing this childish delusion. But when he sees the Jews starving the families of his fellow sneaks, railroading them into jail, shipping them to mental health "hospitals," smearing and blasting them for just the teeniest weeniest little attempt to stand up to Jewish power, he ought to get the idea quickly. Any man who spends 30 or 40 years pretend-ing to imagine there is such an easy way, while our country and our White Race go down and down, is not a dreamer or ignorant. He is a coward!

卐 卐 卐

"Conservatives" are the world's champion ostriches. They mutter to each other down under the sand in "secret," while their plumed bottoms wave in the breezes for the Jews to kick at their leisure. Conservatives are fooling no one but themselves.

One of the conservative leaders I contacted was William F. Buckley, Jr., the publisher of *National Review*. My friend here in DC, Sam Jones, was his correspondent, and we got together at a meeting in New York. It was an intellectual thrill, just talking with Buckley and his staff. There is more pulsating brainpower and genius than any place else on Earth. Bill, himself, is personable in the extreme, and brighter than all the rest. But his staff contains three or four Jews, one of them particularly Jewish-looking, and the atmosphere there is different than with other "conservative" groups.

Buckley is extremely cagey on the Jewish Question; and even when you get him alone, it is difficult to elicit information as to his awareness. The best you can get are guarded implications from which you are at liberty to infer what you want. I have since learned the reason for this: Buckley's millionaire father had a major interest with the Jews in Israel, and the result, even today, is that his anti-liberalism and anti-communism stop at the borders of Israel and the Zionist meeting halls.

However, at the time, I too was playing this silly "I've-got-my-eyes-closed" game, so I felt that much could be accomplished by helping Buckley, and I agreed to promote *National Review* for him. He deposited a thousand dollars in a Washington bank to my account and I started on a project designed to get mass circulation for *National Review* in colleges and universities. In those days, however, I was heavily involved in my own effort to launch the AFCO and the newspaper, and I am ashamed to have to admit that I did a rotten job for Bill. I made some efforts, but they were without the drive and full enthusiasm necessary in such a promotion, and nothing happened. I returned the money to Bill, less expenses, with a guilty conscience.

Outside of being too cagey on the Jewish Question, which is, of course, his privilege, Bill Buckley was 100% square as a man, and unlike the situation with other right-wingers with whom I have worked or tried to work, my failure to accomplish anything with Buckley was entirely my fault—in spite of all the money I poured into it and all the work and inspiration I gave it. My effort to "unite the conservatives" and beat the champion sneaks of the world—the Jews—by sneaking didn't work. I ran out of money and went to work for two right-wing millionaires, first Bob Snowden of Memphis, Tennessee; and then Russell Maguire, who used to publish *Mercury Magazine*—I was his assistant. Maguire talked a good fight. But when the real fight began, he took off. I have exposed the whole ugly story in a previous book (without libel suits by either of them), but I will not repeat it here. Suffice to say that these millionaires, while sincere, simply did not and probably still do not really believe that we are in deadly danger. They figure there will be some easy way of saving their enormous wealth, short of "coming right out with it."

Many right-wingers are sincerely concerned, I know, about my battles with men such as Maguire, Snowden, Welch, Hargis, et al., and my revelations of what they really are. "They are doing good," I am told, "Why not let them go about their business their own way. They are helping. Don't hurt them." I maintain they are only giving the *appearance* of helping—but are actually hurting.

Before a mass of people will rise up and do anything effective and forceful about a tyrannical situation, there must be built up a certain emotional pressure. A firecracker has not the force of a rifle bullet because it explodes harmlessly in all directions. But the gas from a rifle bullet cannot escape, except by forcing the bullet out at terrific speed, because it is confined and directed into useful channels. As long as Welch and all the rest of his ilk, rich and poor, can give themselves the illusion of "fighting the Jews" by exploding the pressure inside of them verbally and harmlessly, in all directions, and without ever hurting a Jew traitor, they stop the pressure we need to get mad and fight from ever building up.

The Jews know this, and so they permit these hundreds and hundreds of harmless rightwing organizations to spout endlessly in silence behind the Jewish "paper curtain." They don't reach any significant number of people outside their own group. Even when they do, their approach is so feeble and so psychologically wrong that they win only a few rare types. They never, *never* get out into the public, into the streets, and reach the masses with an inspiring and driving masculine movement, which alone can win the hearts of the masses! They pass literature and talk only to each other.

If just one tenth of the money which pours every year, year after year, into such "firecracker" movements were to be contained, directed, and used behind an "ideological bullet" forced out by fighting men, the Jews would stop at nothing to crush and destroy that deadly projectile. Even without that money, with only a few grains of "powder," but confined and directed with force, my movement has already earned the all-out hate of the Jews; this is the only sure sign that we are not firing the eternal right-wing "gas" at them, but the deadly bullets which they know will eventually destroy their illegal, tyrannical power.

This does not mean that we must work ourselves up to a "pitchfork-and-barricade" revolution by violence. This old-fashioned attack won't work, as our side learned in the Civil War and the Klan prosecutions. There are plenty of people already awake in America. They are afraid and they are frustrated by their inability to do anything about the terrible evil they see growing. *Mercury* magazine did indeed "inform" a lot of people. So does the Birch Society. But we don't need any more informed people who won't stand up and fight to oppose tyranny!

Such things as *Mercury* and the Birch Society also kept the "steam pressure" of emotions down in millions of Americans who were already informed—who feel that as long as such things as *Mercury* are published and Welch is petitioning to impeach Earl Warren, "something" is being done. These good people are fooled by the constant advice to "write your senator" into imagining that we can somehow petition or talk our way out of tyranny. Worst of all, these papers and societies are financial "leaks" which keep the rightwing bled to death and anemic. There simply is no money for the battle, no money for the bullets and powder, because it has all been spent on firecrackers, uniforms, the band, pictures of the enemy, exciting rallies, and bed-time stories for the troops.

You can't get these myriad stamp-licking and squawking societies to-gether—as I found out, and as every experienced "patriot" knows. And even if you could, they would be worse hitched up together than they are squabbling separately. As Hitler puts it so masterfully,

> [E]veryone who couldn't stand on their own feet joined one working federation, believing that eight cripples hanging on to each other could surely form one gladiator.[7]

Clearly, eight lame men do not make a gladiator. These weak rightwing leaders—who, for 40 or 50 years, have been preaching a million different tricks to avoid the desperate, dangerous fight which is always the price of any victory—are approaching the end of the road. They cannot much long-er pretend that we can save ourselves with their sugary nostrums. When the patient feels the death rattle in his chest, as White America can feel it now, our people will become disgusted with the quack physicians and their sugar syrups and pills, and will welcome our rough and tough, but powerful medicine.

Our motto here is "White man, stand and fight for survival with us, or stand out of our way!"

卐 卐 卐

But it is not just the pantywaist "conservative" dabblers who stand in our way and must be pushed aside if we are ever to win. Even more deadly are the Judases, *the Kosher Conservative "leaders" that the other side sends over to lead our side.*[8]

Consider!

---

[7] *Mein Kampf*, vol. 2, sec. 8.5. See the Dalton translation, p. 150.
[8] Today this is known as "controlled opposition." There are a number of current or recent, prominent right-wing Jews, including Ben Shapiro, Milo Yiannopoulos, Paul Gottfried, Mark Levin, Andrew Breitbart, Joel Pollock, Ezra Levant, Dennis Prager, and Dave Rubin.

- A Jew, Kivie Kaplan, leads the NAACP, while other Jews like the Rosenwalds, the Sterns, and the Lehmans provide the millions in gold to promote communist race-mixing in America.
- A Jew, Milton Rosen, leads the most dangerous and violent communist group in America, "Progressive Labor."
- A Jewess, Bettina Aptheker, leads our college intellectuals and leftist revolutionaries.
- A Jewess, Dorothy Schiff, publishes the leftist *New York Post*, while her fellow Jews publish most of the other "liberal" papers such as the *New York Times* (Sulzburger), *Washington Post* (Myers), and so on, *ad nauseum*.

If it's *left*, you will find one of God's Chosen leading it and/or financing it, sometimes with a "shabbos-Goy" out front, but always with the Jews holding the purse strings and providing the sparks of life for leftist revolution, race-mixing, and perversion.

You would think that with this undeniable record of leading the attack on America, Jews would have a tough time getting themselves accepted as *our* leaders, too. You would think that the rightwing would *at least* be suspicious of Jews, let alone accept them as leaders. In fact, the Protocols[9] (and Lenin) have openly said that the way to emasculate and smash the opposition is to *lead it yourself*—lead it to perdition and frustration. And is not the whole rightwing in perdition and frustrated as few such large movements in history have ever been frustrated? Knowing the brilliance of the Jewish and communist conspiracy, can anyone believe that these master-plotters would fail to install some of their best men and women over on *our* side?

It was a little difficult to *see* all this about Barry Goldwater, in spite of his sponsorship of more integration legislation than any other senator, his sell-out of Taft for Ike, his backing of "terrible 1313",[10] and his origination of the Alaska Mental Health concentration camp laws. If Goldwater was really trying to get elected in 1964, can you think of anything more stupid

---

[9] Rockwell refers to the Protocols of the Elders of Zion, a notorious 1900-era document that lays out a rough plan for Jewish domination of the world—recall the discussion in Chapter 9. For a full recent translation, see *Protocols of the Elders of Zion: The Definitive English Edition* (Clemens & Blair, 2023).

[10] A reference to the Public Administration building of the University of Chicago, located at 1313 E. 60th Street, Chicago. It was long home to a variety of private and public organizations dedicated to housing laws, zoning changes, public health, and related activities.

than to go to Appalachia and preach cutting down aid for the poor; go to Tennessee and preach cutting cheap TVA electricity to poor farmers; to go to St. Petersburg, Florida and preach cutting aid to the aged? Or, when the people were up in arms about nigger crime in the streets and the Republicans had made an excellent movie on the subject for national television, can you think of a better way to ensure not getting votes than by banning this film, as Goldwater did, so that it was never shown?

It was downright funny for millions and millions of White Christian Americans to be working so desperately hard to elect a Jewish president of the United States!

卐 卐 卐

But there is nothing funny about the man behind Goldwater—and behind Buckley, behind Young Americans for Freedom, behind the Committee to Keep Red China Out of the UN, and a dozen other "fronts" operated from 79 Madison Avenue, New York City—the 100% Jew and "ex"-communist *Marvin Liebman!*

Liebman's latest front is the "Friends of Rhodesian Independence" and, like all his other "committees" and fronts, it is raking in the influential names—and the cash, to the tune of millions of dollars. He is getting free advertising from dozens of good and sincere patriots and their papers. So long as this Yiddish faker can be made to appear to be "doing something" to help our White brothers in Rhodesia, nothing real can be done to help them. It is a vile and sickening fraud which angers me more than any such Jew fakes in the recent past.

To present my case against Mr. Liebman, let me dissect one of his earlier "committees" which is still doing business sabotaging America, even while the best Americans are still pouring out their souls and their substance to help this Jewish "right-wing leader."

Liebman set up the "Committee to Keep Red China Out of the United Nations" at his patriotic money-mill, 79 Madison Avenue, New York City. Like all Liebman fronts, this one was beautifully calculated to grab right-wingers and patriots in a sensitive spot, with a consequent rich haul in cash. It did and it continues to do so. But few or none of the patriotic victims of this Hebrew political swindle have ever examined the letterhead of Liebman's "Committee." There they would have found the names of such sterling "conservatives" as Sen. Paul Douglas, Rep. Paul Fino, Rep. Seymour Halpern, Sen. Jacob Javits, Hubert Humphrey, and dozens of other rabid leftists.

Why? How come? Why would leftists want to keep Red Chinese out of their beloved, Red and Black UN? The answer is that on the day Red China gets *into* the United Nations, there is an excellent chance that the USA will get *out*. Public opinion has taken a lot from the UN, but these leftists cunningly calculate that Red China in would mean the USA out.

Meanwhile, Mr. Liebman gathers up literally millions of dollars, holds mass rallies in Madison Square Garden, etc., and keeps good, patriotic American all busy as beavers fighting to keep Red China out of the UN so that the USA will stay in this filthy mess.

When it became obvious that tens of thousands of patriotic young Americans at our colleges were fed up with the rabid beatniks and leftist traitors rampaging on college campuses, Mr. Liebman got some assistant Jew (Robert Schuchman) to organize "Young Americans for Freedom" (YAF) and once again he rounded up all the opposition to Jewry and set them to harmless sputtering in carefully-controlled, pro-Jewish patriotic meetings.

As usual, the Goy herd of rich and influential patriots could hardly wait to pour their names and cash upon this wonderful Jew, Liebman. When I speak on college campuses, some of the most violent and vociferous opposition comes from the poor, Liebman-dominated YAF'ers who wave the stupidest, and most pitiful picket signs imaginable at me. (Incidentally, I have also had some of my most heartening successes with these poor kids in Liebman's "YAF." They have basically good instincts, and my speech always astounds them. Often they gather with me later and it is only a matter of an hour or two to disgust them with the way Liebman and the finks running YAF have deceived them.)

Back in February 1962, in the ninth issue of the *Rockwell Report*, I started a long series of exposes of Liebman and his money-mill at 79 Madison Avenue.[11] I exposed the fact that, although Liebman was supposed to have nothing to do with YAF, Liebman's postage meter number appeared on YAF mail, and YAF mail was opened and signed for by Liebman's office! That included cash! As soon as this exposé was out, Liebman hurriedly shifted operations to cover up.

But I have continued to follow his nefarious operations and expose them to college students at every opportunity. Especially have I been able to make progress with college students in YAF when I reveal Liebman's

---

[11] *The Rockwell Report* was a semi-regular periodical issued by Rockwell from 1961 through 1967. See Appendix D for some pages from that series.

atrocious communist background. Finally, when the facts could no longer be hidden, YAF admitted them.

Here are the facts, admitted by YAF in its own publication, *The New Guard,* for May 1966. You read them and then judge whether Mr. Liebman could possibly be the right man to lead the kids in YAF, the patriots in the Red China Committee, the White Men in the Rhodesia Committee, and all the other fronts he uses to pump the rightwing dry and keep it frustrated and miserable. Marvin Liebman was recruited by a Jew civics teacher (!) in his native Brooklyn into the American Students Union, notorious as the way-out front for young communists. Within months, Liebman rose into the disciplined ranks of the Communist Party itself, openly joining the Young Communist League. YAF admits "few even of New York City youth were as active in the Party as young Marvin."

Liebman himself confesses that, in typical Jew fashion, he didn't like the open, "rough stuff" like picketing, preferring to become what he calls a "manipulator" of others!! (As he is now doing.) Jew Liebman did all the right Jew things: matriculated at New York University, took an apartment in "the Village," wrote leftwing propaganda, and affected all the "literary" pretensions of the dirty beatnik Reds, Negroes, and general scum.

Drafted into the Army, YAF admits that Liebman discovered a "clever" system to avoid KP and any other details he didn't like. In typical Jewish style, Marvin simply "broke his glasses," allowing the Goyim boobs to do all the work. When this no longer worked, Jew Marvin managed to get a "cut finger." (No kidding! YAF actually admits all this in print!) This sharpie communist Jew also managed to flunk basic training!

In spite of ducking all KP by either breaking his glasses or malingering with a hangnail, the Jew was able to fast-talk his way into writing the KP manual for the Goyim to work harder! Finally, Marvin managed to get himself discharged from the hated Army—for a sunstroke!

The courageous Jew, fresh from "battle" in the Army, scurried back into the communist sewer pipe and became editor of *The Spotlight* for American Youth For Democracy. YAF says, at this point, "Liebman flourished under communist discipline and was proud to be a communist functionary." No broken glasses or hangnails here for this hebe.

Liebman became a satellite of communist leader Earl Browder and his Jewish wife, Raisa Berkman. When Browder fell from grace, Marvin found himself out in the cold with the straight commie gang, and, like most Jews, became a follower of the top Jewish communist of all time (outside of Marx, himself), Trotsky.

As a Trotskyite, Liebman signed on with the Israeli terrorist gang, the Irgun, and helped in the torture and murder of British young men. Then he tried to join the Greek communists, but was discouraged by lack of funds, and decided there was a way to be a communist and wealthy and comfortable. Marv went to work as a fund-raiser for the United Jewish Appeal. These professional Jew money-gatherers sent him to school on how to make a "pitch," how to design a tear-jerking campaign to rake in the shekels, how to beat the bucks out of the faithful by veiled pressure, and how to gather names and influence.

Once he saw these professional Jew moneychangers operating, Marvin knew he had discovered his life's work. But he was still so Red, so passionately left, that he felt impelled to put his talents to work for his Jew communist "cause." He raised money for Henry Wallace's campaign for president. He campaigned for the rabid leftist Rudolph Halley for New York City Council. Finally he wound up working for the man who set him on course for what he is doing now: a rabid leftist named Harold Oram. Oram put Liebman in charge of smuggling Chinese out of Red China (and, it must be presumed, into our USA). Liebman raised huge sums doing it and learned the techniques of squeezing money and big names out of his causes with which to get more money.

In 1953, when patriots were worried about a sell-out to Red China, Oram and Liebman saw their golden opportunity to:

- Rake in millions
- Mislead the anti-communists
- Prevent the anti-communists from effective action
- Keep real anti-communists broke
- Discredit real anti-communists, and
- Hide the real facts about communists.

They formed their "Committee of One Million Against the Admission of Red China to the United Nations." They herded in Herbert Hoover, Charles Edison, Walter Judd, and many other real patriots. But mostly they gathered in the money! How it rolled in!

After that one, it was easy. Using the techniques learned in the Communist Party and at the United Jew Appeal school on fund-raising, Liebman set up one outfit after the other to rake in the millions from gullible patriots who never stopped to consider how odd it was that with the leftwing led almost 100% by Jews, only a rabid Jew Zionist-terrorist "ex"-communist seems to be available to "lead" our side in opposing all these Jews!

卐 卐 卐

Now let's take a look at Liebman's latest, his committee on Rhodesia. At the head of it he has placed no other than Miss "Taylor Caldwell." Caldwell is supposed to be a great novelist, and also a great "rightist." I used to wonder how a strong anti-communist can get her books sold so vigorously all over the world in every Jew bookstore.

Then I learned something. Miss "Caldwell" wrote me a vile letter after she read one of my *Rockwell Reports* about the "Berlin Crisis," in which I exposed the printed material by the Jews in which they predicted, before World War II, exactly how they would divide Germany, as it has been divided, and how they would eventually exterminate the Germans as a people, by mass sterilization.[12] Miss "Caldwell's" letter was a staggering document. It was stupid and uninformed beyond my possibility of belief.

She wrote pages of foolishness of which I will give one example: in order to discredit my claim that Jews have something to do with communism, she rages that the two most anti-communist papers in New York are the *News* and the *Mirror* (this was in 1961) and that they are owned by Jews! On the other hand, says this "great" writer, the most leftwing paper in New York, the *New York Times*, is 98% Christian! (*The Times* is owned by the Sulzburgers and the Ochs—both Jews; while for new readers, the *News* is owned by the Christian Pattersons).

To top off her hysterical display of ignorance, and "prove" communism is not Jewish, she writes that notorious "Sidney Hook of Columbia University is deeply conservative"! Here's a direct quote from this crazy female: "The majority of Jews…are deeply conservative." (!) She adds that millions and millions of Jews were murdered by "Russian communists"! She ends her letter with the word, "Sh-t." A real "lady."

I was simply flabbergasted by this dose of madness and utter stupidity. I could not understand it, no matter how I tried. Finally, I dug into the lady's background a bit and began to learn that there is a reason for her "insanity," and a reason for her great "success" as a "writer." She isn't really "Taylor Caldwell"; she is really "Mrs. Marcus Reback" and is married to Mr. Reback, a Jew. Her daughter married a Jew by the name of Gerald Fried. Another daughter married a Jew named Goodman.

Now do you see why "Miss Caldwell" had such a fit when I printed the evidence of Jewish involvement in communism and the plan to exter-

---

[12] See *Rockwell Report* no. 1, Oct. 1961.

minate the German people? And why she can peddle her books by the millions in Jew bookshops all over the world even while she is a top Birch Society functionary and author? And why such a filthy-mouthed woman can be hailed far and wide as a brilliant authoress, just as Jewess Barbara Streisand is worshipped in every Jewish paper and magazine as the world's greatest singer, etc. etc.?

While "Taylor Caldwell" is one of the big wheels of the John Birch Society, she is also listed as a "contributing editor" of the magazine that attacked Goldwater as a psychopath, the great "conservative" magazine *Fact*, published by Ralph Ginsburg, recently sentenced to prison for his utterly filthy "Eros." *Fact* is about as far left as you can get, and this "Taylor Caldwell" (Mrs. Marcus Reback) gets away with posing as a great "conservative" even while she helps Mr. Ginsburg smear her supposed conservative "friends"!

So now "Miss Caldwell" (Mrs. Reback) has been made the head of the Friends of Rhodesia, under Marvin Liebman. With such a nice brace of Jew "friends," Rhodesia doesn't need any enemies.

卐 卐 卐

But even this Jewish manipulator, Liebman, isn't the worst cause of the endless failure in the anti-communist camp. The most deadly danger of all are the capable "conservatives" who have somehow fallen into the clutches of the Jews. These Jew-directed "Kosher Conservatives" have enormous amounts of money, industrial power, and national influence. Were they ever to take a united stand against the Jewish tormentors of our people, the game would be over in the morning. So, knowing this, the Jews have developed for these sincere but shortsighted wealthy right-wingers a sort of playpen in which they can thrash around to their heart's content, without ever doing any damage to the plans of our mortal enemies.

The very word and idea of "conservatism" guarantees that the victims of this delusion will merely try to "conserve" what is already *gone* (such as the Constitution, etc.), thus condemning themselves to a pitiful, rear-guard *defensive* action. They are very much like white-whiskered old Calvary Generals, long retired, cackling and fuming for the restoration of their beloved cavalry, long after tanks and rocket-launchers have swept the last horses from the battlefield.

Those committed to "conserving" something are doomed to think so strongly in terms of defense that the very idea of attack seems sacrilegious to them. Whenever I propose action, such as beating the daylights out of the traitors who burn American flags, these "conservatives" react as though I had belched in the middle of the silent prayer in church.

The Jews have made it relatively safe for patriots who agree tacitly to remain in the official Jewish playpen. And the boundaries of that Jewish playpen consist of avoiding mention of just two things: *race* and *Jews*.

You are allowed to be an economic conservative; you are allowed to be against all sorts of pet hates of "conservatives," such as "big government," Earl Warren, low tariffs, taxes, unions, etc. But let any conservative mention the Jews publicly and he will promptly find himself attacked with maximum Jew terrorism. Let him say that he thinks there is some evidence that perhaps Negroes are not biologically equal to White People, and the floodgates of Jewish hate and sewage will be opened to pour upon his head such a torrent of abuse and smear that he will run like a rabbit. He will be termed a "racist," a "bigot," a "hater," a "fascist"—and finally, a "Nazi"!

The poor, scared inmates of this Jewish "conservative" playpen are so terrified of the Jews getting even the least idea that they might even be thinking about sneaking an inch or two out of the playpen, that they usually seek to assure and reassure the Jews of their meek submission by endless attacks on "racists" and "Nazis." Such organizations as The Birch Society, Billy James Hargis, Fred Schwartz, the Constitution Party, all stay in their playpen, although most of the leaders know "the score." But they have decided that it is "clever strategy" to cooperate with the Jews in order, thereby, to build a larger membership and financial power.

But did you ever in your life hear of anybody winning a war by agreeing first never to mention the enemy, and then never doing anything to attack the enemy which was not first approved by the enemy? That's precisely how we lost the Korean War and are now wasting thousands of American lives losing in Vietnam. When an enemy has you down and almost whipped, it is pure insanity to accommodate him in *any* way. And to pretend he is your pal, and then allow him to dictate your strategy is pure suicide, not to mention cowardice.

In addition to emasculating your fight before it begins, this conservative defeatism and lack of aggressiveness convinces our side that the enemy is all-powerful. Cocky self-confidence is a might weapon, and has more than once given victory over a big man to a little man. But any man, little or big, who cowers and cringes before the enemy, rubbing his hands and smiling and hunching his shoulders and reassuring his deadly enemy that he is just crazy about him, has disarmed himself and made it impossible for himself to *fight*. There's nothing clever or smart about that.

Our nation and our people are perishing from an overdose of political sneaks, demagogues, liars, and cowards. The people may not be able to articulate that thought in these words. But they know it in their hearts. They long for a man to come forth who disdains compromise, sneaking, demagoguery, and slick lies. They want to hear a man say—nay, shout— what is in the hearts of the people without fear and without compromise. They want a real *leader*, not another slick politician. They will accept, vote for, and cheer a substitute only so long as the real thing is unavailable. The light of the moon is appreciated only when there is no sun.

卐 卐 卐

Before such a strong leader can come forward and reach the hearts of millions of the people, the people must first be made ready for the battle that will be made inevitable by any such a leader. The Jews, Blacks, communists, liberals—and the entrenched Kosher Conservatives—will fight desperately to prevent such a man from coming forward, because they know it will mean their own death knell as "leaders." They will fight with furious passion against the leadership of an honest man, because it will expose their own miserable failure and cowardice.

The people already sense this. But they do not yet want the all-out, bloody battle, in which they would probably lose their color TV, their two cars, and their electric lawnmower. They still hope they can win by some *easy* way.

And George Wallace (as I write) represents that hopeful, "easy" way, to America's millions. But the enemy cannot allow the victory of a Wallace because they know Wallace would be only the forerunner of a new, all-out "Hitler"—if he won.

At the same time, Wallace has built into his campaign the same weaknesses and guarantees of destruction as the Birchers, etc.; he has insisted on trying to win a life-and-death battle the same way we are "fighting" in Vietnam—by fighting only on terms and grounds allowed by the enemy. Instead of fighting on the grounds of *race*, on which he could unite the squabbling and divided "right," he fights on the untenable grounds of "states' rights," "segregation," and the rest of the Kosher Conservative shibboleths which are so easily demolished by the brutal enemy.

The clever campaign and pressure of the Jews upon America first produced such compromising economic kosher "conservatives" as William F. Buckley. When he was unable to stop the Jewish juggernaut (because he was with it), the few who could see the need for something more flocked to the banners of the Birch Society. But today, that too is failing, because the Birch Society also consorts with and "loves" the enemy—the Jews—and gives patriots' contributions to send Negroes to college on scholarships, all while calling honest men who name the enemy "communist agents provocateurs."

The next phase of this American movement toward the right must be and is "Wallace-ism"—the covert and sneaky racism, which is now the fashion in the South and conservative circles. For the same reasons that Buckley-ism and Welch-ism failed, Wallace-ism will also fail. We can't win in Korea and Vietnam when we won't fight, and we can't win here in America either when we not only will not fight, but we won't even name the enemy.

Are we not damned fools to continue to let the enemy dictate the terms of the struggle?

Are we not idiots to continue to fight on the enemy's brutal terms when we suffer nothing but defeat, and see the end only months away?

Are we not worse than mad to tolerate almost nothing but Jews and "ex"-communists or pro-communists like Liebman, Goldwater—and now Ronald Reagan—to lead us, when there are millions of pure, unadulterated Americans willing and capable of leading?

How long will we continue to believe we can "out-sneak" and out-wit the Jews by "smart" demagoguery, when they are the world's champion sneaks and demagogues? For every sneaky lie we can tell (such as that we are "not racists,") the Jews can tell ten much better and more convincing lies.

How long before our masses of great Americans get mad enough to say the truth? —as we must, "To hell with all the pretense and fancy talk! It's time to name the damnable Jewish, Zionist, "nigger," and communist enemy, fight him, and kill those who are trying to commit treason, enslave us, or kill us! It's time to fight!"

The answer to that question is that it will not be long. Wallace must have his day. The people must learn that our race of people can't win by any kind of sneaking—even when it is considered *clever* sneaking, such as denying that one is a "racist," and even saying that "racism is evil." Wallace-ism is a phase that must be *grown out of*, as a teenager passes through im-mature phases of development. Racism is not only *not* "evil"—racism is our only hope!

America will soon be ready for a leader who has gone through hell to preach pure racism, to fight for our White people, as a race, without any pretty excuses or cover-ups. The people, when they have been robbed of their savings by inflation and economic catastrophe, when "niggers" are raping their mothers, wives, sisters, and daughters, when their country is in flames and being looted by "nigger" mobs, when Jews have become only a tiny bit more arrogant and monopolize everything, parading around as our teachers, musicians, comedians, actors, philosophers, writers and finally our owners—when the people have had only a little more of this, then the radical racial stance and record of the American Nazi Party will bring us the hearts and love of the masses of Americans.

It is tempting for a rightist political group to make all sorts of compromises right now in order to attract, hold, and gain the financial support of large numbers of people who do not yet see the desperate need for radical measures. This is what all the big, successful rightwing organizations are now doing. They say everything calculated to bring them flocks of frustrated people, and they avoid saying anything that might shock and distress these flocks of poor, frustrated Americans, even though they may know that our people need to hear and know the bloody, deadly, and dangerous truth. These presently "successful" rightwing organizations, including the Wallace promoters, are like a mother who is too chicken to take her son to a dentist to have his tooth pulled when it is rotten and diseased, but instead gives him doped-up soothing syrup. None of these "soothing syrup" patriots dare to go after the deadly germs which are causing the trouble, recommend killing the germs (which represents the Jewish traitors in our midst) and getting rid of the aching tooth (which, in this analogy, represents the 20 million "niggers" causing America the worst "ache" we have ever had.[13])

But the time comes when even the worst coward about going to the dentist can no longer fool himself with soothing syrups, and scrambles in to a real dentist to have the radical treatment which alone can solve his problem: to have the tooth jerked out and the germs of decay *killed*.

Nothing less can stop a real toothache. And nothing less than killing the enemy germs and extracting the "nigger" hell-raisers can stop the disease and pain which is killing America and the White Race.

Our job is to be good dentists, remain steadfast, and keep our pliers and germicide ready to extract the black aching tooth and disinfect our nation of the germs of Jewish treason and decay, when the patient is ready. Fifty years of "conservative" failure is enough!

---

[13] Now, 48 million.

CHAPTER 14

WHITE IMPERIUM

In the previous chapter, I have presented the almost unbelievable evidence that, faced with the ultimate catastrophe in all human history, the only response of most of our side has been to follow the enemy.

Before I proceed with a presentation of what can and must be done to stop this suicidal insanity, I must pause to reinforce in the mind of the reader that this struggle is not only "for keeps," but that loss of the struggle will mean slaughter and terror such as this planet has never before experienced. The Jews and their colored allies behind the hell in the world today are not fooling; they do not use half-measures. They kill their enemies. For an unimpeachable witness to the bloody, murderous nature of the Jews, one has only to inspect their own words. They boast about it.

In the early centuries of human history, all races and groups did plenty of killing. But only the Jews and other Orientals have ever wallowed in the blood and gloried in the agony and bizarre slaughter of their victims, with a depraved hate. If this sounds too extreme, pick up the Jewish Torah (the Old Testament) and read the first few chapters as history. The men whom the Jews worship as their "saints" and "prophets" were the bloodiest gang of massacre-artists in all history, by their own testimony. Everywhere they went, they delighted in slaughtering all those who "pisseth against the wall" (as they like to put it),[1] sometimes going still further and murdering even the pigs, cattle, and cats, and dogs of their enemies.[2]

Historian Edward Gibbon provides another historical example of the oriental-Jewish propensity for murder, in his monumental and authoritative *Decline and Fall of the Roman Empire*. On page 384 of the 1783 edition, Gibbon writes:

> From the reign of Nero to that of Antoninus Pius, the Jews displayed a fierce impatience of the dominion of Rome, which repeatedly broke out in the most furious massacres and insurrections. Humanity is shocked at the recital of the horrid cruelties that they [the Jews] committed in the cities of

---

[1] 1 Samuel 25:22.
[2] 1 Samuel 15:3.

Egypt, of Cyprus, and of Cyrene, where they dwelt in treacherous friendship with the unsuspecting natives. In Cyrene they massacred 220,000 Greeks; in Cyprus, 240,000; in Egypt a very great multitude. Many of these unhappy victims were sawed asunder according to a precept to which David had given the sanction of his example The victorious Jews devoured the flesh, licked up the blood, and twisted the entrails like a girdle around their bodies.

Too few Americans are aware of the fact that in modern times the most frightful gang of killers ever spawned in America is not the Mafia, but a gang of Jews from the Lower East Side of New York City. "Murder, Inc." was based in the Greenpoint District of Brooklyn and run by the Jew, Louis "Lepke" Buchalter. In the tradition of the Torah Jews and the Jews mentioned by Gibbon, who sawed people asunder and danced in the streets wearing the entrails of their victims, the bloodthirsty Jews of Murder, Inc., specialized in trussing up their victims alive and then stabbing them to death slowly with ice-picks—for cash! No other group of killers for pay has ever equaled the bloody, Jewish, Murder, Inc.

From a hard-to-find book called *Murder, Inc.* about the clean-up of this gang by the former Attorney General of New York, Thomas E. Dewey, I copied down the choice characters as they appeared in the book. Take a look at the names of the people involved in this Jewish murder-mill for money:

Al GLASS	"Big Harry" SCHACTER	Charlie YANOWSKI
Carl SHAPIRO	Meyer LANSKY	Moses "Moey Dimples" WOLINSKY
Max "The Jerk" GOLOB	Joey AMBERG	Max SHAMAN
Irving "Chippy" WEINER	"Gangy" COHEN	"Happy" MELTZER
"Abbadabba" BERMAN	Emanuel "Manny" KESSLER	Moses "Moe" SEDWAY
"Waxey Gordon" WECHSLER	"Puggy" FEINSTEIN	Al SILVERMAN
Bo WEINBERG	"Dandy Phil" KASTEL	Harry "Big Greenie" Greenberg
Emanuel "Mendy" WEISS	Frankie TEITELBAUM	Lou GLASSER
"Tootsie" FEINSTEIN	"Longy" ZWILLMAN	Willie SHAPIRO
Sholem BERNSTEIN	"Lulu" ROSENKRANZ	Jacob "Gurrah" SHAPIRO
Hyman KASNER	Isidore "Curley" HOLZ	Max BLECKER
Jacob "Hooky" ROTHMAN	Charlie SOLOMON	Sam GASBERG
Mickey COHEN	Paul BERGER	Harry MILMAN
Charlie WORKMAN	Lou COHEN	Arnold ROTHSTEIN
Mert WERTHEIMER	"Wolfie" GOLDIS	"Muddy" KASOFF
"Pittsburg Phil" STRAUSS	Abe SLABOW	Joey SILVERS
"Pretty" AMBBERG	"Nig" ROSEN	Hyman YURAN
"Bugsy" SIEGEL	Yasha KATZENBERG	"Fatty" KOPERMAN
"Dopey Benny" FEIN	"Fat Sidney" BLATZ	Solomon "Jack" GOLDSTEIN
Benny "The Boss" TANNENBAUM	Max RUBIN	Izzy FARTISTEIN
Abraham "Misfit" LANDAU	Allie "Tick Tock" TANNENBAUM	

and many others, all *Jews*.

During World War II, the Nazis were supposed to have been the ultimate in brutality and ruthlessness. But the fact is that they failed precisely because they were not as ruthless and brutal as the enemy. Almost all the guerrilla fighters behind Nazi lines have since turned out to be communists—and Jews. When these communist "partisans" started shooting German soldiers in the back from ambush during World War II and murdering troops and civilians by blowing up trains, the Germans responded by shooting some hostages, but almost always with a certain restraint. The inevitable result was always a more bitter resistance by the Reds, because when you strike a blow at a determined enemy, it must smash him completely—or it only fires him up to greater resistance, hatred, and strength. When you use terror, as the Jews know all too well, it must be total.

Observe what these communist lovers of humanity did in the Katyn Forest in Poland during World War II. The US Senate investigated this unspeakable atrocity, and you can check the facts in the Senate report on the massacres there. As soon as the communists overran Poland, the Jewish commissar in the Red army gathered all the officers of the Polish army—not just the top ones, but every officer in the Polish army—15,000 of them, marched them out into the Katyn Forest, and systematically slaughtered them. They buried these 15,000 Polish officers in acres of mass graves.

When the Germans got control of Eastern Poland they found the mass graves. They called in the International Red Cross to inspect the site right after they found it, and then invited two top US Army Colonels to see, with their own eyes, this bloody evidence of the nature of the Jews who were leading our "gallant Soviet allies" (as I was being told at the time). Roosevelt and his gang gagged these two US officers and threatened them with court martial if they ever opened their mouths!

My point in picking out this tiny bit of evidence of the nature of the monsters we must fight is to show you a pattern—a pattern of systematic extermination that will quickly destroy us, our people, and our whole civilization, unless we stop it!

The Jewish masters of world revolution never take any chances on attacks behind their lines. They know that most people don't move without leadership of the elite of their group—the natural leaders—just as your hands won't move without the leadership of your head. So the Jewish revolutionists systematically, coldly, smash the "head." That is why they killed all the Polish officers (not a few hostages, as the Germans might have done)—the whole leadership corps of Polish strength. Beheaded, the Polish people never again caused the Reds any real trouble.

One of the latest refinements in the Jewish technique of "beheading" whole peoples and movements is used more and more frequently in the Soviet satellite states of Europe (which were given to the Reds by traitors in the US government). The wily Jews running things from behind the scenes in these unhappy Soviet work-colonies have discovered and put to use an absolutely devilish scheme to keep any resistance to Jewish tyranny from ever succeeding.

From time to time, these calculating communist friends, just like their brethren in Murder, Inc., cold-bloodedly plot, organize, and pull off a "rebellion" *against themselves*.[3] Secretly, they permit the arming and organizing of a "resistance" they themselves have promoted. They watch it develop, sometimes helping it if it seems to falter. Their "Radio Free Europe" has this devilish purpose, for example. As soon as they feel sure it has rounded up all the best and most daring potential leaders of the people, they precipitate open rebellion, which lets them swoop in and exterminate the latest and newest crop of leaders—which is what they were after in the first place! This actually happened in Hungary in 1956!

This calculating deviltry has the added advantage that the tortured people begin to be aware of how they have been suckered, so that any future leaders who try to organize any resistance are instantly treated as enemy *agents provocateurs* by their own peoples, no matter how sincere. It is impossible for resistance to develop in such a fog of suspicion.

In recent centuries, the Jews have found an even easier way to kill off the hated goyim. They get *us* to do it.

My brother used to be the bouncer in a roughneck dance hall. Since my brother is anything but a tough guy, I asked him how he survived as a sort of "cop" among all those brutal hoods. He answered, "Whenever I find a tough who is drunk and causing trouble, I go find a bigger tough, usually just as drunk, and tell him I need his help. I build up his ego, make him feel important, and convince him the other guy is an 'enemy.' He goes over and throws the other guy out, and then I lock 'em both out."

For a least a hundred years now, the Jews have been working this diabolical scheme on White nations the world over. Whenever I travel from our Arlington, Virginia, headquarters to our printing and production plant, down in the Virginia countryside between Washington and Richmond, I pass through some of the most blood-soaked ground in America: battlegrounds of a war in which more White Americans were slaughtered than all the rest of our wars combined! (People forget that the so-called Civil War was our greatest bloodletting, far surpassing World Wars I and II and all our other wars.)[4]

---

[3] Today this is known as a "false flag" operation.
[4] Around 800,000 Americans died in the Civil War, versus 115,000 in World War One and 400,000 in World War Two.

Sometimes when I see one of the little historical markers on the highway, I stop the car and walk out into the quiet hills and meadows where armies of brave young Americans killed each other. As I stand there on those long-silent battlefields of Bull Run, Manassas, Fredericksburg, Spotsylvania, or Chancellorsville surrounding the national headquarters and printing plant of the American Nazi Party, I can almost hear the bugles and shouts of those hundreds of thousands of the finest youth on both sides; the rebel yells—stopped suddenly by a thrust of cold steel in the gut and changed to a scream of terror and death. I can hear the animal grunts as my brothers, on both sides, work hard at the bloody job of stabbing, shooting, cannonading, and clubbing their own White brothers to death by the hundreds of thousands, all on behalf of swarms of half-ape Negroes who are now tearing up America!

I am not ashamed to admit that, standing there in the peaceful silence of the countryside and visualizing thousands of our heroic young lads killing and dismembering each other on those battlefields, I cannot hold back the tears. The so-called Civil War is far enough back in history, today, so that many Americans on both sides of the Mason-Dixon line can begin to see, at last, the tragic folly of this fratricide. For many years now, as I write this, the "Southern Democrats" and the "Conservative Republicans" of the North have been standing together, at least in some Congressional struggles, to try to repair some of the crazy damage done to our White Race on the bloody battlefields of the Civil War.

The Civil War was not fought to "preserve the Union," as the propaganda goes, but to serve the commercial interests of the racial agitators who provoked that war with their "Uncle Tom's Cabin" propaganda and their sob-sister, hypocritical "love" of the Blacks. These same racial agitators happily and greedily brought their colored friends over to America by the boatload when it paid (up until 1808, when the slave trade was stopped). But as soon as Southern commercial competition seemed inconvenient to them, as soon as there was no more cash in selling the Blacks, then their hearts went out to the poor, persecuted half-apes they had so recently delivered in chains from Africa, for gold, for cash, in the great sailing ships of the North.

The Civil War was only the first of the "Wars of Racial Suicide" of our people, the first of the hundred-year marathon of mutual slaughter of White Brother by White Brother (and now that air-bombing is possible, the slaughter of White Sisters, too, by White Brothers, as we did during World War II when we slaughtered a quarter of a million of them fleeing from communism in the beautiful, nonmilitary, defenseless city of Dresden).

Nothing is so completely insane and suicidal as the eager rush of White men all over the world to murder each other by the millions whenever it suits the Jews and their lying, liberal friends to set us at each other's throats. The Jews have only to use their newspapers, television, radio, books, magazines, and school texts to poison our minds, and different groups of White men can be fired up to murderous rage against each other, time after time. The Jews have only to tell us of the "atrocities" committed by some other group of White men, and we slaughter them by the millions. Always it is the best manhood among us that is killed off in these fratricidal wars, since the less able are left home as "4-F's" while the best potential fathers go off to the slaughter. And of these "best" who do go to the slaughter, it is always the cream of the crop of the best of our manhood who get killed first, since they are the ones whose idealism and courage lead them to be the volunteers in the first assaults and on especially dangerous missions.

Whenever any segment of the White Race appears to the Jews to be on the road to recovery of national health (and therefore ready to flush out the germs of Jewish degeneracy and disease), the Jews simply go to work on all the rest of the White world (exactly as predicted in the Protocols) to inflame the rest of us against our own brothers. They lie to us that our White Brothers are the "enemy," that our White Brothers are "torturing and murdering babies and innocent people," that they are planning to "conquer" us and enslave or murder us, that they are "beasts," that all humanity cries out for us to go and smash our brothers—always on behalf of these Jews and/or Negroes—and for the last half century, on behalf of the communists.

What did the American majority get out of World War I or World War II? Did we save the world from tyranny? No! Did we make the world "safe for democracy"? No! Did we gain any land or great, rich prizes, any mines or colonies? No! All we got were headaches, responsibilities, and more little spit-in-the-eye wars, anti-American hate, Berlin Walls, "Foreign Aid" handouts, Koreas, Vietnams, Cubas, and endless riots and crime at home. That is the standard pattern of our "wars" today—mutual suicide of White against White, followed by the handing over to communists, Jews, and Negroes of more and more of our territory, wealth, rights, and power, and the disarming of any real opposition to Jewish-led scum as a form of treason to the "American dream."

As long as the conservatives are too cowardly to face up to this fact, and continue to blast real anti-communist fighters such as the German National Socialists, and now the American Nazis, we will be utterly defenseless against the wily Jews. You cannot claim the "truth" as your biggest weapon, and then crawl at the feet of the Jews to tell the biggest lies of all times about Adolf Hitler and your own fighters!

To see the psychological folly of the conservative position on Hitler and the "Nazis," just imagine the effect if there had been large numbers of rich Mexicans living in the United States at the time of the fight at the Alamo. Further, let's suppose that most American newspapers were owned and controlled by Mexican-Americans, so that our people heard nothing else but that Davy Crockett and his gang of "war-criminals" were committing "aggressive war" by seizing Mexican property at the Alamo, while Santa Anna led the "democratic" forces of "justice and mercy." Any American who questioned the evilness of Davy Crockett or who doubted the goodness of Santa Anna would never get a hearing, but would be immediately dubbed a "Mexican hater," an "anti-Mexican"—and then be driven into poverty and disgrace. Unless somebody had the guts and integrity to tell the truth about the heroism of Davy Crockett and his men at the Alamo, America itself would soon be completely in the hands of the Mexicans. That's what the Jews have accomplished by scaring or swindling American conservatives into joining the Jews in their hate-Hitler and anti-Nazi campaign of lies and filth.

Without the inspiration and heroism of men like Crockett and Bowie and Travis, we can't win our wars. When you become so depraved and cowardly that you can be scared into cursing your own heroes, you have lost the power to survive; history has already marked you for the ash-heap.

In 1932, when the conspirators managed to get Franklin Roosevelt and his Jewish gang into the White House, they planned an open takeover for their communist world revolution. America had been lied to, primed with a terrible depression, and sold the Roosevelt bill-of-goods. It would have been a cinch. But the monkey wrench in their machinery of world revolution was Germany, which was the key to the control of Europe. Unless Germany could be seized, or at least rendered powerless (as it now has been), world communist victory would be impossible.

At the last moment, a strong man arose and seized the initiative from the scheming Jews. Adolf Hitler managed to win back to sanity and honor so many millions of good German people that the weak government was forced to give Hitler legal power, by the will of the people. Adolf Hitler fought the Alamo of the White Race. He held off the colored forces of racial suicide, the forces of communism, the forces of arrogant Zionism, and the forces of international money-manipulation long enough for a few men like myself to wipe the Jewish cobwebs out of our brains and start the long battle to awaken our people and free them from the menacing specter of Jewish and colored world tyranny. Hitler purchased, with his own life and the lives of millions of young German men, the precious time for us to be able to wake up and organize to resist the Jews and Negroes, just as Crockett and his men purchased with their lives the time for General Sam Houston to organize to resist the Mexicans.

To get back to our Mexican-American analogy, can you imagine how the Mexicans would have been doubled up laughing (in private) if at the time of the Alamo, all American leaders were denouncing Crockett and his men as "a gang of hoodlums," "war criminals," "bullies," "Huns," operators of Mexican "slaughter camps," etc., while at the same time these American leaders were heaping endless praise on their wonderful, patriotic Mexican "friends" here in America, and sending every kind of help and aid to Santa Anna, calling him "Good old Uncle Santa"—just as Truman referred to Stalin as "Good Old Uncle Joe"?

But there's more to the Conservative madness. Today the Jews have actually got the conservatives in America repeating in chorus, like a bunch of parrots, "communism and Nazism are the same thing"! (This allows the conservatives to "prove" to the Jews and Red terrorists that they, the conservatives, are just as anti-Nazi as they are anti-communist.) This bit of madness must have the Jews rolling on the floor, holding their sides in agonies and paroxysms of laughter.

To get the full flavor of this "communism-and-Nazism-are-the-same-thing" madness, I must ask the reader to bear with me a moment while we return to the Alamo analogy. Imagine, if you can, all the "respectable" men and patriots of the time, all doing lots of profitable business with Mexicans, swearing up and down to their Mexican friends that while they were pro-American, they were certainly not "anti-Mexican." To equal the madness of the present day "patriots" saying "communism and Nazism are the same thing," these "patriots" of the Alamo days would have to be bowing up and down before their Mexican business partners like figures in Black Forest clocks, repeating over and over, "We're not Anti-Mexican. In fact, we're just as much against Crockett as we are against Santa Anna. In fact, Crockett and Santa Anna are the same thing! They are both shooting and using guns!"

It's really as simple as that; although, when you are right in the middle of it all, and you yourself are subject to the terrorism and smear and loss of job and fortune arranged by the Jewish lovers of democracy, it may be hard for you to realize the full depth of this anti-Hitler madness for a while.

From a historical perspective, William Buckley putting Max Lerner, Jacob Javits, and a long parade of vile, pinko, Red, and Zionist Jews on his TV program and treating them like noble and honest Americans while he cannot find enough words to curse and damn me or anybody else who dares tell the truth about Adolf Hitler, will be downright funny (if we survive long enough to laugh).

For a hundred years, the Jewish agitators have doubled and redoubled the rate at which we are killing off our best, by pitting brother against brother in endless, silly wars we always lose and they always win. The Jewish aim is and remains the wiping out of "the best of the goyim," as the Talmud puts it.[5] They keep getting us killed—now by the millions—while they increase and grow stronger.

In the beginning of this chapter, I mentioned that there was one other Oriental group beside the Jews that has distinguished itself in history for the magnitude of its slaughter and bloodthirstiness—the Mongols. There is nothing else in all history to match the record of hideous mass cruelty and murder of the "Golden Horde" of Genghis Khan. The same Asiatic strain in the Jews that produces such a love of slaughter and cruelty is found in its pure, original form in the savage Mongol. When this yellow beast of Asia rises up and stalks the earth, the Great Writer of history dips his pen in blood and prepares to write chapters of death, suffering, and destruction.

But that was hundreds of years ago. What could Genghis Khan have done with a hydrogen bomb, today? Unless you, White Man, can muster the will to make yourself think that chilling thought, and do something about the approaching time when it will happen, you will find out, and your children will learn the ancient meaning of the "Yellow Peril"—the colored peril. The Jews have gathered up the colored peoples of the earth, armed them with the ultimate weapons of atomic energy, and agitated them to unlimited dreams of world conquest.

As I write, our "experts" keep expressing more and more "surprise" at the speed with which Red China is progressing with a deliverable H-bomb! Only a fool could fail to see that the world is rapidly approaching a terrible climax in which the most historic decision in all human history will be made: the long-awaited Armageddon, or "Ragnarok." Every year, every month, every week, and every hour, we get closer to that terrible moment

[5] Relevant quotations include: "Kill the best of the heathens [in time of war], crush the brains of the best serpents" (Soferim 15, 10); "The best among the Egyptians, kill; the best among the serpents, crush its brain" (Midrash Tanchuma, Beshalach 8, 1); "The best among the Egyptians, kill him… The best among the serpents, crush its brains" (Rashi on Exodus 14:7, 2).

when Red China, allied with black Africa, India, black America, and the rest of the colored world, will have the power to launch rockets with H-bomb warheads at the White nations of the world. China already is within months of being able to devastate White America and White Europe.

We comfort ourselves with the thought that "they wouldn't dare"—because we would blast them right back. If they kill a hundred million of us, we'll kill two hundred million of them. How silly can you get?

Immediately after the Reds took over China, they purposely murdered 40 million people to "thin out" a population far too thick to support. All the colored nations have this same over-population problem, as we have already shown in the first parts of this book. China, India, and Africa would be blessed by the destruction of several hundred million extra hungry mouths.

If these colored races launch a swarm of H-bombs at us, a possibility our experts already admit, we could stop only a few of them. Most of them would get through, wiping out such cities as Los Angeles, New York, Chicago, Detroit, Boston, Dallas, Denver, Minneapolis, Houston, St. Louis, Philadelphia, and Washington. We'd lose not only more than a hundred million of our people, but all the complex machinery which supports a modern, industrial society. What we would destroy in "retaliation" against the colored world would not be "people" in the American sense of the word, but swarms of illiterates, miserable, barely existing coolies, cannibals, untouchables, beggars, who are worthless—an actual burden to their government. The colored leaders do not fear "retaliation"; it would be a help to them!

Russia is realizing this more and more. There is a growing hostility and fear between Russia and China, because Russia realizes that China is less a communist nation than a colored nationalistic nation. Russians are "White," and the Chinamen hate and attack them as "imperialists and exploiters"—just the same as they attack us "dirty American fascists."

What's ahead for our world, in your lifetime, is not a war between communism and capitalism, but a war of annihilation between the elite White minority of mankind and the swarming, inferior, colored majority. Communism is becoming—in fact is—a colored world mutiny against the White Race. And the colored Chinese are within days or months of possessing the power to destroy all of us with our own atomic weapons (which our liberals and Jews have given to them).

While Johnson, De Gaulle, Kosygin, Wilson, Kissinger, and the rest of the white ninnies, posing as "statesmen," bicker and haggle with one another, Red China, harboring and training colored world revolutionists and terrorists, is organizing, on a worldwide scale too terrible and bloody for the Western mind to contemplate, a Genghis Khan horde of colored death for the White Race. Once these colored men of the East possess the H-bomb and the ability to deliver it, nothing can stop the attack—and thus the destruction of the West. They have everything to gain—and we have everything to lose. They openly write about it, talk about it, gloat about it! And still our "statesmen" play medieval games of economic sanctions, power-balances, disarmament, etc., ad nauseam.

As long as the vast masses of the White men in all nations tolerate puppets and damned fools in positions of leadership, these puppets and liberals will play their childish games of 19th-century "power politics" while the colored world and the Jews prepare for the racial Armageddon, using the White Man's atomic weapons to destroy him.

To survive, we must get these puppets and fools out of positions of power and influence, and install some tough, realistic leaders who will unite and organize us for survival. Such men will realize and make use of the basic fact of life that is so thoroughly forgotten by the fatheads in power today. The central fact that is being forgotten in today's insane world is *force!* Liberalism and intellectualism have so blinded Western Man that the majority of us have forgotten the absolute and total primacy of force. Every grain of sand on every beach in the world is where it is because of a force that put it there. When superior force meets weaker force, superior force always conquers and annihilates the weaker. The liberals and mush-heads wish it were otherwise, and today's artificial world of machinery makes it appear possible to them that force can be replaced by "reason."

But this is as irrational and superstitious a bit of jungle "thought" as that of any witch doctor waving a lizard's tail over a cannibal with a broken leg. If good men abandon and denigrate force, then bad men will take it up and beat us to death with it. When good men lay down their club, bad men will smash them with that club sooner or later.

If I get across only one single point in this entire book, let it be this fact: that civilization, peace, and order depend, not on "good will" but on force, policemen, armies, and weapons. Hitler put it more succinctly and more poetically than I could hope to: "The gentle Goddess of Peace can only walk in company with the God of War!"[6]

Those who truly want to see a world of real order and peace, a world where men can live their lives with reasonable expectations of planning their futures and achieving goals without being shot, bombed, blown up, raped, burned, beaten to death in insurrections, eaten in the Congo, sent off

---

[6] *Mein Kampf*, vol 2, sec. 7.7 (Dalton translation, p. 127).

to insane wars to die by the millions for nothing, and forever kept in spiritual turmoil and misery, must decide right now to work for the establishment of White unity and White mastery of the world. There is no other alternative.

Only the White Race—always the White Race—has demonstrated, over the centuries, the ability to enforce peace and order in this world. Ever since the British Empire abdicated, exactly as Adolf Hitler predicted, the world has plunger deeper and deeper into chaos, bloodshed, and terror. Nothing can stop this continuing plunge, outside of an all-out drive by White Men to quit arguing about petty, relatively minor differences among them, unite as a Master Race, and enforce peace and order.

The whole world is in a state of riot, much like that in our cities. The only way to restore order in a riot is with force: instant, sure, and dramatic force, applied with intelligence and as much justice as possible—but, above all, force.[7]

That word, "force," has been made a dirty word, today, by the Jews and their suckers who dream of peace through wormy weakness. What used to be called our War Department, for instance, has been renamed the "Defense Department"—a subtle and apparently minor change, but a psychological retreat of enormous significance. This psychology of retreat and "defense" has robbed us of Nature's primary gift to all her creatures: the will to fight to live and protect one's own. The whole White Race has been poisoned with this subtle defeatism and weakness.

The White Race was once the policeman of the world, and the world was orderly. Compared to the bloody upheavals of today, it was also relatively peaceful. Unless the White Race can find the leadership, the wisdom, and the will once again to police the world, the planet will continue in the grip of increasing chaos and terror, until the jungle reclaims the survivors hiding in caves and holes like frightened beasts. Only a united White Race, supremely conscious of its natural destiny, a destiny bequeathed it in the gift of superior birth, as a master race, a noble race able to create the wonders of Western Culture—only such a united race can muster the will and the strength to restore order to a world in the process of suicide and disintegration. And yet, faced by the most hideous threat of all times, outnumbered ten to one, we find ourselves disorganized, demoralized, wallowing in defeatism, crawling at the feet of our own destroyers, and losing strength every moment. It is easy to fall prey to despair.

---

[7] It cannot be over-emphasized that all current global conflicts of "White" nations are instigated by Jews—who are not White.

卐 卐 卐

But there is another element in this cosmic crap-game which must be taken into account if we are to make a correct judgment about the survival of our people and culture in the face of the Jewish-Negroid-Mongoloid threat. That element is *timing*—or, if you will, destiny.

The mighty White Race is brainwashed, filled with suicidal self-hatred, crazy about its deadly enemies, trivialized, doped-up on drugs and lies, and apparently rushing headlong toward oblivion. But the strength of the blood is still there, as we have shown in every war where the Jews have "turned us loose." Whenever, as in World War II, the Jews wish us to be our ancient, ferocious, mighty selves, able to smash anything in our way; whenever they allow Natural Law to return to us, even in a temporary and wrong way, our people show themselves still heroes and fighters, not decadent weaklings, or in any way like the people of a dying culture.

The rumors of our death, to quote Mark Twain, are "greatly exaggerated." They are appearances only. Let only a strong leader appear, let our people once see the real nature of their Jewish and colored "friends" (as is already beginning to happen), and the blood of our Viking ancestors will well up in a berserker rage which will sweep away the miasma of Jewish and colored poison gas from our lives as a lion sends a pack of vultures flapping with one lunge.

It is not yet our "time" to die. Destiny has a way of doing her will in spite of all human efforts to foil her, both when she is creating and when she is destroying. Destiny brought forth the greatness of Rome when it was time. And, when it was time, she cast it aside and made a way for the mightier Barbarians, sweeping down from the cool northern forests. Destiny brought forth the British Empire, when it was time. And, after centuries of rule, Destiny withdrew her blessing and the British Empire died—when it was time.

Destiny is even now, in America, conceiving the new imperium of our time, the *White Imperium*—the unification of the White Race and its conscious racial mastery of the lobe.

In spite of all signs of death and disease, deep within the vitals of our race is growing the embryo of that unity and that White Imperium which will last for its thousands of years, and destroy all which stands in its way. Destiny simply will not be thwarted or swindled, even by such master swindlers as the Jews. The Jews have let the colored genie out of the bottle, armed him, agitated him, directed him to "sic" the White world, and set him galloping on a mission that the Jew hopes will turn the world over to the Chosen Ones.

But the latest moves of the African and Asian hordes remind me of that dramatic paragraph—one of the most dramatic in all of English literature—written by Somerset Maugham, which conveys my meaning as no other exposition could:

DEATH SPEAKS

There was a merchant in Baghdad who sent his servant to market to buy provisions, and in a little while the servant came back, white and trembling, and said "Master, just now when I was in the market place I was jostled by a woman in the crowd, and when I turned I saw it was Death that jostled me. She looked at me and made a threatening gesture; now, lend me your horse and I will ride away from this city and avoid my fate. I will go to Samarra and there, Death will not find me."

The merchant lent him his horse, and he dug his spurs in its flanks and as fast as the horse could gallop, he went. Then the merchant went down to the market place and he saw me standing in the crowd, and came to me and said, "Why did you make a threatening gesture to my servant when you saw him this morning?" "That was not a threatening gesture," I said, "It was only a start of surprise. I was astonished to see him in Baghdad, for I had an appointment with him tonight in Samarra."

Today, the colored *untermenschen* of the world—the scum, the beggars, cannibals, untouchables, and all that sorry swarm let loose by the Jews— are riding hard upon their horses, charging at full speed, spurring their mounts to furious gallops, racing faster and faster, to Samarra.

CHAPTER 15

NATIONAL SOCIALISM

So far, this book has been mostly critical. Now it is time to present constructive plans for building and creating.

I have put a year of research and hundreds of pages of writing into the effort to help the reader see and understand that Western Civilization is within a very few years of the end reached by Roman civilization-oblivion; and that he, personally, will suffer the fate of millions who have already fallen into the hands of the Jewish mortal enemies of Western Civilization—enslavement or, more likely, murder—unless we can find the will and the wisdom, somehow, to stop running away from the enemy and attack him with a White revolution!

Just how do you go about creating a revolution? Are we all to grow beards, rush into the streets and begin shouting, waving our arms, throwing bombs, and otherwise acting the part of stereotype "revolutionaries"? *No!* Of course not. Our revolution has been all laid out for us. Hitler inspired, organized, and pulled off a relatively peaceful revolution, a revolution which took far fewer lives than the American Revolution, and an insignificant number of lives compared to any ever pulled off by the Jewish Bolsheviks. Not only that, but Hitler's revolution, as he promised in *Mein Kampf*, was 100% "legal"—legitimate—the formally expressed will of the majority of the German people, sanctioned by both the top executive officer of Germany, von Hindenburg, and by the German "congress," the Reichstag. Hitler had many opportunities to seize power by force and could have done it easily in 1931. But he believed that a revolution against the will of the people, a revolution that gains power only by force, cannot long endure. Hitler, as I do, believed that a leader is an enemy of civilization unless he has the will of his people behind him.

How, then, can I be calling for "revolution"? How can I write of "killing and being killed"? Is not the very essence of revolution violence? Not necessarily. There may be an element of violence, yes. When you are attacked by a killer and faced with the choice of death or dealing death yourself, then violence is the only possibility. And Western Civilization is indeed under attack by an enemy who regularly, as a matter of policy, kills and massacres more ruthlessly than any other group in history. So we must be violent enough to put a stop to the communist enemy's killing and ruthless enough to smash his power.

In 1923, when the Reds threatened to seize power in Bavaria, the Nationalists, the conservatives, and General Ludendorff asked Hitler to lead a "Putsch"—a revolt—in Munich. Then the weakling leaders double-crossed him at the last moment. The "Putsch" was crushed and Hitler was sent to prison. But this was not a revolution against the will of the people, as events proved later.

But the essence of a real revolution is never *just* the bloodshed and upheaval. In a genuine and lasting revolution, violence and killing are only one expedient means to the end of a radical change in over-all spiritual outlook—the outward manifestation of a supreme human will to establish a new arrangement of physical affairs to conform with an inner ideal.

The authority exercised by most of those in power today is unadulterated tyranny, though it is hypocritically disguised as "democracy." It is not the benevolent, intelligent authority to maintain order and justice established by the Founding Fathers for the benefit of White men.

Our revolution must be based firmly on the ideal of destroying the illegal power of tyrants, and restoring a just social order that is based on a firm authority that comes straight from our people, and is freely granted to a leader. That, believe it or not, is precisely what Hitler did for Germany, and what we must do for America. Our revolution, in short, must have as its driving force and goal, not merely the hatred and destruction of the enemy, but it must be imbued with an absolute determination to establish a just social order in which each man can achieve his maximum potential as a successful, happy, and productive part of our great White Race.

What is such a just order of society? There is no need for this understanding of the scientific principles of successful group living among those in healthy societies where natural instincts are unimpaired. Animals, for instance, have orderly, successful "societies" because Nature gives every social creature all the instincts he needs for successful group living. Wolves, ants, bees—and apes—for instance, have highly organized and thoroughly healthy, orderly societies.

Early men had healthy societies. Then man's growing control over Nature allowed him to escape his natural environment, and surround himself with artificialities and luxury until he became decadent and full of arrogant conceit—a conceit that is today called "liberalism." Only by going back to the simpler and more primitive life-situation of the unthinking and uncivilized animal world, and observing the workings of the instincts given them by the Creator, can we catch a glimpse of the wonders of what has also been given us—and which we have thrown away.

Nature has created "breeds" with which she can experiment and seek always better breeds, just as does a good farmer. The Creator, being an infinitely wiser farmer than any human, absolutely insists on the purity, the sanctity, the *biological integrity* of each group. But Nature, like a farmer breeding cows, can improve the breed only by fostering the breeding of the better type, and eliminating the poorer type. Nature accomplishes this task with the most powerful instincts we are given: *love* of our own, and *hatred* of those who intrude—the "outsiders."

These two instincts are equally important: Love is not "good" while hate is "evil"—which is the canard so dearly loved by the Jews, liberals, hippies, queers, and half-wits. Love is indeed incredibly powerful, and good, when it is natural. Love, the natural, healthy kind, is indeed what makes the world go round, and is the most beautiful, holy miracle we ever see here on this Earth. *But without a deadly hate of that which threatens what we love, love is an empty word, a catchword for hippies, queers, and cowards.*

I should like to write much more of this particular law of social living, because, as we shall see, *biological integrity* is the essence, the be-all and end-all of National Socialism when applied to Aryan society—and, indeed, of every healthy human society which has ever existed. But there simply is not space in this work for the book that could be written on this subject alone. I can only sum up by saying that the first law of all group living by social creatures is biological integrity: absolute, total, and uncompromising loyalty to one's own racial group based on a consuming love, and absolute, uncompromising hatred of any outsiders who intrude and threaten to mix their genes with those of the females of one's own group. The everyday way in which this law is manifested is love of one's own kind, and hatred of aggressive intruders (which is why most healthy Whites have such instinctive abhorrence of "niggers," Jews, and other aliens).

The second most important law is the law of *territory*. For example, ten or twenty males of the tiny tropical fish called "swordtails" will each stake out a section of a tank as soon as they are placed in it, and they will attack any intrusion by another male. If females are introduced into the tank, the males will fight over them, as expected. But the surprise to science was that sex is not the strongest motive in the life of these little fish. If you start cooling the water in their tank, you can reach a point where the water is so cold the males no longer give much of a damn when you introduce the females. When the water gets so cold as almost to kill the little fish, they pay no attention at all to the females. But even when they are on the point of almost freezing to death, they will still come out ferociously to defend their territory—their private property! National Socialism is based, among other things, on this concept of private property. The law of territory comes out as "nationalism" and private property in human society.

Throughout the animal kingdom, the leader is never chosen by vote, but always by the natural selection established by Nature as the only sure method of ensuring that the group is led by the best. This I have called the law of *leadership*. Once each member of an animal society learns his or her place in the natural biological order of toughness, wisdom, and cleverness, each member settles down into his own niche and the group is relatively peaceful and orderly. Only when young males begin to mature and have to fight their way up or down the ladder is there serious battles. And then, as soon as each male learns who he can whip, and who can whip him, he settles down and lives peacefully and contentedly in that place he has found for himself. Thus is established two more of the fundamental principles or laws of all group living: leadership by the best, and a natural hierarchy or scale of leadership of all the other members of the group—*status*.

Finally, a study of the animal world establishes that females stay out of the affairs of males, and specialize in producing and rearing the young by organizing healthy families.

To summarize: There are five basic laws of all group living, which I call "The Laws of the Tribe":

1) The law of *biological integrity* (love inside, hate outside);
2) The law of *territory* (private property and nationalism);
3) The law of *leadership* (by the best);
4) The law of *status* (or the natural place of every individual in a group); and
5) *motherhood* for females.

With these natural principles in operation, as they are throughout the whole world of social animals, there is a relative peace and order in the group. It is only when the group somehow is forced into unnatural conditions that the God-given instincts to obey these iron laws of Nature fail.

In evaluating all this in your own mind, think of the apparently "crazy" pattern of juvenile delinquency. We have the sons and daughters of some of the most advantaged and wealthy people suddenly seeming to go mad, beating up old folks, tearing things up senselessly, taking poisonous drugs, and becoming arrogant, anti-social criminals. At the same time, we find the children of some of the poorest groups in our society producing almost no delinquents at all. Until very recently, for instance, young Chinese were never delinquents (and they still have a far lower delinquency rate than other groups). The young of tightly knit, even though very poor, groups are often untouched by the modern madness of juvenile delinquency.

Why is this? Why should a wealthy young boy or girl become a thief, a vandal, and be violently anti-social in spite of all conceivable advantages, while the children of some of the poorest people in America are well-adjusted and constructive? The answer is that children who are brought up in a group which has managed to maintain some semblance of the laws of natural group living (the "Laws of the Tribe"), who feel that they are loyal members of a group, a "tribe," that they belong to something or somebody worthwhile, and who therefore have a sense of the five basic laws of all group living, are not frustrated, not lost and not empty.

The Jews, with their spreading of liberalism and communism, have consciously and scientifically gone about the process of wiping from the souls of our people all memory of the sacred "Laws of the Tribe," which, alone, can make a group of people healthy, happy, and peaceful. No human being can live in peace and productive happiness outside of some kind of "tribe" to which he is supremely loyal and which in turn supports him spiritually. The Jews have spread the unspeakably destructive idea of "universalism," "one- world-ism"—one mob of raceless, stateless, and atomized individuals—as the supreme idea of mankind. Even the conservatives have been suckered into paying lip-service to this same unnatural, fragmented, super-individualistic, *Jewish* disease of society.

We are told by the Jews that the Law of Biological Integrity (love inside, hate outside) is "racism"—the "ultimate evil" of all time! We are told that if we do not love Yellow men, Black men, and especially Jews, as much as our own people, then we are vicious, perverted, and doomed—we are "racists." Millions of pitiful White suckers believe that Jewish lie!

We are told that the Law of Territory (private property) is an unnatural greed, and that decent men must wish to share everything and have no desire for their own private property. They call this "Marxist socialism," "communism," and various other names indicating a concern for "society" and "community"—but all of them striking at the heart of the most powerful and only motivation in living creatures to build, create, and produce. More millions believe these Jew liars.

We are told by the Jews that the Law of Leadership (rule of the best) is "dictatorship" and that we must strive for "democracy" (rule by mob). Millions of White Aryans have been suckered into believing this siren song of "democracy," until mobs of human garbage are now terrorizing our whole nation.

We are told by the Jews that the Law of Status (the establishment of the natural order of ability of each person in his right place) is "class exploitation" and that the natural leaders of society—those who have been successful—must be smashed and murdered by those who have not. Whole nations full of good White Aryans have been suckered with this vile Jewish method of dividing and conquering our people through class warfare.

Finally, we are told by these ever-loving Jews that the specialization of women in child-rearing is a beastly enslavement of our females, and that women are intended to be judges, locomotive engineers, army officers, and business executives. The result, of course, is the growing destruction of that sacred and beautiful institution of all healthy civilizations, motherhood, and with it the home and family. Our entire Western world has fallen for this "democratic" Jewish swindle, which has made women the most pitiful victims of the Jewish disease. Millions of "modern" women are hopelessly lost, frustrated, and utterly miserable, even while they are squawking about more "rights" through loudspeakers and marching around in hell-raising, militant, political organizations.[1] Meanwhile, millions of families are without warm, wonderful mothers, and homes are becoming more like luxurious jails than the miracles of love and warmth that were the homes of a century ago.

Have you ever wondered why so many juvenile delinquents congregate in gangs? For years, like most people, I presumed this was an unnatural perversity in "bad" boys, because I was brought up in a sort of bourgeois "cocoon," knowing little of the brutal realities of life. But once one understands the laws of social living for all creatures—the human need to live by the Laws of the Tribe—the gang becomes more understandable. It shows our kids, at least, still have healthy instincts, even though the outward manifestation of these instincts is vicious and antisocial as a result of the unnatural conditions imposed on the kids by their utterly unhealthy urban environment.

---

[1] Extensive data shows that women and girls suffer from exceptionally high rates of depression and other psychological disorders (eating disorders, obsessive-compulsive disorder, manic depression, and so on.)

Observe that gang's very first characteristic is "exclusiveness." They fanatically "stick together." Attack one, and they all attack you. Mess with one of the gang's females, and you are dead. They are passionately loyal to each other. And they hate outsiders and attackers even more passionately. They have reasserted Nature's holy laws of biological integrity, of group loyalty, although they know not why.

Observe that the next thing a gang does is to stake out a "turf"—a territory. Woe unto him who violates that turf and infringes upon the "private property" of the gang! Could anything more obviously exemplify the law of territory? And, the gang is never led by "democratic" elections, but by the toughest, the best (by the gang's standards). Here is a classic example of the law of leadership. Just observe how each of a gang's members is acutely aware of his own exact place in the gang—who is above him, and who below. Let anybody try to move up on him, and he gets smashed. Let him try to move up a notch, and the guy above will smash him. Here is the law of status—just as in Nature.

And finally, observe the females of a gang. Do they give any orders to the leader? No! Do they race around and demand "rights"? Hell no! They act in the manner of females in all the rest of the animal world and do not try to act like males. They glory in their roles as females, as "belonging" to and proudly helping a powerful male. And this is precisely the role of females in wholesome and happy societies.

It is interesting to note that the Jewish Freudian psychiatrist fakers are being forced to return to the laws of the group, the laws of the tribe—to effect "cures" of drug addicts and alcoholics. They form a group and their powerful instincts of loyalty to that group can sometimes overcome lonely, individual weaknesses. The Blacks, too, in their blind and stupid struggling are doing the same thing, instinctively forming Black loyalties, hollering "Black Power" and calling each other "soul brothers."

In spite of the most extreme poverty on the Lower East Side of New York City in the early years of Jewish immigration, even these wretched swarms of Jewish refuse from Europe stuck together with such fanatical group loyalty, obeying all the "Laws of the Tribe," that there was almost no delinquency and no crime against each other among them. In fact, the group loyalty of these Jews is perhaps the most fantastic in the history of the world. It has propelled them into near mastery of the entire world—not because they are braver, work harder, are more intelligent, or more worthy than the rest of us—but because they observe the basic laws of Nature and maintain group loyalty. While all the rest of us have fallen for their rotten

"one world," "we-are-all-brothers" garbage, which disintegrates our society, the Jews maintain their society with a group loyalty such as history has
never before seen, and thus they go from one triumph to another.

Not until Adolf Hitler, 50 years ago, began to see all this intuitively as
a new worldview, the *Weltanschauung* of National Socialism, did non-
Jews gain their first insight into the emerging science of human group-
living. What we have done instinctively for centuries, and the Jews are still
doing instinctively, Adolf Hitler began to see and understand intuitively.

The essence of National Socialism is racism, which, in the simplest
terms, is just the belief that humans differ in excellence of breed exactly
the same as all other living things, and that the White Man is so far the
finest breed to appear, while the Blacks are the lowest. And, as the reader
will recall, this is the very first law of Group Living, "biological integrity"
as I have designated it.

Contrary to the abominable lies of the Jews (and the "conservatives"),
private property was powerfully protected by Hitler; Krupp and the other
large or small property owners and businessmen never lost a cent under
Hitler, nor did the German princes. At one time, rabid "leftists" in his party
wanted to dispossess the German princes, and Hitler had to put down a
mutiny in his own ranks to protect their property rights, which he did. Hitler was a nationalist, a believer in territory and private property.

Needless to point out, Hitler gave his people *leadership*—not sweet-
talk or demagoguery, and they loved him for it. They followed him lovingly and willingly as do the members of all happy, successful, wholesome
social groups. There was peace and order among Hitler's people, because
he taught that a man deserved, and must get, as much respect for being a
good ditch-digger (if that was the limit of his capacity to serve his people)
as the man who was able to invent a new and wonderful machine, or be a
political leader. Each person in Hitler's Germany was honored for his own
place in society, provided he filled it to the best of his ability. They were
not goaded eternally (as our people are by the Jews) to demand jobs only
as presidents, chairmen of the board, and executives, when some people
are not born with those particular talents. To fail at what one could do,
while raising hell and aiming for what one can't do, is to disrupt orderly
and happy society, not to mention hopelessly frustrating the individual who
refuses to recognize his natural place in the world. Thus Hitler's state recognized the law of *status*. Each man was honored for what he did loyally
and with his best effort, regardless of whether he was a farmer, a warrior, a
laborer, a factory worker, or whatever.

Finally, Hitler saw to it that women were restored to their ancient birthright and honored as wives, mothers, and producers of happy, wholesome homes—as the authors of good people.

The lies about the Hitler-times are now so enormous and powerful that it is almost impossible to doubt them. But if you meet an honest and courageous German who lived through these great times (and he is willing to talk in spite of the terror which is abroad today for those who dare tell the truth), you will learn that the German people found out what good leadership and a natural healthy state is like, under Hitler. To prevent that knowledge and that natural state of society from spreading (and thereby destroying the parasitic existence of Jewry), those Jewish devils provoked the rest of us to go and slaughter and smash this miracle of White Aryan renaissance. But natural law cannot be smashed, any more than you can "smash" the fact that two plus two equals four. You may terrorize people out of saying it and get them all parroting "two plus two is seventeen"— but two and two is still four, and there will always be someone with the guts and wisdom, sooner or later, to strike down the terrorists and liars to reassert the truth. Already, this is happening all over the world. The young gangs I have mentioned are only one sign of what is really going on. People will find their way back to the natural "Laws of the Tribe."

What Hitler gave the world, as National Socialism is, in a sense, only a modern form of the ancient, natural "tribal law," the prescription for happy and healthy group living given by the Great Spirit to all living creatures, including man. National Socialism is nothing more or less than *natural order* (a name which would, in some ways, be more descriptive of the reality than "National Socialism"). Hitler had to design the name of his movement to succeed in a specific political situation, and was therefore forced to use names and terms which would accomplish his purposes. In Germany, there were millions and millions of Germans who thought of themselves as "socialists," but were in the manipulating clutches of the Jews. Rather than fight any more battles than he had to, Hitler said, in effect, to these millions, "If you must be 'socialists', let us not be Jewish 'socialists'— Marxists; let us be 'National Socialists', meaning a national society. Let us be 'socialists' for Germany, not the Jews."

And it worked! Millions and millions of good men and women who had been seduced into communism by the Jews were won back to their own people and the Natural Order of healthy group living by Hitler's methods.

卐 卐 卐

Beyond the fundamental elements of natural order, which I have set forth above, National Socialism embodies something far higher and nobler than any mere set of rules or principles. National Socialism, as a *philosophy*, embodies the eternal urge found in all living things—indeed in all creation—toward a higher level of existence: toward perfection, toward God. This "aristocratic" idea of National Socialism—the idea of a constant striving in all Nature toward higher and higher, more and more complex, and more and more perfect existence—is the metaphysical, supernatural aspect of our ideal.

In other words, concepts of social justice and natural order are the organs and nerves of National Socialism, but its *personality*, its "religious" aspect—the thing that lifts it above any strictly political philosophy—is its worshipful attitude toward Nature and a religious love of the great gifts of an Unknown Creator.

Christianity, for instance, is a far higher thing than its rituals, the words of its prayers, or any of its creeds. It is a spiritual striving toward the believer's ideals of spiritual perfection. National Socialism is the same sort of striving toward ever higher and higher levels here on this Earth, while Christianity is striving toward a future and later life not of this Earth.

For the ordinary "soldier" in our "army," building and fighting for Natural Order—National Socialism—it is sufficient that they respect and obey the laws and doctrines established by the lofty ideals of our philosophy with merely an instinctive love of those ideals, perhaps not with complete understanding of the highest forms of our philosophy. But just as the greatest Christian leaders have been those not preoccupied with details and rules but rather those who were "God intoxicated" with the highest ideals of the religion, the leaders among our National Socialist elite must share this fundamentally religious approach. For them, the true meaning of our racial doctrine must be part of their idealistic "striving toward God." Through total identification of ourselves with our great race, we partake of its past and future glories. When we contribute in any way, especially by self-sacrifice toward helping our race along the path toward a higher existence, we reach toward God—the Creator of the Master Race,

In short, while the mechanics and rules of National Socialism, as codified and set forth here, are sufficient for most of us, for the few idealists ready and willing to sacrifice their very lives in the cause of their people, National Socialism must be a very real religious ideal—a striving toward

God. National Socialism is the only movement that has gained sufficient self-knowledge and insight to be able to understand this movement away from liberal artificiality and shortsightedness and toward the eternal wisdom of Nature. Our all-out belief in race, our insistence on the natural laws in society, economics, and every other field of human activity are, in every case, the conscious, scientific application of Nature's iron laws, instead of conceited and short-sighted perversions of these laws, as pushed by the arrogant, peanut-brained liberals and Marxists.

Our liberal and Marxist opponents are just as blind to what they are doing. But in every case, it will be found that they are basically haters of the laws of Nature: conceited, hall-educated "intellectuals" who are victims of the truisms about "a little knowledge being a dangerous thing." Because they have found they can teach a Congo Negro to recite poetry or even act like a lawyer or a doctor, they get all puffed up with their ability to wrench Nature around to suit themselves, and imagine they can make self-starting, Western White men out of any Hottentot. The fact that Nature has already made of the Negro what he is, and no human agency can make a "silk purse out of a sow's ear," they simply refuse to acknowledge.

National Socialism is the distilled essence of the love of and respect for Nature, and the loving, conscious, and scientific application of the eternal, just, and beautiful laws of Nature to every moment of Man's existence. At the same time, National Socialism recognizes Man's need for a higher culture than that of the unthinking animals of the jungle and there raises the application of natural law from the naked, tooth-and-fang competition of the animal world, for instance, to regulated and orderly competition, under fair rules. Our opponents want to eliminate competition altogether—an utterly unnatural idea.

National Socialism insists that man can refine and enrich the application of the Natural Laws of life for the benefit of man, but insists also that Man cannot escape or defy Natural Law. Between the states of social health ("National Socialism" or Natural Order) and social disease (Jewish Marxism) lay the "no-man's-lands" of nothingness—the place where humans are neither dead, nor really alive. Democracy, "liberalism," and "conservatism" are pure, unadulterated states of nothingness. They have no basic, fundamental outlook on life, no understanding, no vital force deep down inside them. They are fancy tricks with pretty words and phrases, meaning nothing at all. They lead only to chaos and prepare the way for the Jews and their damnable, unnatural communism.

The only way we can ever put a stop to this Jewish con game and capture the minds and hearts of our people is to restore to our people Natural Order—the Laws of the Tribe—which, alone, will give us the strength and the will to reassert the natural, biological superiority of our White Race, and thus save Western Civilization.

Destroy the cohesive forces of Natural Order in any group, and that group will become chaotic, hopeless, frustrated, lost, empty, vicious, and finally helpless before any other group that is united and obeys the Laws of the Tribe. That's why the Blacks, in so many cases, terrify whole cities. They stick together. Hit one, and a million Blacks roar out at you. That's why police often no longer dare arrest them, even for the most outrageous offenses. And the Jews are even more powerful among us, for the same reason. They stick together.

卐 卐 卐

Adding the Laws of the Tribe to the Laws of Race that we examined earlier, we can now synthesize a new law of modern society: the *Law of Group Dominance*.

In a state of Nature, that animal or primitive human group that is biologically superior, the group composed of the best individuals, carrying the best genes and chromosomes, will dominate all inferior groups, because all groups in Nature (superior or inferior) obey the Laws of the Tribe equally. Thus, the only factor operating competitively in the animal world is biological excellence of breeding. But scientific gadgetry, luxury, and Jewish "liberalism" have so greatly destroyed the modern, civilized White Man's ability to feel and obey Nature's "Laws of the Tribe" that he has lost his group cohesiveness; he has come "unglued" as a social animal; he is fragmented and atomized into millions of isolated individuals and hundreds of thousands of selfish "pressure groups," classes, etc. This almost complete fragmentation of the great "tribe" of White men has reduced us to impotence, as a group.

The law of *group dominance* among men is the rule that any group which fanatically adheres to the Natural Laws of the Tribe will be able to dominate any group which disobeys those laws, no matter how inferior may be the "tribe" which does obey the laws. This is why Negroes and Jews lord it all over the White Man in the America built and owned by White men. This is why we suffer "minority" tyranny. Any organized minority of scum and human trash have power—while the great White, non-

Jewish majority is a sprawling, helpless, paralyzed giant. The goal, then, of our National Socialist revolution is the restoration of the Laws of the Tribe to our people, to enable their natural biological superiority of breeding once again to give the White Man dominion of what he built and should dominate.

This is exactly what Hitler and National Socialism did in Germany for millions and millions of fragmented, atomized people who were sunk in the depths of hopelessness and chaos. Hitler did not win such astounding success with his people because he was a "tough guy," because he put on big, exciting rallies, because the Germans are natural "beasts," nor any of the other reasons put forth by the lying Jews and their toady liberal and conservative allies. The reason Hitler was able to accomplish a social miracle in Germany was because he intuitively understood all that I have written, and he restored his people to *natural social order*.

Hitler taught his people to quit hating each other as isolated, lonely, and frightened individuals, and gave them back that holy sense of nationhood, of "tribe"; yes, of real brotherhood (not the artificial kind peddled by the Jews). There is nothing wrong and everything right about "brotherhood" with your own people. It is when the Jews slyly and falsely try to extend "brotherhood" to pull the hood over the "brother" and try to make us "brothers" with Zulus, pygmies, Chinese, Bushmen, and Jews, that "brotherhood" becomes a byword for racial catastrophe, as it has. Hitler gave his people the same sacrificial spirit of warm love for one's family and one's people (which is a big "family"), which unites and blesses every natural social group of creatures in creation.

As I have pointed out many times, no man can live happily, successfully, and productively as a lonely, bitter individual at war with all his fellows. Every one of us has a deep need for the warmth and love of his group, of those in his biological family of people. Modern man has lost that feeling of group warmth, loyalty, and love, and the result is the chaos and spiritual emptiness we see all around us in this disintegrating Western society. The horrors depicted in the second chapter of this book are the direct result of America's almost total disobedience of the laws of the tribe. These horrors would continue, even if all the Jews and Negroes were to disappear overnight, unless we restore to our people, as Hitler did, the natural order, "Laws of the Tribe."

Our revolution, therefore, is not material and physical, but a radical spiritual change in the feeling of our people: The elimination of selfish atomism and greedy, narrow "individualism"; whether it be called "liberalism," "conservatism," or "democracy," and the restoration in the hearts of Western White men of the deeply satisfying feelings of love of our own kind. This love of one's group manifests itself in the willingness to sacrifice and give for one's family—and the larger family of one's race.

CHAPTER 16
WHITE POWER

Make no mistake about it, I am advocating total and complete *White power* in this world! White men can no longer shilly-shally around with compromises and half-hearted measures to protect their own lives and interests. What we face is not a social, philosophical, economic, religious, or territorial battle, but a struggle between *quality*—the elite, but minority, White Race—against *quantity*: the vast swarms of sub-human scum who have been gathered up under the banners of Jewish Marxism to be used as a giant battering ram against the White Race.

Our beleaguered Race will organize itself and fight for its own survival, or the scum of the Earth will inundate it. If we continue to hesitate, to rationalize, and to temporize with half-hearted measures, we will be obliterated from the face of this planet. This is truly *"scum power"* with a vengeance—like some horrible multiplication of roaches who, if there be only enough of them, can literally smother the greatest thinker or fighter in history; the scum of the world are gathering for the attack. There are seven of them for every one of us!

The only answer to scum power must be, and is, White power. The power of the elite of the world, the White human beings who have already proved their natural, God-given superiority over this gathering swarm of scum, must drive it back, re-establish order and culture in the world, and maintain that order the only way order has ever been maintained—*by force!*

Today, there is no segment of the White Race left on Earth with the possibility of turning back the scum except the White Men of the United States of America. America is the only nation, as a matter of cold fact with the *physical* power to master the scum.

The center of Jewish power and money is here in New York City, USA—not Moscow, and not even Jerusalem. And the American working man and farmer still has in him the good and wholesome racial instincts of our ancestors who, time after time, drove back the mongrel hordes by sheer force of guts and will.

I am well aware of the upwelling of revulsion which comes over many Europeans at the thought of the sort of "Americans" they have seen and experienced ever being able to re-establish Western Culture. And they can hardly be blamed. "American" representatives in Europe today are, for the most part, *Jews*. The "American" foreign policy they have seen, which destroyed their countries, slaughtered their people, and turned half of Europe over to communism, and which today continues to give aid and comfort to White Men's enemies while destroying their friends, was and is directed, inspired, and instigated by Jews. In short, Europeans have seen America only through Jewish eyes—they have seen "Americans" who are not Americans at all, but Jews.

But my fellow White Men of Europe, believe me when I tell you that America is brimming over with good and brave men—men who share your blood, and who will bring honor to our race when finally they see the urgent necessity of rolling up their sleeves for an all-out fight.

But aside from that point, the eternal jealousies, rivalries, and blood feuds between segments of the White Race must be stopped as a matter of strategic necessity—not to be continued for the benefit of united world Jewry. White Men of Europe: Put aside, if you can, the memory of two world wars in which we joined hands with our mortal enemies to slaughter your finest young men—we too shed our blood in those unholy wars. Forgive us for being so blind, for turning the deadly power of our might against you, instead of the Jewish communism that is now devouring us all. Forgive us for the misery and degradation we forced upon you, and join us in a last-ditch fight for our race and respective nations.

This time it will be different!

This time we shall stand together as brothers against a common foe.

This time the traitors will find no White Man anywhere who will listen to their lies and fight their battles for them.

This time we shall have no mercy for those who have caused untold suffering among our people; we shall give no quarter to those who have lived among us for no purpose other than to destroy us.

This time—together—we shall drive the bastards to the wall!

How is this to be done? Believe it or not, it is not terribly difficult. The only obstacle in our path at the moment is the unbelievable ability of our people to *rationalize* and *temporize* in the face of deadly danger. The horse is infinitely more powerful than a man, and could stomp him to death if he ever realized it. But he doesn't realize it, and so he goes on in harness, pulling and hauling and tied up. The vast majority of Americans are fed up to the teeth with arrogant Jews stealing their wealth and rioting Blacks tearing up their streets, but—like the horse, they know not their strength.

Here in America, White Men outnumber alien scum by enormous margins. If ever they realize the strength their numbers represent, nothing on Earth can stop them from stomping to death the filthy subversives and traitors who have been beating them, lying to them, stealing from them, and finally turning a mob of black African savages loose on them. Once a horse finds he *can* stomp a man and get away with it, he is an "outlaw" and nothing more can be done to make a drudge of him.

The only reason the White Men of America cannot now feel their strength, even though they are the overwhelming majority with unheard of strength, is that the Jews, through their control of our entire system of communications, have been able to keep them apart. Most White Men *in their hearts* agree with the things I've said in this book. But they think they are alone!

The Jews have recognized the inborn sense of fair play in the White Man. They have recognized the White Man's deep-rooted desire for order, and his innate repugnance for that which upsets his order. *And they have taken advantage of those good and wholesome qualities—they have used the best in us to destroy us!*

TV, radio, movies, books, magazines, newspapers, schools, and even our own government officials, tell us constantly and repeatedly that:

- It isn't "nice" to believe an African ape is not our equal—albeit the facts conclusively prove our superiority in all matters pertaining to a civilized society.
- It isn't "nice," we're taught to believe, to want our bloodline kept pure—to want our grandchildren to be White.
- It isn't "nice" to point to the filth, immorality, crime, and disease that move into a neighborhood on the heels of Black "neighbors."
- It isn't "nice" to want our children educated on their own level, instead of being held down to that of the stupid Black.
- It isn't "nice," we are told, because it isn't "fair."

But let's turn it around. Is it "nice" to have our women live in constant fear of being raped or murdered by a Black ape on the rampage? Is it "nice" to have our children adopting the language, attitudes, and morals of sub-human scum? Is it "nice" to have our men competing with illiterates for their livelihood—and having the illiterates come out on top? Is it "nice" to tolerate taxes and inflationary prices to support the multiplication of Black scum, when it drives our mothers from the home and family into the factories? Is it "nice" to leave our children the inheritance of a world governed by alien scum? *Hell no; it isn't nice—and it isn't fair.*

You're a slave in your own country, White Man. Each year you get to keep less of the fruits of your labor; each year it gets more difficult to carry the burden the aliens have placed upon you; each year the cheap labor of aliens makes your future less secure; each year you retreat a few steps more into the world of slavery. Where will it all end? *I'll tell you*—it will end with the complete and total annihilation of "Whitey."

Stop rationalizing a situation you know to be deadly serious. *Stop* temporizing with halfway measures in a situation that screams for decisive action. *Stop* using business, social etiquette, family, and security as an excuse for downright cowardly behavior. If you hesitate very much longer, the fight will be over—and the White Man will have lost.

STAND UP AND FIGHT!

APPENDICES

APPENDIX A

"Lincoln Rockwell: A National Socialist Life"
By William Luther Pierce

On the eighteenth of June, 1945, a little over six weeks after the death of Adolf Hitler, Rudolf Hess wrote the following words in a letter to his wife, from his prison cell:

> You will readily imagine how often during the last few weeks my thoughts have turned to the years gone by: to this quarter of a century of history, concentrated for us in one name and full of the most wonderful human experiences. History is not ended. It will sooner or later take up the threads apparently broken off forever and knit them together in a new pattern. The human element is no more and lives only in memory. Very few people have been privileged, as we were, to participate from the very beginning in the growth of a unique personality, through joy and sorrow, hope and trouble, love and hate, and all the manifestations of greatness, and further, in all the little indications of human weakness, without which a man is not truly worthy of love…

Even when one has been privileged to witness the manifestations of greatness, it may be exceedingly difficult to describe adequately in words those manifestations and thereby to paint a true picture of a unique and great personality. When one has not the basis of a quarter-century of participation in the growth of such a personality, but less than two years, the task is especially difficult. It would be a vain hope, then, to expect the pages which follow to reflect the true greatness of the man. That greatness will be best reflected in the fruition of his life's work in years to come.

Here, however, we can at least hope to evoke an image of the man, imperfect and incomplete though it may be, which will serve to inspire those National Socialists who did not have the privilege of knowing him personally.

George Lincoln Rockwell was born on March 9, 1918, in Blooming-ton, a small coal-mining and farming town in central Illinois. Both his par-ents were theatrical performers. His father, George Lovejoy Rockwell, was a twenty-eight-year-old vaudeville comedian of English and Scotch ances-try. His mother, born Claire Schade, was a young German-French toe-dancer, part of a family dance team. His parents were divorced when he was six years old, and he and a younger brother and sister lived alternately with their mother and their father during the next few years.

The young Rockwell passed the greater part of his boyhood days in Maine, Rhode Island, and New Jersey. His father settled in a small coastal town in Maine, and Rockwell spent his summers there; attending school in Atlantic City and, later, in Providence during the winters. Some of his fondest memories in later years were of summer days spent on the Maine beaches, or hiking in the Maine woods, or exploring the coves and inlets of the Maine coast in his sailboat, which he built himself, starting from an old skiff. Rockwell acquired what was to be a lifelong love of sailing and the sea during those early years spent with his father in Maine.

Aside from a bit more traveling about than the average child, it is dif-ficult to find anything extraordinary in his childhood environment. He lived in the midst neither great poverty nor great wealth; he had an affec-tionate relationship with both his parents, despite their divorce; he was a sound and healthy child, and there seems to be no evidence of prolonged unhappiness or turmoil in his childhood. If he later recalled with greater pleasure the times spent with his father than those spent with his mother, this can be attributed either to the greater opportunities to satisfy his youth-ful longing for adventure that life on the Maine coast offered relative to that in the city, or to the fact that his mother lived with a domineering sister of whom young Rockwell was not fond.

And yet, even as a boy he displayed those qualities of character which were later to set him off from the common run of men. His most remarka-ble quality was his responsiveness to challenge. To tell the boy Rockwell that a thing was impossible, that it simply could not be done, was to awak-en in him the irresistible determination to do it. He has described an expe-rience he had at the age of ten which illustrates this aspect of his character.

A juvenile gang of some of the tougher elements at the grammar school he was attending in an Atlantic City coastal suburb had singled him out for hazing. He was informed that he was to be given a cold dunking in the ocean, and that he should relax and submit gracefully, as resistance would be futile. Instead of submitting, he ferociously fought off the entire gang of his attackers on the beach, wildly striking out with his fists and feet, clawing, biting, and gouging until the other boys finally abandoned their aim of throwing him in the water and retired to nurse their wounds.

Later, as a teenager, he found that the challenge of a stormy sea affected him in much the same way as had the challenge of the juvenile gang. When other boys brought their boats into dock because the water was too rough, young Rockwell found his greatest pleasure in sailing. He loved nothing better than to pit his strength and his skill against the wild elements. As the wind and the waves rose so did his spirits. Wrestling with tiller and rigging in a tossing boat, drenched with spray and blasted by fierce gusts, he would howl back at the wind in sheer animal joy.

This peculiar stubbornness of his nature—call it a combative spirit, if you will—coupled with an absolute physical fearlessness, which led him into many a dangerous and harebrained escapade as a boy, gave him the willpower as a man to undertake without hesitation ventures at which ordinary men quailed; throughout his life it led him to choose the course of action which his reason and his sensibility told him to be the right course regardless of the course those about him were taking; ultimately it provided the driving force which led him to issue a challenge and stand alone against a whole world, when it became apparent to him that that world was on the wrong course. This trait provides the key to the man.

Two other characteristics he displayed as a boy were an omnivorous curiosity and a stark objectivity. He attributed his curiosity, as well as the artistic talents which he early displayed, to his father, who also exhibited these traits, but the source of his rebellious spirit and his indomitable will is harder to assign. They seem to have been the product of a rare and fortuitous combination of genes, giving rise to a nature markedly different from that of his immediate forebears.

He entered Brown University in the fall of 1938, as a freshman. His major course of study was philosophy, but he was also very interested in the sciences. He used the opportunity of staff work on student periodicals to exercise his talents in drawing and creative writing. In addition to his curricular, journalistic, and artistic activities, he also found time for a substantial amount of skirt chasing and other collegiate sports, including skiing and fencing; he became a member of the Brown University fencing team.

While at Brown he had his first head-on encounter with modern liberalism. He enrolled in a sociology course with the naive expectation that, just as in his geology and psychology courses he would learn the scientific principles underlying those two areas of human knowledge, so in sociology would he learn some of the basic principles underlying human social behavior.

He was disappointed and confused, however, when it gradually became apparent to him that there was a profound difference in the attitudes
of sociologists and, say, geologists toward their subjects. Whereas the authors of his geology textbooks were careful to point out there were many
things about the history and the structure of the earth which were as yet
unknown, or only imperfectly known, it was clear that there were indeed
fundamental ideas and well-established facts upon which the science was
based and that both his geology professor and the authors of geology textbooks were sincerely interested in presenting these ideas and facts to the
student in an orderly manner, with the hope that he would thereby gain a
better understanding of the nature of the planet on which he lived.

In sociology, he found the basic principles far more elusive. What
was particularly disturbing to him, though, was not so much the complexity of the concepts as the gnawing suspicion the waters had been deliberately muddied. He redoubled his efforts to get to the roots of the subject or, at
least, to understand where the hints, innuendoes, and roundabout prompt-
ings led: "I buried myself in my sociology books, absolutely determined to
find why I was missing the kernel of the thing."

The equalitarian idea that the manifest differences between the capabilities of individuals and between the evolutionary development of various races can be accounted for almost wholly by contemporary environmental effects—that there really are no inborn differences in quality worth
mentioning among human beings—was certainly one of the places his sociology textbooks were leading:

> I was bold enough to ask Professor Bucklin if this were the
> idea, and he turned red in anger. I was told it was impossible
> to make any generalizations, although all I was asking for
> was the fundamental idea, if any, of sociology. I began to see
> that sociology was different from any other course I had ever
> taken. Certain ideas produced apoplexy in the teacher, par-
> ticularly the suggestion that perhaps some people were no-
> good biological slobs from the day they were born. Certain
> other ideas, although they were never formulated and stated
> frankly, were fostered and encouraged—and these were al-
> ways ideas revolving around the total power of environment.

Although he did not clearly recognize it for what it was at that time, young
Rockwell had partially uncovered one of the most widely used tactics of
the modern liberals. When the clever liberal has as his goal miscegenation,

say, he certainly does not just blurt this right out. Instead he will write novels, produce television shows, and film motion pictures which, subtly at first and then more and more boldly, suggest that those who engage in sexual affairs with Negroes are braver, better, more attractive people than those who don't; and that opposition to miscegenation is a vulgar and loutish perversion, certain evidence of being a ridiculous square at best and a drooling, violent redneck at worst. But if one tries to pin him down and asks him why he is in favor of miscegenation, he will reply in a huff that that is not at all what he is aiming at, but only "justice, or fairness," or "better understanding between the races."

And so when Rockwell naively went right to the heart of the matter in Professor Bucklin's sociology class, he got an angry reprimand. The racial equalitarians have gotten much bolder in the last thirty years, but at that time Rockwell was merely aware that they wanted him to accept certain ideas without actually those ideas out into the open arena of free discussion where they would be subject to attack:

> I still knew little or nothing about communism or its pimping little sister, liberalism, but I could not avoid the steady pressure, everywhere in the University, to accept the ideas of massive human equality and the supremacy of environment.

Typically, this pressure resulted not in acquiescence but in his determination to stand up for what seemed to him to be reasonable and natural. He satirized the equalitarian point of view, not only in his column in the student newspaper, but also in one of his sociology examination papers! The nearly catastrophic consequences of this bit of insolence taught him the prudence of holding his tongue under certain circumstances.

As he began his junior year at Brown, the alien conspiracy to use America as a tool to make the world safe for Jewry was shifting its propaganda machine into high gear. National Socialist Germany was portrayed as a nation of depraved criminals whose goal was the enslavement of the world—including America. Hollywood, the big newspapers, and his liberal professors—always the most noisily vocal faction at any university—all pushed the same line, unabashedly appealing to the naive idealism of their audience: "Hitler must be stopped!"

And, like millions of other American patriots, Lincoln Rockwell fell for the smooth lies and the clever swindle, backed as they were by the authority of the head of the American government. Neither he nor his millions of compatriots realized that the conspiracy had reached into the White House, and that its occupant had sold his services to the conspirators:

> It is typical of my political naivete of that time that when the propaganda about Hitler began to be pushed upon us in large doses, I swallowed it all, unable even to suspect that somebody might have an interest in all this, and that it might not be the interest of the United States or our people. ... It became obvious that we would have to get into the war to stop this 'horrible ogre' who planned to conquer America so we were told, and so I believed.

Thus, in March, 1941, convinced that America was in mortal danger from "the Nazi aggressors," Rockwell left his comfortable life at the university and offered his services to his country's armed forces. Shortly after enlisting in the United States Navy, he received an appointment as an Aviation Cadet and began flight training at Squantum, Massachusetts. He received his first naval commission, as an ensign, on December 9, 1941—two days after the Pearl Harbor attack. He served as a naval aviator throughout World War II, advancing from the rank of ensign to lieutenant and winning several decorations. He commanded the naval air support during the American invasion of Guam, in July and August, 1944. He was promoted to lieutenant commander in October, 1945, and shortly thereafter returned to civilian life, where he hoped to make a career for himself as an artist.

While still in the navy, he had married a girl he had known as a student at Brown University. The marriage was not a particularly happy one, although it was destined to last more than ten years.

The first five years after leaving the navy were spent as an art student, a commercial photographer, a painter, an advertising executive, and a publisher, in Maine and in New York. Then in 1950, with the outbreak of war in Korea, Lieutenant Commander Rockwell returned to active duty with the United States Navy and was assigned to train fighter pilots in southern California. There almost by chance, the political education of thirty-two-year-old Lincoln Rockwell began.

It was in 1950 that Senator Joseph McCarthy's investigations into subversive activities and treasonous behavior on the part of a number of United States government employees and officials began to receive wide public notice. Rockwell, like every honest citizen, was horrified and angered by these disclosures of treachery. But he was puzzled as much as he was shocked by the violent, hysterical, and vicious reaction to these disclosures which came from a certain segment of the population. Why were so many persons—and, especially, so many in the public-opinion-forming media—frantically determined to silence McCarthy and, failing that, to smear and discredit him?

McCarthy was an American with a distinguished record. A war hero, like Rockwell he had entered his country's armed forces as an enlisted man and emerged as a much-decorated officer. He had won the Distinguished Flying Cross for his combat performance in World War II. Now that he was flushing from cover the rats who had sold out the vital interests of the country for which he had fought, Rockwell could not understand why any responsible and loyal citizen should seek to defame the man or block his courageous efforts:

> I began to pay attention, in my spare time, to what it was all about. I read McCarthy speeches and pamphlets and found them factual, instead of the wild nonsense which the papers charged was his stock-in-trade. I became aware of a terrific slant in all the papers against Joe McCarthy, although I still couldn't imagine why.

At this time an acquaintance gave Rockwell some anti-Communist tracts to read. One of the things he immediately noticed about them was their strongly anti-Semitic tone. Although manifest public evidence obliged him to agree with some of the charges made by the authors of these tracts—for example, that there were extraordinarily disproportionate numbers of Jews both among McCarthy's attackers and among the subversives his investigations were unearthing—he found many of their claims too far-fetched to be credible. In particular, the charge that communism was a Jewish, not a Russian, movement seemed ridiculous when Rockwell considered the fact that Jews were so firmly entrenched in capitalistic enterprises and always had been; capitalism, supposedly the deadly enemy of communism, was the traditional Jewish sphere of influence.

One anti-Communist tabloid went so far as to cite various items of documentary evidence in support of its seemingly wild claims, and Rockwell decided to call its bluff by looking into this "evidence" for himself. On his next off-duty day he went to the public library in San Diego, and what he found there changed the course of his life—and will yet change the course of world history. In his own words: "Down there in the dark stacks of the San Diego Public Library, I got my awakening from thirty years of stupid political sleep...."

Rockwell was staggered by the evidence he uncovered in the library; it left no doubt, for instance, that what had been described in his school textbooks as the "Russian" Revolution was instead a Jewish orgy of genocide against the Russian people. He even found that in their own books and periodicals the Jews boasted more-or-less openly of the fact! In a Jewish biographical reference work entitled Who's Who in American Jewry he found a number of prominent Bolsheviks proudly listed, although by no stretch of the imagination could they be considered Americans. Among them were Lazar Kaganovitch, the Butcher of the Ukraine, and Leon Trotsky (Lev Bronstein), the bloodthirsty Commissar of the Red Army, who was given credit in the book for liquidating "counter-revolutionary forces" in Russia.

Another book, written by a prominent "English" Jew, boasted that "the Jews to a greater degree than . . . any other ethnic group . . . have been the artisans of the Revolution of 1917." An estimate was given in the book that "80% of the revolutionaries in Russia were Jews."

Musty back issues of Jewish newspapers told the same story, and they were backed up by official US government records. One volume of such records, which had been published twenty years previously, contained ministerial reports from Russia of brutal frankness. Typical of the material in these records was the following sentence written by the Dutch diplomatic official, Oudendyk, in a 1918 report to his government from Russia:

> I consider that the immediate suppression of Bolshevism is the greatest issue now before the World, not even excluding the war which is still raging, and unless as above stated Bolshevism is nipped in the bud immediately it is bound to spread in one form or another over Europe and the whole world as it is organized and worked by Jews who have no nationality; and whose one object is to destroy for their own ends the existing order of things.

Shocking as were these revelations, Rockwell was even more disturbed by the fact that the general public was oblivious to them. Why were these things not in school history text? Why was he told over and over again by the radio and newspapers and magazines of Adolf Hitler's "awful crime" in killing so many Jews, but never told that the Jews in Russia were responsible for the murder of a vastly larger number of Gentiles?

Other questions presented themselves. He had been told that England's attack on Germany was justified by Hitler's attack on Poland. But what of the Soviet Union, which had invaded Poland at the same time? Why no English declaration of war against the Soviet Union? Could it be because the government there was in Jewish hands? Who was responsible for the conspiracy of silence on these and other questions? He grimly resolved to find out. And, later, as the facts gradually fitted into place and the whole, sordid picture began to emerge, he saw before him an inescapable obligation.

An honest man, when he becomes aware that some dirty work is afoot in his community, will speak out against it and attempt to rouse his neighbors into doing the same. What if he finds, though, that most of his neighbors do not want to be bothered; that many of his neighbors are already aware of what is afoot but prefer to ignore it because to oppose it might jeopardize their private affairs; that some of his neighbors—some of his wealthiest and most influential neighbors, the leaders of the community —are themselves engaged in the dirty work? If he is an ordinary man, he may grumble for a while about such a sorry state of affairs, but he will adapt himself as best he can to it. He will soon see there is nothing to be gained by sticking his neck out, and he will go on about his business.

Human nature being what it is, he will very likely ease his conscience by trying to forget as rapidly as possible what he has learned; perhaps he will even convince himself eventually that there is really nothing wrong after all, that his initial judgement was in error, and that the dirty work was really not dirty work but merely "progress." If, on the other hand, he is an extraordinary man with a particularly strong sense of duty, he will continue to oppose what he knows to be wrong and bound to work evil for the community in the long run. He may continue to point out to his neighbors, even after they have made it clear that they are not interested, that the dirty work should be stopped; he may write pamphlets and deliver speeches; he may even run for public office on a "reform" ticket.

But even so, being a reasonable man and no "extremist," he will feel himself obliged to give the malefactors the benefit of the doubt which must surely exist as to their motives. And perhaps their position is, indeed, not wholly wrong? Surely, some sort of reasonable compromise which will be fair to all concerned is the best solution. If the evildoer had been working alone when discovered, hanging would, of course, be the only admissible solution to the problem: a fitting and total repudiation by the community of his evil deeds. But when so many criminals, with so many accomplices, have been engaged for so long in such an extensive undertaking and have already done such profound damage, surely the most reasonable solution must be just to admonish the criminals—if, indeed, it is fair to call them criminals—try to install a few safeguards against their renewed activity—safeguards which, to be sure, would not be too grossly inconsistent with the "progress" (or was it damage?) already wrought—and then, letting by-gones be bygones, try to live with things as they are.

But, it is only one man out of tens of millions—the rare and lonely world-historical figure—who has, first, the objectivity to evaluate such a situation in terms of absolute and timeless standards and, unswayed by popular and contemporary considerations of "reasonableness," to draw the ultimate conclusions which those standards dictate; and who then has the strength of will and character to insist that there must be no compromise with evil, that it must be rooted out and utterly destroyed, that right and health and sanity must again prevail, regardless of the commotion and temporary unpleasantness involved in restoring them.

Rockwell had seen the facts. To him, it was unthinkable to attempt to wriggle away from the conclusion they implied. And, as he realized the frightening magnitude of the task before him, instead of attempting to excuse himself from the responsibility which his new knowledge carried with it, he felt rising within him his characteristic response to a seemingly impossible challenge.

It was a straightforward sense of commitment which had led him to volunteer for military service in March, 1941, as soon as he had been tricked into believing that Adolf Hitler was a threat to his country, instead of waiting for Pearl Harbor. And in early 1951, when he began to understand that he had been tricked in 1941 and when he began to see who had tricked him and what they were up to and the terrible damage they had done to his people and were yet planning to do, that same sense of commitment left only one course open to him, namely, to fight! He did not stop to ask whether others were also willing to shoulder their responsibility; his own was perfectly clear to him.

But how to fight? Where to begin? What to do? The name of one man who had done something naturally came to his mind: Adolf Hitler. Rockwell has described what happened next:

> I hunted around the San Diego bookshops and finally found a copy of *Mein Kampf* hidden away in the rear. I bought it, took it home, and sat down to read. And that was the end of one Lincoln Rockwell...and the beginning of an entirely different person.

He had not, of course, spent nearly thirty-three years completely oblivious to world events. Many things had bothered him deeply, and he had spent years of frustrating effort trying to fathom the apparently meaningless chaos into which the world seemed to be descending. It seemed to him that there must be some logical relationship between the events of the preceding few decades, but he could not find the key to the puzzle:

> I simply suffered from the vague, unhappy feeling that things were wrong—I didn't know exactly how—and that there must be a way of diagnosing the disease and its causes and making intelligent, organized efforts to correct that something wrong.

Adolf Hitler's message in *Mein Kampf* gave him the key he had been seeking, and more:

> In *Mein Kampf* I found abundant mental sunshine, which bathed all the gray world suddenly in the clear light of reason and understanding. Word after word, sentence after sentence stabbed into the darkness like thunderclaps and lightning bolts of revelation, tearing and ripping away the cobwebs of more than thirty years of darkness, brilliantly illuminating the mysteries of the heretofore impenetrable murk in a world gone mad.
>
> I was transfixed, hypnotized. I could not lay the book down without agonies of impatience to get back to it. I read it walking to the squadron; I took it into the air and read it lying on the chart board while I automatically gave the instructions to the other planes circling over the desert. I read it crossing the Coronado ferry. I read it into the night and the next morning. When I had finished I started again and reread every word, underlining and marking especially magnificent passages. I studied it; I thought about it; I wondered at the utter, indescribable genius of it...
>
> I reread and studied it some more. Slowly, bit by bit, I began to understand. I realized that National Socialism, the iconoclastic world view of Adolf Hitler; was the doctrine of scientific racial idealism—actually a new religion.

And thus Lincoln Rockwell became a National Socialist. But his conversion to the new religion still did not answer his question, "What can be done?" Eight long years of struggle and defeat lay ahead of him before he would gain the knowledge he needed to effectively translate his new faith into action and begin to carry on Adolf Hitler's great work once again. While he still lacked the wisdom that could only come in the years ahead, he lacked nothing in energy and determination. For a year he continued to explore the ramifications of the new world view he had adopted and also continued his self-education in several other areas, including the Jewish question.

Then, in November, 1952, the Navy assigned him to a year of duty at the American base at Keflavik in Iceland, where he was executive officer and, later, commanding officer of the Fleet Aircraft Service Squadron there, "Fasron" 107. His promotion to commander came in October, 1953, after he had requested an extension of his Icelandic assignment for another year. He also met and fell in love with an Icelandic girl, who became his second wife in the same month he was promoted. This marriage was far happier than his first. The relative isolation and solitude he enjoyed in Iceland gave him a further opportunity to consolidate his thoughts and to plan a campaign of political action based on his National Socialist philosophy. Feeling that his most urgent need was some medium for the dissemination of his political message, he considered various ways in which he might enter the publishing business. He needed to establish a bridgehead in this industry which would provide him with operational funds and living expenses as well as give him a vehicle for political expression.

He finally decided to begin his career with the publication of a monthly magazine for the wives of American servicemen, primarily because the complete absence of any competing publication in the field seemed to offer an excellent business advantage. He felt that he could not only capture this market, thus assuring himself a steady income, but that service families would provide a particularly receptive audience for his political ideas. His idea was to employ the utmost subtlety, disguising his propaganda so carefully that he would not jeopardize any Jewish advertising accounts the magazine might acquire. He naively thought that he would deceive the Jews and move the hearts and minds of his readers in the desired direction simultaneously.

Rough plans had been laid by the time his service in Iceland was over. His return to civilian life came on December 15, 1954. Nine months of more planning, hard work, fund-raising, and promotion led to the realization of his ideas with the publication of his new magazine, for which he chose the name *U.S. Lady*, in Washington, in September, 1955.

At the same time, he was getting his magazine underway, he began making personal contacts in right-wing circles in the Washington area. He attended the meetings of various groups and then began to organize meetings of his own. Before he could put his magazine to use as a medium for disguised propaganda, however, he found himself in serious financial difficulties, due to his lack of capital, and he was forced to sell the magazine in order to avoid bankruptcy.

With undiminished enthusiasm, he continued his organizing efforts among the right wing. Making the same mistake that nearly every other beginner makes, he assumed that the proper way to proceed lay in coordinating the numerous right-wing and conservative organizations and individuals—bringing them together into a right-wing superstructure where they could work effectively for their common goals. He felt that such a coordination could make an almost miraculous transformation in the strength of the right-wing position in America.

To this end he bought radio advertisements, spoke at dozens of meetings, wrote numberless letters, and devoted every waking hour to the promotion of his plan for unity. He created a paper organization, the American Federation of Conservative Organizations, and continued his tireless efforts to inspire and mobilize even a few of the hundreds of right-wing groups and individuals with whom he had established contact, but to no avail: "Our meetings were better and better attended, but there was no result at all—nothing accomplished."

He sadly learned that all the right-wing groups had one weakness in common: their members loved to talk but were incapable of action. A substantial portion of them were hobbyists—escapists obsessed with various pet projects and absolutely invulnerable to reason, or masochists who delighted in moaning endlessly about treason and decay but who were shocked at the suggestion that they should help put an end to it. Many were so neurotic that the idea of engaging them in any prolonged cooperative effort was untenable. Some were simply insane. Virtually all were cowards. Years of inaction or ineffectiveness had drained the ranks of the right-wing of the type of human material essential for any serious undertaking. Very little was left but the sort of dregs with which nothing could be done.

Unfortunately, he had failed to heed the Leader's warning that eight cripples who join arms do not yield even one gladiator as a result:

And if there were indeed one healthy man among the cripples, he would expend all his strength just keeping the others
on their feet and in this way become a cripple himself.

By the formation of a federation, weak organizations are
never transformed into strong ones, but a strong organization
can and often will be weakened. The opinion that strength
must result from the association of weak groups is incorrect.

Great, truly world-shaking revolutions of a spiritual nature are not even conceivable and realizable except as the titanic struggles of individual formations, never as the under-
takings of coalitions.

It has been said that experience keeps a dear school, and in Rockwell's
case it was dear indeed. He had exhausted all the money left from the sale
of *U.S. Lady* by the time the last meeting of his American Federation of
Conservative Organizations, on July 4, 1956, failed to produce any concrete results. He had to find a new source of income and considered himself fortunate to obtain a temporary position as a television scriptwriter.

This lasted only a few months, however, and then he took a position
on the staff of the New York-based conservative magazine, *American
Mercury*, as assistant to the publisher. He had learned the futility of trying
to achieve effective cooperation between the various right-wing groups and
had resigned himself to forming a new organization.

Rockwell still had two bitter lessons to learn in the school of experience, however—lessons which the Leader had set forth clearly in his immortal book, but which Rockwell, for all his careful study, had failed to
take to heart, just as with the admonition against hoping to gain strength by
uniting weaknesses. He still believed that the enemies of our people could
be fought effectively by the "respectable" means to which conservatives
have always restricted themselves. He thought to avoid the "stigma" of anti-
Semitism by working silently and indirectly against treason and racial subversion. This method had the great advantage of not provoking the enemy,
so that one could proceed peacefully and safely with one's "silent" work.

Thus, while working at *American Mercury* he began to formulate
plans for an underground, "hard-core" National Socialist organization,
with a right-wing front and financing by wealthy conservatives. Since the
organization was to be, in effect, National Socialist, with National Socialists
at the helm and carrying out the significant activities, and the conservative
front only a disguise, he happily thought he had a plan which would not be
subject to all the flaws of those of his conservative efforts of the past.

His new project rapidly foundered on the shoals of reality, however. First he found that wealthy conservatives suffered from most of the character defects that he had already observed in not-so-wealthy conservatives. Money could be gotten from them for "pet" projects—but not for any serious effort which smacked of danger, particularly danger of exposure. A more fundamental weakness of the "secret" approach, however, lay in the fact that it is the surface disguise, the front—not the hidden core—which determines the quality of the personnel attracted to an organization. Thus, when his anticipated source of funds balked and his one National Socialist recruit became discouraged and left, Rockwell was faced with the prospect of scrapping his new idea and starting again from nothing.

Sadly he re-read the words the Leader had written more than thirty years previously:

> A man who knows a thing, recognizes a given danger, and sees with his own eyes the possibility of a remedy, damned well has the duty and the obligation not to work 'silently,' but to stand up openly against the evil and for its cure. If he does not do so then he is a faithless, miserable weakling who fails either from cowardice or from laziness and incompetence. ... Every last agitator who possesses the courage to defend his opinions with manly forth-rightness, standing on a tavern table among his adversaries, accomplishes more than a thousand of these lying, treacherous sneaks.

It had taken two years of repeated discouragements and failures to bring this lesson home to him, but now he understood it. He had finally seen the fallacy underlying the conservative premise. In his own words:

> Although it is made to appear so, the battle between the conservatives and liberals is not a battle of ideas or even of Political organizations. It is a battle of terror, and power. The Jews and their accomplices and dupes are not running our country and its people because of the excellence of their ideas or the merit of their work or the genuine majority of people behind them. They are in power in spite of the lack of these things, and only because they have driven their way into power by daring minority tactics. They can stay in power only because people are afraid to oppose them—afraid they will be socially ostracized, afraid they will be smeared in the

press, afraid they will lose their jobs, afraid they will not be able to run their businesses, afraid they will lose political offices. It is fear and fear alone, which keeps these filthy left-wing sneaks in power—not ignorance on the part of the American people, as the conservatives keep telling each other.

Beyond this however, he was coming to an even more fundamental conclusion: Not only were conservatives wrong in their evaluation of the nature of the conflict between themselves and liberals and wrong in their choice of tactics, but their motives were also wrong; at least, he was beginning to see that their motives differed fundamentally from his own. Basically, the conservatives are a-racial. Their primary concerns are economic: taxes, government spending, fiscal responsibility; and social: law and order, honest government, morality. At worst, their sole interest is the protection of their standard of living from the encroachments of the welfare state; at best, they are genuinely concerned about the general decay of standards and the trend toward mobocracy and chaos. But, as a whole, they show very little concern for the biological problem of which all these other problems are only manifestations.

Certainly the right wing was preferable to the left wing in this respect. At least conservatives tended to have a healthy anti-Semitic instinct. But as long as their inner orientation was economic-materialistic rather than racial-idealistic, they would remain primarily interested in the defense of a system rather than a race, they would continue to look for easy and superficial solutions rather than fundamental ones, and they would continue to lack that spirit of selfless idealism essential to ultimate victory. Thus, as the year 1956 drew to a close, Rockwell was certain of one thing: Conservatives would never, by any stretch of the imagination, be able to offer any effective opposition to the forces of degeneration and death. As he wrote later, anyone, when he first discovers what is going on, might be forgiven a certain period of nourishing the delusion and hope that there is a safe, easy, and "nice" solution to the problem. But to pursue the same fruitless tactics year after year is evidence of something else: Conservatives are the world's champion ostriches, muttering to each other down under the sand "in secret", while their plumed bottoms wave in the breeze for the Jews to kick at their leisure. They are fooling nobody but themselves.

The answer would have to be found elsewhere—but where, how?

The years 1957 and 1958 were difficult ones. As a representative of a New York management-consultant firm, he spent most of 1957 traveling in New York, New Jersey, and Pennsylvania, writing and consolidating his thoughts whenever he could find time. The winter of 1957–58 saw a brief interlude in Atlanta, where he sold advertising.

During this period, Rockwell had an experience about which he has never written and which he related to only a few people. Always a skeptic where the supernatural was concerned, he was certainly not a man to be easily influenced by omens. Yet there can be no doubt that he attached special significance to a series of dreams that he had then. The dreams—actually all variations of a single dream—occurred nearly every night for a period of several weeks and were of such intensity that he could recall them vividly upon waking. In each dream he saw himself in some every-day situation: sitting in a crowded theater, eating at a counter in a diner, walking through the busy lobby of an office building, or inspecting the airplanes of his squadron at an airfield hangar.

And in each dream a man would approach him—theater usher, diner cook, office clerk, or mechanic—and say something to the effect, "Mr. Rockwell, there is someone to see you." And then he would be led off to some back room or side office in the building or hangar, as the case may have been. He would open the door and find waiting for him inside, always alone—Adolf Hitler. Then the dream would end.

One can most easily interpret these dreams as a case of autosugges-tion, but in the light of later developments Rockwell considered them as a symbolic summons, a beckoning onto the path for which he was then still groping, whether that beckoning was the consequence of an internal or an external stimulus.

Early in 1958 he returned to Virginia. His first effort there was in *Newport News*, where he produced political cartoons in collaboration with the publisher of a small racist magazine which shortly went bankrupt. In *Newport News*, however, he met a man who was to play a critical role in changing the course of his political career: Harold N. Arrowsmith, Jr.

Arrowsmith was a wealthy conservative with a "pet" project—but he was not like any other wealthy conservative Rockwell had met. Inde-pendently wealthy as the result of an inheritance, he had formerly been a physical anthropologist. He had stumbled into politics rather by accident when a friend on the research staff of a Congressional investigating com-mittee had asked him for some help with some library research connected with a case under investigation. In the course of this work he had, to his surprise, come upon some of the documentary material that had so startled Rockwell a few years earlier in San Diego.

Being a trained scholar, a linguist with a dozen languages at his dis-posal, having access to all the major libraries and archives of the Western world—and with unlimited time and money—he was able to follow up his initial discoveries and soon had unearthed literally thousands of items of evidence. The story they told was a shocking and frightening one: world wars and revolutions, famines and massacres—not the caprices of history, but the results of deliberate and cold-blooded scheming.

Although he had filing cabinets bulging with military intelligence reports, court records, photostats of diplomatic correspondence, and other material, he had not been able to publicize any of his finds. Scholarly journals returned his carefully written and documented papers with rejection slips, and it soon became apparent that no publisher of general periodicals would accept them either. He approached Rockwell with the proposition of printing, publishing, and distributing some of his documentary material, with full financial backing.

They formed the "National Committee to Free America from Jewish Domination," and Rockwell moved to Arlington, Virginia, where Arrowsmith provided him with a house and printing equipment.

Rockwell had already reached the conclusion that if any progress were to be made, it was necessary to break out of the right-wing milieu into fresh territory. Right-wingers had been exchanging and reading one another's pamphlets for years, with no noticeable results. They always used the same mailing lists and sent their propaganda to people who, for the most part, had already heard at least a dozen variations on the same theme. What was needed was mass publicity, so that some fresh blood could be attracted into the Movement.

As the normal channels of mass propaganda were closed to most right-wingers—and certainly to anyone whose propaganda might prove distressing to Jews—Rockwell had decided that radical means must be used to force open those channels. He placed this objective before all others. For, he reasoned, if one is to mobilize men into an organization—secret or otherwise—for the purpose of gaining political power, one must first let those men know of one's existence and communicate to them at least a bare outline of one's program. Until a mass of new raw material—potential recruits—could be stirred up by making a really significant impact on the public consciousness, there was simply no sense in proceeding further; he had already spent too much time doing things the old way. He was, in fact, prepared to take the next-to-last step in his progress from just another goy to the heir to Adolf Hitler's mighty legacy. He decided on public agitation of the most provocative sort—agitation of such a blatant and revolutionary sort that the mass media could not ignore it.

In May, 1958, Eisenhower had sent US Marines to Lebanon to help maintain the government of President Chamoun in power, against the wishes of the Arab citizens of that country. The Lebanese Arabs desired closer cooperation with the other Arab states, but Chamoun, much to the pleasure of the Jews, did not. The threat of the overthrow of Chamoun and of a pro-Arab government coming into power in Lebanon, thus adding another member to the Arab bloc opposing the illegal Jewish occupation of Palestine, led U.S. Jews to press the course of US intervention upon Eisenhower, always their willing tool. The issue was much in the public eye during the summer of 1958, and Rockwell decided to use it as the basis of his first public demonstration—a picket of the White House. Calling on many of the contacts he had made around the country during the past few years, he was able to arrange for a busload of young demonstrators to come to Washington and also to organize protest groups in both Atlanta, Georgia, and Louisville, Kentucky.

Then on Sunday morning, July 29, 1958, Rockwell led his group of pickets to the White House, while the groups in Atlanta and Louisville began their demonstrations simultaneously. Carrying large signs which Rockwell had designed and printed himself, these three groups made the first public protest against Jewish control of the U.S. government since the Jews had silenced their critics in 1941. It was indeed a momentous occasion: not yet an open National Socialist demonstration, but a vigorous slap in the face for the enemy—a slap which could not be ignored, as all the "secret" right-wing activity had been for years.

Ten weeks later, on October 12, a synagogue in Atlanta was mysteriously blown up. Police immediately swooped on Rockwell's men in Atlanta who had demonstrated in July. Newspapers around the world carried front-page stories implicating Rockwell and Arrowsmith in the bombing. Arrowsmith, who felt he was getting more involved in politics than was comfortable, retrieved his printing equipment and withdrew Rockwell's financial support. For the first time, Rockwell began to get a taste of the difficult times which lay ahead. Hoodlums, instigated by the newspaper publicity, attacked his home. Windows were broken, and stones and firecrackers were thrown at his house late at night. Both by day and by night he and his wife received obscene and threatening telephone calls. Finally, for the sake of their safety, he felt obliged to send his family to Iceland.

With its financial backing gone, the "National Committee to Free America from Jewish Control" was no more. The last of Rockwell's conservative friends evaporated in the harsh glare of newspaper hate propaganda which was heaped upon him. As the new year, 1959, came in, he

found himself alone in an empty house, without friends or money or pro-
spects for the future. He had dared to seize the dragon by the tail and had
survived. Yet, in the bleak, cold days of January and February, 1959, this
gave him little comfort as he faced an uncertain and unpromising future.

> As I sat alone in that empty house or lay alone in that even
> emptier bed in the silent, hollow darkness, the full realization
> of what I was about bore in upon me with fearful urgency. I
> realized there was no turning back; as long as I lived I was
> marked with the stigma of anti-Jewishness... I could never
> again hope to earn a normal living. The Jews could not sur-
> vive unless they made an example of me the rest of my life,
> else too many others might be tempted to follow my exam-
> ple. My Rubicon had been crossed, and it was fight and
> win—or die.

And then something happened which, in its way, was to be as decisive in
his life as had been his finding Adolf Hitler's message in *Mein Kampf,*
eight years before, in San Diego. Again, it was like a guiding hand reaching
to him from the twilight of the past—from a charred, rubble-filled bunker in
Berlin—and showing him the way. Waiting for him at the post office one
morning at the beginning of March was a large carton. In it, carefully fold-
ed, was a huge swastika banner, which had been sent by a young admirer.

Deeply moved, he carried the banner home and hung it across one
end of his living room, completely covering the wall. He found a small,
bronze plaque with a relief bust of Adolf Hitler, which had been given to
him earlier, and mounted it in the center of the swastika. Then he found
three candles and candle holders, which he placed on a small book-case he
had arranged just below the bronze plaque. He closed the blinds and lit the
candles:

> I stood there in the flickering candlelight, not a sound in the
> house, not a soul near me or aware of what I was doing—or
> caring.

On that cold, March morning, alone before the dimly lit altar, Lincoln
Rockwell underwent an experience of a sort shared by few men in the long
history of our race—an experience which comes seldom to this world but
which may radically alter the course of that world when it does. Nearly fifty-

three years before, a similar experience had befallen a man—that time on a cold, November night, on a hilltop overlooking the Austrian town of Linz.

It was a religious experience that was more than religious. As he stood there, he felt an indescribable torrent of emotions surging through his being, reaching higher and higher in a crescendo with a peak of unbearable intensity. He felt the awe-inspiring awareness for a few moments, or a few minutes, of being more than himself, of being in communion with that which is beyond description and beyond comprehension. Something with the cool, vast feeling of eternity and of infinity—of long ages spanning the birth and death of suns, and of immense, starry vistas—filled his soul to the bursting point. One may call that Something by different names—the Great Spirit, perhaps, or Destiny, or the Soul of the Universe, or God—but once it has brushed the soul of a man, that man can never again be wholly what he was before. It changes him spiritually in the same way that a mighty earthquake or a cataclysmic eruption, the subsidence of a continent or the bursting forth of a new mountain range, changes forever the face of the earth.

Slowly the storm subsided, and Lincoln Rockwell—a new Lincoln Rockwell—became aware once again of the room about him and of his own thoughts. He has described for us his feeling then:

> Where before I had wanted to fight the forces of tyranny and regression, now I *had* to fight them. But even more, I felt within me the power to prevail—strength beyond my own strength—the ability to do the right thing even when I was personally overwhelmed by events. And that strength has not yet failed me. Nor will it fail. ... I knew with calm certainty exactly what to do, and I knew, in a hard-to-explain sense, what was ahead. It was something like looking at a road from the air after seeing only the curve ahead from the ground. ... Hitler had shown the way to survival. It would be my task on this earth to carry his ideas...to total, world-wide victory. I knew I would not live to see the victory which I would make possible. But I would not die before I had made that victory certain.

And just as Adolf Hitler had said of his experience on the Freinberg, "In that hour it began," so in that hour it began for Lincoln Rockwell also. He did not realize it then, of course, but this climactic event had come almost exactly in the middle of his political life; he had run just half the course from that fall day in 1950, in the San Diego Public Library, to a martyr's death in Arlington in the late summer of 1967.

Before, he had been a right-winger, a conservative, albeit a more and more openly anti-Jewish one; before, he had felt the need to keep his National Socialism concealed; before, while he had admired Adolf Hitler as the greatest thinker in the history of the race and *Mein Kampf* as the most important book ever written, they had not been wholly real to him—and this attitude had resulted in his failure so often to apply the Leader's teachings to his own political efforts. Now, however, he was no longer a conservative, but a National Socialist, and he would bear witness for his faith before the whole world; now, at last, he recognized in Adolf Hitler not just an extraordinarily great mind and spirit, but something immortal, transcendental, more than human; now he saw the Leader as an embodiment, in a way, of that Universal Soul with which he had briefly communed; now he was prepared to follow the Leader's teachings without reservation, in all things.

At the same time that these fundamental changes in his outlook took place, he saw the need for a fundamental change in his political tactics. He recalled the Leader's words:

> Any man who is not attacked in the Jewish newspapers, not slandered and vilified, is no true National Socialist. The best measure of the value of his will is the hostility he receives from the mortal enemy of our people...
>
> Every Jewish slander and every Jewish lie is a scar of honor on the body of our warriors.
>
> The man they have most reviled stands closest to us, and the man they hate worst is our best friend.
>
> Anyone who picks up a Jewish newspaper in the morning and does not see himself slandered in it has not made profitable use of the previous day; for if he had, he would be persecuted, reviled, slandered, abused, befouled. And only the man who combats this mortal enemy of our nation and of all Aryan humanity and culture most effectively may expect to see the slanders of this race and the efforts of this people directed against him.

And further:

> It makes no difference whatever whether they laugh at us or revile us, whether they represent us as clowns or criminals;

the main thing is that they mention us, that they concern themselves with us again and again, and that we gradually appear to be the only power that anyone reckons with at the moment. What we really are and what we really want, we will show the Jewish journalistic rabble when the day comes.

Rockwell had already recognized the need for gaining mass publicity by radical means, but he had flinched at the thought of the slander and vilification, the misrepresentation and ridicule which must inevitably accompany any publicity he received through the alien-dominated mass media. He had been living in the conservative dream world and had shared with other right-wingers the comfortable illusion that one can keep the enemy fooled—even make him think one is his friend—and fight him effectively at the same time.

Even as he gradually became more forthright in his statements with respect to the Jewish question, he retained the feeling that to speak out openly for Adolf Hitler's National Socialist world view would be nothing short of suicide.

Thus he had fallen between two stools after his demonstration of July 29, 1958. He had been numbed by the virulence of the hatred unleashed against him, and at the same time found himself crippled by self-imposed limitations in his own campaign.

Now, however, he had decided that not only would he never again flinch under the torrent of abuse and slander which his activities were sure to bring down on him, but he would provoke such attacks by the enemy, looking upon each one as a "scar of honor" and also as another small step toward his eventual general recognition as the opponent of everything the enemy stood for, as "the only power with which [that enemy] reckoned." And he saw that an open avowal of his National Socialism was not only the strongest irritant he could bring to bear against his enemy, but it was the only realistic basis for gathering around himself those elements of the population needed to build a viable and lasting movement with which eventually to destroy that enemy and restore his own race to the position of strength and health and honor from which it had abdicated.

Actually, he carried the Leader's counsel about the use of the enemy's own propaganda to its logical extreme. Looking at the task before him realistically for the first time, he saw that the problems he faced were so severe that, in order to make any progress against them, he would be obliged to concentrate all his energies upon one aspect of those problems at a time.

The first step was general recognition. His earlier conviction that that goal must be attained at the expense of every other consideration was now stronger than ever. Thus, instead of following the natural urge to dissociate National Socialism from the Hollywood image that Jewry had been building for it for more than three decades, he temporarily threw all hopes of "respectability"—even among other National Socialists—aside and set about turning to his own advantage all the Jews' previous efforts.

Toward this end he deliberately pinned on himself the label "Nazi," rather than "National Socialist," using this bit of journalistic jargon which had been coined by the enemy during the early days of struggle in Germany, a term looked upon by National Socialists with about the same feeling that convinced Marxists must look upon the designation "commie," or "pinko." Behind this step—one which was to cause much misunderstanding and suspicion in days to come—was the cold-blooded realization that a strutting, shouting uniform-wearing, Hollywood-style "Nazi" was vastly more newsworthy, had vastly more "shock value," than any mere National Socialist.

As he pondered over his soul-stirring experience and began to lay new plans for the future during the next few days, events began flowing in the new channel marked out for them by the finger of Destiny. Three men, a right-wing acquaintance and two other men who were strangers to Rockwell, dropped in to see him one evening. Initially shocked and repelled by the swastika banner in his living room, they were soon won over by his passionate exposition of the new cause. Two of the three remained to become his first disciples.

Then he opened the blinds on his windows, making his swastika banner visible from the street. He issued swastika armbands to his two recruits, and the three of them swaggered about the house wearing holstered pistols. Later he mounted an illuminated swastika on the roof.

The crowds came to laugh and jeer and throw rocks—but a few remained to listen. His "stormtroopers" grew in number from two, to four, to ten.

These March days in 1959, which witnessed the first genuine rebirth of National Socialist activity after nearly fourteen years of terror and total suppression, marked the beginning of the stormiest and most difficult times Rockwell faced. Harassed by the police with illegal searches and confiscation of his property and materials, assaulted by thugs and vandals whom the police made no efforts to apprehend, he and his small group of followers printed and distributed tens of thousands of leaflets and talked to throngs of curious and hostile visitors who came to see the "American Fuehrer," as the newspapers laughingly called him. He first chose the name

"American Party" for his embryonic organization, but soon changed the name to "American Nazi Party."

Keeping his initial objective foremost in his mind, he concentrated the activities of his small group primarily on the distribution of inflammatory leaflets, on creating public incidents, on haranguing crowds under circumstances especially chosen to provoke violent opposition—anything and everything, in other words, to gain mass publicity, to become generally recognized as the opponent of the Jews and everything they represented, from Marxism to unprincipled capitalism, from racial degeneration to cultural Bolshevism.

His first soapbox-style public address was delivered on the Mall, in Washington, on Sunday, April 3, 1960, and became a regular occurrence for some time thereafter.

A letter he wrote to his mother during this early period of public speaking gives an idea of a few of the difficulties he faced:

> 7 July, 1960
> Dear Mother:
> Thank you for the letter and the help. It is much appreciated... Don't pay too much attention to what the papers say, Mother they lie unbelievably. Last week they tried to murder us again on the Mall here and almost killed Major Morgan, whom you met, when they dragged him out—ten of them— and stomped him and left him for dead. But we prevailed, and even though the police, much against their will, were forced to arrest us for "disorderly conduct" (for being attacked by a murderous mob!), the people are with us. This sort of thing is inevitable, and it will get worse. Now they have tried—yesterday—to have me heaved in an insane asylum to shut me up, but they were surprised, as I was relieved, when people rushed forward to offer the huge cash bond they set for me and I will have a psychiatrist of my own choosing deliver a report, instead of the two Jews they planned for me. Do not worry about all this. It is dangerous, painful, and bitter when our own people do not understand what we are doing and suffering for them, but I am sure that the Lord will not permit liars and villains to win in the end. You will yet be mighty proud...
>
> Love,
> Link

In May, 1960, the National Socialist Bulletin made its appearance as the first periodical published by the American Nazi Party. It evolved in to the *Stormtrooper* magazine after eight issues. Meanwhile, on February 5, 1960, the United States Navy, under pressure from Jewish groups, forced Rockwell to accept a discharge from the Naval Reserve.

Despite the news quarantine imposed on him, despite beatings and jailings, despite a chronic lack of funds, despite serious personnel problems, and despite a thousand other troubles and difficulties, his campaign to gain public recognition made steady progress. Newspapers found it impossible to completely avoid mentioning his brash and daring exploits; editors and columnists found irresistible the temptation to denounce or "expose" him. Even radio and television emcees, ever on the prowl for sensation, yielded to temptation and defied the ban on publicity for Rockwell.

The image of George Lincoln Rockwell and the America Nazi Party created by the mass media for public consumption was, of course, a grossly distorted one. Rockwell had succeeded in forcing the media, more or less against their will, to give him publicity. Unfortunately, he could not force them to be impartial in their treatment, or even to be truthful. An interview with him published in the popular magazine, *Playboy*, was prefaced with such editorial remarks as: "Unlike controversial past interviewees Rockwell could not be called a spokesman for any socially or politically significant minority. But we felt that the very virulence of Rockwell's messianic master-racism could transform a really searching conversation with the 48-year-old Fuhrer into a revealing portrait of both rampant racism and the pathology of fascism."

Another commented: "The question of George Lincoln Rockwell boils down, then, to the question of how far can America let the hate-mongers go. Will an unsound branch on the tree of American democracy fall off or will it poison the organism?"

The really ambitious writers, editors, and reporters did not restrict themselves to such mildly prejudicial remarks but vied with one another in concocting outrageous lies about Rockwell. He was accused of cowardice, sadism, selfish gormandizing, kidnapping: "Like the late Adolf Schickelgruber, on whom he models himself, he believes in leading from behind—as far behind as possible." In one magazine, he was "quoted" as boasting that he had once castrated a heckler with his bare hands," and another reported: "George Rockwell's hysterical raving has already whipped up the lunatic fringe to the breaking point. Last summer three of his stormtroopers decided to please the Fuehrer by kidnapping a small Jewish child in Washington, DC, and holding him at the Party Headquarters for several hours. How many more innocent citizens will be subjected to harassment before Robert F. Kennedy and the Justice Department move in?"

Topping them all was the story that "Like a true Nazi top dog, he avails himself of top-dog privileges and orders private meals served in his room. He partakes of such fancy fare as turtle soup, lobster, and steak while the men eat hash. Between meals he enjoys sucking kumquats." This last flight of fancy is reminiscent of articles published in the German press (before 1933) which portrayed Adolf Hitler as a drunken profligate (Hitler only drank once in his entire life: the night of his High School Graduation) and lecher who dissipated the contributions of his followers in high living, champagne parties, and whoring.

Rockwell accepted these lies and slanders philosophically, for the alternative to this Jew-designed public image even was no public image at all. As a matter of fact, the Jews-and non-Jewish publicists anxious to demonstrate their affection for the Jews—cannot be given all the blame for this poor image. Rockwell himself lent a conscious hand to its creation, as he admitted when he said, "When I have the rare opportunity to use some mass medium, as was recently the case when I gave an interview to *Playboy*, I am forced to walk a careful line between what I should like to say and what the enemy would like to hear me say. Unless I deliberately sound at least halfway like a raving illiterate with three loose screws, such an interview would never be printed."

The price he paid for becoming generally recognized as "Mr. Nazi" was a high one indeed. Other men with sound racial instincts but without Rockwell's understanding of political realities were, naturally enough, appalled by what seemed to be Rockwell's ridiculous antics. Most people, even relatively sophisticated ones who talk knowingly about "managed news," simply find incomprehensible the Jewish Big Lie technique.

These sound but simple citizens all too often jumped to the not-implausible conclusion that Rockwell was a kind of agent provocateur, a traitor hired by the enemy to discredit honest racists and patriots. His correspondence with some of them displays a mixture of impatience with their inability to perceive the essence of the real problems facing our race, and a sincere desire to evoke understanding. The following extracts from a letter to a member of a snobbish racist group calling itself the "European Liberation Front" are typical:

Dear Mr. ... :

I realize that I am only a stupid, silly American, but I do love
this country, in spite of your denunciation of it. What you
hate about it is what the Jews have done to it, and you are
like a man who permits his wife to be debauched by rapists
and then tosses her in the garbage can for it. Shame on you!
"American" influence on Europe is not American at all, and
you damned sure should know it. The real American influence was Henry Ford, our West, and the like.

Europe is a tired old man—more like a tired old lady—
and if Western culture is to be saved, it will be saved by the
last Western barbarians, the American barbarians I love.
Men like you, suave, polished, educated, supercilious, and
"above" nasty physical violence, cannot save themselves, let
alone a nation, a culture, or a race. You people with your
"European Liberation Front" are going at it backwards. You
can't liberate Europe any more with Europeans. Hitler gave
that effort every bit of holy genius within him, and he was
mashed by the American barbarians. You and your egghead
gang of dandies are in love with what is gone and insist on
ignoring what is here. Rome is no more. You keep trying to
resurrect it, and you can't, because there are no more noble
Romans over there, at least not enough to make a real fight
of it, Europe is like one big France—all empty shell, fine
words, pretty songs, and dead men. We helped kill Europe. If
you did liberate it, like France was "liberated," it would sink
into degeneracy again in a century.

There are, of course, good, vigorous fighting men in Europe, but they are swamped by the human garbage left in the
wreckage of two wars promoted by Jews and fought by
Americans. I am building National Socialism here, by such
expedients and methods as may be possible, and I am succeeding, in spite of your looking down your nose at me...

Whenever I can get some or the other of you to ditch the
"We're-the-real-National Socialists" game and start being
National Socialists, I give strength to the cause to which I
have given my life, my family, my comfort, and everything
else I have to give, no matter what you may have been told.

Frankness, not diplomacy, was his strong point.

In order to allay hostility and suspicion as much as he could, he was soon obliged to divert some of his energies from agitation and publicity garnering to a more sober exposition of his ideas. His first major effort in that direction was the publication of his political autobiography, *This Time the World*. Written hastily in the fall of 1960 between speaking engagements, court appearances, street brawls, and desperate attempts to raise money to sustain his small group, he was not able to publish it until a year later. The printing and binding of the book were done entirely by his untrained stormtroopers, and their only machinery was a tiny, office-style duplicator. The absolute sincerity of its tone failed to convince few of its readers, but the difficulties of distribution, due to the Jewish "quarantine," limited its circulation to a few thousand copies.

In October, 1961, the first of his *Rockwell Reports* appeared. Varying in length from four to thirty-six pages, the *Rockwell Report* appeared semi-monthly at first, then monthly, occasionally lapsing into bi-monthly publication during particularly difficult periods. The *Rockwell Reports* contained a lively mixture of National Socialist ideology, current political analysis, prognostication, political cartoons and drawings, reproductions of pertinent news clippings, and photographs of Party activities. They all bore his unique stamp and, more than any other one thing, were responsible for drawing to him the idealistic young men who formed the cadre of the growing movement.

From the beginning, Rockwell had understood the necessity for the National Socialist movement eventually to operate from a worldwide basis. For the ultimate political goal of the Movement was the establishment of an Aryan world order, a pax Aryana, as a prerequisite for the attainment of the long-term racial goals of the Movement. From the spring of 1959, this concept had existed on paper as the "World Union of Free-Enterprise National Socialists," but until the summer of 1962 it was not implemented beyond an exchange of letters with individual National Socialists in Europe. In early August, 1962, Rockwell met with National Socialist representatives from four other nations in the Cotswold Hills, near Cotswold, England, and the World Union of National Socialists formally came into existence. On the fifth of August the protocol now known as the Cotswold Agreements was drawn up, pledging the National Socialist movements of the United States, Great Britain, France, Germany (including Austria), and Belgium to a common effort. Annual meetings of the World Union of National Socialists were originally envisaged, but Fate and circumstances prevented this. Rockwell was under increasing pressure in America during the next five years, as the situation there grew steadily more turbulent.

Rockwell's original program was divided into three phases. The first phase, beginning in March, 1959, was to be a phase of provocative but essentially non-constructive activity, intended to generate publicity and build a public image, no matter how distorted. The second phase was to be a cadre-building phase, during which a strong, disciplined, effective, professional National Socialist organization was to be built and capabilities in propaganda and organizing developed to a high degree. The third phase was to be one of mass organization.

Phase one was masterfully executed. Rockwell proved himself an outstanding tactician in the rough-and-tumble game of smashing through the Jewish blackout barrier. With cool objectivity, he watched the press heap bucket after bucket of lies and filth on his image, provoking them to renewed activity whenever they tired. With keen insight he analyzed the Jewish situation. He understood that though they occupied the key positions of control in the public-opinion-forming networks, they were constrained to a large extent by the fact that that control must remain hidden from the public.

Furthermore, he understood the fact that a very substantial portion of the reporters, editors, columnists, newscasters, and even many individual newspaper and broadcast-station owners are not Jews, and, barring direct and categorical orders to the contrary from the key Jews, these people can be counted upon to react in a more-or-less predictable way to a given stimulus. Thus, by taking a position and making statements which seemed extreme and even ridiculous to the "average citizen," he could entice publicists to quote him widely, thinking thus to discredit both the man and the philosophy with these average citizens. What they failed to understand was that before the Movement could profit from any mass appeal, it had to appeal to a large number of very un-average citizens—fearless idealists who could form the National Socialist cadre.

And these men responded in a very different way to Rockwell's message than did the liberal publicists or their average audience. They saw beyond the superficial "ridiculousness" of his message to the kernel of deep truth that it contained. While the average citizen, incapable of thinking beyond the immediate problems of the day, found Rockwell's message "too extreme," just as the publicists intended, those who could extrapolate in their minds the developments of the present to the consequences of tomorrow—and of a century hence—saw the compelling necessity of his demands. But such men are rather sparsely distributed throughout the population, and to reach them Rockwell needed to cast his net very wide; this the publicists helped him do while they thought to smear him. Rockwell also understood that the image of him being erected in the minds of the masses, while a liability now, had a value for the future, when conditions had ripened so that at least some of those masses were ready for an "extremist."

Phase two—cadre building and organizational development—in a sense was co-extant with phase one, for from the very beginning Rockwell's publicity began to attract a few of the idealists needed for phase two, and these men began to constitute the skeleton of the organizational structure which was later to be filled out. Even a bit of phase three entered the picture during the first phase, when Rockwell conducted a campaign to become governor of the state of Virginia in 1965.

This election campaign proved to be a period of extremely valuable training not only for Rockwell but for the leadership personnel of his entire Party. Realizing the eventual need to develop proficiency at mass campaigning, Rockwell decided to begin acquiring experience in that direction soon rather than late. As he later admitted, after winning less than 1.5% of the votes cast, the campaign also provided a more fundamental lesson and helped him to realistically re-evaluate the entire status of the Movement. Before, he had taken overly optimistic view that the Movement would begin to pick up substantial mass following as soon as it had gained sufficient publicity through his phase-one activities; that is, he believed that phases two and three would be largely concurrent.

After the Virginia campaign, having been reminded once again of the stupendous inertia of public opinion, he realized that phase two would be much longer than originally anticipated, and that the beginning of any substantial success from phase-three activity would have to await two things: a considerable internal strengthening of the Movement and a considerable worsening of the general racial-social-economic situation.

With this first thing in mind, he made the decision in 1966 to inaugurate a general activity. As mentioned before, the first two phases of Party activity overlapped to a large extent, and the transition between the two was marked primarily by a shift of emphasis. Phase one was the "Nazi" era of the Movement. Phase two is the beginning of the National Socialist era. In line with this re-emphasis, the American Nazi Party officially became the National Socialist White People's Party on January 1, 1967, and that date can reasonably be considered to mark the transition. Six months earlier, the appearance of National Socialist World was a major step in this direction. And six months after that date—in June, 1967—a historic reorganizational conference of the Party leadership was held in Arlington. There Rockwell set the Movement on its new course, explaining the need for a total professionalization of every activity, from fund raising to propaganda writing, in order to meet the severe demands to be expected during the long period of growth and struggle ahead.

He was now forty-nine years old. For the past eight years he had been working an average sixteen hours a day, seven days a week. The strain on his physical and spiritual resources had been severe. Usually he was obliged to concentrate on the several tasks simultaneously. There was always a demonstration to be planned, a speech to be prepared, propaganda to be written, a court case to be fought, money to be raised, and everything to be done under nearly impossible working conditions, with incessant interruptions. Only the immense vitality of his rugged, six-foot-four-inch frame and a deep reserve of spiritual strength had sustained him in the past.

The course that lay ahead would certainly be no easier; on the contrary, in addition to the old tasks connected with agitation and publicity, there would be many new problems to be faced as the Movement continued into its new phase of activity.

Other men—strong men—might have yielded to the temptation to remain with a prescription to which they had become accustomed and not venture from a beaten path into strange and difficult territory. The slightest trace of subjectivity would allow them to ring forth a hundred reasons for not changing a modus operandi which they had found successful in the past. And yet it was characteristic of Rockwell that he did not hesitate for an instant. When he saw that the time had come for the Movement to change its tactics and accept a different set of challenges, he set himself to the new task with the same determination that he had shown throughout the first phase.

Now it was necessary to build up a whole new public image for the Party, or, rather, gradually to transform the grossly distorted image he had induced the enemy to build for him to one closer to the truth. It was a demanding task, and he spent the summer of 1967 in laying plans for the future and in finishing his new book, *White Power*.

In one of his last letters, written in August to two faithful Party comrades, man and wife, he reveals a little of the introspection which occupied his mind at this decisive time:

> Dear …
> By no means do I get the solid feeling that [you] are clear in your own minds on what has been done, what should be done now, and what might be done (or not done) in the future. For this reason, after much of my favorite recent hobby—tossing and turning—I have arisen as dawn is creeping

over this benighted city to set forth on paper some thoughts which might help. (And often I find that such efforts to help others, help me in the process.) There is no plan or overall approach in this letter; it's just jewels, pearls, and clinkers from a mind which seems to be in a state of near-collapse and rebellion.

First let me present an insoluble problem within me. Doing my best to learn from history, I am aware of a fact of all great struggles. There have been millions of causes, battles, and so on, almost all of them lost. History rarely records the losers, except when they get hacked up in a particularly interesting and dramatic manner. But there are some winners, who do get recorded in history and I have examined these pretty carefully (wishing someday to join their exalted ranks) to see if there is any common pattern to their activity on this planet which might be a key to why they won, when almost everybody loses. There is absolutely no doubt about it; there is such a pattern, even though the causes and struggles vary in content or aim from Lenin's Bolshevism to Adolf Hitler's National Socialism, from a little old lady set on running her neighbor out of town to Genghis Khan and his human hamburger machine. The winners in every case have been more determined, more fanatical in their ruthless refusal to quit, than their competitors. This would seem to indicate that victory is given to him who is most persevering. But this has not been true, either. History abounds with persevering nuts who have repeatedly hopped off hills and buildings wearing "wings" and just as repeatedly landed on their behinds until there was nothing left. …

The conclusion I reach from all this is that it takes three things to make a winner: *a good cause*, i.e., a cause which is in time, in phase, and needed; *a leader* who is unshakeable in his determination to fight as long as he has a couple of stumps for legs and who can inspire that same will in his troops; and some *plain good luck*. As I examine my own cause, leadership, and luck, I find that it is absolutely impossible for me to make a detached judgment on whether I am one of the fanatics hopping off a hill with a pair of Woolworth, glue-and-feathers wings, or whether I am one of the guys who gets modeled into stone images for the benefit of pigeons. ...

I do not think either of you knows the answer to that one, either. However, I have the advantage over both of you in that I long, long ago made up my mind that the best thing I can do with my life—what's left of it—is to take aim, do my best to control the inevitable shaking, and never take my eye and heart off the target until it goes down...

On the 25th of August, 1967, a Friday, at two minutes before noon, near his Arlington headquarters, an assassin's bullet struck him down.

The murderer, a man whom Rockwell had expelled from the Party a few months earlier for his repeated attempts to inject Marxist ideas subtly into Party publications and for publicly expounding a doctrine of racial Bolshevism, had lain in ambush atop a nearby building and fired into Rockwell's car as it drove by. Ironically, Rockwell had rescued this puffed-up little Bolshevik from the gutters of New York City eight years before, and he had taken an almost fatherly interest in him ever since. He had never given up his repeated attempts to instill a little decency and sense of honor into him, despite overwhelming evidence that the man was a compulsive liar and thief and an incurable conspirator. All his well-meant efforts in this direction were rewarded only with heartache after heartache over the years—and finally with death, when the vicious little punk he thought he could make into a man found a chance to "get even" for being expelled from the Party.

Following a denial by the United States government of Commander Rockwell's right to burial in a national cemetery, his Party comrades had his body cremated, and a National Socialist memorial service was held in Arlington on the afternoon of August 30. His eulogy was short but moving:

National Socialist comrades! Fellow White Americans! Today we take upon ourselves the sorrowful task of laying to rest the mortal remains of our beloved Commander, Lincoln Rockwell, martyred by the bullet of a cowardly assassin. To those of us who worked with him every day, to those Party comrades all over America, and to dedicated National Socialists throughout the world the staggering loss imposed by his death will only be fully felt in the days and years of struggle which lie ahead of us all. His inspiration and his will, the depth of his wisdom and the heroism of his spirit—

these are the things which gave us the motivation and the guidance we sorely needed to keep up the fight on so many dark days in years past.

The stunning suddenness of his departure and the ensuing turmoil of the last few days have kept us from yet assessing the magnitude of our loss. But even harder to bear than this, perhaps, has been utterly shabby—the despicably shameful—treatment of our fallen Commander by a government of the nation he served so faithfully throughout all the years of his manhood. George Lincoln Rockwell gave his life in the struggle against Bolshevism at a time when thousands of other American fighting men on the other side of the world are also falling victims to that same Bolshevism—and yet an American government has denied his request to be laid to rest in the place of his choice.

George Lincoln Rockwell served America for twenty years and through two wars, risking his life again and again in defense of the land and the people he loved so well. He was no armchair soldier, but he chose of his own will that soldierly profession demanding the very highest order of courage and skill: he was a fighter pilot. His dedication to duty, his daring, his proficiency led him from the rank of Seaman to that of full Commander, gave him the leadership of three squadrons, and earned him nine decorations. And an American government does not hold him fit to be buried beside his fellow fighting men.

George Lincoln Rockwell has sacrificed more and fought harder for the things he held dear—his native land, his fellow countrymen, and above all his race—than any man now living. He saw his duty and unflinchingly did it, even when that duty led him into opposition to nearly all those around him. He saw further than other men, and he fought harder. Indeed, in this latter regard he cherished the maxim of the great Leader whose philosophy molded his own thoughts: Those who want to live, let them fight; and those who do not want to fight in this world of eternal struggle do not deserve to live.

He fought, and he died. And yet Lincoln Rockwell is not really dead, for he built a Movement and he spread an idea, and that Movement was not destroyed nor that idea silenced by the bullet that struck him down. And so long as that

Movement remains and that idea continues to fill the hearts and minds of men, the spirit of Lincoln Rockwell lives on.

The ashes of the martyr lie here before us, and we cannot help but be filled with a solemn sense of tragedy. Yet we are not really here to mourn him, but to honor him and to rededicate ourselves to the Cause which he served. In the times ahead we must redouble our efforts, so that he will not have died in vain. We must let his great sacrifice serve to inspire us onward in our struggle toward victory—the victory of our people, of our great White race, over the disease which now afflicts it and the enemies who now oppress it. Indeed at this moment we must bear in mind that old saying which the Commander paraphrased for us: 'The stones and mortar of our Movement are the bones and blood of its martyrs.' It is this aspect of his death that he would now want us to keep uppermost in mind, forgetting our sorrow and filling ourselves with pride at the knowledge we followed such a leader.

For it was he, Lincoln Rockwell, who again picked up the torch which fell to earth twenty-two years ago. Adolf Hitler founded our great Movement and will forever fill a unique position in the saga of our race; but had it not been for Lincoln Rockwell, Adolf Hitler's mighty work might well have been in vain. It was Lincoln Rockwell who set us once again on the upward path when we had faltered and wanted to go back again. It was his example which inspired us to do what we knew we should do rather than that which was easiest to do. It was his hand which led us out of the maze of defeat and degeneration and despair, and pointed the way toward higher things; and his voice which reminded us over and over again that we must continue the struggle for our race.

As we lay to rest the mortal remains of Lincoln Rockwell, it is appropriate to read once again that passage from the Leader's book which he loved best. I shall read from chapter twelve of the first volume of the Commander's personal copy of *Mein Kampf*:

When human hearts break and human souls despair, the great vanquishers of distress and care, of shame and misery, of spiritual slavery and physical duress look down upon them from the twilight of the past and hold

out their eternal hands to faint-hearted mortals. Woe to
the people that is ashamed to grasp them![1]

[1] Originally published in *National Socialist World*, no. 5 (winter 1967). The closing *Mein Kampf* quotation is from section 12.10 (Dalton translation, p. 349).

APPENDIX B

"By This Sign, We Will Conquer"
(*In Hoc Signo Vinces*)

George Lincoln Rockwell

Long lasting success in any human endeavor is never the result of blind luck. The achievement of a clearly defined goal, whether it be the act of walking from point "X" to point "Y," the building of a house, or the organization of a business, is always the product of three things:

- *The intellectual ability* to perceive the problem involved, the opposition which must be expected, and the best way to overcome that opposition to reach the goal.
- *The will and determination* to do whatever may be necessary to reach the desired goal, regardless of opposition.
- *The physical means, strength, and courage* to enforce and carry out the plan conceived by the mind and determined by the will.

If any of these three elements be lacking on one's purpose, failure is the inevitable, predictable result.

A man who is too stupid to understand the various factors involved in trying to walk from point "X" to point "Y," where the path between us is a jungle infested with snakes, dangerous carnivores, and fever, and who fails to arm himself with weapons and maps, medicine and other equipment will never arrive at "Y" no matter how dogged his determination or how mighty his muscles. Another man attempting the same journey, though he clearly perceives the dangers and prepares for them, and though he be mighty of muscle, will yet fail to reach "Y" if he is so irresolute and weak of will that he does not persevere at the struggle and ruthlessly use whatever force might be necessary to crush and destroy the forces opposing him. And a third man who has the intellect to perceive the dangers and to prepare for them, and the will and determination to fight his way through even with the utmost heroism, but who is frail of body and so physically weak that he cannot carry out the commands of his mind and his will, cannot but succumb to the stronger adversaries he will meet.

It is with civilizations as it is with the struggles of individual men. Dozens of great civilizations have perished because of failure in one or more of these three elements necessary in the struggle for survival. Savage societies usually perish, not so much from lack of vigorous will or lack of physical strength, as from lack of ability to perceive the real situation. Drowning in superstition and stumbling in the darkness of ignorance, they are overwhelmed by the physical forces of violent natural occurrences, catastrophes, and diseases which more civilized societies have learned to overcome.

On the other hand, civilizations, for all their intellectual achievements and sciences, perish most often because of *failure of the will*: the diminishing of the savage and ruthless drive for survival and dominance which originally created society. They become "humanitarian," selfish, and soft. They become physically weak and dependent on paid armies and police to do their fighting. The fighting spirit of honor and self-sacrifice and heroism of their ancestors gives way to a growing love of ease and luxury and cowardice masquerading as "humanitarianism."

When a civilization reaches this effete stage in its decay, only a very rare historical occurrence can halt the final collapse of the society, as the decadence grows daily more apparent. Only when the dying society still has enough life-energy to produce a spiritual giant, a godlike throwback to the ancient heroism of its people, one who is able to shock and drive the civilization out of its natural historical night of sleep and death, in spite of the suicidal opposition of the dying peoples who long only for "peace" and the slumber of death, can a society once again rise for a while.

Western, Aryan civilization passed the historical point of no return on its journey into limbo during the nineteenth century, as was duly noted by Oswald Spengler, Houston Chamberlain, and others. Were it not for the unbelievable, miraculous arrival of Adolf Hitler at the last possible moment, the only bearable course for an intelligent, perceptive, and sensitive man surrounded by a disgusting and suicide-bent civilization would have been resigned enjoyment of such momentary pleasures as provided escape from the soul-crushing reality of a Judaized, cannibalized, and boob-ized civilization rushing headlong back to the jungle in the name of "humanitarianism."

But the appearance in history of Adolf Hitler is evidence that there still remains in White, Western civilization a sufficient spark of self-sacrificing, creative vigor to permit, perhaps, another thousand years or so of survival for the White man. This infinitely precious spark will remain just that, however, and quickly fade into darkness, so long as the tiny elite minority of humanity is too selfish, cowardly, and short-sighted to apply the lessons of history before it is too late forever, and fan the spark Hitler gave us into the roaring flame of creative civilization founded by our courageous ancestors.

So far, the fearful punishment meted out to Adolf Hitler's fighting heroes of civilization by Jewish forces of decay and destruction has so unnerved and terrified the world that even those able to see and understand the peril to humanity, and the way to salvation as shown by Adolf Hitler, are so pitifully attached to their lives and liberties and comforts that they dare not pick up the sacred spark of White survival and fan it with their own life's breath. And it must soon be fanned—or go out forever.

Aryan, White humanity is on the precipice of darkness and oblivion. Strewn on the crags in the eternal blackness below are the bones of other know-it-all, pompous civilizations which were doubtless unable to imagine their own demise at the very time when they were surrounded by the outward power and magnificence of empire. They were unable to realize or face up to the *total* threat of a growing weakness and "humanitarianism," unable to muster the *total will* necessary to reverse the historical march to death and oblivion. They were too lazy and selfish, greedy and cowardly to heed the tiny few who have been burned, crucified, stoned, fed to the lions, or handed the cup of hemlock.

If there is any history a thousand years hence, and any people able to study it, they will marvel in disbelief most of all at the stubborn refusal of the White man to use his overwhelming strength, his knowledge, and the providential gift of Adolf Hitler's leadership to save himself from the most incredible and cringing slavery at the hands of a relatively tiny gang of disgusting, pathologically unbalanced, physically weak and cowardly, arrogant, tyrannical Jews.

Our problems today are not "American" problems, "British" problems, "French," "German," or "European" or "African" problems—they are problems of *survival for all White men*. What, in the name of the most elementary reason, is the difference between whether Bartholomew Buckingham is born near the Thames, Hans Schmidt on the Rhine, Pierre Dubois on the Seine, Per Olafson in Stockholm, Eric Erasmus in Durban, Joe Doaks in Podunk, Ohio, or John Smith in Auckland, New Zealand, compared to the question of "Shall there *be* any more Bartholomews, Hanses, Pierres, Pers, Erics, Joes or Johns?"

卐 卐 卐

Our planet swarms with colored creatures who outnumber us by more than *four to one*—and in all of our nations, these inferior beings, we are told, are our "equals," able to vote away our money, our liberties, our lives, and our honor. By the old-fashioned notions of nationalism and democracy, I, Lincoln Rockwell, am supposed to treasure and care for and be loyal to some of the lowest spawn of the jungle, providing only that their Black dam gave them to the world in some American ditch or filthy crib—because then, of course, they are "Americans," and aren't we all out for "America"? Or am I to be loyal and die for these miserable and pitiable half-animals, my "fellow Americans," by slaughtering millions upon millions of the finest biological specimens of my own race, because a gang of Hollywood Jews teaches us that Americans must hate Germans? Or again, is it a certain piece of geography to which I am to be loyal, and for which I must kill my own people and perhaps die myself? Does my loyalty to this hunk of geography stop at the Canadian border?

But perhaps it is "Americanism" to which I am to be loyal and for which I must make war upon German men, women, and children. When I examine what they tell me is "Americanism," however, I find that it consists primarily in being willing to submit meekly to Jewish direction of my culture, government, religion, entertainment, and even my sex life.

No, all this is nonsense. The only thing to which I can be loyal with any deep conviction—the only loyalty which makes any sense—is my *racial*, and therefore cultural, brotherhood with my own people, no matter where they happen to have been born! When that loyalty is challenged, and my people are in danger, it is monstrous to pretend that we must be suspicious of each other just because we live across imaginary geographical lines. It is monstrous that, upon proper preparation and agitation by a gang of international Jews, we White men must march forth to kill each other and bomb each other to ashes and everlastingly hate each other because we are "trade rivals" or for "American democracy" or the "British Empire" or for anything else in the world.

I am a *White man*, and a brother to all other White men, and I mean to stand with all of them and, if necessary, lead them in battle to survive against the unspeakable menace of the colored populations of the Earth rising to slaughter and rapine against the White men—and led by the scheming Jew!

But like the first man in the analogy of the walk through the snake-infested jungle, too many of our White "leaders" fail to perceive the cosmic proportions of the problem and imagine it is something which can be solved in "their" country, and by half measures. The tiny few who do see the dreadful and total urgency of the White man's situation have, until our arrival on the scene, attempted to fight with less than the total weapons required in a total fight for survival. Most of the best leaders have imagined that small groups of beleaguered White men, gathered into little geographical huddles behind imaginary lines and waving different colored bits of cloth bravely in the breezes, can survive by themselves, and the hell with the other White men who have different bits of colored cloth.

The Jews have *never* made the mistake of seriously dividing themselves into these phony geographical "teams." On the contrary, the Jews—with their Bolshevism, Zionism, and mongrelism—are attacking *all* White men, *everywhere and all the time*.[1] They are sending their black armies into all of our nations in an all-out attack against the White elite of the world, with absolutely no considerations of "national" boundaries or flags or languages or cultures. In the face of this total international threat of annihilation by race, millions of those who already see the danger are to be found babbling darkly of "Yankee imperialism," "British Empire," "dirty Catholics," "immoral atheists," "Republicans," "Laborites," "damned Yankees," "Germany first," etc., etc., *ad nauseam*. Like little boys besieged by a mob of kidnappers and murderers, they cannot resist squabbling about who has the most marbles in the face of a deadly danger that they temporarily forget. The battle of our times—if there is to be any battle   is for the *survival of the White race!*

And to survive, the White man will have to *re-conquer* the Earth once conquered and civilized at the cost of so much blood by his ancestors. Under the banners of international Jewry, the colored masses are threatening to return civilization to savagery. Under the swastika banner of Adolf Hitler, White men around the world will master the planet to save civilization.

The Jewish war against civilization has actually been a worldwide, gigantic *revolution*, in the course of which they got millions of us to murder each other, shouting "Democracy!" "*Gott mit uns!*" "Free the slaves!" "Liberty, equality, fraternity!" And now they are preparing for the final bloodbath during which we will shout "capitalism!" and "communism!" respectively, as the two teams of White men slaughter each other with Jew-financed H-bombs.

In the course of these fratricidal and suicidal wars, the Jews have not been afraid to sacrifice thousands of their brethren in their devilish cause, as they did in the last monstrous slaughter in the 1940s. The Jews realize

---

[1] And they have been doing so for literally millennia. See T. Dalton, *Eternal Strangers* (2020).

what *we* must realize: that they are playing for the highest stakes in the knowledge of mankind—mastery of the whole Earth—and they do not shrink from the inescapable conclusions of strategy and tactics dictated by knowledge of such stakes. If we are to survive, then we too must have the wit and the strength of mind to face up to the deadly facts of the situation and act ruthlessly, rapidly, and effectively.

The Jews have almost won the final step in their 4,000-year revolution—open world power. They now have total secret power to manipulate and control all world activities, and lack only a little more brainwashing and breaking of the will of the masses to make their world domination an acknowledged and formal power. They have fought and won their way to this incredible power by unsurpassed determination and iron will over 40 centuries, and only a miracle can prevent the final victory of such fanatical warriors—tragically and viciously wrong as such a victory would be for humanity.

Even the atheist Jews—which is most of them—have an inexplicable belief in the ancient Jewish prophecies that when "the law comes forth from the hills of Zion" and Jerusalem, it will be the millennium for the Jews and they will own and rule the Earth. They are in Jerusalem now, and lack only a few blocks of it for total possession![2] They are experiencing a worldwide frenzy as they can already sense the total victory we are about to give them, and they are even now preparing their sacrificial orgy of victory in Tel Aviv!

In the face of this unspeakable threat, that the whole world and all of us will fall to the tyranny of a gang of criminal paranoiacs, the narrow chauvinism, conservatism, and regionalism of most right-wing leaders is the utmost stupidity! With the masters of mongrels, the Jews, leading millions of savages in a worldwide attack against the White-elite bearers of civilization, and with the end only moments away in terms of history, only the most short-sighted leaders can continue to keep our children divided and helpless into "teams" of Americans, Dixiecrats, Catholics, Germans, Yankees, atheists, Dutchmen, conservatives, Irishmen, etc. down through the whole pitiful, heartbreaking list. The Jew may be all of these things— *but first he is a Jew!*

It is the first task of he who would save civilization—which requires saving the White man—to make White men supremely and totally con-

---

[2] This was written just before the 1967 war in which Israel captured all of Jerusalem, the West Bank, and the Gaza Strip. Currently in 2024, Israel is in the process of destroying remaining Palestinians in Gaza and, more slowly, in the West Bank.

scious of race above all other allegiances. Our people can be Democrats or Germans or Catholics or Englishmen if they want to and if it suits their purposes, *but first they must be White men!* Otherwise, the Jew will keep us divided and helpless and unconscious of our racial unity and strength, while they fanatically fight as Jews, no matter where they are, until it is all over.

The world of TV, rockets, and jet transportation has become too small to permit any group of White men anywhere to enjoy the suicidal luxury of fighting each other on behalf of the Jew ever again, no matter what the reason which may be advanced in the propaganda. We simply cannot afford to fight each other when we are under such overwhelming and deadly attack by such endless hordes led by such a fanatical and devilish enemy as the Marxist, Zionist Jew. The reason that the White man has been losing for so long in the first place is that he has failed or refused to see the enormity and the pressing urgency of his problem. He has permitted himself to be distracted into a million little squabbles over trifles, while his race has been driven almost to extinction.

Like the first man in the analogy, we haven't understood the path, the nature of the obstacles and, worst of all, we haven't even realized the goal we must win—or die. That goal is and must be *mastery of the Earth by the White man,* since civilization depends solely on such White mastery. Any lesser goal is utterly worthless, just as it would be worthless for a man scheduled to hang to take vitamins and attain perfect health.

And such a fantastically difficult and cosmic goal as world mastery cannot be won by luck, sneaking, half-measures, prayers, hopes, fine speeches, pamphlets, or sporadic violence. What we must aim at and achieve is a world counter-revolution against the Jewish Marxist-Zionist revolution. And revolutions are never, never the result of spontaneous and fortuitous uprisings, but always the product of ruthless, scientific planning and fighting, based on the immutable laws of great social upheavals. Behind the pitchforks and the barricades there is always the story of the candle-lit conspiracies by the planners—otherwise the revolution would be over in a trice.

Not only have our handful of leaders so far failed to realize the unheard-of proportions of the goal at which we must aim, but they have singularly failed to face up to their terrifying responsibilities in planning. Time after time, would-be leaders have arisen and led us in pitiful efforts to nip the end of the tiger's tail, only to waste our substance and blood and heroism in a fruitless struggle which always ends in being crushed by a single, smashing blow from the paw of the beast.

The Jewish world revolution can only be broken and beaten by a counter world revolution. Any revolution must be planned with care and precision in accordance with the iron laws governing human conduct in the mass. A world revolution, in the face of the international and staggering power of Jewry, must be planned and executed with a brilliance and ruthlessness unmatched in the history of the world.

The most fundamental rule of such a cataclysmic social upheaval as a revolution is: "The blood of the martyrs is the seed of the church!" Perhaps it sounds cruel and brutal, but it is nevertheless true, that the greater the proportion of human upheaval aimed at, the greater quantity of blood and torrents of tears which must be poured out in vast quantities to gain the goal. The kind of unprecedented, colossal movement which can alone reverse the suicidal trend of the Western world, and usher in even another thousand years of survival for the White man, can never be launched—let alone won—in any safe, painless, or easy way. Even ordinary sufferings and martyrdom are too minuscule for the kind of movement we must set aflame to survive. Everything about the current deadly battle for world mastery is and must be *Olympian*, and we cannot shrink from *Olympian agonies* if we are to hope to win.

Mighty movements always require millions of people to immolate themselves in a passion of self-sacrificing devotion to the cause. And these enormous masses of people can never be moved to fling themselves into the flames of revolution with shouts of "Favorable trade balance!" or "States' rights!" etc. Only the fundamental drives from deep inside the human psyche can lift the slow-moving masses from their ignorant apathy to the wild pitch of emotion which carries them entirely away in the tidal wave of revolution. Nothing so affects these fundamental emotions of the masses as *heroism*, and only the utmost heroism can now save the White man from his lethargy and paralyzing fear of the Jews.

And there is no symbol other than the swastika, and no name other than Adolf Hitler, which is so beautifully calculated to produce the persecution and consequent heroism which alone can unite and inflame the White man into an irresistible wave of anti-Jewish Marxist-Zionist revolution. Until the advent of Adolf Hitler, the White men of the world had nothing, absolutely *nothing* in the way of a common cause, common heroes, common martyrs, sacred shrines, names, and symbols. But now, after millions of young German White men heroically flung their precious lives away in the first real fight in history for the White elite, we finally have the blood-soaked shrines, symbols, and martyrs which are the most elementary stuff of revolution. Millions of equally precious young White men on the opposing side, fighting for the devilish Communist-Zionist Jews, will have lost their lives for absolutely nothing unless we accept this stupendous blood-sacrifice, and use it to ensure that never again will precious White blood be spilled fighting for Jews and negroes.

Nevertheless, and unbelievably, the lucky heirs of all this self-sacrifice and heroism—the recipients of these precious bloodstained banners and sacred names—reject their heritage as "impractical." "We can never win with open adherence to National Socialism and the Swastika," these gentlemen explain feebly. "The Jews have taught people to hate them too much," they add. "If we use the Swastika and praise Hitler too openly, they will throw us in prison or kill us!" And did they not throw all makers of revolutions, including the Jew makers of the Red revolution, in jail—and even kill some of them? Are we National Socialists to be more fearful and cowardly than a gang of Jews? The very persecution and bloodshed such irresolute characters seek to avoid is the *sine qua non* of our victory!

卐 卐 卐

These are not empty words. I have personally proved their truth here in America, the power center of world Jewry, by being beaten, by going to jail and the insane asylum, losing my dear family, and living like an animal. Twelve days from today, as I write this, I face jail again. These things are unpleasant and even heartbreaking—but they *must be!*

I have risen in two years to a commanding position in the worldwide fight for the White man, starting as a penniless, unknown, and unaided single individual like millions upon millions of others—simply and solely because I have gratefully and lovingly used the precious names and symbols which have been bathed and soaked in such oceans of blood and tears—the swastika and the name of the Leader, Adolf Hitler.

Temporary and flashy political successes are always easy. It is always simpler and quicker to put pads in one's jacket that to build the human muscles to fill the coat by months or years of work and sweat. For 50 years now, there has been a steady rise and fall of "right-wing" or White movements built entirely of pads. By endorsing motherhood and virtue and patriotism, etc., and by avoiding brutal statements of the real purpose of such organizations—which must necessarily be the extermination of the communist-Zionist enemies of humanity—great flocks of skittish "patriots," "conservatives," and even a few "tough" anti-Semites could be corralled. But these people are not attracted to such a movement because they are so inflamed with revolutionary zeal that they can hardly be restrained from attacking their tormentors in the streets. Rather they join the "patriot" society to relieve their guilty consciences by pretending to fight the Jews and their treason and terror by what they call "clever underground methods." They relieve themselves of their pent-up frustration at the tyranny of the Jews and negroes once a week at a "rally" (private, of course) and then hurry home happily for another week of profits, parties, and TV. Such Mighty Mouses are horrified when it is suggested that perhaps they should hand out pamphlets in the street, or picket some outrageous example of Jewish-communist arrogance.

And if one exposes not only the Jews for what they are, but also exposes these political loafers who siphon off the support and energy for a real battle, these heroes reply by howling that one is an *agent provocateur* working to get them all crucified as a bunch of Nazis—which, except for their disgusting cowardice, they might otherwise be.

It is not the task of the world anti-Jewish revolution to attract and organize these contemptible sneaks, but to drive them out of the way and out of business, where they will be unable to milk the movement of the tiny bit of available support for useless "projects," as they have been doing for years. Nothing accomplishes that task like the swastika. The political drones, profiteers, prostitutes, and cowards scoot with their tails between their legs from this hooked cross, as the devil does from holy water. On the other hand, the swastika has an irresistible attraction for the kind of daring, bold, devil-may-care fighting young men we need. In America, most of them are simply nigger-haters because of their pure White man's instinct. When they learn the Jews' part in the disgraceful negro situation, they become Nazis in minutes. Then it is the work of only months until they also understand the deeper significance, the idealism, and the true aims of the movement.

But even more important than these advantages, the blood-soaked swastika has a supernatural effect on Jews. It is after all only a few black lines—but it drives the Jews out of their usual sly and calculating frame of mind and makes them hysterical and foolish. To them, it is not just the lines, but the awful threat of ruthless exposure, swift justice, and terrible vengeance which their guilty consciences tell them they richly deserve. It is like a picture of the electric chair to a hunted murderer.

A calm, calculating Jew is the most dangerous beast on the face of the Earth. By the exercise of his devilish, perverted, but brilliant reason, the Jew has almost mastered all the rest of us. But a hysterical, screaming Jew, out of his mind with hate and fear of punishment for his crimes, is helpless putty in the hands of a calculating National Socialist. We have proved this time and again, when Jewish councils have spent millions of dollars to spread the word among the Jews to ignore us. But the hordes of guilty little sinners can't do it! When they see that swastika and hear us praising Adolf Hitler and describing the gas chambers for traitors, they become screaming, wild ghetto Jews who have eternally blown up their victories at the last moment by their insane passions of hate and revenge.

The result is the lifeblood of a political movement: *publicity!* In spite of the Jewish domination of all the media of public information, the parading of swastikas and National Socialists in public streets cannot be hidden or ignored without giving the game away. They can suppress the news, to be sure. But then too many people realize their press power and censorship. And when the young movement is able to force publication of its existence on the giant national TV networks, in magazines, the press, etc., it serves as a clarion call to the frustrated millions who are looking for such a movement. It is only thus that we have been able to contact thousands of people all over the world who have never before been in any "patriot" outfit but couldn't resist the American Nazi Party and the World Union of National Socialists.

The swastika and Hitler, far from being millstones, are actually the answer to the eternal problem of the right wing—*money!* When you don't have money for paper, meeting halls, etc. as our side never does—you can go into the streets and march and distribute homemade handbills and picket, for nothing. The Jews go wild, attack—and you then have free use of millions of dollars' worth of Jewish TV, newspapers, magazines, etc. Of course, you may get bloodied and have to sit in jail awhile recuperating, but this is a small price to pay for the astonishing results.

In addition to the free publicity attendant on open operation as a Nazi, you also find that the very audacity of the thing will attract the young fighting men you need, even though they know nothing and care less about the politics of the business. They admire raw courage and daring. Later, when they have come to know the facts a little better, they will fight for ideals and the White man. But until then, these valuable protectors of your free speech will fight just for fun.

Above all, the swastika will save you from the fundamental error of the right wing—that sweet *reason* will change the world and save us from the Jewish tyrants. Reason is still an infant in human affairs, a precious and rare development found in the mutational brains of an infinitesimal minority of Homo sapiens. And even the few geniuses able to exercise genuine, independent reason are almost entirely incapable of acting in accordance with the dictates of that reason—which is one of the reasons so many of them end up as failures in a world which does not appreciate them or their reason. It is *force, power, strength* which rules the world, from the ebb and flow of the tides to the decision of your neighbor to join the Rotary. Only a negligible fringe of oddball humans change their mind as a result of being convinced by a superior argument. The overwhelming masses, including the mass of today's "intellectuals," change their minds only in order to conform. In other words, the minds of the vast majority always bow to the strongest opinion—the opinion which brings rewards and avoids punishment.

The Right wing examines its reasons and arguments and facts and finds them true and good—as they may be. They then become outraged when the slobs next door cannot see and appreciate this rightness and, very probably, throw them out of the house for preaching "hate." But this is only as things are. The slobs will hold whatever opinion seems to show the most strength and *will to power*. The Right are completely, hopelessly female in their approach to reason and always, always prefer strength to "rightness." When they say "no" to our swastika and National Socialism, they are only the eternal female saying "no," but meaning, "If you accept my no, then you are a weakling and have no right to my favors. Let us see if you have the manhood and the strength to *make* me say yes!"

They hate us now because we are weak and powerless. All the reason in the world will never make them love us or our ideas in any guise, no matter how we try to sugar-coat them, until we command their respect and admiration for our will, our guts, our force! As stupid as they are, their instincts in smelling force and strength are still pure, and the attempt to *sneak* National Socialist ideas in the guise of "patriot leagues" and other nice, safe groups very properly repulses them as being the actions of cowards and sneaks.

To hell with the sneaky, safer approaches! They get us persecuted every bit as much as the direct, open approach, and they doom us to miserable, sneaking failure every time. If we are to be the last of the White men who conquered the world; if we are finally to be overwhelmed by a pack of rats, let us at least face the death of our race as our ancestors faced their death—*like men*. Let us not crawl down amongst the rats begging for mercy or trying to out-sneak them and pretend to be rats ourselves! Let us stand on the scaffold of history—if hang we must—like the martyrs of Nuremberg, tall and proud! Is life so sweet, is comfort so precious, and a job in a Jewish counting house so sacred that we are afraid to grasp the mighty hand of Adolf Hitler reaching down to us from our glorious past? Again, *to hell with sneaking and safety!*

It is part of the Jews to be sneaky and sly. The genius of our people has ever been joyous strength, robust forcefulness, directness, manly courage, and flaming heroism. When the Jews, with their economic terrorism, jails, bullies, and hangmen, scare the White man into laying down his cudgel and goad him into trying to out-sneak Jewish tyranny, the Jews have completely emasculated the once-strong White man, and doomed him to dishonor and defeat. The White man can *never* win by sneaking!

In the dawn of Nordic civilization, lesser races used to cringe in their crude huts and pray, "Lord, save us from the fury of the men of the North!" It was *that* kind of man who built Western civilization. If civilization is now to be saved from the swarms of degenerate Jews, their cannibal accomplices, and their unspeakably depraved liberal friends, it will be *that* kind of man who saves it, never a sneak!

卐 卐 卐

White man! The same iron blood of your mighty ancestors flows in your veins! The towering figure of Adolf Hitler reaches out a giant hand to lift you up to world-conquering power! You have cringed long enough before pygmies! Now rise! Defy the rats and vermin at your feet! Let them feel the toe and heel of your boot! *Stamp them out!*

You have been sleeping. When you rise and stand up, and the masses once more see what a man of force looks like, they will love you as they now imagine they hate you. With the spark of National Socialism, struck by Adolf Hitler, burning in your breast, you are unconquerable! *In hoc signo vinces!* By the sign of the swastika, you will conquer!

White man! Join hands with the heroes in America, Britain, Iceland, Denmark, and other White countries who have raised the holy swastika banner and defended it with their blood. It has risen from the ashes of Berlin, and never shall it be hauled down again. Stand with us before the altar of Adolf Hitler and the world-conquering White race, and pledge your life as we have, to bring the order and justice of Western, White civilization once more into the world. Let us teach the traitors and rats and pygmies once more to cringe in terror in their huts and pray, "Lord save us from the fury of the men of the North!"

APPENDIX C

The *Playboy* Interview (1966)

Editor: In early 1966, G. Lincoln Rockwell agreed to an interview with a major American periodical, *Playboy*. Though best known for their salacious photos of half-dressed young women, the magazine used its notoriety to conduct a long series of significant interviews with major figures of the day. For the Rockwell interview, the journal assigned a 45-year-old black journalist, Alex Haley. (Haley would later earn fame with his books *Roots* and *Autobiography of Malcolm X*.) The interview is remarkable for the frankness of both parties. Equally amazing is the fact that it ever appeared in print. *Playboy* clearly viewed this as an attack piece, something intended to destroy "Commander" Rockwell's public image, but Rockwell more than holds his ground, and gained substantial publicity in the process.

Haley: Before we begin, Commander, I wonder if you'd mind telling me why you're keeping that pistol there at your elbow, and this armed bodyguard between us.

Rockwell: Just a precaution. You may not be aware of the fact that I have received literally thousands of threats against my life. Most of them are from cranks, but some of them haven't been; there are bullet holes all over the outside of this building. Just last week, two gallon-jugs of flaming gasoline were flung against the house right under my window. I keep this gun within reach and a guard beside me during interviews because I've been attacked too many times to take any chances. I haven't yet been jumped by an impostor, but it wasn't long ago that 17 guys claiming to be from a university came here to "interview" me; nothing untoward happened, but we later found out they were armed and planned to tear down the flag, burn the joint, and beat me up. Only the fact that we were ready for that kind of rough stuff kept it from happening. We've never yet had to hurt anybody, but only because I think they all know we're ready to fight anytime. If you're who you claim to be, you have nothing to fear.

Haley: I don't.

Rockwell: Good. Just so we both know where we stand, I'd like to make something else crystal clear before we begin. I'm going to be honest and direct with you. You're here in your professional capacity; I'm here in my professional capacity. While here, you'll be treated well—but I see you're a black interviewer. It's nothing personal, but I want you to understand that I don't mix with your kind, and we call your race "niggers."

Haley: I've been called "nigger" many times, Commander, but this is the first time I'm being paid for it. So you go right ahead. What have you got against us "niggers"?

Rockwell: I've got nothing against you. I just think you people would be happier back in Africa where you came from. When the pilgrims got pushed around in Europe, they didn't have any sit-ins or crawl-ins; they got out and went to a wilderness and built a great civilization.

Haley: It was built with the help of Negroes.

Rockwell: Help or no, the White people in America simply aren't going to allow you to mix totally with them, whether you like it or not.

Haley: The purpose of the civil rights movement is equality of rights and opportunity, Commander—not miscegenation, as you seem to be implying.

Rockwell: Equality may be the stated purpose, but race mixing is what it boils down to in practice; and the harder you people push for that, the madder White people are going to get.

Haley: Do you think you're entitled to speak for White people?

Rockwell: Malcolm X said the same thing I'm saying.

Haley: He certainly was in no position to speak for White people.

Rockwell: Well, I think I am speaking for the majority of Whites when I say that race mixing just isn't going to work. I think, therefore, that we should take the billions of dollars now being wasted on foreign aid to

communist countries which hate us and give that money to our own niggers to build their own civilized nation in Africa.

Haley: Apart from the fact that Africa is already spoken for territorially by
sovereign nations, all but a few of the 20 million Negroes in this country
are native-born Americans who have just as much right to remain here as
you do, Commander.

Rockwell: That's not my point. When two people prove incompatible in
marriage and they can't live together, they separate; and the mass of average niggers simply don't "fit" in modern American society. A leopard
doesn't change his spots just because you bring him in from the jungle and
try to housebreak him and turn him into a pet. He may learn to sheathe his
claws in order to beg a few scraps off the dinner table, and you may teach
him to be a beast of burden, but it doesn't pay to forget that he'll always be
what he was born: a wild animal.

Haley: We're talking about human beings, not animals.

Rockwell: We're talking about niggers—and there's no doubt in my mind
that they're basically animalistic.

Haley: In what way?

Rockwell: Spiritually. Our White kids are being perverted, like Pavlov's
dogs, by conditioned-reflex training. For instance, every time a White kid
is getting a piece of ass, the car radio is blaring nigger bebop. Under such
powerful stimuli, it's not long before a kid begins unconsciously to connect these savage sounds with intense pleasure and thus transfers his natural pleasurable reactions in sex to an unnatural love of the chaotic and animalistic nigger music, which destroys a love of order and real beauty
among our kids. This is how you niggers corrupt our White kids—without
even laying a dirty hand on them. Not that you wouldn't like to.

Haley: It's sometimes the other way around, Commander.

Rockwell: Well, I'll have to admit one great failing of my own people:
The White man is getting too soft. The niggers are forced to do hard manual labor, and as a result, most nigger bucks are healthy animals—rugged

and tough, the way nature intended a male to be. When you take a look at how the average, bourgeois White man spends his time, though—hunched over a desk, going to the ballet, riding around on his electric lawn mower or squatting on his fur-lined toilet seat—you can't help but observe how soft and squishy a lot of White men allow themselves to become; especially some of the skinny, pasty-faced White peace creeps with their long hair, their fairy-looking clothes and the big yellow stripe up their spineless back. What normal woman would want one of these cruds? Unfortunately, some of our White women, especially in the crazy leftist environment on our college campuses, get carried away by Jewish propaganda into betraying their own instincts by choosing a healthy black buck instead of one of these skinny, pansified White peace creeps who swarm on our college campuses.

Haley: Are you implying that the Negro male is sexually superior to the White man?

Rockwell: Certainly not. The average White workingman, the vast majority of White men, are just as tough and ballsy as any nigger who ever lived. It's the White intellectuals who have allowed themselves to be degenerate physically, mentally, and especially spiritually, until I am forced to admit that a healthy nigger garbage man is certainly superior physically and sexually to a pasty-faced skinny White peace creep.

Haley: Do you consider Negroes superior to White men in any other way?

Rockwell: On the contrary—I consider them inferior to the White man in every other way.

Haley: That's a fairly sweeping generalization. Can you document it?

Rockwell: When I speak at colleges, they often ask me the same question. I always answer with a question of my own: How do colleges determine the superior and inferior students? By performance, that's how! Look at history; investigate the different races. The Chinese perform; they've created a great civilization. And the White races certainly perform. But the nigger race, until very recently, has done absolutely nothing.

Haley: How recently?

Rockwell: The past 20 or 30 years.

Haley: What about the contribution of those millions of African Negroes and their descendants—along with that of migrants of every color from all over the world—who helped found and build this country?

Rockwell: I don't dismiss it, but the fact is that any contribution of the niggers has been almost entirely manual and menial. Horses could have done most of it, or well-trained monkeys from the same trees they were flushed out of back in Africa. They've picked up a few more tricks since then—but only what they've learned from the White man.

Haley: Recent archaeological findings have documented the existence of advanced black African civilizations centuries before the dawn of comparable cultures in Europe.

Rockwell: If they were so far ahead of us then, why are they still shooting blow darts at each other while we're launching rockets to the moon?

Haley: The American space program isn't a segregated project, Commander. There are many Negroes working for NASA and in the space industry.

Rockwell: This only proves my point. A few niggers, like trained chimpanzees, have been pushed and jammed into such things as the space program by our race-mixing presidents and the federal government; but niggers didn't originate any of the ideas or develop the fantastic organizations capable of putting men into space. The niggers in NASA are like chimpanzees who have learned to ride bicycles. A few trained monkeys riding bicycles doesn't prove that chimpanzees could invent or build or even think about a bicycle. The fact is that the average nigger is not as intelligent as the average White man.[1]

Haley: There's no genetic or anthropological evidence to substantiate that.

Rockwell: I know you're going to say you can show me thousands of intelligent niggers and stupid White men. I'm well aware that there are exceptions on both sides. All I'm saying is that the average of your people is

---

[1] The average black IQ is around 85, versus the White average of 100. This means that only one in six blacks is even above-average intelligence.

below the average of my people; and the pure-black ones are even further below us. I have living evidence of this sitting right in front of me.

Haley: If you mean me, I'm far from pure black—as you can see.

Rockwell: That's just it: You're an intelligent person; I enjoy talking to you. But, you're not pure black like your ancestors in the Congo. Now, this may insult you, but we're not here to throw pansies at each other. There had to be some White people in your background somewhere, or you wouldn't be brown instead of black. Right?

Haley: Right.

Rockwell: Well, I'm saying that your intelligence comes from the blood of my people. Whenever they trot out some smart nigger and say, "See? Look how brilliant niggers are," what they usually show you is a part-White man with some nigger blood in him. This doesn't prove that niggers are great. On the contrary; it proves that White blood can make a part-nigger more intelligent.

Haley: That's not proof, Commander. Can you offer any authoritative documentation to support your view?

Rockwell: A psychologist named George O. Ferguson made a definitive study of the connection between the amount of White blood and intelligence in niggers. He tested all the nigger schoolchildren in Virginia and proved that the pure-black niggers did only about 70 percent as well as the White children. Niggers with one White grandparent did about 75 percent as well as the White children. Niggers with two White grandparents did still better, and niggers with three White grandparents did almost as well as the White kids. Since all of these nigger children shared exactly the same environment as niggers, it's impossible to claim that environment produced these tremendous changes in performance.[2]

Haley: In his book *A Profile of the Negro American* (1964), the world-famed sociologist T. F. Pettigrew states flatly that the degree of White ancestry does not relate in any way to Negro IQ scores. According to Petti-

---

[2] *The Psychology of the Negro* (1916).

grew, the brightest Negro yet reported—with a tested IQ of 200—had no traceable Caucasian heritage whatever.

Rockwell: The fact that you can show me one very black individual who is superior to me doesn't convince me that the average nigger is superior. The startling fact I see is that the lighter they are, the smarter they are, and the blacker they are, the dumber they are.

Haley: That's an opinion, Commander, not a fact. Can you back it up with any concrete evidence?

Rockwell: The evidence of lifelong experience. I've never met a black nigger—I mean a real black one, so black he looks purple—that can talk, and think as, say, you can. When I do, then maybe I'll change my opinion. All the really black niggers are either what you call Uncle Toms, or they're revolutionists, or they just want to loaf, loot, and rape.

Haley: Most sociologists would agree that the vast majority of Negroes— dark-skinned or otherwise—don't fit into any of those categories.

Rockwell: Like I said, there are always exceptions—but everybody knows that they prove the rule. Evolution shows that in the long run, if the superior mixes with the inferior, the product is halfway between, and inferior to what you started with in the original superior group—in other words, mongrelized.

Haley: The words 'superior' and 'inferior' have no meaning to geneticists, Commander—and neither does mongrelization. Every authority in the field has attested that the world's racial groups are genetically indistinguishable from one another. All men, in other words—including hybrids—are created equal.

Rockwell: You're bringing tears to my eyes. Don't you know that all this equality garbage was started by a Jew anthropologist named Franz Boas from Columbia University? Boas was followed by another Jew from Columbia named Gene Weltfish. And our present Jew expert preaching equality is another Jew named Ashley Montagu. Any anthropologist who dares to preach the facts known by any farmer in the barnyard—that breeds differ in quality—is simply not allowed to survive in the universities or in publishing, because he can't earn a living. You never hear from that side.

But Carleton Putnam has written a wonderful book called *Race and Reason* (1961), showing that there is plenty of scholarly evidence to back up my contention that the nigger race is inherently inferior to the White race intellectually. This equality garbage is straight Soviet, Lysenkian biology—direct from the communist Lysenko, who preached that by changing the environment you could grow one plant from another plant's seeds. This is the doctrine that's destroying our society—because it's not true. You can't grow wheat from corn by changing the environment.

Haley: You can't grow wheat from corn by changing anything. In any case, we're discussing human beings, not foodstuffs.

Rockwell: I don't feel like quibbling. What I'm saying is that I believe the Jews have consciously perverted the study of anthropology and biology and human genetics in order to reach this phony conclusion—and thus destroy the great White race.

Haley: What phony conclusion?

Rockwell: The totally erroneous notion that heredity has nothing to do with why, for example, the niggers have lower scholastic averages and higher illegitimacy rates than Whites.

Haley: According to geneticists, it doesn't. In any case, how would acceptance of this notion lead to the destruction of the White race?

Rockwell: By deluding people into believing that the nigger is only "underprivileged" rather than inherently inferior; into believing, therefore, that he can be cleaned up and smartened up by letting him eat in our restaurants, study in our schools, move into our neighborhoods. The next inevitable step is to take him into our beds—and this would lead to the mongrelization, and hence the destruction, of the White race.

Haley: You said that the Jews are behind this plot. Since they're Whites themselves, how would they benefit from their own destruction?[3]

---

[3] This is a myth; Jews are not White, in any meaningful sense of the term. Jews can be light-skinned, but Whites, by definition, derive from an indigenous European stock. Jews claim to be White only when it serves their purposes.

Rockwell: They won't be mingling like the rest of us. They believe they're too pure to mix; they think they're "the chosen people"—chosen to rule the world. But the only world they could rule would be a world of inferior beings. And as long as the White man is pure, they cannot succeed. But when the White man permits himself to be mixed with black men, then the Jews can master him.

Haley: How?

Rockwell: They already run the niggers. Except for the Black Muslims, the Jews run practically all the big civil rights organizations.

Haley: You're misinformed, Commander. The key posts in all but one of the major civil rights groups—the NAACP—are held entirely by Negroes.

Rockwell: They're just the front men. The Jews operate behind the scenes, pulling the strings and holding the moneybags.

Haley: The Jews who belong and contribute to these groups serve strictly in an advisory capacity.

Rockwell: *You're* misinformed. As I started to say, Jews want to run the White people just the way they run the niggers. Once they get the White people mixed with the black people, the White people will be just as easy to run as the niggers.

Haley: Why?

Rockwell: Because when you mix superior and inferior, like I told you, the product is inferior—halfway between the two. The Jews would be able to outwit and outmaneuver and thus manipulate the mongrelized White man just the way he already does the niggers. That's what the whole so-called civil rights movement is all about; and they're just liable to get away with it if the good White Christians of this country don't wake up and get together before it's too late to restore the natural order of things.

Haley: And what's that?

Rockwell: Separation. In nature, all things of a similar being tend to group together. Chimpanzees do not run with baboons; they run with chimpanzees. This is the natural order of people, too. Even in thoroughly integrated colleges, when I visit them, I notice that niggers usually sit and eat at tables with other niggers—even though they don't have to. And the White people sit with other White people. I think this is the natural tendency, and to attempt to pervert this is to fight nature.

Haley: You fail to make an important moral and constitutional distinction between choosing to associate with one's own race and being forced to do so. Left to themselves, some people will mingle and some won't; and most Americans think this is just the way it ought to be.

Rockwell: That's all very noble-sounding; it brings a lump to my throat. But what does it boil down to in practice? Every time your people move into my neighborhood, the White people move out; and often there's violence—by peaceful, decent White men who never before committed any, but are outraged at the black invasion.

Haley: That's an exaggeration, Commander. The record shows that fewer and fewer White people are moving out when Negroes move into White neighborhoods; and the fact is that violence very seldom occurs because of Negro "block-busting." In most instances, after an initial period of strain, the newcomers are being quietly accepted.

Rockwell: I don't know what neighborhoods you've been hanging around in, but my own experience has been that violence and animosity are the rule rather than the exception. And that goes double when one of my guys moves into a place like Watts. Your people don't just riot; they try to kill him. This is natural. Their instincts are coming out, and they always will. And any effort to override these instincts, or deny they exist, will inevitably be unsuccessful. Nature will prevail.

Haley: Negro hostility toward Nazis could hardly be offered as proof that integration is unnatural. Nor is anti-Nazi violence confined to Negroes.

Rockwell: You're right—the Jews are even better at it.

卐 卐 卐

Haley: You've been quoted as saying that the Watts, Harlem, and Rochester riots, among others, were actually instigated by Jews. Do you have any evidence to substantiate that charge?

Rockwell: I didn't say they started them; I said they engineered them. First of all, they tell the niggers, "You people don't have to obey the laws you don't like"—just like Martin Luther Coon preaches. If a cop arrests a nigger, it's "police brutality." And he's told he should fight back. Whenever a policeman tries to do his duty, the Jew-oriented niggers have been told to try and take the prisoner away from this brutal cop. The Jews turn him into a psychological bomb—so that when a cop comes along and does his duty it's just like touching a match to a fuse. Boom—up it goes! Like it did in Watts. Like they do in Harlem.

Haley: In both the Watts and Harlem riots, the bulk of the property damage was suffered by Jewish-owned stores and businesses. Why would the Jews foment violence that's bound to result in the destruction of their own property?

Rockwell: It just happens that most of the businessmen making money off the niggers in the ghettos are Jews. The big Jews in charge are willing to sacrifice the little Jews, just as a general sacrifices some troops to win a war.

Haley: But what could any Jews possibly win by engineering riots?

Rockwell: They're just natural-born agitators. They just can't help coming in and getting everybody all stirred up—and they're always the ones to suffer for it. Every time! But they just can't quit. It's irrational as hell. With all their liberalism and their preaching about equal rights for niggers, they've promoted disorder and chaos that's eventually going to bury them. The liquor dealers are getting it now. Last summer, all those kike store owners in Watts kept screaming, "Oy! Stop! Listen! We're your friends!" —while the coons beat their brains out. And that's just the beginning, just a sample of things to come. This summer I predict that racial violence even more terrible than Watts will erupt—all because of these two troublemaking inferior races.

卐 卐 卐

Haley: In judging Negroes "inferior" to Whites, you said a while ago that you made this appraisal on the basis of "performance." Do you find Jews inferior for the same reason?

Rockwell: I've never accused the Jews of being incapable of performing. As a matter of fact, I think there's a good chance they're superior to everybody else in terms of actual mental capabilities. I think the average Jew is probably sharper intellectually than the average gentile, because for years and years he's had to live by his wits. Consequently, there has evolved a race of Jews who are more agile mentally than the rest of us.

Haley: In what way do you consider Jews inferior, then?

Rockwell: Spiritually. I believe that a human being, in order to be a successful person, in addition to performing—inventing a rocket or something—has got to have something he believes in, something more than his own survival, something that's a little bigger than himself. The Jews don't. They've even got a rabbi now who admits he's an atheist—Rabbi Sherwin Wine of Birmingham, Michigan.

Haley: Perhaps you didn't know that the current Church movement toward disbelief in God originated among the Protestant clergy. In any case, Rabbi Wine's convictions are a minority voice and could not in any way be said to represent those of the Jewish faith in general. Most Jews continue to believe in God, as set down in the Torah.

Rockwell: Jews talk a lot about God. But actually their god, just like Marx said, is money.[4] Cash! This is where the Jews fail—in their lack of idealism. Most of them are strictly materialists at heart. Wherever the Jews have gone, they've moved into a friendly, unsuspecting country and promptly started to glut on its people and resources. They think they're engaging in business, but actually what they're doing is eating the country up alive. And when people begin to resent their viciousness and greed, and either kick the Jews out or kill them, they always scream "Persecution!" That's not persecution. It's self-defense.

---

[4] "What is the secular basis of Judaism? Practical need, self-interest. What is the worldly religion of the Jew? Huckstering. What is his worldly God? Money." (Marx, "On the Jewish Question," 1844).

Haley: Are you implying that Hitler was justified in exterminating 6 million European Jews?

Rockwell: I don't believe for one minute that any 6 million Jews were exterminated by Hitler. It never happened.[5] You want me to prove it to you?

Haley: Go ahead.

Rockwell: We have the figures for the number of Jews in the world in 1939, before World War II: 15,688,259; and the figures for the number living after World War II: 18 million. Now, if you take the number of Jews for after World War II—and add the 6 million you say were gassed, you get a total of 24 million—which means that there would have to have been a 50-percent increase in the Jewish population during a period of about five years. Even people as good at sex as the Jews couldn't possibly reproduce that fast. So you see, the Jews' own figures convict them as liars![6]

Haley: What's your source for these statistics?

Rockwell: The prewar figures came from the 1947 *World Almanac*, page 219; and the postwar figures from *The New York Times*, February 22, 1948, in an article by Hanson Baldwin.[7]

Haley: Population figures aside, do you deny the validity of documentary photographic evidence showing the gas chambers themselves, and the thousands of bodies piled up in concentration-camp trenches?

Rockwell: I emphatically deny that there is any valid proof that innocent Jews were systematically murdered by the Nazis. The photographs you've seen that have been passed off as pictures of dead Jews have been identified as pictures of the corpses of German civilians—mostly women and

---

[5] Rockwell was an early proponent of Holocaust revisionism. And he was largely correct, even from the standpoint of current revisionist research: far fewer than 6 million Jews were killed in WW2 (and none in gas chambers). Most current revisionists argue for a death toll under 1 million, and perhaps as low as 500,000.

[6] In other words, the 15.7 million prewar Jews would have had to skyrocket to 24 million even as 6 million were being gassed, to reach a postwar figure of 18 million.

[7] There is evidence that Jews self-reported exaggerated numbers beginning around 1900. The likely figure for 1939 is about 12 million globally. A loss of 500,000 during WW2 would bring that down to the 11.5 million reported just after the war.

children and refugees—who were killed in the one-night Allied bombing of Dresden, which slaughtered 350,000 innocent people.[8]

Haley: By whom have these pictures been so identified?

Rockwell: By Matt Koehl, my research chief, who says that you can recognize the buildings in the background of these so-called Nazi atrocity photographs as buildings in Dresden.

Haley: We don't accept the findings of your research chief as authoritative.

Rockwell: I have conclusive evidence to prove that some of these "documentary" photographs are frauds, pure and simple. In interviews published by the Jews and sold all over America, they show a bottle supposedly containing soap made by the Germans out of the poor, dead, gassed Jews.[9]

Haley: What evidence do you have for claiming that it's fraudulent?

Rockwell: Common sense. That soap could have been made out of anything; it could have been melted down from a dozen bars of Lifebuoy. But here's my ultimate proof of just how utterly ridiculous all the anti-Nazi literature you've read really is: an article in *Sir* interviews, March 1958, on how the Nazis gassed and burned and murdered everybody. It's by "a former corporal of the SS" as told to an American Army master sergeant who signs himself "Lew Cor." Well, "Lew Cor" is simply Rockwell spelled backward. I wrote it myself—as a test. I wrote the vilest lies I could think of! And here they all are in print in this interview. Look at the photographs! These are supposed to be actual shots of Nazi victims mentioned in the article—victims that I invented!

Haley: Your own willingness to lie about Nazi atrocities doesn't prove that the Jews have done the same thing, Commander. Do you also dismiss the

---

[8] Most conventional sources cite a figure of about 25,000 killed, but they have incentive to undercount, given that the majority of those killed were women, children, and the elderly.
[9] The myth of Jews turned into soap was documented at the Nuremberg Trials, but is totally discredited by all parties today.

testimony of hundreds of prison-camp survivors who have given eyewit-ness testimony about Nazi atrocities?[10]

Rockwell: I have an affidavit from a Jewish doctor, a prisoner at Ausch-witz, who says there were no gas chambers.

Haley: Do you have that affidavit?

Rockwell: I'll send you a photostat. I believe the gas chambers in these concentration camps were built after the war—by Jewish Army officers. We know this for sure: It was mostly Jewish Army officers who went in there to liberate these camps. And it was mostly Jewish Army CIC officers who were in charge of the Nuremberg trials. It was they who tortured in-nocent Nazis, using any kind of vile method they could to cook up phony evidence.[11]

Haley: Can you prove these charges?

Rockwell: I know of several cases where American personnel resigned in disgust at the methods used.

Haley: That doesn't prove that torture was used to extract false testimony. In any case, you still haven't said whether you dismiss eyewitness testimo-ny of Nazi atrocities.

Rockwell: Certainly I do. I've lost count of the times I've been in court, after being assaulted and beaten by gangs of Jews, and seen these same Jews get up on the witness stand, with tears pouring down their faces, and tell how I attacked them! The Jews are the world's master liars![12] They are geniuses at it. Why, when a kike is up on a witness stand, he doesn't even need onions to start the tears pouring.

---

[10] Jewish camp survivors have made countless false and absurd claims about al-leged Nazi atrocities; see *Holocaust Encyclopedia: Uncensored and Uncon-strained* (2023).

[11] American Jews in fact tortured and coerced evidence from captive Germans. See *Holocaust Encyclopedia* (above), "Van Roden, Edward"; see also *Streicher, Ros-enberg, and the Jews* (T. Dalton, 2020), pp. 14-23.

[12] This has been noted by critics of Jews for millennia. Arthur Schopenhauer, for example, called them "great masters of the lie." For details, see T. Dalton, *Eternal Strangers* (2020).

卐 卐 卐

Haley: It's said that you keep a model gas chamber here at your headquarters. Is that true?

Rockwell: No, but we have an electric chair at Sing Sing that's already done a great deed for America in frying the Rosenbergs; and there are hundreds of thousands more Rosenbergs running around America who need frying—or gassing.[13]

Haley: By "more Rosenbergs," do you mean more Jews or more communist spies?

Rockwell: More communist Jews. They're practically the same thing.

Haley: Are you saying that many Jews are communists, or that many communists are Jewish?

Rockwell: I use the term "communist Jews" in exactly the same sense that I would say "Italian gangsters." Most Italians are not gangsters, but everybody knows that the Mafia is mostly Italians. Well, my experience is that communism is as Jewish as the Mafia is Italian. It's a fact that almost all of the convicted spies for communism have been atheist Jews like the Rosenbergs. And international communism was invented by the Jew Karl Marx and has since been led mostly by Jews—like Trotsky.

Haley: Stalin, Khrushchev, Brezhnev, Kosygin and Mao Tse-tung, among many others, certainly aren't Jews.

Rockwell: The Jews operate nowadays mostly as spies and agitators for the Reds. Mind you, I'm not saying that there aren't vast numbers of Jews who despise communism.

Haley: Yet you say there are hundreds of thousands of Jewish communists in America?

Rockwell: Perhaps more.

---

[13] Julius and Ethel Rosenberg were electrocuted in 1953 for treason.

Haley: What evidence do you have to back up that figure?

Rockwell: Plain statistics. Fourteen of the 16 Americans convicted in US courts of treason as communist spies have been racial Jews and one of them was a nigger. Of the 21 communist leaders convicted in Judge Medina's court, 19 were racial Jews. Of the so-called "second-string Politburo" communist leaders rounded up, more than 90 percent were racial Jews.

Haley: The total number of convicted spies who you say are Jewish comes to 33. That's far from hundreds of thousands.

Rockwell: There's also evidence in black and white. Even in their own publications, the Jews do not hide from the Jewishness of communism. It's there for anybody to see. For instance, the largest-circulation communist newspaper in America is not *The Worker*, but a paper published in Yiddish called *The Morning Freiheit*. Any American can get a copy of this Jewish communist newspaper and read, in the English portions, the open communist treason they're preaching.

Haley: The views of *The Morning Freiheit* certainly can't be said to reflect those of most American Jews, Commander. Can you give a specific example of a pro-Marxist statement by any recognized spokesman for American Jewry?

Rockwell: Just one? That's easy. Let's take a statement made by Rabbi Stephen Wise; he's one of the leading spokesmen for American Jewry.

Haley: He died in 1949.

Rockwell: Well, before he died, he wrote, "Some call it communism; I call it Judaism." That's a direct quote. I'd say that's putting it pretty unequivocally, wouldn't you?

Haley: Can you produce proof of that statement?

Rockwell: Certainly. I'll send it to you.[14]

Haley: Do you have any tangible evidence to substantiate your charges?

Rockwell: Would you accept evidence based on a statistical sampling?

Haley: Let's hear it.

Rockwell: Out of the number of Jews that I have known personally, a tremendous proportion—at least 50 percent, maybe as high as 85 or 90 percent—have been pro-Red; either card-carrying communists or accessories before or after the fact, either openly and knowingly aiding and abetting communism and promoting the communist overthrow of this government, or assisting the communist enemies who are killing Americans, or consciously suppressing legal evidence which would tend to convict such traitors.

Haley: Your own conjectures about the political sympathies of Jews you've known personally, Commander, could hardly be accepted as evidence to support your allegations about them, let alone the "hundreds of thousands" you say are pro-Red. In any case, you say they "need frying—or gassing." On what grounds?

Rockwell: Treason. Everybody—not just Jews—with suspicious records of pro-communism, or treasonable Zionism, or any subversive attack on this country or its people, should be investigated and arrested and the evidence placed before a grand jury. If they're indicted, they should be tried for treason, and if they're convicted, they should be killed.

Haley: How?

Rockwell: Well, there are going to be hundreds of thousands of Jewish traitors to execute, don't forget. I don't see how you can strap that many people in electric chairs and get the job done before they all die of old age; so it seems to me that mass gas chambers are going to be the only solution for the communist traitor problem in America.

---

[14] Rockwell evidently never supplied the proof, and the quotation is likely spurious. Still, communism is a construction of the Jew Karl Marx, and thus is undoubtedly a product of Jewish thinking and values.

Haley: Your suggestion of gas chambers as a "solution for the communist traitor problem" is reminiscent of the "final solution for the Jewish problem" instituted by the Nazis in Germany. Are you planning to lead another anti-Semitic crusade along the lines laid down by Hitler?[15]

Rockwell: The crusade I plan to lead will be much broader in scope than that. In Germany, Hitler produced a local "lab experiment"; he provided me with an ideology in the same way that Marx provided one for Lenin. My task is to turn this ideology into a world movement. And I'll never be able to accomplish that by preaching pure Aryanism as Hitler did—by glorifying the Nordic-Germanic people as a "master race." There is an easily identifiable master race, however: the White race. You can find it all over the world. This is what I'm fighting for—not Aryanism, but White Christian solidarity. In the long run, I intend to win over the people of Greece, of Germany, of Italy, of England, of Canada, of France, of Spain, of Latin America, of Rhodesia, of South Africa—the people of every White Christian country in the world. All the White Christian countries of the Earth I would try to mold into one racial, religious, political, and military entity. I want them eventually to have hegemony.

Haley: Over the non-White, non-Christian nations?

Rockwell: Over the Afro-Asian bloc, which is to me the ultimate danger the earth faces. Worse than the bomb! These people have something both communism and democracy have lost. They're fanatics! They're full of this wild-eyed belief and vitality that the White man has gradually been losing. If they ever unite, there will be almost a billion of them against the White man—a ratio of seven to one. They're breeding so fast that the odds could easily be 10 or 15 to one before too long. When these billions of primitive colored people are able to control an atom or an H-bomb, as Red China may soon be able to do, we could wipe out a hundred million of them, and there would still be plenty more who kept coming. The White race couldn't take that kind of a bloodletting for long. We'd be wiped out! The huge masses of semi-animal colored people would simply sweep over us, and there'd be nothing we could do about it. It would be the ultimate

---

[15] Despite common perception, Hitler's "final solution" never involved homicidal gas chambers. For him, it was always a territorial solution involving ethnic cleansing and enforced deportation. See T. Dalton, *Debating the Holocaust*, or G. Rudolf, *Lectures on the Holocaust*.

victory of quantity over quality—unless the White people unite first. We're in real trouble if they get together first.

But make no mistake: There's going to be a battle of Armageddon, and it's going to be not between communism and democracy, but between the colored millions of the world and the small but elite corps of White men; ideological, economic, and philosophical issues will play little or no part in it. When the time comes—and it's later than we think—I plan to be ready not only to defend myself, but to lead the millions of Whites all over the world who today are foolishly pretending they don't know what's going on.

Haley: Estimates of your nationwide membership range from 25 to 100. Do you propose to lead the White Christian nations with this handful of followers?

Rockwell: In the first place, we're a world movement, just as communism is a world movement rather than a local or a national organization. We've launched a world union of National Socialists, of which I am the international commander. In the second place, you've got those figures wrong. In this country alone, we've got about 500 storm troopers—that's men ready for street action—plus about 1500 Party members. Also about 15,000 correspondents—people sympathetic to our cause who write in and donate. And our membership abroad numbers in the thousands.

Haley: Where abroad?

Rockwell: Let me name you countries. Argentina: Horst Eichmann, Adolf Eichmann's son, is our leader there; he's either in jail or disappeared, but our movement is growing there. In Australia, our movement is temporarily busted up, but my leader—an American—is running around under cover, trying to get his group back together again. In Spain, we've got a pretty good undercover movement, but Franco doesn't appreciate it, so we have to stay under cover. In England, Colin Jordan is operating wide open—and doing very well. In France, we've got a damned good group; they were all arrested just a while back. In Belgium, I've got an ex-SS paratrooper in charge, and he's doing very well. In Sweden, we've got a tremendous group; they were all just arrested. In Austria—our guy is in jail, so things are pretty well broken up there.

In Canada, John Beattie is leading a tremendous and successful movement. Our leader in Chile is in jail. In Germany, we've gone under cover; our leader is going to jail shortly. In Holland, we're doing fine. In

Ireland, they're coming along fast. In Italy, we've got a real tremendous movement. In Japan, one of our guys stabbed the Socialist deputy. Remember? New Zealand is coming along fine. But Norway isn't doing too good. We've a fine group in South Africa now, though, and we've got a group in Rhodesia now, too.

So you see, we've got groups all over the world. They're still little. But after all, it's only been 20 years since Hitler died. Twenty years after Christ was crucified, there were almost no Christians. Right now, the followers of the swastika are in the catacombs, like the original followers of the cross were then. I can't say we're a Christian movement in the ordinary sense; in fact, I personally am an agnostic. But I deeply believe that there is a power greater than ours that's helping us in our fight to keep the world natural and racially pure—as opposed to perverted and mongrelized. We've got an ideology, a dedication, a belief, a vitality to match the zealotry of the fanatical Asian-African bloc. That's why we're going to grow; that's why—eventually—we're going to prevail.

Haley: Can you tell us just how you plan to go about fulfilling this destiny —with or without divine intervention?

Rockwell: I have a four-phase plan. The first phase is to reach the masses; you can do nothing until you've reached the masses. In order to reach them—without money, without status, without a public platform—you have to become a dramatic figure. Now, in order to achieve that, I've had to take a lot of garbage: being called a nut and a monster and everything else. But by hanging up the swastika, I reach the masses. The second phase is to disabuse them of the false picture they have gotten of me, to educate them about what my real program is. The third phase will be to organize the people I've educated into a political entity. And the fourth phase will be to use that political entity as a machine to win political power.

That's the plan. They all overlap, of course. Right now we're about 50 percent involved in phase two; we're actually beginning to educate people—in interviews like this one, in speaking engagements at colleges and the like. The other 50 percent is still phase one—just raising hell to keep people aware that there's such a thing as the American Nazi Party, not caring what they call us, as long as they call us something.

Haley: What kind of hell-raising?

Rockwell: Well, I haven't done it yet, but one of my ambitions is to rent a plane and skywrite a big smoke swastika over New York City—on Hitler's birthday. That sort of thing. Or I might get one plane to do the Star of David, and I'll come in another plane and squat and do brown smoke all over it—on Ben-Gurion's birthday. I've checked federal regulations, and they couldn't do a thing about it. All I need is the money to do it. But that's in the future. One of the biggest things we've already done to propagandize ourselves is our "Coon-ard Lines Boat Tickets to Africa." It's our most popular mail-order item; White high school students order them by the thousands. Would you like me to read you what a ticket entitles one nigger to?[16]

Haley: Go ahead.

Rockwell: Six things. One: a free trip to Africa on a Cadillac-shaped luxury liner. Two: choice cuts of all the bananas and missionaries desired *en route*, and a free jar of meat tenderizer. NAACP members may sit up front and twist to Martin Luther Coon's jazz band. Three: a barrel of hair-grease axle grease delicately scented with nigger sweat. Four: a framed picture of Eleanor Roosevelt and Harry Golden. Five: an unguarded chicken coop and watermelon patch on deck, plus fish and chips for breakfast. And six: plenty of wine, marijuana, heroin, and other refreshments. And on the reverse side, we offer White liberal peace creeps a year's supply of "Instant Nigger." It's described as "Easy-mixing powder! Just sprinkle this dingy black dust on any sidewalk! Just make water on it, and presto! Hundreds of niggers spring up—little niggers, big niggers, fat niggers, skinny niggers, light niggers, midnight-black niggers, red niggers, even Jew niggers." It reads here, "Why wait? With this Instant Nigger Powder, any nigger-loving beatnik peace creep can have all the niggers he can stand!" Want one? Compliments of the house.

卐 卐 卐

Haley: Is mail-order hate literature your main source of income?

---

[16] See image in Chapter 10.

Rockwell: That, plus initiation fees from new members; plus small donations from those who believe in what we're trying to do; plus the proceeds from special events like one of our "hate-nannies".[17]

Haley: What are they?

Rockwell: Big musical jamborees. We hold them on patriotic holidays.

Haley: Would you give an example of a hate-nanny lyric?

Rockwell: Sure. Remember, you asked for it: "Ring that bell, shout for joy / White man's day is here / Gather all those equals up / Herd them on the pier / America for Whites / Africa for blacks / Send those apes back to the trees / Ship those niggers back / Twenty million ugly coons are ready on their pier / America for Whites / Africa for blacks / Ring that bell, shout for joy / The White man's day is here / Hand that chimp his ugly stick / Hand that buck his spear ..." That's just the first part of that song. Do you want to hear more of it?

Haley: No, we get the general idea.

Rockwell: Well, I believe a man ought to hoist up his flag and tell you what he is. And that's just what we do here.

Haley: Are there any anti-Jewish ballads in your hate-nanny song bag?

Rockwell: Oh, yes! One of our favorites is "The Jews Are Through in '72." It goes to the tune of "Mademoiselle from Armentières." Want to hear it?

Haley: We'll listen.

Rockwell: "The Jews are through in '72, parlez-vous / The Jews are through in '72, parlez-vous / We'll feed them bacon till they yell / And send them all to kosher hell / Hinky dinky, parlez-vous ..." The chorus repeats, and then comes the next verse: "We'll steal the rabbi's knife and

---

[17] A play on the word 'hootenanny,' which is hillbilly slang for an impromptu folk music festival.

sheath / And make him do it with his teeth / Hinky dinky, parlez-vous."
The rest of it I don't remember.

卐 卐 卐

Haley: The song says the Jews will be "through in '72." Is that date significant in some way?

Rockwell: 1972 is the year I'm going to be elected President on the National Socialist ticket. Five years of the Johnson administration will leave
the country so torn with racial tensions that some Republican will be a
cinch to win in 1968. Then, in 1969, a great economic catastrophe is going
to hit this country.

Haley: The nation's economy has never been healthier than it is today, and
most economists predict that the end of the boom is not in sight.

Rockwell: Nevertheless, there will be an economic catastrophe, though of
what nature I'm not sure. It could be an inflation. I say so because all this
build-up is based on sand. America's so-called prosperity is based on debt,
war, and inflationary money which has no backing and is bound to collapse. Along about 1969, it's all going to come tumbling down like a house
of cards, and the president is going to be blamed for it. In the ensuing economic chaos, plus all the racial warfare, the people will welcome a man
who stands unequivocally for the White Christian majority.[18]

Haley: What makes you think so?

Rockwell: As I travel, I find that people everywhere, from the smallest
towns to the biggest cities, are looking for what I offer. Most of them
won't agree with me openly, but if you take them aside, ask them privately, they'd probably tell you, "Rockwell has the right idea: White Christian
people should dominate." By 1972, with the economy coming apart at the
seams, with the niggers pushing, with the communists agitating, with all of
this spiritual emptiness, with all this cowardice and betrayal by our government, the masses of common, ordinary White people will have had it up
to here. They'll want a real leader in the White House—no more spineless

---

[18] In fact, inflation rose to 6% in 1970, dropped and then rose to 12% in 1975, and
dropped again and then rose to 14% in 1981.

jellyfish, no more oily, two-faced demagogs, no more queers in the White House like Walter Jenkins and his friends. They'll be looking for a White leader with the guts of a Malcolm X, with the guts to stand up and say, "I'm going to completely separate the black and White races and preserve White Christian domination in this country, and I'm going to have the Jew communists and any other traitors gassed for treason. And if you don't like it, you know what you can do about it."

Haley: Do you seriously think you can be elected on that platform?

Rockwell: I know so. Things are going to be so desperate by then that it won't matter whether I've got two horns and a tail; I'll be swept into office.

Haley: If you are elected, who from among contemporary public figures would you appoint to your cabinet?

Rockwell: If he were still alive, I'd have General Douglas MacArthur as Secretary of State. For Secretary of Defense, Retired General of the Marine Corps "Chesty" Puller. For Attorney General, J. Edgar Hoover. For Secretary of the Interior, Governor George Wallace of Alabama. Let me think, now, others: Senators William Jenner and Harry Byrd, Charles Lindbergh—and William Buckley; he won't appreciate that, but I think his brilliance could certainly be valuable. You'll have to agree that this is a cabinet to give nightmares to any Jew alive. They'd start swimming for Israel even before I was sworn in. But I don't think there's a man in that cabinet who is known as anti-Semitic.

Haley: How about anti-Negro?

Rockwell: Well, I'd prefer to call them pro-White.

Haley: If you had carte-blanche power to do so as the Chief Executive, would you create a dictatorship along the lines of Hitler's?

Rockwell: No, I'd reinstitute the American Constitutional Republic the way it was set up by our authoritarian forefathers—who were, in essence, nothing more than National Socialists just like me.

Haley: In no way did the founding fathers attempt to abridge the democratic right to "liberty and justice for all." How can you call them Nazis?

Rockwell: In the first place, I don't believe in democracy. In the second place, neither did our White forefathers. I believe, as they did, in a republic—an authoritarian republic with a limited electorate—just like the one the writers of our Constitution meant this country to be. When these White Christian patriots sat down to write the Declaration of Independence, there were no black citizens for them to worry about. In those days, all the niggers were slaves; but today, thanks to several misguided amendments, our Constitution provides even the blackest of savages with the same rights as his former White masters.[19]

Haley: Then you advocate the disenfranchisement of Negroes?

Rockwell: And the revocation of their citizenship.

Haley: And the restoration of slavery?

Rockwell: No, we have machines to do their work now. I would simply revoke their citizenship and then offer them the alternatives of either returning to Africa with our generous help and assistance in establishing a modern industrial nation, or being relocated on reservations like the Indians were when they became a problem to the survival of the White people. This will apply to you, too, by the way. Nothing personal, you understand; I like you, personally; but I can't make any exceptions.

Haley: Of course not. What would you do with America's 6 million Jews?

Rockwell: I think the Jews can be dealt with individually rather than as a group—like the niggers must be because of their race. As I said earlier, I think all Jews—in fact, all those connected in any way with treason, whether Jews or not—should be investigated and their cases put before grand juries; if they're indicted, they should then be tried, and if convicted, they should be killed.

---

[19] Rockwell is correct. He might also have added that only landowners were allowed to vote, and that, of course, no women could vote. The Founders in no sense endorsed a popular mass-democracy like we have today.

Haley: Having disposed of Jews and Negroes, would that complete your list of those slotted for removal?

Rockwell: Not quite. I'd also purge the queers. I despise them worst of all. They're one of the ugliest problems of our society, and they must be removed—I don't know if with gas, or what, just so they don't poison society. If they insist on being queers, put them on some island, maybe—but certainly not around the rest of society. They're the ultimate symbol of a decaying civilization.

Haley: Since you're concerned about the problem, Commander, would you like to reply to a frequent charge by psychiatrists that the womanless atmosphere of military asceticism and institutionalized hostility that characterize your "hate monastery," as you've called your headquarters here, make it an ideal sanctuary for those with repressed homosexual tendencies?

Rockwell: My reply is that this is the standard Jewish charge. The biggest charger that we are a bunch of homosexuals is Walter Winchell, whose real name is Isadore Israel Lipshitz, or something like that.[20] He's always calling me "George Lincoln Ratwell, Queen of the Nazis," saying I'm a fairy, and so forth. Universally, I have found that the Jews themselves, as Hitler said, are the greatest people in the world for accusing others of their own crimes.

Haley: You haven't answered the charge that your Party is a haven for homosexuals.

Rockwell: Well, I do think there is a tendency for queers to come here, because to a queer, this place is as tempting as a girls' school would be to me. Whenever I catch any of them in here, I throw them out; and I have caught quite a few of them in here. We had one case where we had reason to believe that the police would catch two guys in the act. The two of them left here hand in hand. I tried to get them prosecuted. We won't tolerate that sort of thing.

Haley: How about heterosexual relations? Are they *verboten*, too?

---

[20] This appears to be untrue; 'Winchell' was apparently his real name.

Rockwell: Absolutely not. Any man who didn't vigorously enjoy normal sex could never be a National Socialist. One of the best American Nazis I've ever known used to use a vulgar expression, "Those who won't fuck won't fight." I wouldn't put it so crudely myself, but I heartily subscribe to that doctrine. I never knew a good fighting man who didn't enjoy a lusty sex life.

Haley: Are any of your men married?

Rockwell: A few, but most are either single or divorced, like myself. I believe very strongly in the importance of basic morals to protect civilization, but it's almost impossible for a guy in this kind of work to have a normal marriage and family; so most of us have no choice but to make other arrangements. And I might add, to paraphrase a French bon mot, *vive les arrangements*. But I must admit that it's damn difficult—especially for me—to have any sort of normal contacts with women, since I'm so often approached in this regard for political blackmail.

Haley: Is it true that you require your Party members to swear an oath against drinking, smoking, and cursing?

Rockwell: All my officers take an oath against drinking, including myself. Most have also taken an oath against smoking. I, myself, would not smoke except that the corncob pipe I've smoked for so long has become sort of a trademark. As for cursing, it's hard to stop cursing in the rough situations in which we live, just like in the Armed Services; but I do all I can to discourage it.

Haley: You've used swearwords in this interview. Is this setting a good example for your men?

Rockwell: Well, I exempt myself from that oath for professional appearances such as this. In talking to you, I've used words like "nigger" and "kike" because this is a big interview in a national interviews, and I want to attract attention—to shock people into listening to what I have to say. If I were discussing, say, the favorite word of niggers—"motherfucker"—I'd say it strictly as a factual observation and to make a point. But in private conversation, neither I nor any of my members ever use that word—or any other foul language.

Haley: Do you also forbid the use of drugs?

Rockwell: Certainly. I've had a few guys in here who I think were marijuana smokers, but I've thrown them out and turned them in. Addiction to any drug is degenerative mentally as well as physically, and we're dead serious about our dedication to the healthy-body-healthy-mind philosophy.

Haley: Is karate or judo instruction part of your training program?

Rockwell: Not so much of that. I've found that unless you're a real expert at karate or judo, it doesn't help you much. Unless you use it instinctively, it's no use at all. So we concentrate on physical education, boxing, and weapons training.

Haley: What sort of weapons?

Rockwell: Rifles and pistols.

Haley: For what purpose?

Rockwell: Self-defense. I believe the White people of America should learn methods of surviving in the event of racial anarchy and general bedlam in this country, which I think is likely.

Haley: Do you share the belief of the Minutemen in the importance of being prepared for an armed communist invasion of the US mainland?

Rockwell: The Minutemen are kidding themselves. If there is a total communist takeover, they haven't got a prayer in the world of surviving it, let alone stopping it—running around in the weeds with a few guns like little boys playing cops and robbers. All they're doing is giving themselves an emotional catharsis. They're wasting millions of dollars, and in the process they're getting a lot of good kids sent to jail for illegal possession of weapons. I think it's like the Klan. Their aim, insofar as being ready is concerned, I'm for. I'm for the Klan's principles, ideas, and so forth—except the anti-Catholicism—but from my point of view, their methods stink!

Haley: What methods?

Rockwell: Their partial terrorism. I feel that terrorism is a valid weapon in guerrilla warfare, or any kind of warfare; and under the circumstances in which our country finds itself, I would favor terrorism *if* it could be complete—if it would work. A hundred years ago, I'd have been a Klansman with a rope and a gun and the whole business. I'd have really gone all out during the Reconstruction to save the White South. And make no mistake about the terrorism: It did the job. But today, it plays directly into the hands of Martin Luther Coon; it manufactures martyrs for the Northern press, for the liberals, and it doesn't scare the niggers out of hell-raising anymore.

Haley: But apart from your belief that racial violence against Negroes has become self-defeating, you have no moral objection to it?

Rockwell: None at all. What I object to is wars among White men. This is what we've been doing for centuries—fighting among ourselves and wiping each other out. The North versus the South is a perfect example: the biggest bloodletting we've had, the cream of the White population wiped out, all because of the niggers. It solved nothing; it really changed nothing—except that a lot of good White kids got killed.[21] I'm agin that! If we have any more wars, I want to fight the Red Chinese or the Jews, or go over to Africa and fight the niggers. This I can see some point to.

As far as violence on an individual basis is concerned, well, when I come to power, I plan to have dueling for officers in the Armed Forces. I'll have two purposes in that: first, to maintain a corps of officers unafraid to face death—not just in case of war; and second, to restore the concept of personal honor. I don't think going to court and suing somebody is really a deterrent to libelous, vicious talk. But people don't flap their mouths quite so freely when they're liable to have to back it up with a gun. Right now, dueling isn't legal, but the moment it is, I would be eager to face Billy James Hargis and Robert "Rabbit" Welch on a field of honor for going around calling me a communist.

Haley: Have you considered the possibility that you might be killed in such a confrontation?

---

[21] Around 750,000 soldiers were killed in the US Civil War, and roughly another 50,000 civilians. This is more American deaths than in World Wars One and Two combined.

Rockwell: I've not only considered it; I expect it. And I'm ready for it. Being prepared to die is one of the great secrets of living. I know I'm going to go—probably in some violent manner; the only question is when and how. But I don't think that's going to happen to me until I complete my mission. I know this is irrational, but I believe that I was placed here for a purpose and I think God has something to do with it: Our country needs a leader. So I think I'll be spared. As Rommel said, "Stand next to me; I'm bulletproof."

Haley: Do you think you're bulletproof, too?

Rockwell: Not literally, of course, but I firmly believe that the more arrogant and defiant you are of danger, the safer you are from harm. I think that's the reason I've survived so many times when people have shot at me. If you're fearless enough, it implants a certain psychology in the guy that's trying to shoot at you. It's almost as if he could smell your fearlessness, the way an animal smells fear. But the effect is the opposite: Instead of being emboldened to attack, he's so unsettled that his hand shakes when he goes to pull the trigger; and this makes it almost impossible for him to hit you. Either that, or he'll back down entirely. When I go out in the street and toughs come up threatening to whip me, I look them straight in the eye and say, "Go ahead. Start." Maybe they could whip me, but so far nobody's tried.

Haley: What's the closest you've come to getting killed?

Rockwell: The closest, I guess—though I didn't get hurt—was the time we had scheduled a picket by 14 of us of the movie "Exodus" in Boston. The other men were in a truck, and I had registered in a nearby hotel as Nathan Ginsburg, where I waited until the scheduled picket time of two p.m. The newspapers and radio estimated that 10,000 or more Jews were packing the streets waiting for us, and my truck full of boys couldn't get through the crowd. Well, our picket had been the subject of headlines for days, so I couldn't possibly chicken out at that point. I had to get through the crowd somehow to picket in front of the theater; so I put on an overcoat, went through the crowd quietly, and when I got in front of the theater, I took off the overcoat in the middle of all those Jews and stood there in full-dress uniform. They were shocked into silence for a moment; their jaws dropped. Then somebody hollered, "It's Rockwell; get him!" And the whole huge mob marched in on me with their clubs and baling hooks. If I hadn't been rescued by a flying wedge of tough Irish cops, I would certainly have been killed. I was taken into protective custody and put in a cell.

I'll tell you, I was glad I was out of that; it could have ended horribly. But I had to show my men that I wouldn't ask them to do anything I wouldn't do myself. Another reason I did it is the effect the Nazi uniform has on Jews: It turns them into insane hatemongers—easy to beat, outmaneuver, and outthink. The most dangerous man on the face of the Earth is a rational, carefully planning Jew, but a raging, hate-filled Jew will act foolishly; you can whip him.

Haley: How many times have you been jailed for this kind of agitation, Commander?

Rockwell: Up to now, 15 times. But never for very long; two weeks was the longest—that was in New Orleans. We'd gone down there with our "Hate Bus" to make fun of nigger agitators who were calling their bus the "Love Bus." Without so much as a warrant or any real cause, the Jew-dominated officials of New Orleans had us all thrown in jail on phony charges that were later dropped. We finally got out by staging a hunger strike; 11 of us went eight days without a bite. On the fourth day, one of our men began to crack and said he was going to eat, so we had to let him know that if he did, it would be his last meal. He changed his mind. Another time in Virginia, they put me in jail, and I was facing ten years' possible imprisonment for "starting a war against the niggers." You've never seen a man act as guilty as the sheriff who arrested me.

Haley: Guilty about what?

Rockwell: He felt he was doing the wrong thing. Here was a fellow White man fighting for the same things he believed in, and he was throwing me in jail. But this town is in the clutches of this Jew who owns two huge department stores and grocery stores there; so the sheriff was acting under leftist political pressure.

But that leftist hotbed is a sanctuary of segregationist archconservatism compared with Philadelphia. Believe it or not, my men and I were jailed there for picketing a hotel where Gus Hall, the head of the American Communist Party, was speaking. As far as I'm concerned, Philadelphia is the enemy capital. They've practically got Jewish flags flying from the flagpoles.

In most cities, though, I've found that they're only bluffing when they threaten me with jail. I tell them, "You'd better start arresting, 'cause I'm going to start speaking." Nine times out of ten, they chicken out. They're used to nonviolent niggers being willing to go to jail—not White supremacists. Well, here's one White supremacist who ain't afraid to go to jail. And neither are my men.

As a matter of fact, we've got at least two or three Party members in jail somewhere in the United States almost 365 days a year. Every Sunday night we honor them in ceremonies that we hold on the parade grounds in front of this building. We also award special decorations for conspicuous achievement on behalf of the Party and for acts of heroism above and beyond the call of duty. Our top award is the Order of Adolf Hitler, then the Gold, the Silver, and the Bronze awards. The highest award I've given yet was the Silver; that was to a man who couldn't contain himself in Birmingham and belted Martin Luther Coon on the head for calling that nigger Jew Sammy Davis, Jr. "an example of the finest type of American."

Haley: You know, of course, that Dr. King is widely respected and admired by the majority of the American public, black and White—while you, a champion of White supremacy, are regarded by most people as a "nut" and a "hatemonger," abominated by almost everyone—including the John Birch Society.

Rockwell: Martin Luther Coon may go on pulling the wool over the public's eyes for a while longer, but sooner or later they're going to find him out for what he is—an 18-carat fake, a fraud on the Negro people. When the black revolution comes, I wouldn't be surprised to see him get it first—from his own people.

As for my being a nut, that name has been applied to some of the greatest men the world has ever known, from Christ to the Wright Brothers. I say it's therefore one of the highest accolades I could be given. My father once told me that his Jewish friends ask him, "How could you spawn such a viper?" Well, I'm proud that communist Jews think me a viper. As for the threats and the beatings and the investigations and the assassination attempts and all that, when I hung up the Nazi flag, I counted on being jailed and hated and hounded. If I hadn't been, I'd figure I was a flop. Harassment is par for the course in the embryonic stages of any new movement that's opposed by the established powers—especially one as revolutionary as mine. I wouldn't be surprised if the Anti-Defamation League already has a cross built for me, with the nails ready.

But I don't consider myself persecuted. Maturity is to accept the consequences of your own acts. I think it's a symptom of paranoia to feel that it's anyone's fault but your own if you fail to accomplish what you set out to.

Haley: We read a newspaper interview a few years ago in which you claimed you were being "gagged and slandered by the Jewish press," sabotaged by a nationwide journalistic conspiracy in your fight to put your case before the nation. When "the Jewish press" wasn't pretending that you didn't exist, you said, it was either deliberately misquoting you or doctoring your public statements to remove the sense and retain the shock value —in order to make you sound simple-minded or to portray you as a racist monster.[22] Only this conspiracy of silence and misrepresentation, you claimed, was preventing you from getting your revolutionary message across to the White, gentile masses and rallying them to your flag. To some people, Commander, these might sound like the remarks of a man who's trying to blame his failures on someone else.

Rockwell: You think I'm being paranoid, is that it?

Haley: Some people might.

Rockwell: In the *Columbia Journalism Review* about three months ago, Ben Bagdikian, a frequent writer for the Anti-defamation League, wrote an article called. "The Gentle Suppression" which asked the question, "Is the news quarantine of Rockwell a good thing?" Bagdikian openly reveals that the press maintains as much silence as possible about our activities. So you see, the Jew blackout on us is as real as a hand over my mouth. They know we're too poor to buy air time or advertising space, so they ban our publications from all channels of distribution, and they refuse to report our activities in the daily press. I could run naked across the White House lawn and they wouldn't report it. I'm being facetious. *But I'm dead serious when I say that the only kind of free speech left in this country is that speech that doesn't criticize the Jews.* If you criticize the Jews, you're either smeared or silenced. They have that same kind of "free speech" in Cuba, Red China, and Russia and every other communist country: You can say anything you like as long as it doesn't criticize the dictator. The Jews

---

[22] This is still true in the present day, especially with the most dangerous critics, such as Holocaust revisionists.

are never going to let me reach the people with my message in the American press; they can't afford to.

Haley: How do you reconcile that statement with the fact that you're being interviewed at this moment for a national publication?

Rockwell: I've been interviewed, taped, and photographed thousands of times for just such presentations as these, but they never appear. The fact that you come here and get this interview doesn't prove that you'll print it, or that if you do, you'll print it straight. After the editors read over the transcript, they'll decide it's too hot to handle, and they'll chicken out rather than risk getting bombed by the Jews and the niggers when it comes out.

Haley: We'll take our chances, Commander—if you will.

Rockwell: I'll take any chances to get my message read. But it's never going to happen. We've been kept out of the news too many times before. I'll bet you a hundred dollars this whole thing has been nothing but a waste of my time because it's never going to reach the people who read your interviews.

APPENDIX D

Pages from *The Rockwell Report*

Editor: By the early 1960s, Rockwell had had a fair amount of experience with publishing journals and periodicals. In 1961, frustrated by mainstream media, he decided to publish his own humble periodical, titled *The Rockwell Report*. The inaugural issue came out in October of that year, and subsequent issues appeared roughly monthly until Rockwell's demise in 1967. The following are pages from selected issues.

THE U S RIGHT WING PICTURE

About a year ago, in response to many requests, particularly from overseas - I reproduced a letter to our Italian comrades picturing clearly the situation of the right-wing in America and sent it around for information to right-wing leaders in the U. S.

With the sudden immense growth of the right-wing during the past year, that analysis has been somewhat outdated. Further, I think an accurate picture of the rapidly proliferating right-wing groups in America would be most helpful to our leaders.

I am therefore printing a new appraisal and analysis of the right-wing in America in this issue of the Rockwell Report.

While it is impossible to categorize all right-wing groups accurately, we have nevertheless produced a working chart which will be helpful to the student of politics in evaluating the left-right orientation of these groups.

In spite of all the wishful thinking and sloppy humanitarianism, in the final analysis the laws of nature prevail in the affairs of men as well as in all other things. Man can USE these laws and manipulate them perhaps, but he cannot change or eliminate the laws themselves. Whether it suits man or not, might makes right in the sense that the winners in mass human conflicts are always "heroes" and "saviors", while the losers are "traitors", "war criminals" and "monsters". The end does justify the means as every father who punishes his child and every nation which sends its young men out to die in wars, perhaps, must tacitly admit.

It is this respect for the immutable laws of the natural world which we believe provides the best criterion for establishing the relative left-right positions of political organizations. The ultimate and utopian idealists - the anarchists - represent the farthest possible political extreme to the left, while the brutal and highly personal conquerors like Genghis Khan, who don't care a fig for any idealism whatsoever and establish a social order based on the most brutal and naked tyranny represent the farthest possible extremity to the right. We believe that both the soft-headed wishful thinking anarchists and the brutal natural tyrants are equally "bad".

As usual in human affairs the extremes are bad and the golden mean is the only tolerable situation.

The American Nazi Party believes that the golden political mean for civilized western men was

achieved with the authoritarian republic established by our slave-holding, aristocratic American forebears who never considered franchising any but white, responsible male property holders and who were ready to fight and die for their ideals, regardless of threats and atrocity propaganda. To us, such a constitutional authoritarian republic is "dead center" between naked tyranny and the chaos of anarchy.

The world, however, driven by a century of Jewish democratic, equalitarian propaganda, has moved so far to the left that the authoritarian republic of our forefathers, which, with its slaves and aristocratic leaders would now be considered "right-wing extremism" even worse than Hitler's National Socialist Germany, were it to re-appear today.

As a result, what is called the "center" today is, in terms of relative distance from absolute left and absolute right,   at least 75% away from center toward the left.

In short, the so-called "democratic" world is actually MARXIST and differs from the openly Communist world only in symbols, catch words and the gang in charge.

In the OPENLY Marxist world the leaders are atheist, Jewish Communists who set up non-Jewish fronts like Khruschev. In the "democratic" world the "leaders" are a gang of Zionist-Capitalist Jews and their billionaire, plutocrat accomplices like the Rockofellers, the Fords of today, etc.

Because of this disparity in actual left-right orientation and the conceptions of these groups which have become so accepted that they are hard-to-break habits of thought, we have been forced to produce TWO charts. One is the left-right orientation of the various groups as they appear to political observers so steeped in democratic-Marxis thinking in spite of themselves that our present government appears to be substantially different from a Marxist system. The other chart shows the ACTUAL left-right orientation of these groups in terms of absolute left and right values. On the first chart, the one depicting the situation as most observers see it in the U. S. today, the American Nazi Party is as far right as it is possible to get and all other groups are found progressively to the left of us based on what they CLAIM.

What they claim and what we know to be the truth are quite different things.

2

the Rockwell Report

GEORGE LINCOLN ROCKWELL MAY 1965

THE REAL STORY:
LEFT vs. RIGHT

WHITE MAN... UNITE & FIGHT!

Official Publication of the American Nazi Party

THE ROCKWELL REPORT is published monthly by the American Nazi Party. Write Box 5505, Arlington, Virginia, U.S.A. Single copy: $1.00. One year, mailed in an unmarked envelope: $10.00 Air Mail: $11. One month: $1. Clippings always welcomed.

there is NO ORDER, and no safety for the decent citizen. During the Boston police strike in the twenties, before Coolidge put it down with the National Guard, there was bloodshed and looting all over Boston in the police-less city, and no decent citizen could come out of his home. Even IN his home, the decent citizen was likely to be attacked, robbed, raped and outraged.

Never in this world will ALL humans be "noble" and full of "love" for fellow men. And as long as there is just ONE louse who would use force to rob, rape, loot, kill, etc., then there must be SOME government and some kind of force available to society to protect itself from even the small minority of predators.

In other words, absolute tyranny is intolerable.

But so is absolute freedom.

As with most human affairs, the answer lies not in the extremes, but in what Plato called the "golden mean"--a BALANCE between the two extremes.

However, in struggling away from the misery of the total tyranny of the feudal middle ages, Western man had no choice but to move to the LEFT-- from total tyranny and order, toward the other extreme of total freedom and NO ORDER--chaos. And I would have been forced, therefore, to move LEFT with the struggle for some freedom from absolute tyranny.

But humanity has a terrible habit in correcting evils.

Often it moves and fights long and hard to correct an evil, only to keep moving in the same direction to make AN EVIL OUT OF THE CORRECTION!

This is precisely what has happened in Western Civilization.

"Freedom" has become an insane fetish, a crazy, illogical shibboleth toward which everybody bows, regardless of whether it is REAL, responsible freedom such as America knew during the eighteen-hundreds, or the wild, murderous, vicious libertinism masquerading as "freedom" of savage Africa and the American "left".

We of the American Nazi Party believe that Western Man necessarily moved left for a thousand years, away from the total tyranny of the right, until he reached the "Golden Mean" of perfect balance between the need for order (and some government) and the need for liberty.

4

the Rockwell Report

George Lincoln Rockwell Nov.-Dec. 1966

The REAL NATURE of WHITE BACKLASH

White People! Unite & Fight!

Official Publication of the American Nazi Party

mutter to the managers up in the office, "Look at them down there: they're trying to run your business and grab all the profits! We've got to put these swine down! Lock them out! Speed up! Longer hours! Bust the unions!"

The only reply of the majority of the ⁓i-Communist right in America, with minor exce ⁓tions, has been economic, has been "reactionary", has been precisely the economic "royalism" and conservatism" which can be used by the Jewish Communist propagandists to show the workers that they are, indeed, being exploited by the "filthy capitalists", etc., etc., and must united and rise up, etc., to "save themselves" from the "greedy plutocrats".

So far, all according to the Yiddish plan, and exactly as the dodge has been working in every country attacked by the "Red Plague": so far the Jews have been eminently successful in starting class warfare, in pitting the Buckleys, Goldwaters, Welch's and the wealthy against the United Auto Workers, against the masses of workers, farmers and ordinary Americans who keep voting for Roosevelt, Truman, Ike, Kennedy and Johnson on economic grounds.

But now there is a new element appearing in every country attacked by the Jewish parasites.

According to Red plans, by now, everybody in America should be neatly divided into either the united "downtrodden", who hate the "capitalists" --the power structure--and, on the other, opposite hand, the embattled upper classes, completely isolated from and full of hate for the "workers and peasants".

The upper classes have been most accommodating and have duly developed a snooty economic attitude, even promoted the utmost in snooty rich candidate for President, Goldwater (best typified by the Jew, pinko cartoonist to the Jewish Washington Post, Herbert Bloch (Herblock), in his cartoon of Goldwater saying to the starving "worker", "Go get your own department store!") The "conservative" upper classes have acted just like the

P ⁓ ⁓ czar, the French aristocrats, Marie Antoinette, and all the short-sighted snobs of history, and done everything to alienate and isolate themselves from their people.

But the lower classes, the American workers, have not accommodated the Jews as per plan--not QUITE.

Into the usual Jewish Communist economic revolution has come an unwanted and powerful element--RACE!

The Communist "Worker", "Workers World", "Militant", and all the rest of the Red propaganda apparatus (including the New York Times), have endless exhortations and cartoons, editorials and tirades showing that the welfare of all workers, black and white, are in direct conflict with the interests of the "ruling classes".

The Communist and Jewish press is downright rabid on the subject of the Black and White poor joining forces.

The Jews and Reds being materialists whose short-sighted doctrines force them to believe that human beings have no ideals and will never sacrifice anything except for cash and material gain, cannot imagine that they could fail to unite black and white when they hold out huge economic gain as the reward to the White Man for ignoring all his racial instincts.

The Jews have believed, and continue to believe, that, for money, for cash, for position and praise in Jewish press, the White workers will join the blacks in the usual economic class uprising against the wealthy, the managers and the natural leaders of the Gentile world.

But it is precisely the white workers who are forced to suffer the jungle habits and nature of the Negro, not the rich people. It is the White worker in the big city like Chicago who does not have to be "educated" about what "niggers" are like in the mass. The White worker is physically repulsed by the mass (ghetto) nigger and his savagery and filth.

SF Jeers Rockwell, Nazi Rally

SAN FRANCISCO (UPI)—An angry mob of about 1,000 persons Saturday shouted down American Nazi leader George Lincoln Rockwell when he tried to stage a "white power" rally in front of city hall.

A neatly dressed unidentified man, about 68 years old, suffered a heart attack and died at an emergency hospital.

The outburst occurred when the gray-uniformed Rockwell climbed atop a camper truck and began to speak through a public address system. "The white people must unite," he declared.

Rockwell managed to speak for about five minutes over shouts of "Ratfink!" and "Nazis aren't funny!" and name-calling obscenities before a policeman took the microphone and said, "Quit shouting or he'll have to go."

The crowd, predominantly white, yelled even louder and Rockwell got into the truck.

A squad of policemen formed a wedge to escort the vehicle away from the area. Several persons pelted the truck with eggs.

No arrests were made.

Several hundred persons then surrounded a paddy wagon and refused to let it move. Sgt. Edward Epting climbed on top of the wagon and shouted, "Please, please disperse for the peace of San Francisco!"

After a few minutes the crowd thinned out and the police vehicle drove away.

Rockwell was accompanied to the civic center plaza by 16 khaki-clad Nazis who stood guard around the camper truck. One of them was splattered with an egg.

Before he was shouted down, Rockwell denounced the Viet Nam Day Committee, an anti-war group, as "a bunch of pigs." He also declared, "People who want freedom [or] Communists deny it to others."

The Nazi leader, who has also threatened to stage a march

(Turn To Page A2, Column 2)

Here's a clipping from the front page of the Santa Ana Register in California, about our battle in the Plaza in San Francisco. The papers minimized what the Jews did. But thousands there, and more thousands on TV, saw that these Jews, who are so sickening in their demand for "free speech" for Reds, queers and dope fiends, came down there to murder us, if possible. They used every form of violence and mobbing they could against us, and the politically-dominated police meekly bowed to this filthy Jew terrorism. They stopped our legal speech, and permitted the mob to free even those arrested and placed in police patrols. There were some humorous sidelights to this affair. Among these was the old kike who keeled over with a heart attack at seeing 26 uniformed Nazis guarding me and the camper, and who was given mouth-to-mouth resuscitation by a cop. When the niggers saw the cop bending over the downed Hebe, they ran through the crowd screaming that the brutal, fascist cops had beaten the old man to death, and tried to start one of their brotherhood riots, in addition to the Jew riot already going on. Another old Jew lady began pounding on the cop, with an umbrella, not realizing the poor guy was trying to help this noble fallen Hebrew.

Finally, on San Francisco, here are some of the results in the local college newspapers around the area. Read 'em for yourself, and see how the Jews cut their own throats, when we give them the Nazi treatment.

The Register

SOUTHERN CALIFORNIA'S WATCHFUL NEWSPAPER

SANTA ANA, ORANGE COUNTY, CALIFORNIA SUNDAY OCTOBER 23, 1966

D

Pages A16, 18 and 59-11

Harbor Area News — A18
Horoscope — A16
KHJ-TV News — A16
Military Beat — B16

9

Germans Bewildered by Nazi Rockwell

By David M. Nichol
Chicago Daily News Foreign Service

BONN, Oct. 28—George Lincoln Rockwell, America's homemade mini-Hitler, is the object of some bewilderment in Germany.

To most people here he seems unbelievable, and ridiculous in a menacing way, and most of their countrymen caricature from a nightmare they are trying to forget.

If they are old enough to have had some first-hand experience of the original, they are likely to shudder, at least in private, at the recollection of the ease with which they were recruited for Adolf Hitler's evil aims.

What they cannot understand is that Rockwell is permitted to parade his swastikas and to agitate in public in the United States for a re-run of the Auschwitz gas chambers. In Germany he would be clapped into jail.

Among the genuine pro-Nazis here, of whom there still are some, Rockwell probably is considered in addition to be stupid. The smart ones in Germany have learned, also from bitter experience, that any revival of the "movement" must rely on much subtler forms of propaganda.

"Approved speakers" for the far-right National Democratic Party, many of whom are former Nazis, have been cautioned that they will be expelled from the organization if they relapse too readily into the jargon and slogans of Hitler's "Thousand-Year Reich."

There is a danger that the Party would be dissolved by the Constitutional Court.

There is also the fact that such outworn, utilizing as they may be to a handful of "old fighters" do not win the Party new votes.

There is almost no market for genuine Nazi relics. Copies of "Mein Kampf" are available, but not many people want them. Most of them didn't read it 30 years ago, when it was first published, and it has even less attraction now. Recordings of some of Hitler's speeches were a short-lived sensation.

This does not mean that there is no interest in the past. A scholarly study of the origins of "Mein Kampf," which showed that most of Hitler's ideas had been formed by 1913 and changed very little after that, was considered sufficiently important to run as a serial in the weekly news magazine, Spiegel.

One of the most widely circulated illustrated weeklies has begun to publish the serialized memoirs of Emma Goering, the widow of the No. 2 Nazi, Hermann Goering. The publication coincides with the

20th anniversary of Goering's suicide in the U.S. jail at Nuremburg shortly before he was to be hanged.

The first episode is a banal and sentimental account of Emma's last meeting with Hermann.

"Do you want me to appeal for mercy?" he asks.

"No, Hermann, you can now die in peace."

Hermann is quoted as saying, "You can be assured they will not hang me."

A week later when the Goering family heard of his successful suicide, Edda, the daughter, then 8, is quoted as saying:

"I know, mommy, how he got the poison. An angel pushed aside the ceiling of the cell and dropped the capsule to him."

On that same morning writes Emma, an Evangelical pastor came to assure her that "in the eyes of God it was not a suicide."

"ICH WÄRE GERN MIT HIMMLER VERWANDT"

SPIEGEL-Interview mit der US-Nazi-Sekretärin Erika Himmler

Chicago-Nazi-Sekretärin Erika Himmler, Parteigenossen, Maschinen

After years of doing their best to pretend that the American Nazi Party doesn't exist or is a joke, the Jew-dominated German press has finally been forced, by our smashing successes in Chicago, to start reporting the rise of National Socialism in America.

Here's one of the articles in Germany's biggest periodical "Der Spiegel" and a comment from the American press.

10

Appendix E

"The shadow of an assassinated American Nazi commander hangs over Charlottesville" (2017)

Editor: On the night of 11 August 2017, a large contingent of 'alt-right,' dissident right, and White nationalist protestors held a nighttime rally in Charlottesville, Virginia; the event was known as "Unite the Right." The open appearance of so many "far right" dissidents horrified local authorities, and hence they covertly instigated violent attacks against the peaceful protestors in order to justify a police crackdown. The mainstream media lost no opportunity to portray the event as evidence of a growing presence of anti-Semites, neo-Nazis, and White supremacists in the US. A major paper, the *Washington Post*, published the following article on the rally about a week later. Though horribly slanted and biased, it does show the continuing influence and importance of Rockwell's work, even decades after this death.

Shortly before noon on Aug. 25, 1967, a pale '58 Chevy pulled into a shopping center in Arlington [Virgina]. Out stepped one of the most hated men in America.

As the founder of the American Nazi Party, George Lincoln Rockwell had hung swastikas on the Mall and picketed the marches of Martin Luther King Jr. He had called for shipping blacks to Africa and sending millions of "Communist Jews" to the gas chambers—all at a time when memories of World War II were still fresh.

Now, dressed not in his Nazi uniform but a simple white shirt and dark slacks, Rockwell grabbed his dirty laundry and headed into the Econ-o-wash, only to realize he had forgotten the bleach. As he climbed back into his car to return to Nazi headquarters—a large house a block away dubbed "Hatemongers Hill"—two shots rang out.

Rockwell died amid a flurry of Ivory Snow soap flakes.

For years, he had claimed his enemies were stalking him. But when police arrested the gunman minutes later, they identified him as 29-year-old John Patler: Rockwell's neo-Nazi protege.

The killing made international headlines and led to a bizarre standoff over the Nazi's body. It also crippled his party, which soon sank back into obscurity.

But Rockwell's death did not dispel his ideas.

Half a century later, they were on display last weekend when hundreds of torch-carrying neo-Nazis and white nationalists marched in Charlottesville.

Among today's white supremacists, Rockwell's hate-filled books remain widely circulated. Even Rockwell's assassin, now an old man, still struggles to shake off his influence. And "White Power," the term Rockwell coined months before his death, lives on in the movements of David Duke and the alt-right, which advocates for a whites-only state.

The Charlottesville rally was "infused with Rockwell's ideology," said Martin Kerr of New Order, the successor to the American Nazi Party.

"He is the grandfather of the white racialist movement as it exists today," he said of Rockwell. "To see these many hundreds of racially conscious white men on the streets of Charlottesville, I'm sure he would have been very pleased."

'Barnum of the Bigots'

When Martin Luther King Jr. arrived to the southwest side of Chicago on Aug. 5, 1966, to march for housing desegregation, he was met by thousands of angry white residents. Some waved Confederate or Nazi flags. Others pelted him and other civil rights activists with bottles and bricks. Many of them chanted "White Power."

"I've been in many demonstrations all across the south," King told reporters, "but I can say I have never seen—even in Mississippi and Alabama—mobs as hostile and hate-filled as I've seen here in Chicago."

Rockwell, who had spent the day egging on the crowd and distributing "White Power" T-shirts and posters, considered it his finest hour.

Chicago marked a turning point for Rockwell. Tall, handsome, and sporting a corncob pipe in the style of Gen. Douglas MacArthur, Rockwell had studied philosophy at Brown but dropped out to join the Navy after becoming convinced the school was a breeding ground for communism.

After serving in World War II and rising to the rank of commander, Rockwell stumbled upon a copy of Hitler's *Mein Kampf* in a used bookstore and became obsessed with the racist manifesto. Rockwell, who once had fought against fascism, became convinced only it could save America. He moved to Arlington in 1955 and launched his party a few years later.

He initially ran his party out of a ramshackle house on Randolph Street in downtown Arlington. When police raided the swastika-draped den in April of 1959, they walked in on Commander Rockwell—as he liked to be called—and his followers celebrating Hitler's 70th birthday with a cake.

When "Exodus," a movie about the founding of Israel, opened in Boston in 1960, Rockwell stood outside the theater in his Nazi uniform—earning him mention in a Bob Dylan song. He and his troopers followed the Freedom Riders around the country in a "hate bus" covered in swastikas and picketed clubs that booked Sammy Davis Jr., whose wife was white. Rockwell's parents had been successful vaudeville performers and he had inherited their showmanship, earning himself the nickname "Barnum of the Bigots."

But those tactics gained him few followers. When Rockwell ran for governor of Virginia in 1965, he got one percent of the vote.

He saw the rapid rise of Black Power and decided to emulate it. At the urging of Patler—a short, dark-haired Greek American who had changed his name from Patsalos to Patler to sound more like Hitler—Rockwell began pitching his party to all whites, including southern and eastern Europeans it had previously shunned. Rockwell would eventually change its name to the National Socialist White People's Party and even eschewed the swastika, according to the biography "American Fuehrer."

"We will make White Unity the biggest thing in history," Rockwell wrote to Patler, a Marine marksman who had been discharged for wearing his uniform to Nazi rallies.

Rockwell believed White Power would carry him to the White House.

In a 1966 *Playboy* interview, which began with Rockwell pulling out a pearl-handled revolver, Rockwell told black journalist Alex Haley that he planned on being elected America's first National Socialist president in 1972. "The people will welcome a man who stands unequivocally for the white Christian majority," he said.

Behind the scenes, however, his party was in turmoil. Some did not like the denazification. Rockwell and Patler, once like father and son, had a personal falling out that ended with Patler's expulsion from the party in the spring of 1967. A few months later, two men—one of whom reportedly looked like Patler—shot at Rockwell as he returned to Nazi headquarters, then escaped.

On the morning of his death, Rockwell worked on his magnum opus —posthumously published as *White Power*—before heading to the Dominion Hills shopping center. Seconds before gunshots broke the midday humdrum, bystanders heard what sounded like footsteps on the roof.

The first bullet nicked Rockwell's shirt. But as he peered up through the shattered windshield at a figure perched atop the shopping mall's roof, a second bullet tore through his chest.

Rockwell's pipe fell from his mouth to the car seat. As the Chevy rolled backward, Rockwell crawled toward the passenger door and tumbled onto the asphalt. Witnesses said the fleeing gunman wore a yellow shirt, hat, and a trench coat.

Fifteen minutes later, Arlington police officers spotted Patler, wearing a yellow shirt, his pants wet at the ankles, standing at a bus stop 1.5 miles away. They found a hat and trench coat hidden nearby. And the next day, they fished a German Mauser pistol out of Four Mile Run in Bon Air Park, between the bus stop and the crime scene.

The story stayed on *The Washington Post*'s front page for more than a week as it took one strange twist after another. Before Rockwell's family could organize a burial, his Nazi followers attempted to inter him at Culpeper National Cemetery in Virginia—in a Nazi ceremony, complete with a swastika-draped casket.

Soldiers blocked their entrance. The American Civil Liberties Union backed the Nazis, but before a lawsuit could be settled, the Nazis smuggled the body out of an Arlington funeral home and secretly cremated it.

"You don't mean they actually stuck the ... in an oven?" Hank Burchard, a *Post* reporter who had infiltrated Rockwell's group while in college, asked Rockwell's second-in-command. Burchard was, he wrote, "struck by the irony of the end of a man who had dreamed of sending 'the Jews that Hitler missed' to the ovens."

At trial, Patler denied killing his mentor. His attorney suggested it could have been another Nazi, upset with the direction Rockwell was taking the party. But the jury found Patler guilty. He was sentenced to 20 years.

'Becoming poisoned again'

The script in Charlottesville could have been cribbed from Rockwell's speeches.

"White lives matter! You will not replace us! Jews will not replace us!" the men chanted as they carried tiki torches around the University of Virginia. "White power!" they shouted at counterprotesters the next morning.

If white nationalism is now resurgent in America, it is partly due to Rockwell.

Rockwell paved the way for white nationalists like David Duke and Richard Spencer, according to Heidi Beirich, director of the Southern Poverty Law Center's Intelligence Project, which tracks hate groups. "I don't know if we'd have this type of activism or even this kind of president [Trump] if there hadn't been a figure like that," she said.

"He had a very big influence on the resistance movement in this country to the destruction of European Americans," agreed Duke. "He brought attention to a lot of issues."

In Charlottesville, Duke echoed Rockwell, telling a crowd in Emancipation Park that "European Americans face massive discrimination" and were being "ethnically cleansed in our own nation."

Spencer said Rockwell's Nazi uniform was "unproductive" but admired some of his tactics. "There was a trolling aspect to what he was doing, so you could connect him to some of the trolls on Twitter," he told *The Post*. "Shock can be a positive means to an end."

Among the millions of Americans dismayed by the violence in Charlottesville was an adjunct professor of African American history at West Virginia State University.

Sitting in a McDonald's in Mississippi, where he is doing research for a book on black leaders during Reconstruction, Nicholas Patler saw the hatred on a television screen and couldn't help but think of his father.

John Patsalos, as he is again called, served a decade in prison before being released in the early 1980s. He is now 79 and lives in New York City. The man who once illustrated hate magazines for Rockwell now ekes out a living as a freelance cartoonist.

Patsalos refused multiple interview requests, including one left on his door, which is covered in Dr. Seuss-like cartoons and an "I voted" sticker. He is a staunch online defender of Donald Trump.

Patler said he learned of his father's crime as a child. His parents divorced when his father was in prison, and his mother moved the family to Staunton, Va., near Charlottesville.

His father's hatred "inspired me to explore different things," he said of his decision to study African American history. His students don't know about his father, he said. But in 2013, Patler penned an afterword to another Rockwell biography, *For Race and Nation*, in which he said his father had been traumatized as a child. Patsalos's father had killed his mother, and Patsalos was now ashamed of his time as a Nazi. "Today he describes that time as a period of 'temporary insanity,'" his son wrote.

Over the past two years, however, Patler has seen his father change again. "I don't know what the climate is doing to him," he said. "Now it seems like, little by little, he's becoming poisoned again."

Two days after Charlottesville's "Unite the Right" rally left a 32-year-old counterprotester dead and many others injured, Patsalos praised the neo-Nazis and white supremacists who descended on the college town.

"It was a peaceful parade, with a coupl'a hundred white men, neatly attired, expressing their to free speech and objection to the removal of the statue of Gen. Lee," he wrote on Facebook, where he uses an alias. "White Pride, Black Pride, Gay Pride, Transgender Pride, Greek Pride, Your Grandmother's Pride ... Hey, this is the United States of America, so can we not all exhibit pride?"

The remains of the man he killed are kept in an ivory urn with a photo of Rockwell on one side and a swastika on the other, said Kerr, who helps run New Order, the successor to Rockwell's American Nazi Party. Kerr refused to reveal more about Rockwell's ashes. "We want to keep them in a secure location until a time when we can inter them properly," he said.

"We're not at the end of the Rockwell wave," Kerr added. "We're at the beginning."

www.ingramcontent.com/pod-product-compliance
Lightning Source LLC
Chambersburg PA
CBHW020916140626
46545CB00015B/64